A BOOK
TO FREE
THE SOUL

*You live in a prison, but you do not see the bars;
you hold the keys, and you do not know what they
are. Make on your journey a companion of the
book; you will find the answers where others do
not look.*

YVES CADOUX

ISBN: 9798696271392 (paperback)
ISBN: 9798747798762 (hardcover)

CONTENTS

Prolegomenon

Each reader in the act of reading is the very reader of himself. The writer's work is but a sort of optical instrument offered to the reader so that he can discern in himself what he might have been unable to see without this book. The reader's recognition in himself of what the book says is proof of its truth.

—Marcel Proust, *Time Regained*

The volume before you is your Ariadnean thread out of the trap of materialism, the maze of institutionalized religions, the endless circuitous discursions of occultism, and the blind alleys of the pop spirituality industry, which no longer satisfy the longings of the soul and stunt the spirit.

To open *A Book to Free the Soul* is to open a new window of perception; to probe its matters is to build a bridge between physical reality and aethereality[1]; to follow its drift is to undergo an inner initiation; to solve its many riddles is to unearth the keys to the liberation of your soul. But before we pursue, a few remarks are in order:

I am not going to sedate you with recycled platitudes and trite abstractions. I am not selling tickets to the ultimate psychical or astral thrill. I am not here to lead you on a journey that can only be yours. There already are enough teachers in the enlightenment business doing all of the above; I am not one of them. Furthermore, I do not teach a scheme: my writings

---

[1] In this book, I use the spelling *aethereal* and *aethereality* for the more common "ethereal" and "ethereality." This isn't out of snobbery but to differentiate the actual trans-material plane of existence from what is merely considered non-physical, heavenly, delicate, or refined.

i

stand as a mirror to show you something that is already in you; they are not didactic but revelatory, like a breach into the wall of earthly conditioning. Nor is this work a rehash, a compendium of other peoples' ideas, or a commentary thereon. As stated plainly, my sole purpose now is to free the soul.

Traditional religions have devolved into the craft of a tarnished priesthood and an erring leadership. Alternative spirituality has morphed into a materialistic mysticality. Everything in this book began with reasonable premises anyone can test:

1) I perceive, therefore I am. And even if what I perceive might prove to be unreliable, it does not change the fact of there being a distinct primary observer.

2) I am a prisoner of the material world because:

   a) What I can construct in imagination only eclipses anything I can possibly accomplish on the physical plane of existence and leaves in the shade all human accomplishments or feats of nature.

   b) I am subjected to horrors, violence, pain, suffering, and misery that I cannot avoid, and which are beyond my control.

   c) My choices are conditioned by the circumstances of my physical existence.

   d) I am subjected to human laws although I might not agree with them. Even in the smallest conceivable form of society, individuals are obligated to submit to the leader of the clan or the head of the family, to respect cultural taboos, traditions, and to abide by the rule of the majority or consensus. There is no such thing as a sovereign earthling; the sovereign self belongs to a kingdom that is not of Earth.[2]

3) If nothing in the world can appease my longings, a sensible explanation worth exploring is that this world is not my true home.[3]

Many people will not read past the two lines in c) above because they would not allow for even a remote possibility that they may not be the free agent they think they are. Thus, this book will only have value for a few persistent searchers. In matters spiritual, there is a fundamental difference between seeking and searching. The spiritual seeker is looking to validate their assumptions and shore up their beliefs. The searcher is looking to answer a nagging feeling that something is amiss, but they remain open to all possibilities, including those they do not favor.

The transcendent awareness you will garner from these pages cannot be confirmed or refuted by anyone else. It is the sum of profound and powerful mystical in-sights, or illumination—a liberating cognizance with a distinctly introvertive, experiential, and subjective quality that can never be measured by outside standards and is never verifiable for as

---

[2] "He noblest lives and noblest dies who makes and keeps his self-made laws" Richard Francis Burton once declared boldly and eloquently. But even he, despite an extraordinarily rich life that afforded him much freedom, could not escape all the normative restraints of his time.

[3] Here I paraphrase C. S. Lewis:

If I find in myself a desire which no experience in this world can satisfy, the most probable explanation is that I was made for another world. (From *Mere Christianity*)

Or, as Thomas Ligotti puts it sardonically:

The only value of this world lay in its power - at certain times - to suggest another world. (From *Songs of a Dead Dreamer*)

long as the soul is trapped in matter. But its value can be validated and its validity assessed against one's objective observations. The rocket engineer-cum-occultist Jack Parsons emphasized this notion:

> *Objectively, we know nothing at all. Any system of intellectual thought, whether it be science, logic, religion or philosophy, is based on certain fundamental ideas or axioms which are assumed but which cannot be proven. This is the grave of all positivism. We assume but we do not know that there is a real and objective world outside our own mind. Ultimately we do not know what we are or what the world is. Further, if there is a real world apart from ourselves we cannot know what it really is; all we know is what we perceive it to be. ... Absolute truth ... can only exist for the individual according to his whim or his inner perception of his own truth-in-being.[4]*

What follows is not a self-help book but a book to help the self; a lifetime companion to remind you of who you are, thereby unlocking the mysteries of infinite life. There is no method, no system, no ideology here to (mis)direct your inner journey. I open before you a large box that contains all the pieces of the puzzle; put them together, and you will have the whole picture in sight. Apply yourself diligently to this work, and you will break the seesaw pattern of human hope and despair. Delve into the riddles of the book, and you will find the answers along with the keys to free your soul.

---

[4] John Whiteside Parsons, *Freedom is a Two-Edged Sword*

Essentially, people approach all religious or spiritual matters from different but often overlapping angles. The literal is the worst—a blind alley littered with piles of garbage. The academic is not our concern here. We will dwell partly on the philosophical, the metaphorical, the mystical, and the initiatic. Yet, the true import of this book is theurgic: it opens the pathless, aethereal domain of the god-beings.

To perceive reality is only to experience what has already occurred, whereas to hear a myth is to penetrate the realm of endless possibilities. All legends are true because we dream them up ourselves. They are what we are. Thus, we begin with a tale of two realities...

Part One

You must be ready to burn yourself in your own flame;
how could you rise anew if you have not first become
ashes!

—Friedrich Nietzsche
Thus Spoke Zarathustra

Theirs is the responsibility, then, for deciding if they want
merely to live, or intend to make just the extra effort
required for fulfilling, even on their refractory planet, the
essential function of the universe, which is a machine for
the making of gods.

—Henri Bergson
The Two Sources of Morality and Religion, 1932

PORTENTS OF THE GODS

A Tale of Two Realities

1 So much is revealed in the lambent realm of the night that is veiled in the glaring reign of the day. Unfortunately for John, his own aphotic sibylline moment was irremediably butchered by the morning alarm. Like Odysseus marooned on the beach of Ogygia, he landed on the shore of the day, begrudgingly and dazed, with for sole companion the dread of having been tossed once again away from his true home. The castaway dragged himself to the bathroom and stood before the vanity mirror to examine his reflection: solar lentigines; crow's feet; eyebrows out of control; at least, the slight facial asymmetry that bothered him terribly in his teenage years had been mostly elided in the late sagging of his features. But now, the downturned corners of his mouth made him look perpetually dissatisfied. *Certainly, mirrors do not lie,* suggested the reflection, *but everything else can and will.*

John— John— John— He had read somewhere that Lord Alfred Tennyson found the "only true life" by repeating silently his own name without ceasing. It was worth a try, though not today; he was late again for work, and enlightenment would have to await the end of the rush. Still, one mirror realization had come before breakfast on the go: Death isn't the great equalizer, aging is. It gnaws at its victims steadily, troubling their minds and bodies until the end comes as a relief.

He splashed water over his face.

* * *

Why do they have to keep the water cold when it could easily be warmed alongside the potage in the kitchen hearth? Yet another trick of Father Ricaud who seems to view self-inflicted discomfort as a gateway to heaven. He would have been happier joining a stricter observance, Fèlyx murmured to himself thinking of the prior. To the contrary, the oblate drew closer to God in the experience of soothing sensations: the thick pattering of the summer rain on the wooden blinds at night; the petrichor of the humus when the mushrooms and the minuscule, damp-loving creatures feast on the rich decay of the autumnal forest; the farinaceous-sweet taste of the chestnuts roasted over the winter fire; the fresh wetness of the moss engorged with spring dew under the sole of one's naked feet.

That early morning, Fèlyx was in a hurry and would dispense with his habitual ruminations of daybreak toilette time. With sprinkles used economically, he refreshed his sleepy eyes and tamed unruly hair. Thursday was the day he had the exclusive permission from noon to midnight to use the hours for himself, away from studies, devotions, and chores. Abbot Gilbèrt entertained lofty designs for his protégé and therefore was willing to relax the monastic rules to some extent in order to secure the pupil's willing cooperation. But the fulfillment of the abbot's glorious vision of his charge becoming a renowned scholar, even a grandee of the Church, would require years of patience. The youth was not a novice yet and shared quarters with the secular servants of the monastery.

The young scholar-to-be worked through his schedule dutifully, if absentmindedly, and by the time the sun put on its most flamboyant attire to enter the hall of the zenith, he was running down the hill of Girocens, toward the Agot. The portion of the river he sought glided languidly less than an hour away from the abbey for a pair of young legs, and the boy felt he had wings.

In early spring, the waters could still be chilly. Still, the cloudless sky bore the promise of warmth aplenty to delight in the contrast. Soon, the student turned vagabond for a few hours trod through the thicket of ashes, willows, alders, and bushy, riparian undergrowth the hidden passage he had discovered three years gone that led to a secret destination: an old, abandoned watermill, forgotten by all but the intrepid children who did not hesitate to brave the sting of the nettle and the prick of the brambles in their playful quest to seize a castle and assert sovereignty over the purlieu. The remains of the edifice stood in a precarious equilibrium and collapsed chunks of walls in a curl of the river framed a deep pool where one could occasionally spot the darting gleam of a perch. The monastery escapee was not the only recurrent visitor to the mill: Brother Kingfisher also frequented the haunt to eye its lunch from the sill of a vanished window. Presently, the bird plunged like a bright, blue bolt into the fluid element. The boy followed his winged acquaintance and jumped.

* * *

Just as a slight, glistering curve formed on the edge dividing the realm of the living from that of the dead, an aethereal figure emerged from the low tide: first a buoyant tangle of golden-brass locks, then the head, neck, shoulders, torso, and hips dripping with liquid shimmer. The apparition arched the full length of his body backward like a bow and smoothed his hair from the forehead to the nap with a stroke of his two hands before extending his arms skyward: a worthy salute to the dawn. Hymnoneos returned ashore and, facing the rising sun, sat on the wet sand, his feet and buttocks still lapped by the tongues of the sea. His sight aligned with the horizon, he absorbed the spectacle that brought him to the same place every clement morning: Helios pulling his chariot from the deep and ascending the heavens swiftly, surrounded by a spellbinding display of pyrite, copper, and amber light that played for a moment on the pupils of the solitary spectator. On his roundish face, the soft, juvenile curvatures were complemented pleasantly by symmetrically full, proud lips. His nose was wide with rounded nostrils. The high cheeks, and broad, ovaline eyes rounded off his preternatural allure: eyes pellucid and green like the waters clapping gently in the silence of the coves; to be captured in their gaze gave the captive a feeling of wandering in a labyrinthine cluster of marine grottoes. There was in the lad's stare an indefinable dolefulness that presaged ill-fated fortunes. Few knew how the boy inherited his strange features. Some repeated exaggerated hearsays that he was the spawn of Poseidon himself. Persistent and more realistic rumors placed his birth at a time when pirates raided the coastal area, which would have made him the seed of a brigand. There were other mysteries surrounding the orphan, and the question none dared articulate aloud was why a lowly goatherd would be under the protection of the powerful priestess Agdomenis.

Lost in the contemplation of the sunrise, Hymnoneos was considering what it would be like not to have a name: everyone with a name seemed bound to places, duties, and expectations. With that thought the boy rose to his feet and, turning his back to the sea, rejoined his little herd, which was busy licking eagerly the salt off the rocks. Although he had not named the animals, their young protector knew them individually and used for each of them a different whistling call to which they responded separately: a trick he had learned from the birds whose cry is recognized by their chicks amidst a cacophony of cheeps and tweets. The noisy birds and insects, the cool springs and rivulets, the plants with healing properties and the shady groves, the warm sunsets and crystal sunrises, the tides and the Zephyr were the goatherd's life. The goats were his friends: their milk nourished him; their proximity kept him snug. Many a Summer night he had spent with his head resting on the flank of a doe. Calmed by the slow lull of her breath, his gaze searching the Zodiac, he could hear whispered in his ear the strange and mystical secrets of the god of the wild, companion of all the shepherds. There was nothing he desired more than the carefree roaming he had known for the most part of his juvenile years, and he wondered why the villagers and the townspeople, the fishermen, craftsmen, and tradesmen, the slaves and the officials in the world at the threshold of his were perpetually trapped in a web of superfluous endeavors.

2 John let two buses pass by and waited for the one less crowded. At the stop, he stood apart from the commuters whose proximity made him cringe. He had been told once by a co-worker that he was ochlophobic—he looked it up—but he was prey to no irrational fear of crowds, he simply loathed them. It was the masses, not he, who sweated irrationality and stank of abject conformism.

A crow alighted on the utility pole nearby to evaluate the situation below with a disdainful eye. John could not blame the bird and hoped he himself would not be judged too harshly by the winged observer. He wasn't with the others; he was the only creature on the sidewalk without a mobile phone in hand, and, unlike his fellows, he had not positioned himself strategically to board the bus ahead of the rest of the commuters. The group was ballooning around the stop sign; John retreated even farther. The bus arrived, and the little drove pressed forward, vying to be admitted first in the funnel. All surveyed the layout inside the vehicle, tallying a series of environmental factors and computing an outcome followed by swift selection. A few of them were anxious to secure a two-seat space. Where a passenger could lay his butt would be his most thought-through decision in a working day. Even nearing 60, John cut a reasonably thin figure that, under the circumstances, was an unfortunate attribute: it worked as a magnet for assertive bipeds in search of roomier territory. At the next halt, he found himself shoulder to shoulder, thigh to thigh, and knee to knee with a fellow whose earphones leaked a riling assault of cadenced percussion beats. Another hellish commute had begun.

From his own seat, John resumed his study in behaviorism. He remembered, when he was a child, entertaining himself in public transportation by imagining an occupation for individual passengers based on outer characteristics. But that game could no longer be played these days, he decided, observing the riders: at the dawn of the 21st century, the face of our species is turning into a paragon of blandness strangely highlighted by the glare of our handheld electronic devices. Our soulful composure is ravened by smart parasites: apps, virtual games, social media, texting deplete us of genuine human expressions at best, cultivate in us deranged emotions at worst. This Thursday morning, John himself was too weary to manage further considerations; he dozed off.

"I have something for you," announced his supervisor in a singsong voice—the habit she had of formulating her requests as if to compensate for being resented by everyone. Without a word or even looking at her, John took the file she was handing him. It was far easier to accept a task on the spot and find imaginative ways to eschew its unreasonable constraints later than to argue futilely about its infeasibility with someone deaf to logic and practicality. It was disingenuous, but he had an excuse: he profoundly disliked his job. The nature of that work had one major advantage though: it was so mindlessly routine that John could allot a good portion of his on-the-clock mental capacity to thinking about matters unrelated to business as usual. If individuals whose passion is their career are often envied, it is frequently the privilege of those with unenviable professions to nurture consuming passions. John's passion was a lifelong interest in all things esoteric since the day he stumbled upon a crate filled with his grandfather's books in the attic. The Pandora box opened by the twelve-year-old had released the strangest, eclectic collection: volumes authored by mysterious writers such as the Abbé Julio, Peryt Shou, Mouni Sadhu, or Lobsang Rampa; books on Rāja Yoga and the chakras; impressive titles like "The Eye of Revelation," or "le Matin des Magiciens"; gems of occultism written by retired career officers with dubious ranks and unverifiable tales of time spent among the natives of remote regions learning their mystical lore. There was no shortage of antediluvian records conveniently made available on the immaterial shelves of Akashic libraries by the ancient priesthoods of Atlantis, Mu, Shambhala, Agartha, or Thule. A couple of authors from the crate had been afforded the luxury of a trip around the cosmos in a flying saucer piloted by space aliens (at the time they were handsome, Nordic-like people, not the repulsive insectoid and reptilian creatures of more recent abductions). Other esotericists unchained were on familiar terms with the likes of Cagliostro, Saint-Germain, and Rosenkreuz or had penetrated the secret chambers and underground passageways of the great Egyptian sphinx and pyramids of Giza. The more fantastical the matter, the more it engrossed the child John in the same way the timeless folktales and legends of the past preoccupy the mythologist. Scarcely little of that corpus past-middle-aged John would take seriously, but it had once set his youthful imagination ablaze. There was a sweet nostalgia attached to the heydays of the New Age that, in retrospect, appeared almost profound in the dawning era of "conspirituality." Over the years, he had ingurgitated vast amounts of such literature until he had his nauseating share of the wondrous, hermetic feast: the secrets of shamans, lamas, magicians, and witches; the ultimate guides to attract prosperity or to repel evil, to fill the soul or empty the mind, to destroy the ego or embrace the shadow; the holy books and the grimoires; the hidden history and the forbidden archeology; the sacred and the taboo. *What did it all amount to?* he wondered one evening while attempting unsuccessfully to organize his bookshelves. He formulated for himself a threefold answer:

1. Nobody really knows what's taking place on the backstage of life, no matter how loud and imposing the pretense to the contrary is. (And what kind of a fool anyway would unquestionably accept from the dead or the living a claim of having privileged access to the ineffable, of being privy to the salon conversations of the gods, spirits, angels, and demons?)

2. A monumental library of metaphysical works is also a labyrinth fraught with hazards.

3. In the center of his own labyrinth lived a persistently gluttonous sprite in the shape of a question mark.

John no longer wanted to play the part of the spiritual enthusiast who reads one book after another, seeking to confirm the answers of the one with those in the next. Here and now, he would stop being so obsessed with answers that he did not have the time to reflect on the proper questions. We learn nothing when we are too busy sorting through the myriad conflicting ideas in circulations instead of paying attention to how and why beliefs form, rise, and fall, he decided. Henceforth, his quest for the grail of eternal wisdom would be less single-minded: rather than stretching and huffing to pluck the best fruits high in the tree, he would seek the best trees and wait for the ripe fruits to fall. There is great theurgical grace in store for those who surrender to their spiritual destiny instead of sweating in vain to pave its path.

3 *Inasmuch as you enquired about the origin of evil amidst all things created, I must turn your attention to the natural world where two principles can be plainly observed to be at work: one creative and benevolent from which proceeds life in all its aspects and all things that are beautiful and give joy to the human soul; the other, destructive and unpredictable from which proceed illnesses, plagues, and death, and all that which is afflicting our bodies and spirits. Does it not beseem reason, then, that man who is at the center of the natural world be under the sway of the two principles as well? For man is capable of great deeds in the arts and thoughts, and of generosity and compassion just the same as he is prone to greed, wanton destruction, and acts of violence. Even those who profess the good in the name of God often commit unspeakable evil...*

Felice di Caraman strained for the right words. The mental equipoise he considered a prerequisite to every reasoned thought was eluding him in the moment. He chose to postpone his task and let the peacefulness of the panorama stretching before his eyes work on his soul. The sun was setting over the lake. The countryside fragrances warmed by the summer day and moved by the light evening breeze had the savor of comforting quietude. As older men who have nurtured a keen intellect throughout their life sometimes do, he pondered again the intricate, uncanny circumstances of his existence. Destiny! How it relishes toying with our expectations. Happy is the soul who comes to realize her will is naught, the mere corollary of a primal, titanic conflict between powers unseen. The man whose prospects are all fulfilled is the one who learns the least, and he who believes he can rein the two horses that pulls the chariot of his life is a fool with no understanding.

From the open window, Felice allowed the spirit to reach out and caress the expanse within his gaze until essence blended with essence. He would not have foreseen such a favorable lot for his latter years. But that too, he reflected, may pass. The protection and hospitality of which he was the beneficiary might not extend many more years with the political uncertainties and shifting alliances of the times. Would he have once again to journey farther, to the East perhaps? Presently, memories crowded his reflective mood. Forty years had passed since he had taken leave of his adoptive mother in Collioure and sailed to the kingdom of Italy to pursue his studies in Bologna. After the death of Aurèlia, he had stayed in Lombardy. If he could not read the future, the past now lay in sharp relief before his mind's eye. He remembered the scrawny boy, famished and sickly, sitting on the ledge of the public fountain in La Vaur where the monks had found him. The fountain, the forlornness, the want for food and shelter, the despair of the heart were indelible imprints on his memory. But of the events prior to his encounter with the Felicians, he had little recollection: a few scattered images of places and faces on an indistinct timeline; a nomadic struggle to survive always at the edge of poverty. He did not know his exact age, or where he was born, and had imagined it was by chance or through angelic providence that the pious brethren took him under their wing. In truth, they had acted on a tip. They named him Fèlyx, and he could not remember having had any other name before that. Straightway, the foundling had been carried to the abbey, fed, bathed, and examined thoroughly by the infirmarer. From his apparent frailty, none would have guessed how resilient he was, although he would remain underweight for the rest of his life. From the lay brothers to the superiors, everyone had taken a liking to the child who displayed an endearing personality one could read openly on his face. Long lashes and thick eyebrows that nearly joined at the root of the nose accentuated the deep setting of his dark eyes. They had the welcoming obscurity of the confessional in which even the weakest soul could find relief and absolution. His lower lip was plumper than the thin upper lip in the shape of a slack Cupid's bow with its long lines osculating a soft, shallow philtrum. Dimples in the cheeks and little folds of extra skin under the eyes made him look perpetually mischievous.

Soon, Fèlyx had been baptized. He delighted in the care and concern lavished on him; he marveled at the magical atmosphere fostered by the play of lights between the walls of the church; he cherished the scent of incense and burning candles lingering between the colonnades of the abbey. One day, he too would be a monk, he had resolved. The newcomer demonstrated a remarkable ability to see through human pretense, paired with a precocious intellect that did not escape his benefactors. Indeed, it was that latter trait Abbot Gilbèrt found especially appealing in the youth to whom he had given his sacerdotal protection.

4 Hymnoneos was expected to show up for class on a grassy promontory close to where he tended his flock. For a few hours every week he joined a dozen other boys and a smattering of girls, ranging from age 8 to 16, who were taught the precepts of wisdom, science, and virtuous life under the tutelage of Xenoastares. The reputation of the elderly man they called the Wise had spread beyond the locality; leading families were competing to have him mentor their heirs and complement the formal schooling of their progeny. It was not unusual for the sons of embittered enemies to sit side by side before their tutor who was the sole arbitrator of whose children he would instruct; a few of them he picked among slaves and beggars. The Wise did not require or accept payment and could not be bribed.

Hymnoneos was not uncouth. He sojourned in the city when visiting Agdomenis, Priestess of Poseidon, his protector and de facto guardian since his infancy. Who his true parents might have been, the boy did not know. His curiosity was sufficiently satisfied when he was told his mother had died in childbirth and his father had vanished at sea. Meanwhile, to the effect he was believed to be favored by the gods, the priestess had carefully circulated and cultivated rumors that the child was the sole, miraculous survivor of a shipwreck. At the end of his formal education he had been given lodging and work with the superintendent of husbandry for the temple less than a half-day walk from the urban center. Unbeknownst to all, Agdomenis, who moved in the highest circles of power, intrigue, and influence was slowly grooming her protégé for a long-planned purpose.

From the Wise, Hymnoneos would acquire the lofty aspects of learning and refinement; but over mental things, he preferred the simple pastoral life befitting the nourishment of a serious mystical bent. It was not the intricacies of geometry, astronomy, music, or logic that endeared the teacher to the boy but the secrets of nature the older mentor was imparting to him, the mystagogic marvels he seeded in his imagination, the love of the gods and the understanding of their manifestations he instilled in his mind. The Master had given the would-be disciple a single thread of reasoning to which the youngster could apply himself for the remainder of his life:

"If we are created by the gods, we share in their substance and attributes. It ensues that by understanding ourselves we can explain the nature of the gods."

The Wise habitually pursued the arcane portions of his lessons with his most eager student (if not the brightest) once everyone else had been dismissed from class. The two were often seen walking along the seashore in the early evening, accompanied by Xenoastares' scribe, a servant who shadowed his master every way he went to record on beeswax tablets the substance of his words. The adolescent who fancied himself a storyteller claimed that he was the son of a deposed ruler. He even made a boast of having been sold into slavery thrice, remarking mystifyingly that he was freer than all his masters. No one knew how he ended up in the service of the Wise; Xenoastares always kept silent about personal lives, his or others'. The young scribe hardly spoke to anyone but became voluble with the goatherd boy to whom he relished relating the most astonishing tales of crossing the seas on a fantastic vessel, braving many dangers, and visiting many lands, the wonders of which he described with much lyricism. If some details stretched credibility, Hymnoneos saw no need to press for evidence. Truth be told, the goatherd was very fond of the handsome ephebe who, one had to admit, cut a princely figure even in his plain garb.

5 Riding a self-balancing unicycle, an app-development company employee rudely cut in front of John, mobile phone in hand.

Do they really need gyro-wheels to travel a six-block distance from an urban condo to a high-scale tech space? A caricature-like image flashed through the pedestrian's mind: a future generation of gnomes with atrophied legs and over-developed thumbs. Even without their paraphernalia, he was confident in his ability to profile the "tech" guy. "They shine by lack of originality," he had explained to a co-worker who was politely feigning interest.

"It's remarkable how, for people who are on the cutting edge of technology, they can be so bland. They are not aware of copying one another's style because their insular world of endless team meetings and insiders' socials is the only frame of reference they have, with little or no interest in anything non-tech. And there are obvious demographics too..."

He resented the kids who were less than half his age though paid twice as much as he was in an industry that encouraged a narrow set of hyper-developed skills over a broad education.

"They work to conjure heretofore inexistent consumer needs, which they subsequently satisfy with ever-encroaching, useless technology. They move in cliques and cramp the elevators where they love to hold superlative conversations over ambulatory coffee as if they were the artisans of a wondrous betterment of humankind. But the only life they are improving is their own."

From this perspective, John saw the "techs" as a new privileged class, self-centered, short on good manners (although that could just be part of a modern indifference to one's surroundings), unaccustomed to manual labor, unconcerned by realities, unadjusted to the forces of nature from which they were shielded by the increasingly intrusive, artificial, intelligence they championed.

John was in a despondent, distracted mood. Dragging his feet just a few blocks away from work, he let his mind wander back to his latest night dream:

The dwelling appears ancient; a sort of yurt or circular tent like those used by nomads and encamped armies in remote antiquity; made of animal skin possibly, stretched on a light, wooden frame. It stands in the blackness of a void, nowhere. The abode is dimly lit inside yet illuminated by the presence of its eremitic occupant. Is he a starets? A Bön abbot? A holy man certainly; and when I the dreamer approaches him, I am overwhelmed by a tide of boundless empathy. There is nothing apparently remarkable about the bald fellow of uncertain age, but his radiating presence is awe-inspiring. Reaching for my hand, he places in its palm a few pebbles with rough edges, one of which stands out with a deep blue color. With his own hand, the dweller of the dream closes mine still holding the stones and blows on it. Then, he takes the pebbles back before receding into hypnopompic blur.

* * *

The dead awoke from reality, the larger cosmic dream that encompasses all the dreams of the sleeper. There was indeed a rush of memories; or rather it was as if all the memories of his existence were woven and presented to him in a vivid, aethereal tapestry from which not the minutest detail was omitted: the plenitude of his life, the limpid spectacle of his soul. Nothing is ever forgotten: the trivial, the unpleasant, the joyful are only playing a game of hide and seek until a clever child drives them out. And in timelessness, John was not just remembering everything, he was the remembrance of all things while also distinct from it. There was no weighing of the soul against a feather, no life review, no moral implications, only the sum of a lifetime gushing out of his reality, evading at once the clutches of matter and the chain of neural connections to be free like an immense flock of starlings, compact, fluid, and shifty, flying as one toward the spiritual sun. The experience, strangely, was that of being entirely and authentically present to himself as he had never been before. He felt no regret, no pain, no contrition for the reprehensible because he was that which observes all phenomena as a thread of cause and effect that did not taint his eternal being. He was the amoral knower who has left childhood but still owns the child, born of the future that lies before the past in the ronde of the entirety. In that sphere, John was solitary but not alone: there was another presence, mutable, both tangible and incorporeal. Her shapes were many, now a child, now an adolescent; and then a fully developed person— male, female, both and neither, but always exuding an irresistible, mystical sensuality and an intoxicating aura. And John was filled with a fathomless desire for the radiant being. He could only comprehend her as different aspects merging into one: a pervading voice and a silence; a reflection and a guide; a primordial desire and an otherworldly lover, a daimon, an angel. And in her hands was a small book with iridescences of blue that penetrated John's psyche like an anchor lowered in the depth of the sea.

* * *

When John regained earthly consciousness, his mouth was dry with a bad taste, and his body felt limp. But the perception was unencumbered as when one occasionally awakes in the middle of the night without a transitional state. Then followed like a sudden dark fog the realization that he had been tossed back into the physicality of the cosmic dream: a tenacious nightmare he could not shake off; a make-believe lingering obstinately; a usurping illusion of being in charge. He furiously wanted to return where his will was no longer his own but that of an all-knowing daimon, where certainty sprouted not from faith or science but out of a transcendent determination. Instead, his mind was forced again into the clamps of the conditioned world, compelling him to re-visit the instant of a routine day when the habitual suddenly fractured.

The closer he got to the office, the more he dragged his feet. His mobile phone rang. The second he reached into his pocket, he knew a "bot" was calling, and yet, before a conscious decision reached the prefrontal cortex, he was already grasping the device, taking it to his ear: the perfect man-machine osmosis he so abhorred. He stepped absentmindedly onto the pedestrian crossing...

Evelyn too was preoccupied: that all-important text-message from the team had to be answered on the spot. A swift glance sideways assured her the light had just turned green; she took a right turn...

The impact was not particularly violent, but John was thrown out of balance and his head met the curb. There was a gash, blood, and a rush to the emergency room, but no loss of consciousness. The wound was cleaned and stapled; X-rays were taken. The patient was sent home with an admonition to come back to the hospital without delay should he feel any discomfort. He resumed work the following week. A few days passed before a severe headache prompted his return to the emergency room. The condition had taken a turn for the worse and soon called for an urgent medically induced coma, from which John did not resurface.

6 In a midsummer afternoon, Fèlyx again was *en route* to his private sanctuary. Ambling on the dusty paths, he kicked pebbles and chased after butterflies, but the grip of the heat reverberated under a polished sky soon forced him to slacken his pace. As usual, Farmer Delrieu's old dog accompanied him to the edge of the verdant overgrowth that enfolded the river protectively and stopped in his tracks as if heeding an ominous threat on the threshold of the unknown. The boy alone advanced through the thickets knowingly and negotiated the treacherous slant down to the water expertly until he reached his secret destination. With reverence, he approached the ruined mill cradled in a fold of the Agot.

The roof was long gone, but saplings grown in the cracks of the masonry formed a shredded canopy of overhanging branches. In places, roots, and the rhizomes of ferns had replaced the mortar to hold together stones shifted from position. Of the walls, three were still partially standing; a lump of the fourth had tumbled flat in the center where it rested unperturbed, enduring the erosion of the elements. In joint effort, the rain and the cyclical overflow of the river had shaped the slab into a smooth bed matted with moss, suitable for a weary tramp on a hot day. Fèlyx lay down and waited for the sun to dispatch a scattering of its best golden flickers and choreograph for the solitary audience an intricate dance with the green translucence of the leaves overhead. The spectacle reminded him of the magical display of lights in the nave. The church's windows had colored glass panels that filtered the sun rays in their rush, stealing and redistributing their essence into aethereal light. Presently, Fèlyx left his hidden retreat to lower himself into the coolness of the swimming hole. He was not a very good swimmer and trod the water close to the bank and toward a nearby bend where the flow relented and yielded to stillness. The sandbar was a favorite haunt for enormous carps who basked immobile in the warmth of the sunny shallow. The fish barely stirred when Fèlyx walked ashore but signs of another visitor to the secluded riverside startled the boy. A folded, white tunic lay over a hauberk tossed on the ground and, alarmingly, there was a sword too, planted in the sand next to the garb. Fèlyx noticed a man, almost camouflaged, sitting under the low-reaching foliage of an alder. The mysterious intruder was looking straight at him, and the bather—naked and wet like the carps—felt awkward. Yet, awe replaced his initial apprehension when he glimpsed, sewed on the stranger's tunic, the unmistakable emblem of the Poor Knights of Christ.

"Come and sit," called the knight. "You are the oblate from the abbey, aren't you?" And Fèlyx was surprised the warrior monk already knew this much.

The boy walked diffidently toward the young man but stood at a respectful distance, uncertain about what he should do or say, or if he should speak at all.

"Don't stand there gawking; sit down!"

The lean, taut physique and graceful demeanor of his interlocutor impressed the oblate; his own shyness, weak frame, and maladroit behaviors embarrassed him. He flushed, betraying the juvenile combination of being at once smitten with someone and feeling terribly inadequate. The impassive, controlled features of the stranger cracked with a slight, knowing smile. His soft but determined gaze carried an unmistakable message: *Tread carefully in your dealings with me, for I am capable of great kindness or implacable violence.*

Fèlyx was fascinated by the stranger' skin tone that, for lack of a better description, reminded him of the inner lining of the almond shells he had cracked at one of his patron's elegant soirées. (Only much later would he hear the rumor about the half-blood knight whose mother had converted to the true faith.)

"I am Saint Amant," interrupted the interlocutor, "and there is Mithras." He pointed at his destrier. "I named him after the guide of the souls who accompanied the legions of ancient Rome on the battlefield. By what name should I know you?"

The overture had the effect of putting the boy somewhat at ease, and he introduced himself.

"Ah, Fèlyx! I am a friend of your friend, the Lady de Caraman. I noticed you at her latest, fine evening gathering. You were so wrapped up in the Lady's aura of sweetness, you did not pay attention to me!" Saint Amant laughed at his own joke, but he was not mocking: his laugh was brotherly and congenial. Fèlyx uncomfortably flushed for a second time, but he accepted the jest as a child accepts a nudge from an elder brother. Instinctively, he lowered the drawbridge of his irreproachable heart to let in the friendly traveler.

7 On one of their didactic promenades by the sea, the trio opted for a recess at the beach. The sun was on its descent to the depths of Oceanus at the ends of Earth; the day had come to that pleasant turn when the aroma of the flora inland, extracted by the heat of the afternoon, wafted to the shore as if carried by the sound of the gently lapping waves, to mix with the smell of salt and the sand. Xenoastares absented himself, and the lads took advantage of a little recreational time to look for shellfish they could roast, play a game of knucklebones, and start a campfire. Selene had already stolen Helios' light when the teacher reappeared carrying a smallish round shield left behind by some marauding platoon. Close to the blaze, the incongruous object at the feet of the Master gleamed with the dancing glares of Vulcan's forge. The Wise kept silent. The youths were expecting one of those ancient, epic sagas of warriors and conquest—best narrated by the flames rising in the dark—with which the teacher often regaled the students. Instead, he began tracing lines on the diminutive aspis with a piece of charred wood; the boys knew a lecture was imminent.

"See how everything around you is changing with the cover of the night and the contours of all things are blurred by darkness and shadows. To your eyes, the landscape appears different from what it was erewhile, and yet, with the return of the first light, you will know it has always been the same. Think of the marine creatures who live in the depths of the seas. They are ignorant of the limits of their watery world, yet the sea is self-contained. The fish has no understanding of the land on which we walk, and we have never probed their abyssal abode. Consider the realm of the Somnia that vanishes as soon as you awake. Or is it that you are sleeping now and truly arise from slumber in your dreams? Night and day, sea and land, dream and wake, all the paired sides of the dual world are concurrent, but we know not how to experience them at once."

Xenoastares' audience of two did not interrupt and remained attentive. Meanwhile, the Wise had finished drawing to adorn the plain shield with a geometrical design: a circle held snugly within a square, and the square hugged by a triangle with the three peaks osculating the circular metallic rim.

"We live in the dream of the gods, and in that dream, we dream the gods into existence—I represent them with the triangle. The circle is Apeiron, the boundless whole, both the inner—inside the square—and the outer, the circumference that encompasses everything else; there is nothing beyond, not even a void. Because Apeiron is the All, where could nothingness be? The square is the world of physicality where we live and evoke the gods who draw from Apeiron the substance for their dreams. Thus, we, and the gods are reborn forever because of the endless soaring of their desire and our longings, and they know themselves in our memories that become their own eternally. We see cyclical time, eternal recurrence, moving in one direction only, but continuous, infinite time is an eternal sameness that flows backward as well as forward. Thus is the entirety pulsating, inhaling and exhaling, breathing."

Many a great secret Hymnoneos learned from his teacher about the gods who, he was taught, do not live on the top of a massive mountain, or in the vault of the sky.

"They are everywhere, penetrating all the elements with desire, riding the waves of the sea, the flames of the fire, and the clouds of the sky. They speak to us in the murmurs of the stream, the breath of the wind, and the calls of the birds. They are the vitalizing movement in the blade of grass and in the minerals even. Their limbs extend everywhere, but their heart is in the heart of men. They have no memory of their own but man's memories. We give them life with our oblations, and they give us birth so we can worship them. Only when we give the gods the proper worship do they let us partake of their substance in us."

8 John had been in a vegetative state for three days when he was declared brain dead. However, barely an hour after having been issued his ticket to a trip onboard Charon's vessel, the dead, apparently, was having buyer's remorse. A slight, almost inaudible gasp, and a jerk of the arm alerted an attendant that the traveler to the underworld was venturing to return to the upper one, causing quite a stir in the facility.

By the measures and criteria of the medical center, John had been dead and was alive again, defying the scientific paradigm. The resurrected was welcomed back with a mix of awe, congratulations, cheering words, and even a few feeble jokes. Unsettled by a phenomenon that eluded their grasp, confronted their expertise, and could challenge their procedures, the doctors preferred to eschew the subject of one of their patients crossing the Styx both ways. For the most part, they kept mum. Once the essential tests and procedural post-surgery care had been completed, this modern Orpheus was released without mentions of his foray into the beyond or words of advice. The atmosphere of reluctancy from the medical establishment carried over to John's circle of friends, coworkers, and acquaintances. There was no lack of merry observations, but the merriment was not contagious. And when John broached the metaphysical specifics, they were met with a blank stare and an air of refrained dismissal. He found the imposed dumbness and numbness even less bearable than the pretentious, pointless, and lengthy, existential arguments his know-it-all French relatives would have loved to end abruptly with the ineludible conclusion (voiced in a solemn tone): "Faut pas chercher! C'est un mystère."

For John, whatever meaning could be scrapped from life was justified by the words of Thomas the dissentient Apostle: "He who seeks, let him not stop seeking until he finds." He believed in solving mysteries. He believed knowledge could wake the latent god under the spell of nature. The depression bouts that had plagued him since childhood might not have been chronic, he opined, if not for a psychic fatigue caused by his inability to answer a nagging call from the innermost. Now, at the heart of his dejection was his visit to the netherworld, the stupefying event that had remained unspoken and unprocessed for lack of an audience. The depression he had learned to do with, to assuage and probe as one would do with a temperamental teenager in order to understand his motives. He had come to regard anxiety, and a depressed mood as intuitive, natural mechanisms of recognition that there is something inherently wrong with this world and the standardized lives we live in the name of normalcy. His present, persistent state of mind was different, however: it was a sullen anger; the directionless resentment of the dreamer jolted out of a wondrous dream by the morning alarm and thrown back into the world of stifling conditions that everyone seemed to take for their only home. He decided to contact the Jungian analyst a sympathetic nurse had recommended to him off the record before his discharge from the hospital.

9 The abbot of Girocens was alarmed, in a state of panic even. Henri de Marciac and his troops were closing in on the gates of La Vaur, having sided with Raymond V in the petty disputes between the Count of Toulouse and his thorn in the side Rogièr Trancavel, Viscount of Albi. Beyond the political maneuvering though, it was well known that the Cardinal's main ambition was to subjugate the Cathari to the Church of Rome or eradicate them altogether. The abbot of Clairveaux's suggestions had been heeded by the Third Council of Lateran, and his views on the heretics instigated the 27th canon with its radical measures aimed at dissenters. Yet, it remained unclear how de Marciac himself would deal with his foes once he faced them, and the papal legate did not worry Father Gilbèrt as much as the zealots who might follow on his heels. The canon had pronounced under anathema the Cathari, their hearers, supporters, and well-wishers, enjoining the populace to take up arms against all dissentient believers and their acolytes, drive them out of their land, and confiscate their wealth. Now, any adventurous fool or vulgar mercenary could gather a band of brigands and seed chaos and mayhem in the region with the sanction of the Church. The simmering pot of gruel could soon boil over, and Gilbèrt was certain great injury would be inflicted to the inhabitants of peaceful Girocens. The abbot felt somewhat responsible. Had he been perhaps too complacent, unwittingly letting a poison infect the populace? Had this same poison already infiltrated the very walls of his abbey? Now, his flock, and the monks under his care were possibly in great danger.

* * *

Roused by the preaching of Bernard de Clairvaux, Félicien Verdeau, then an idealistic young man, had enthusiastically joined Alphonse Jourdain *en route* to the Levant. After the assassination of the Margrave of Provence, he had remained behind with the French army in their ill-fated attempt to take over Damascus. The unfortunate results for the young crusader were a life-threatening wound inflicted by the Turkish archers, the scarring of his soul caused by the senseless violence of the crusade, the machinations of power seekers, and the ubiquitous cruelty of man. Ill and in low spirits, Félicien claimed to have had on his trip back from the land of the Saracen a glorious vision of the Virgin flanked by the boy Jesus and surrounded by angels. The Mother of God spoke to him saying that his calling was not to combat the Mohammedan overseas but to reform the heretic at home through benignant persuasion and example. This he would do by gathering sympathizers and laying the foundations for the congregation of the pious brethren of the Mother of God, usually known as the Felician order, or simply "the Felicians." He saw the *opus dei* as a three-thronged approach: the brethren would commit in equal parts to devotional, charitable, and scholastic endeavors. The order was approved and fast-tracked by the bishop of Albi, and Félicien's goodwill and candor was welcomed by the villagers of Girocens who only three months before had chased away the local priest with stones and sticks. Soon, the congregation attracted the patronage of wealthy families. But poor Félicien would not see the fruits of his labor as he died nine months into the consummation of his lofty objectives. An ambitious monk by the name of Gilbèrt would take over at the helm of the order.

Abbot Gilbèrt hoped the constitutions of the congregation of the pious brethren would eventually be approbated by the pope himself, and he was satisfied the religious community was a success under his leadership. At the same time, most of the region remained under the sway of the bons hommes who thoroughly took care of their own. This left scarcely little charitable work for the monks to perform, and instead, they shifted their emphasis toward worship, scribal work, and the copying and illuminating of books. The abbey now boasted a renovated church, a small hospital for travelers, and a sizable library that was known by repute at home and farther among men of letters and religious scholars. As far as reforming the heretics—the initial concern of the brethren at the inception of the order—the results were meager, though. The abbot was aware of the persiflage that, far from having brought the heretics into the flock, he had watched the flock flying to the heresy. It was an exaggeration, yet there were indeed within the bounds of the monastery tares that had grown together with the wheat. Whenever possible, Father Gilbèrt had taken swift action to unroot the weeds; but the mores and beliefs of the Albigensians all around were persistently insidious. In retrospect, the head of the congregation of the pious brethren saw that lacunae in his past achievements might carry a cost in the future, and he reproached himself for a lack of foresight, too much leniency, and, above all, his compromises. Now, two large thorns pricked his side: his own protégé the young Fèlyx had fallen into the grip of a Manichean preacher; and then, too many dangerously unorthodox books sat on the shelves of the library. At least, should things take a turn for the worse, he would know exactly on whom to redirect the blame: Aurèlia de Caraman,

Chatelaine of Les Martels, widow of the late Knight Pèire-Raimon Tourlareine.

10 The Wise never meandered far from the source of lofty knowledge and higher meaning; but downstream, Hymnoneos turned to Alkedoron for everything practical. Indeed, the superintendent was as experienced in the ways of men as the revered teacher was knowledgeable in the ways of the gods. The absence of real parents did not feel abnormal to the boy whose extended family had included the goats, his herding dogs, the birds of the field, and even the trees as far as he could remember. His protector the high priestess of Poseidon had generously provided for him, and the overseer of the temple livestock had been his conscientious guardian. Not that there was much to guard in the self-sufficient youngster who, from the earliest age on, had demonstrated a stubborn, independent streak. When not outdoors with the animals, Hymnoneos and his foster parent lived in a small, sober, but adequately furnished house on the bluff.

Alkedoron was a colorful character. He came from the islands and had spent more years of his life on deck than inland. By his own admission, he had also been a raider, long ago. The vivid and varied recollections of his past were difficult to sort out for authenticity; but parts of his adventures at least could be substantiated on account of the amazing scars he sported on his body. There was hardly any parcel left of the mariner's flesh that did not bear the lacerations of reckless times. Apparently, he had been found washed aground and unconscious, and that is how he turned up on the shores of the peninsula. The maroon had been brought to the high priestess who nursed him to recovery. A few years after the events of his rescue, she made the survivor a curious offer: she would grant him a better occupational position for life on the condition that he would care for the boy Hymnoneos. Thus were two destinies entwined, and the pair was well matched: the mature man who uncannily kept death at bay, quite the raconteur, never shy to speak his mind, and very liberal in sharing the content of his thoughts; the youth, a virgin substrate eager to absorb the dramatic memories of his elder. The goatherd boy thirsted to drink of the flavorful flow of others' existences as if under an ominous premonition his own sojourn in the mansion of the day would be brief. Also, Alkedoron was the only link to Hymnoneos' origins and infancy that wasn't tenuous.

"I did not know your mother, but your father and I were friends, briefly, when I was in the service of our king. Your father was a foreigner of noble descent, and a warrior. He journeyed from a land unknown, through the mountains, at the head of a small detachment. The following months, a hundred more of his people arrived: men, women, and children whom the king permitted to settle in the area. But after twelve years, they left as inexplicably as they had come."

Alkedoron had made the youth swear not to breathe a word of his revelations to anyone.

"Your father departed when you were still a newborn, and you were named by an oracle. He did not abandon you; I do not think he knew of your mother's pregnancy. Perhaps the two already lived apart by then. Whatever his motivations to disappear were, I cannot believe for an instant he would have forsaken you, had he been aware you existed."

The story comforted Alkedoron's young companion, and the benignant man promised he would soon take his charge to the hills, to the forgotten shrine Hymnoneos' progenitor had built for the mysterious god worshiped by his forebears.

11 Dr. S. A. Wood was not much help; at least not the sort of help John thought he could use. He was uncertain of the exact nature of what he expected, but they had to do with validation, affinity more than sympathy or even empathy, and an understanding of the implications of his experience. He did not know how to deal with the inescapability of being thrown back unwillingly into the dread of material existence after having visited the exultation of a pleroma. Maybe with time he could bear that burden; but the resentment lingered painfully, and the sense of alienation from his daily surroundings was excruciating. Yet, suicide was no longer the option he had mulled when he was a teenager, as it was plain to him now that it would only disrupt a process of a higher order.

Sue Ann was a reasonably competent psychotherapist, and that was the problem, he reflected: she stood too close to what she knew best without taking the risk of venturing beyond her academic framework. She had a near cultish propensity for deferring to Jung as the final voice of authority and betrayed too much confirmation bias in accepting his unproven theories. At times, she lost herself in the goals, the work to perform, the steps to be taken, until they completely obfuscated what was truly at stake. Near death experiences are but the archetypal actualization of an unconscious wish for individuation, she maintained. She added that paranormal and visionary events gain validity and meaning only through an application to wholeness of purpose in life—this life! He begged to differ, having been shown by a numinous power that the living are not alive until they are dead. He did not care to mend the psyche's split between anima and animus, to out the shadow from some dark closet, or to reconcile the unconscious with the conscious. All those aims suspiciously felt like extra tentacles on the body of the Magna Mater, and John was not inclined to fall deeper in her embrace; he wanted out and had no further patience for Jungian labyrinthine speculations.

"The unconscious is a pseudo-scientific discovery, a new suit for the Devil" he rejoined, "a fable concocted by a handful of 19th century white men to whom is given too much credence. Besides, our current cultural obsessions with the unconscious and a DIY approach to it looks suspiciously like yet another detour to keep us away from what really matters. Our lives are not dictated from a vast hidden reservoir of powerful urges and repressed memories but by the power of our beliefs. In any case, considering what a poor job we do with our conscious mind, perhaps we would be well advised not to tamper with an unconscious one. And why would I go milling about in a gloomy, dank basement in the first place when the treasures of a sunlit attic are beckoning me?"

Paraphrasing Jung, the therapist had the misfortune to mention that one does not reach enlightenment by imagining figures of light outside but by peering into the darkness within:

"Those who look outside dream; those who look inside awake."

"Aren't all things dreamed and imagined born inside?" John retorted, all fired up. "Would peering in the darkness be an awakening or the tumbling into another dream just as unpleasant? How can we make the unconscious conscious when consciousness itself is subjective? How do you know darkness would not beget darkness or worse yet, deceptive enlightenment? It is deceitful to say that there is no way to the angel of light without first encountering the shadow. I did not have to plunge into a sea of repressed instincts and drives to be lifted with the rising sun. I have peered into the numinous center. I have not encountered an archetypal projection; I have communed with the quintessential manifestation of the 'dioscuric other,' fully alien and yet completely myself, not just an image but a living, aethereal being. There is nothing more to achieve, only something awaiting. I am not the artisan of my individuation but the instrument of a transcendent individuality. An angel showed me the multitudinous windows of existence which are the dreams of a god. The god dreams and re-dreams souls so that the best versions, or the most mature and accomplished of them can dream the god to whom they belong. Everything is only the dream of a dream; the entirety is but the reflection of a reflection. Reality and aethereality are the two mirrors facing each other, and nothing is created outside of perception. The waste that should be discarded to oblivion is sifted through the warp and weft of destinies, which is recombined in all necessary possibilities to weave the perfect fabric that will last in eternity."

"You see," John continued, "everything possible is manifested at once in the sight of the god, and spirit is perpetually pervading all material planes in search of soul. In one window of possibilities, the odds favor him because of all the permutations and combinations of reality allowed by necessity that are played out simultaneously. Like the fibers in the strands plied into the yarns, themselves entwined to make up a cord, possibilities are compounded into destinies, destinies into anamnesis, and anamneses into souls. Fate is the narrative that holds all the stories together. Spirit on its many courses will encounter many soul stories; but only some of them have the right chain of cause and effects, the distinctive plot leading to a forever-after happy ending. There is only one story that becomes a ladder to the heavens—so to speak—the others unravel unless, I surmise, the god chooses to preserve and remember what he wills. I know how I can be liberated; I do not know all the secrets of liberation.

"Because a strand of destiny requires choices and decisions, from a shallow perspective we are left with the impression we are the shapers of our own path. But from a vantage point, individual lives are the unfolding of one possible path, one possibility among untold other possibilities, all known and present at once in the dream of the god. Versions of ourselves live the many different lives we could have led had we made different decisions. I think it takes many souls to make a god. And when a soul facilitates at last the release of the spirit from the bonds of matter, that god is reborn. I call the soul, the totality of our memories, the unique window into the world that makes us individuals. The soul doesn't need to be whole; the god does! A god is a god only when he dreams the proper story, and that is the one with the soul perpetuated out of material existence. Therein lies the liberation I understand: not in performing good deeds, or useful ones, but by belonging to the exact chain of events ending in a soul-god conjunction. In short, what liberates us is necessity."

John took a few measured breaths for reflection before resuming.

"It's like different scenarios for a same actor playing on the screens of a multiplex theater: some with unhappy denouements; some with a bitter-sweet end; and one with the perfect resolution. Can you see how it works? The soul does not need to progress through successive lives and be purified, as some think, it is distilled by the concurrent, varied destinies that disrobe becoming and predictability to reveal naked being and spontaneity. There is no reincarnation of the soul, but there is a perpetual incarnation of the Spirit. Just as light is both particle and wave, we are both physical and aethereal, subjective and objective, divided and whole: the limbs of Dionysos scattered upon many soils and collected by his brother Apollo. The soul/Dionysos and the Spirit/Apollo are two aspects of the same observer, a reciprocal perception through different pairs of eyes. When spirit looks through the eyes of Dionysos, we are physical reality; when soul sees through the eyes of Apollo, we are aethereality. If my vision was the result of a subconscious wish, in the end, it has become consciously objective—the birth of something ineffable and new in the center of my subjective universe."

John's soliloquy had poured out with the assurance of self-evidence, and the psychologist had listened patiently as one would listen to the babble of the child. She remarked cleverly that if he could figure all that out on his own, he was more in need of a publisher than a therapist. John could appreciate the josh but was in no mood to laugh at himself. He interpreted Sue's bantering attempt and lopsided smile as condescension.

Dr. Wood acknowledged that John would not make any progress under her care and proposed to put him in touch with an acquaintance of hers, a prominent investigator in the field of NDE studies who conducted her research here in Washington.

"You must tell your story to a person who has walked in your shoes. Retelling your experience in detail to someone with a thorough background in NDE, metaphysical, and occult studies will bring about the catharsis you need," Sue Ann expressed confidently. "And you won't have to pay the fees I charge!"

She told him he could have the opportunity to participate in an ongoing case study. Three weeks hence, John was sitting on a rickety chair in a modest two-room office on the sixth floor of the Pioneer Building.

* * *

Marguerite Swanson had a quick errand to run and invited John to make himself comfortable. He wondered if she meant that ironically in consideration of the wooden chair with its one leg shorter than the others, and it signaled the difficulty he would have in gauging his interlocutor.

In contrast to Dr. Wood's professional, generic office, with its cozy furniture and unfortunate *objets d'art*, Marguerite's workspace was sparsely furnished but for the books, binders, and folders ubiquitously scattered in meticulous disarray on all available flat surfaces and piled up to the ceiling. Unexpectedly, he relaxed: for the first time since his release from the hospital, the agitation and anxiety that had gripped him were relenting. On the walls hung a few assorted etchings, woodcuts, watercolors, and ink drawings together with an ostentatious display of diplomas, and certificates. John found the artwork tasteful and the show of credentials a bit too pompous. There was no doubting the researcher's qualifications though, and her résumé was impeccable. She had written several books on NDEs, and her extensive groundwork had earned her the respect of academia. She pursued her case study work with the help of grants and the proceeds from her publishing endeavors. John felt he was in the right place. Besides, he enjoyed the epochal atmosphere of the vintage building with its smell of old wood and dust, the filtered luminosity of the large skylight, the hefty steel beams traversing the space of the atrium, and the heavy, red-brick walls that smothered the urban noise down to an otherworldly silence.

Presently, Marguerite returned. With her underweight frame, outrageous makeup, and mismatched, colorful attire, she reminded him of a school counselor he had in seventh grade. They both affected the poise and self-confidence of those rare individuals who are genuinely and completely free from the universal compulsion to blend in. They are also the most problematic persons to gauge. Her comical appearance made it hard not to stare, and perhaps it was all on purpose. John was slightly bothered he wouldn't be able to break through the extravagant façade and appraise the mental furnishing, but Marguerite's frank, open-minded, and direct demeanor set him suitably at ease. The state of disorder that surrounded her balanced appropriately his obsessive rigor. John was given another chance to make himself comfortable when he was motioned through the dangling bead curtain of an open doorway. Marguerite followed carrying the rickety chair, a notebook, and a voice recorder. The adjacent room was oddly sparse. In the right corner next to the door, a worn leather club chair (with its obligatory bouncy, bellied cushioning) seemed to be patiently awaiting its next occupant. Against the facing wall across the room stood a vintage pendulum clock nearly seven feet high. John held fond memories of a similar antique at his uncle's place. When he was a child, he would never fail to caress the belly of the clock and feel titillated by the brush of his fingertips on the smooth patina skin of the hardwood. When nobody was home, he would sit cross-legged before the *horloge*, watching time being moved rhythmically by the sway of the pendulum, listening absorbedly to the loud ticking (more "tock" than "tick") of the second hand that punctuated the silence, waiting for the chime that broke the hour.

The visitor sank in the armchair while Marguerite sat out of his sightline in the opposite corner of the same wall. Next, she asked her guest to gaze effortlessly at the pendulum and to let the beat of the seconds transport him back to his own death. She could not have found a better way to set things in motion. Soon, John would fling open his psychic gates and let the anamnesis flow.

12 The evening at Les Martels was spectacular in the eyes of the child. The queen of the assembly had invited two troubadours who jousted with the fervor of their verses to win her favors. Musicians too, and other entertainers attended the reception. The gentry mingled with scholars, craftsmen, and artists. The festive atmosphere and the abundance of foods bedazzled Fèlyx who had never seen such refinement. He had an appetite for cured meat but decided to abstain and chose the fish instead in deference to the bon homme Jérôme who was also present. The youth fluttered from tables to invitees and tried to avoid the ladies-in-waiting and women servants who always teased him with exaggerated amorous displays and pinched and kissed his cheeks; the more he resisted the more encouraged they felt. He was the darling boy of the estate, but his own secret affections were ever for Aurèlia. "Ma Dame des Martels" he had called her since the day of his introduction to the Mistress of the manor, when he was still a young child. Everybody found it charming, and, with no one correcting the boy, the appellation persisted.

The Lady de Caraman was once married to Pèire-Raimon Tourlareine, a knight 20 years her senior. The contract benefited both, and the relationship grew over time into a stable, fulfilling friendship. Clearly, they liked each other. The knight had the reputation of an eccentric. He claimed there was somewhere on his estate a forgotten necropolis that was both the final resting place of Visigoth aristocrats and a cache for coffers when their people retreated before the Franks. If not at war, Tourlareine could be spotted with his servants digging holes in search of the elusive treasure of his land on the plateau overlooking the river Agot at the foot of Girocens. He was also vigorously vocal about his opposition to the Capets and was often heard saying he would be found dead before he bowed to the king of France. In that, the knight's prediction had come true as he died in a skirmish fighting the brigands who often raided the purlieus. He had left behind a surprisingly large inheritance for someone of his status, which led the populace to believe he had indeed unearthed the "treasure of the Visigoths." In the wake of being widowed, the alluring and wealthy Aurèlia attracted many a suitor, as could be expected. From wandering bards to local gentry, she cleverly dismissed them all, quipping that her only true love was Fèlyx who, sadly, would be a monk. The truth was, she had forgone the futilities of romance and had no longer a need for the security a pragmatic matrimony could provide. Free from the compulsion of giving birth to an heir, she used a substantial part of her fortune to sustain charitable works, encourage the arts, foster learning, and promote education. To Fèlyx, Aurèlia was the epitome of femininity. He was fascinated by her hair that had the color of the chestnut's crown in autumn, and the scintillas-like freckles on her skin, which reminded him of the golden dust on the sheer of sunbeams. He thought she should act the part of the Mother of God in a mystery play; a feeling that did not seem sacrilegious in any way for, he reflected, there can be no conflict between beauty and the religious sentiment. This reasonable angle put his mind at ease while he would not admit that his mystical admiration for the Lady and captivation with her entourage were drawing him increasingly into free-thinking circles and away from the sanction of the Church he was called to serve.

Aurèlia herself was an individualist who delighted in organizing religious debates. Publicly, her allegiance was with the mother Church, and she was known for her devotions to the Magdalena. Most of her company however accepted the Albigensian faith, and she opened her doors to its proponents and followers. Of late, she had befriended the charismatic Jérôme whom she allowed to lecture at Les Martels.

Fèlyx thought highly of Jérôme whom he regarded as a father figure. In return, the bon homme showered with paternal affection the boy whom he saw as his *filius spiritualis*. He hoped Fèlyx too would receive the consolamentum someday but never coerced him in any way, remarking that the *spiritus principalis* does not have terms or a cutoff and works differently with each soul. The largest hands and strongest arms he had ever seen on a man intrigued the oblate. The long, white hair and beard gave the Elder a stately presence while making him appear somewhat more advanced in age than he might have been. Few facts were known about Jérôme, but a quasi-legend preceded him. He was the son of a wealthy merchant in Lyon and, as a child, he followed his father on the trade routes both by land and by sea. He had little schooling but was a precocious and strong-headed youngster. By age 15, Jérôme had left the family business to join a string of wandering heresiarchs and soon gained the reputation of a rabble-rouser who incited the populace to rebel against the Church authorities and trample the holy cross and the relics. He claimed that God never intended for his children to worship an instrument of torture, or body parts, and that His grace was open to all through the words of the Apostles and the gift of the spirit without a need for the intersession of priests or saints. Those who knew him (or pretended to know him) said he could have turned the most dedicated eremite into a heretic. Such was the power of his sermons. He confronted many a dignitary and led a multitude away from the Christian flock until he nearly avoided, through a daring escape, being burned at the stake by a mob beneath the walls of Tonnerre. After that, he disappeared and was thought dead (though conflicting reports of his whereabouts constantly circulated) only to resurface twenty years later, alive and well, by the side of the young Baron de Caraman who was an ardent believer in the faith of the Cathari. Shortly thereafter in Sant Felitz, a series of high-profile meetings took place to settle matters of doctrine and administration, which attracted many eminent dualists, Manichaeans, and Bulgars. Jérôme won the respect and admiration of the assembly for his profound knowledge and ability to expound on the nature of the two gods: the one who rules over the celestial element, the invisible Father; the other who sprung from the Nihil and assembled the four elements of matter, the Rex Mundi visible through the evil deeds of men and the wickedness of priests. However, he seceded from the council because of his fierce opposition to the hierarchical structuring of the good Christians into diocesan boundaries ruled by bishops and deacons. Subsequently, he was spotted in Rabastens and La Vaur before settling in Girocens where he became the spiritual father and a leader of the bons hommes and bonnes femmes in the area. Much to the annoyance of Abbot Gilbèrt, Jérôme contended he held the power, in direct lineage from John the Beloved, to confer the Paraclete.

13

Hymnoneos awoke elated and rose before the night surrendered its last corner to the push of the day. Following a slapdash ablution, the boy headed to the craggy hillock where he habitually made his devotions. He knew his way to reach the even top, scaling the accumulation of boulders. From the heights, he looked straight into the brightest patch of the emergent dawn, then he kneeled and bowed, lightly touching the stony ground with his forehead.

"Desire unbound who lifts the breathing dew of existence; primordial, perfect shine; I bow before you like I bow before the flame of the shrine. May my name be remembered forever."

Still kneeling, he pivoted in the direction of the late summer and autumnal storms as they reached the shores. He straightened his back and stretched his arms as if to touch the line of the horizon with the tips of his fingers.

"Unblemished, two-natured eternal youth born of the sun-parched and the ever-blooming lands, let me partake of your cup of ecstasy like I drink the honeyed milk of the libations. May I serve you in your abode."

He stood again, facing the expanse where the sun is last seen before plunging daily into the underworld. Raising his hands skyward in the pose of the Orante, he prayed.

"Bestower of liberation and freedom, deliver me from the foes of life and the shackles of death. May my destiny be entwined in yours."

Such were the ways his teacher had told him to invoke the primigenial, liminal, benignant god. But on that day, anticipating his journey to the shrine at which his own father prostrated, he raised his eyes and gazed at the aerial pathway of the migratory birds when they flew over the peninsula, returning from their sojourn in the vast lands of the south beyond the seas.

"O god of my fathers, I listen to you in silence as I listen to the silence in the temple."

Hymnoneos trotted back home and was met midway by Alkedoron who had made the preparations for their excursion. They would travel light. He had packed a bow and arrows, his kopis and two knives, two blankets, some cheese, oil, bread, and wine. The rest they would glean on the way. With that, they headed toward the hills. The pair was in high spirits. For the elder, the trip was a welcome throwback to his youthful adventures minus the violence and warfare: a smooth interlude to delight in drinking once more of the cup of uncompromised freedom and to breathe in sync with the wilderness. Man as he was meant to be, he thought, without a care for duties or allegiances, free from bonds or attachments except those he chooses on his own. For the younger, it was his first occasion to venture beyond the boundaries of the familiar and the predictable. Furthermore, he hoped to make a connection with his own history—not to find roots (in common with his traveling companion he did not wish to be a stump attached to any soil) but to grasp the thread by which he could secure his place in time and be remembered by the gods in the tapestry of life they weave by design.

As expected, the terrain turned arduous as soon as they reached the hills, but they enjoyed the challenge thoroughly. Hymnoneos wondered aloud why anyone would erect a sanctuary so distant from the roads most traveled, and Alkedoron answered that it was to protect the holy from false and plebeian religious sentiment. The former warrior found in the intergenerational hike the perfect outlet for his voluble self, and he resumed recounting what he knew of the boy's father and ancestors.

"They came through the mountain range, most of them on foot, and a few riding horses the likes of which no one had seen before in this country. Who knows how far they had journeyed? Their mores and fashion were very foreign to us. They refused to eat any meat, especially that of the waterfowl; they revered the cryless swan. We did not know what brought them to our regions, but the men offered their services as mercenaries. They soon arose to fill the ranks of the king's elite personal guard owing to their stupendous fighting skills. Your father was their leader and the strongest; he had no match in combat. It is said he was of noble birth. They learned our tongue, honored our gods, and made a great effort to adopt our customs. After three years among us, the king granted them funds and assistance to establish their own place of worship in these remote parts. And yet, in the twelfth year of their dwelling amidst our kind, they left, seemingly and strangely disappearing overnight without a warning or a reason. Some of their men had married women from our people. Many wives—but not all—followed their husbands with the children. Your mother who was pregnant with you stayed behind."

Alkedoron was discernibly unwilling to expand on the subject of Hymnoneos' mother and instead steered the conversation back to the object of their pilgrimage.

"I was one of those who helped scout the area and build the sanctuary to the silent god. We called him the silent god because he does not speak like the other gods through the priests, the Oracle, or in dreams. He makes himself known only to those who are initiated in his mysteries. That was the purpose of the temple we constructed. I was told those shrines are everywhere to be seen in the land of your ancestors. They erected them only for the benefit of those who underwent the sacred ritual because otherwise, they made their daily devotions at home or outdoors. They did not have a large temple as we do. They said that once the god has made himself known to them, he lives in them and they cannot know death; and though their body would rot before our mortal eyes, they are reborn forever in the image of his being, invisible to us."

The young interlocutor who wanted to learn everything about the silent god assailed Alkedoron with a hundred questions, and the recounter obliged as best as he knew.

"I heard the story from their own mouth:

"When the primordial egg cracked open, it released twins: a male child as white as ivory, and a female child as dark as the obsidian. The male offspring escaped unscathed, but the female one was swallowed whole by the mighty, cosmic serpent who was crushing the egg in his coil, intent on devouring its living substance. Yet, having ingested its prey too fast, the serpent disgorged the infant while flying over the largest lake of the land. And when the girl twin tumbled into the deep, blue waters, the rising plume spewed myriad droplets that fell on the earth, each turning into a polished pebble of Lapis Lazuli. And from every gem arose a human being. This, according to them, is the genesis of the human race. Now, the boy twin was in the throes of agony over the loss of his sister. They said that henceforth he was bound to the physical world looking for her. And when he sees her image in those who willingly offer an irreproachable heart to him, he digests their thymos and makes their memories his own to perpetuate their being into his own being.

14 "When you are a stone, you care for nothing. I have no feeling, no wish, no need, only a subtle awareness of a universal becoming about and within me. And when I am a blade of grass, I have no care but for being grass. Yet, I can sense the proximity and movement of my environment, the forest, the insects— I go through considerable such transformations before getting to the awareness of being me— as I am now— but in a more essential or superlative quality. There is either something added to my being or subtracted from it— or both perhaps— as if I were in a dream but sharper, more delineated: someone entirely me, and yet beyond the habitual perception I have of myself. Then, I have a rush of memories— no, I am the memories; all of them: my lifetime's, my ancestors', and even memories of the story of mankind. It isn't like a life review, let alone a judgment; it is my very soul being rescued from the confines of matter: a total anamnesis drifting gently both inside and toward the center of the light, soft, diffuse, palpable. I can feel that light as much as I see it; and I am part of it. First it is an amber shimmer, and then phosphenes that gradually organize themselves in concentric, polychrome, translucent shapes of striking, daedal beauty. It gives me the impression of peering through an old-fashioned kaleidoscope and falling through its aperture. My memories move toward the center, but the center keeps retreating. There is no notion of good or evil, no regrets, no moral considerations in those memories—like looking at one's childhood from the standpoint of adulthood: the experiences of the child we were are still with us—they are us—but we cannot own them because the mind and the will of the child are no longer."

John spoke for a half-hour, frequently reverting from his narrative to analytical comments, but Marguerite did not interrupt or intervene. She knew the nature of her research implied an acceptance that the objective and the subjective could not be separated.

"An aethereal being appears whom I may have subliminally conjured out of myself. Her otherworldly, overwhelming numinosity inspires divine passion, but words to describe her on our level of perception have no value. Her presence is formidable and intoxicating; her appearance is like that of the entrancing androgynous angels of the Renaissance. But I know she is not the embodiment of any objective reality; she is an immaterial being to whom I give shape. Her form possesses me; and yet it does not subvert my own individuality. At that moment, I feel I am two beings in one, but her vitality rules over mine. My will and essence are purified in being swallowed by her intent and desire. She speaks with a sweet, musical voice— almost a murmur—and says to be my spiritual sibling who is called by many names in tradition: daimon, *syzygos*, heavenly twin, guardian angel, *spiritus angelicus*, divine Self. And she reveals to me that she is the one who gathers all the memories I behold. Then, the angel tells me she is an eidolon of light reflected by my soul. Memories, soul, and the heavenly twin are sealed together eternally by providence and necessity. Man is but an arrow of primordial desire that pierces through chaos, violence, suffering, and travels unhampered toward the limpid expanse of the sky. All that pain I can behold in sharp relief, but it no longer affects me; it is absorbed—digested, I could even say—in the radiant light of my angelic sibling. It is like the tears of infancy we still remember though they have long dried, the wounds that healed into innocuous scars. At last, the stream of my life is drawn by the memories to empty itself into a breathing sea of perfect joy."

John responded favorably to the three sessions the researcher had scheduled, and the benefits were reciprocal: she was impressed by the wealth of new material elicited; he was able to steady his mental turmoil and paint a picture of rich perspectives. Life is not the painting, he reflected, but the canvas: what we see on it is but perception; what really matters is how we look at it. A masterful work of art is shaped layer upon layer: false starts are covered, mistakes are blended in, corrections are added, and effects are created until the masterpiece surfaces and the painter becomes his art. John's state of mind improved with the ability to observe his moods with detachment instead of letting them overrun his spirits. He gladly gave up the human obsession with purpose, knowing that his own will was but accidental in the run of a mystical, uncreated, primordial desire to manifest its foreordained, unimpeachable ends. He took on writing a more carefully detailed account of his spiritual journey, not omitting the things he had withheld in his interviews with Marguerite Swanson. The writer was in the process of emending his story when he received the unexpected phone call that once again would send him toppling other the edge of the ordinary.

15

The evening gathering had drawn to an end, and most of the guests had dispersed. Fèlyx noticed his mood had shifted from cheerfulness to something inexplicably more somber. He failed to recognize the nagging constriction in his throat as the warning sign of terrible things to come. Unbeknownst to the group of friends and believers who prolonged their stay in the core of the night, mad clouds were gathering rapidly, casting over their lives the shadow of an ominous presage: by a violent turn of destiny, fury was about to rain onto the guests whose lips were stained with the wine of the Albigensians. An oppressing atmosphere weighed on the night when Jérôme began his lecture.

"Do not fear what may befall the fleshy garment fashioned by the usurper to imprison your soul. For this life is but death and the true life is given by the Living Father in the seventh heaven where the celestial spheres never stop shining over the truthful. The invisible Father is not the one who walked in the garden of our first parents because he is hidden in the light that is not of this world. He who appeared to Moses in the fire is the great deceiver who created a garden in Eden. The prelates of Rome who gorge themselves on luxuries and never work with their hands worship him as their father; but in truth, he is Satanael, the father of all lies, and Samael the blind god who proceeds from the Nihil to combat the true god and his angels. Satanael reigned on the waters over the Nihil, and he gathered the waters until dry ground appeared. He planted a garden in Eden that he called Paradise to entice down by its strangeness the angels of God. And Lucifer—he who brings the light of knowledge—was the second born of the invisible Father. Curiosity was his strength and his weakness. He came down from the celestial abodes and drew too close to the material world until the pull of matter was so strong that he could no longer escape. Behind him, a third of the lights in heaven also fell because they had been attracted to the strangeness of the garden, and they were imprisoned first in clay and then in flesh. The bodies of flesh Satanael differentiated by sex to fetter with the chains of births and rebirths the souls that had fallen. But Lucifer could not be tamed or made to forget because his light was too bright. Nor was his numen impaired. He remained in the garden and repented of his error, and he planted a tree in the middle of Eden, in which he made his dwelling. Satanael planted three other trees in paradise: the tree of water, the tree of earth, and the tree of air, for the book of genesis tells that he used water from the sea, air from the sky, and soil from the land to form the earth. Those are the three elements and the three trees. Lucifer planted the tree of the knowledge of good and evil to instruct our parents so they could know the good god from the false one. It is from the seed of the fruit of knowledge that grew the tree of life, the fifth tree. Hence it is said that there are five trees in paradise. Satanael could not give life to the bodies of clay he created. They became living beings because of the spirit of God that was breathed into them. Thus, it is said that the spirit of God was hovering over the water. After that, Satanael barred our first parents from the tree of life and from the tree of knowledge so that the children of Eve would die in ignorance. And it became necessary that the invisible Father would send his first born to guide the souls back to the light. He is he who is called the Christ. He had the power to give the Paraclete by the laying on of hands. And the authority of the laying on of hands was passed from the Apostle John to the good

Christians down to this day to administer the consolamentum some of you will receive tonight. When you receive the consolamentum, your spirit is made whole again because it is reunited with your soul. Thus, the Paraclete will guide you to the end of your days, thereupon you will return to the presence of the good god. But those souls who are not consoled must be reborn in the world of matter for another life until they are consoled at last. The prelates of Rome have hidden the keys of this knowledge. Because they obey the Rex Mundi, they cannot enter the presence of the good god and would not let anyone else enter either."

Thus taught Jérôme, and he answered many questions from the audience that night. Fèlyx admired him for his knowledge of the scriptures and the writings of the ancients, which he used to great effect in demonstrating the doctrine. It surpassed all that which the abbot and the prior together knew, and even the scholar monks at the abbey did not have such wisdom.

Toward the eleventh hour of the night, Jérôme gave the consolamentum to those in attendance who had chosen to be consoled. It was the first time Fèlyx witnessed the ceremony, and he was unimpressed. He did not doubt the sincerity of those who were made *perfecti* but he wondered about the efficacy of the ritual. There was no liturgy in beautiful Latin, no wafting incense, no gutting candles. Not that those were necessary in themselves, but they created the atmosphere that seems to draw down the very presence of the angels from heaven. The consolamentum was sober to the extreme, one may say dry, even. In contrast, the boy was easily moved by that which delicately appeals to the senses, the image especially: the

67

colorful frescoes on the walls of the church; the intricate tapestries at the manor of Les Martels; the illuminations in the precious books through which he liked to leaf, feeling the texture of their pages under the tip of his fingers. Though the senses are of the flesh, he reasoned, they also permit apprehending beauty. And he was satisfied that all things beautiful ought to be permitted by God to apprehend. At least, it was his earnest opinion. Creeds lacking in imagery are lacking in holy presence, Fèlyx asserted to himself. He knew the power of the mystical image, having soothed a troubled sleep oftentimes with beautiful imaginal compositions. Most of the bons hommes lived exemplary lives, and they spoke the truth. But who is to say their authority was any more valid than that of Rome in spite of her weaknesses? On reflection, the ends of the consolamentum did not seem much different from those of the extreme unction or of the baptism, which were so despised by Jérôme. And Fèlyx was beginning to think that prescribed rites—or the lack thereof—couldn't save or damn anyone. Jérôme himself had said that the tree of life grew from the seed of the fruit of knowledge. Knowledge, then, was perhaps all that which was needed to save. Henceforth, he would make it his calling and his mission to seek the knowledge of the truth wherever it might be found. A scholar he would be. There was still enough rightness in the Church despite the wickedness of the priests. He, Fèlyx, would redeem the good in the mother Church, and he would be a friend of all men of good will everywhere. His own guardian angel had guided him when he was little, even though he had not been consoled (and he wasn't even sure he had been baptized before joining the monks). In the darkest hours of his early childhood, long before he set his eyes on the holy images or read the books of Honorius of Autun, he had beheld the messenger's haloed face, his fine hands like those of the musicians, and his smooth feet like polished shells. And though he had been enfolded in the wings and arms of the resplendent envoy, Fèlyx was bound by a promise never to speak to anyone of the angelic visitation.

Saint Amant had been in attendance the whole evening at a reserved distance from everyone, and Fèlyx, under the impression he was being ignored as well, was upset. They spent the few remaining hours of the night together though, for they had to sleep in the horse stable. Saint Amant had promised he would take the boy back to the abbey at the break of dawn. Over the past months, the pair had become friends, although the oldest kept affecting a remoteness that saddened the youngest who was inclined to offer his affection without reserve to whom he liked. Fèlyx was unsuccessful in breaking through the emotional ramparts with which his comrade habitually surrounded himself, and he felt clumsy and somewhat embarrassed for being foolishly forward. Hardly a word was spoken before the boy fell asleep exhausted, but in sporadic jounces out of slumber, he sensed over him like a soothing nimbus the abiding vigil of the warrior. At the hour the monks at the abbey were having their nocturnal convocations, the oblate in the stable was still dreaming. He dreamed of a hen courageously defending her chicks against the vicious attacks of an eagle.

16 Hymnoneos and Alkedoron trekked six days before arriving at their destination, a towering peak as high as twelve sea-vessel masts, on the face of which a modest man-made structure clung precariously, supported by an outcropping of the cliff. At first sight, Hymnoneos was underwhelmed. The site certainly was breathtaking, but he had expected a magnificent edifice, perhaps even grander than the temple of Poseidon. So small the building appeared from the distance that the boy asked how it could possibly accommodate more than a handful of visitors at once. Alkedoron smiled knowingly. "You will see."

The early evening was pleasant and the scenery idyllic. The two travelers settled at the foot of the geological monument to recover from the trip and feast on a roasted hare who had been struck by the misfortune of crossing their path earlier that day. A spring poured out of a crevice nearby, making the spot an ideal place to camp. They would visit the temple in the morrow.

That night, the goatherd's sleep was agitated by a nightmare: a large bird of prey goring defenseless chicks and eating their viscera. But the troubling dream evaporated with the glow of dawn, and, before the day would affix its colors on the landscape, the pilgrims were standing at the base of the titanic pylon, contemplating the vertiginous climb ahead.

The shrine was accessible through steps carved in the scars that the passage of the ages had etched on the rock: a steep, sinuous path that held the promise of a heart-quickening ascent. Spurred by exhilaration, Hymnoneos took a fast-paced lead. He negotiated the climb with the skill and agility of a wild goat, leaving the man far behind panting and lagging. As he gained elevation, the agile excursionist realized the structure he had observed from afar was only a pronaos. Soon, he could marvel at the extraordinary ingenuity of the builders who seamlessly integrated their architectural prosthesis onto the wounds inflicted by nature to the scarp. The goatherd turned explorer felt dizzy. He had been running up the last portion of stairs and was out of breath. The boy rested awhile to take in with awe the sheer heights he had reached. But soon, the boy fell in the grip of a different, stranger sensation that pulled him forcibly toward the mouth of the sanctuary as if the hoary crags themselves were willing to swallow his youthful ardor. He stepped through the vestibule and entered the hidden, cavernous naos bored in the center of the truncated peak just below the summit, a broad, unbroken space bathed in weakened sunlight descending from shafts pierced in the stone. The youth had removed his sandals out of intuitive reverence. The skin of his soles rubbed the slight bumpiness of myriad smooth pebbles assembled into a massive mosaic that filled the floor with repetitive geometrical patterns in black and white. And then, to his right, painted on the wall exposed by a sunbeam, stood the silent god, the lord of the waterfowls, surrounded by the images of the birds who move freely on land, in the waters, and through the air. The fowls were exquisitely rendered perched on stumps or gliding on a river. So lifelike they looked that Hymnoneos wanted to brush their colorful plumage with his hand, half expecting the animals would take flight. He did not dare graze the fresco though, as he sensed falling on him the gaze of the regal ephebe prisoner of the rock. The visitor's eyes met those of the divine resident, which seemed full of painful longing—a fluid sadness that instantly found its way to the heart of the young mortal. What was the name of the immortal? Hymnoneos yearned to worship him, grieving he did not know how. He reached with the tip of his finger to touch the navel of the god as if to breathe life into his petrified figure. But the effigy remained unmoved, unable to respond to the fervent, mystical desire of a mere herdboy.

Alkedoron called from outside the grotto, and the forlorn suppliant walked back to the heartening closeness of his human companion who had preferred to wait sitting outside under the portico. The adult forcibly suggested they needed the afternoon to find food; but the child noticed in his friend's demeanor a strange, inexplicable reluctance, unapparent until then, to linger on the temple's grounds. In silence, the pair trekked down the serpentine path and returned to camp.

They spent the late afternoon leisurely hunting for food. Alkedoron did most of the light talking, and they did not speak of their visit to the holy place. In the evening, the two sat by the fire. The adult kept the conversation sparse while the child kept at his poking the embers with a stick. Hymnoneos ate little. Early in the evening he washed in the mist from the spring and retired to rest. Slumber would not come easily despite the fatigue. Relentless thoughts kept sleep at bay. Why had his true people come to the peninsula? Why had they left? Who was the mysterious god with no name? What did he want from him? Eventually, the exhausted mind relented, and the boy gave in to the swaddling clasp of the silent darkness.

He awoke feeling alert and spirited, with that pleasurable remembrance there was reason for excitement before the mind could even recollect the object of his anticipation. Alkedoron was still fast asleep and snoring loudly; but upon the child, the sacred aerie again exerted a spell spurred by the enchantment of the night. Nudged by the gentle touch of an unseen hand, Hymnoneos surrendered willingly. Carried speedily on the wings of a trance, he found himself once more at the threshold of the hallowed cave. The night was now nearly as bright as the day; the immense lunar corona elided the gleam of the stars. The goatherd boy walked straight to the fresco. Touched by streaks of moonlight, minute particles in the pigments that colored the image made it sparkle. The god shone even more sweetly seduced by the lesser sphere than he did when wooed by the mighty orb. His wings—one white, the other black—were like unto those of the graceful swans who flanked him on each side. With his right forearm he held a shield; in his left hand rested an unadorned cup.

The visitor turned his attention to the back of the consecrated cave where more steps had been hewed along the slant of a passageway. On the threshold of the stairs once hung a veil, had mentioned Alkedoron, through which the mystai were led before proceeding further into their initiation. But not a shred of it remained. The boy hesitated and removed his tunic as a substitute rite. A pearlescent light bathed his naked frame while he advanced charily, treading softly toward its source. At the end of the tunnel, he emerged in the exuberant shine of the moon over the aerial haven.

The summit afforded a narrow platform on the edge of which lay a sarsen that had been further cut and polished into an altar by the hand of man. With his feet dangling over the void, Hymnoneos sat on the monolith and looked in the distance where the day would break. He wanted to stay and watch the sun rise but soon fell asleep instead.

The boy was awakened by a sweep of his bangs as if his forehead had been brushed by invisible fingers. He rose and stretched, rubbed his eyes, and surveyed an extraordinary panorama of the swelling hills. Between two peaks, the silver, thin sliver of sea on the horizon turned to ashes before glowing anew with brassy shimmers. The pleasant numbness in Hymnoneos' limbs spread to his mind, and his own will left him. Presently, a preternatural esthesis took hold of him: he could feel the elements cradling his body. And he became the soft air infused with a morning freshness that mixes the scent of the night with that of the early day; he became the dew crawling up the stems of the ferns that clung stubbornly to the cliff. Now he was the dry soil tamped in the slits and crannies of the bare bedrock; now he was the changing light coloring the expanse with strokes of muted shades and bright hues. The sun rose timidly, boldly, brashly, and the boy became the sun, Lord of the two horizons. He became the voice within and its enveloping power.

I am the wind that gives the sea its swell. I am the fire of primordial desire that inflames the heart of the gods and gives them glory. Though I would be bound, I can never be tamed. I stood at the beginning to rise with you at the end. My name is one and many, alone and everywhere; I am known only by the silence that holds the truth. I perish in the heart of man; through their sacrifice I am reborn.

The words became a thin pearlescence that hung momentarily over the consecrated landscape before disappearing. A jolt bored through Hymnoneos' chest as if an incorporeal hand had clasped his heart. He fainted.

Only half-conscious, the boy who bore a god in the hollow of his bosom was carried away by Alkedoron. For the last time they passed the enchanted fresco of the resplendent ephebe whose eyes were now inexplicably shut. *So much occurs when the glimmer of the night surrenders to the first light of the day,* thought the traveler. He had a premonition that no one would ever again behold in the sacred enceinte the countenance of its guardian who had stolen the heart of a goatherd boy.

17 *Flapping his wings furiously to confuse the attacker, the fowl, talons jutting forward, thrusts itself at the adversary, breaking the defense of its foe. Overwhelmed by its prey's instinctive, combative skills, the eagle retreats, weakened for loss of blood. At the victorious call of the rooster the sun rises...*

The landline phone rang, and the dreamer awoke with a jolt. Barely out of hypnopompic confusion, John walked gingerly through the semi-darkness. He had not talked to Davy Sicard in over three years, though he and the professor had kept in touch through increasingly sparse emails. The cryptic phone call at 6:20 in the morning mystified him.

"Meet me around 3:30 at the Blessed Sacrament Church on 8th NE, and wait for me if I'm not on time," had asked Sicard after briefly enquiring about his interlocuter's health and availability. "It's important."

John and his friend had met at the Seattle Antiquarian Book Fair. In addition to their passion for musty books, they had discovered a common interest in all things esoteric. For John, it was the drive to unearth the missing pieces in the puzzle of life; for Davy Sicard it was a mere hobby, a zeal to gather and research the most outlandish and obscure occult theories in the same way older generations used to collect rare stamps. The two had developed a casual friendship and commonly stretched the evening hours after dinnertime discussing arcane topics. John still had a vivid memory of such a conversation, the last they held together. It started with Davy making a distinction between Spiritualism and Spiritism and soon branched out into a lengthy exposition of his ideas, to which John listened patiently as was most often the case.

"I have no doubt whatsoever that some individuals possess tremendous psychical abilities," had emphasized Davy, "but I categorically reject the notion of external entities or agents being responsible for paranormal phenomena. The problem is we are looking in the wrong direction—that is outwardly. We think angels are envoys from God and that demonic possessions are the work of a devil; we take past events recollections to be a proof of reincarnation; we assume UFOs come from beyond the solar system or from other dimensions; the dead, the discarnate, the spirits, the aliens, all essay to communicate with us, we expect. No one asks why no two alleged spaceships look alike; or why their manifestations are always in line with the technological and mythological vision of the historical period in which they are observed. Nobody wonders why crop circles grow increasingly complex as we give them more enthusiastic attention. ETs and 'hidden Masters' are equally, annoyingly, and forever elusive. And to those they contact, they always relay the same tedious vapidities that unsurprisingly mirror the human concerns and preoccupations of the times. Not one paranormal communication has ever added anything of substance to scientific knowledge or conclusively answered metaphysical questions. Let me ask you: why would a supposed advanced civilization care a fig for the inhabitants of our planet when the far reaches of the universe could not even notice if Earth exploded? There are no visitors from outer space or celestial regions, but there are multitudinous creatures bursting from our inner sphere! Fundamentally, there is no difference between Marian apparitions and ghost sightings, angel visitations and alien abductions. Automatic writing or painting can be explained alongside artistic and scientific genius. Stigmata and spontaneous healing have their origins in the same source, and it is in us."

Davy was convinced that a subliminal consciousness in autopilot mode acted independently from our conscious meddling.

"Its reach," he observed, "is far beyond what we realize."

Never one to be satisfied with half propositions, the professor pushed his reasoning to further conclusions.

"Even the entire universe exists only by virtue of mind. Without our perception of it, there would be no universe. In fact, there is no reason why the perceivers who sustain the galaxies could not sustain themselves past physical death, choosing a form of their liking, and perhaps taking along human memories to simulate continuation."

Sicard was at least ten years older than John and taught Linguistics at the University of Washington. He had confided that he was once part of a small group of esoterica enthusiasts— a coterie started in the 1880s that had numbered a few prominent members of the community. Eventually, the company had dwindled to a handful of hardcore occultists who took their vocation a lot more seriously than he ever did. In the 1970s they had begun to call themselves the Vintage Club after the name of the private party room where they hold their assembly once a month in the old downtown.

"Vintage indeed they were," had quipped Sicard. "At the time, I was the youngest of the bunch. We disbanded when most participants were too old and frail to attend."

John sat in the sixth row from the altar. He was early. The church was empty and silent except for a maintenance man who paced the length between each row, pushing a mop before him and casting equivocal glances at the lonely visitor. John could only relax after the caretaker had left to busy himself elsewhere. The lapsed Catholic could now revel in the familiar, entrancing atmosphere of a traditional church that he always enjoyed but was sorely lacking in the bland quarters of evangelical Christianity and the plethora of so-called "non-denominational" churches. He fell into a hypnagogic spell and lost sense of the passing of time. He let his eyes follow the course of the sunrays that swept each subsequent stained-glass window until they reached the altar panel and pierced at its center a haloed glass host. The sun flooded the translucent image of the elevation act, and beams emanated from the Grail, raised like an offering to the sun by the High Priest Jesus.

"Remarkable, isn't it?"

Davy startled his friend who had not heard him coming.

"Hey! How long have you been sitting behind me?"

"About half an hour; I did not want to disturb you."

"Well, that's creepy," answered John half-jokingly.

Davy suggested they go to their habitual haunt in the U-district: "I buy you coffee; we have a lot of catching up to do." Indeed, the two fellow esotericists kept a spirited, casual exchange on the way, and John appreciated how his friend's jovial nature never failed to lift his own alternate somber moods. Once at the coffee shop however, Davy abruptly turned to a more focused conversation.

"I asked you to meet me at the Dominican Parish, because the place is linked to the story I'm about to tell you," started Davy mysteriously while imparting small circular movements to his cup to stir his oversweetened mocha. The terse words were enough to capture John's immediate attention.

"In 1908, a group of Dominican friars were sent to Seattle to establish a parish in the community of the university. Among them was a certain Olivier Cesoux who had become Brother Christophe when he joined the order rather late in his life. He was quite the character reportedly, having been a sort of adventurer and a hedonist in his youth before turning unexpectedly to God. He remained a conflicted monk though, and not just because he was drawn to both the Spirit and the spirits." Davy laughed at his own feeble joke. He could not help himself dropping one of those even in the most serious of situations. John cracked a smile politely, and the professor resumed.

"Anyway, he died eventually of liver complications. But you see, he too had a secret passion while alive—the same as we have. Like many an ecclesiastic before him, he entertained a double pious life split between exoteric orthodoxy and an esoteric, inner tradition. More importantly, he was in possession of an old manuscript; God knows how he had acquired it."

In John's mind the story took the appearance of a thread that lengthened and connected to the memories of his out-of-body experience, when he temporarily exited the realm of the living (or of the dead, depending on one's angle). He made an effort to remain impassive but blushed slightly, realizing his facial expression had already betrayed him. Davy took great pleasure in toying with his friend's heightened receptivity and kept an unnecessary drama tic tone throughout the story.

"I don't think Cesoux had a very happy life, which he most likely spent with each of his two feet planted on the opposite sides of a widening gully. He must have been rather lonely with his mass of existential anxiety and unsolved riddles for companions. Kind of like you!"

Davy laughed again, and this time, John chuckled.

"So, you have it?"

John could not refrain from casting side glances at the age-worn leather satchel the academic perpetually carried along. Davy playfully withheld an answer and continued with his train of thought.

"The manuscript did not do our friend much good: couldn't keep it, couldn't part with it. A torture for a tortuous monkish mind. Well, the dear friar eventually gave it away to two of his rare friends just before he died: Thomas and Edwin Gaggin, who were both active freemasons. While the Dominicans were supervising the construction of their church, the Gaggins were completing their own architectural project, the Smith Tower— a barely disguised Masonic building, if you ask me. How the three met, I have no idea. But during their visits to Seattle, Thomas and Edwin frequented the society that would become the Vintage Club. That's how we ended up in possession of the manuscript.

"One of our members who had done extensive research found out through his contacts in French esoteric circles that there might have been another, larger portion of the parchment. It was apparently acquired by a German lady in the 70s. But we could only put so much stock in what he told us because he was already showing signs of senility.

"The piece we had became for us a sort of relic, the glue that held the group together. We even developed a ritual around it and had an oath never to reveal its existence or content. In retrospect, it all looks so ridiculous. For all I know, the lines on the manuscript might have been penned by a raving medieval mystic. Anyhow, it was passed from one senior member to the next until everyone died and I was left alone."

"But, is it authentic?" interjected John.

"Oh yeah! I had the ink analyzed and the parchment carbon-dated by a colleague at U-Dub; everything is consistent with a 12th century work."

Davy now fell silent, gauging his interlocutor for reactions. But John, concerned he would appear too eager, did not say anything, and spoiled the crescendo the professor intended to build. The pause felt awkward. It was broken by Sicard who transitioned to a solemn, matter-of-fact tone that took John by surprise.

"I'm weary. My health is failing me, and frankly, I do not expect to live much longer. Even the enthusiasm I once had for teaching is gone. I have no family or friends left besides you. The closest I felt to having relatives was with the odd bunch at the Vintage Club, even though I could never subscribe to their out-of-touch theories and fantastical outlook. You know me: forever the agnostic."

John was unable to react appropriately to Sicard's unexpected declaration, having known the man solely through his jovial demeanor. He felt embarrassed by his inability to reach out and consoled himself with the thought that no matter how surrounded, supported, or loved, we are all solitary travelers: our innermost is forever out of others' sight. He did not want to be that person whose contrived words of empathy come across as self-serving. Yet, he surprised himself in putting his hand on Davy's forearm and finding something to say.

"People are often so obsessed with answers, they are oblivious to what the right questions might be."

Sicard did not want to make the situation any more uncomfortable and reverted to his trademark self-satisfied smile. He opened his satchel and pulled out a legal-sized blue folder.

"If anyone should have it, it is you. The vellum is badly damaged and was unwisely folded until it tore in two pieces. But its content is still of interest."

The professor produced the fragments neatly protected in archival sleeves. With the tip of his index he grazed each segment while explaining:

"The parchment is ripped at the bottom and has many stains. Part of the content is illegible. And the narrative stops abruptly. So, we don't have much to work with. It looks syncretic, with elements borrowed from the Gospel of Thomas; but otherwise, I couldn't link the text to any precedent. I am not the expert on the matter though. The whole document appears to have been copied in haste with sloppy writing. It was transcribed in medieval Latin, and I will give you my own translation—certainly not the best that can be managed. I have reasons to believe the Latin is actually a translation from a previous work in Greek. There were more of those arcane texts in circulation during the first millennium than there were relics in the Catholic Church. But most of them have been obliterated in the making of religious history. The whole thing looks like a draft, somewhat garbled, with sloppy handwriting—something that was intended for later publication. Marginal annotations were made too, but unfortunately, they cannot be read."

Sicard paused briefly.

"Well, it is yours now. You can do whatever you want with it; even make a bit of money if you wish. I no longer care. People put so much disproportionate value on things of the past, trusting the voices of the dead more than they trust their own. There is such a craving for ancient texts. Maybe it presages the decline of our own literature. Maybe it's the indication of a latent fear over the uncertainties of our future."

John had listened patiently to his friend's monologue, not wanting to appear himself afflicted by naive spiritual acquisitiveness. For his part, Sicard was showing signs he was ready to leave. Then he got up unceremoniously and offered a bemused John a heartfelt handshake.

"I'd better go.

"John, my dear fellow, I passed you the torch; do not let it burn you. I do not think we will see each other again— At my funeral perhaps!" And he laughed so loudly, the patrons were distracted from their cup of coffee.

John stood awhile looking in the direction his friend had left. It occurred to him he had not breathed a word to Sicard of his marvelous escapade into the beyond. Yet, he had no urge to know why. He sat again, took a few sips of coffee absentmindedly, and let his thoughts enter the strange world of synchronicities and conjectures that had just opened before him. He felt like a combustible projectile that had been hurled to crack a safe. What awesome fate had brought in his life the conjunction of two extraordinary events when most everyone around him seemed to live their own life so ordinarily? Had another strand of himself walked a different path in the co-existent plane of another existence—a divergent outcome woven into the fabric of physical reality? He glanced at the bracelet on his wrist: amber beads on a string; universes arranged on a ring, each closing where the other opens, at once parallel and sequential; God in the center. Was he at this juncture the recalcitrant thread destined to hang beyond the fringe and dangle into a state of complete, unconditional freedom? Was this life of him a script written so that an eternal determination could escape at last the entanglement of matter? Presently, John could only see the barista expecting him to free the table forthwith and make room for other customers.

18

Before daybreak, Mithras was dawdling back to the abbey, carrying both Saint Amant and Fèlyx. The half-asleep oblate rested his head with the cheek pressed between the cavalier's shoulder blades. Saint Amant obviously was in no hurry, having taken a detour under the pretext that it was a safer route. He broke the silence first and grew unusually chatty, perhaps encouraged for not having to face his interlocutor.

"You are a man of the book; I am a man of the sword. Do you know a blade can be yielded for other purposes than shedding blood? The sword is in the shape of the cross to symbolize a lofty endeavor: it cuts through the lies and delusions of men and slices the tether that the flesh keeps on their spirit."

Fèlyx decided he could risk the few questions he had not dared to ask since their encounter on the riverbank.

"Why did you come here, to Girocens? Why are you always traveling alone? Why are you always in the proximity of the same people I am close to?"

Saint Amant hesitated for a minute, stroking with a thumb the amber gemstone on his mantle brooch. The boy had noticed the knight's idiosyncrasy when mulling, and he feared having overstepped.

"I'm here for a book that is of great interest to me and the brotherhood. Your friend Jérôme is quite the collector, would you know it? One of his books he gave to Aurèlia de Caraman. The Lady was not as disinterested as you may think in granting favors to the *bougre*. For her part, she loaned the new acquisition to some of the scholars at the abbey who had expressed great interest in it. And that's where it is now."

"Ah— the books." The boy's voice quivered reproachfully. "Is that why you befriended me then?"

At once, the knight realized he came short of using the necessary skills to navigate the skerries of adolescent emotions. He continued with a more tactful approach.

"Young friend. Do not be upset; do not doubt my affection for you. Friendship has nothing to do with the affairs of the world. Some of my most trusted friends are among the Saracen while others who call themselves my Christian brothers would betray me for thirty pieces of silver. I set about my mission considering all my options, and indeed I knew you had easy access to the library. The books should not be a dividing issue between us; they should be our bond. Do you know what the greatest sin is—? Deliberate ignorance, the disregard for everything that does not justify one's actions and beliefs. I have many hopes for you. I want to open your mind to many horizons from which your abbot, and even Jérôme, would rather have you avert your gaze."

Fèlyx did not answer but Saint Amant figured he was regaining the trust of the youth whose chest was now heaving softly on the warrior-monk's back.

"There is so much in the world you have yet to apprehend. I have read the wisdom of the Brethren of Purity and witnessed the rapture of the Mahometan Sufis, and yet, there is alway more I want to understand."

The knight's voice was soothing, his words seducing. Was it the way the serpent held Eve under his spell? thought the boy. But the serpent might not have been the deceiver, and all may be but appearances. Had not the lord himself enjoined his followers to be wise as the serpent? Saint Amant continued:

"Like you, I want to see the Church purified. But I am willing to use my cunning in equal measure to that of the adversary. The god of the Albigensians can do nothing but wait for his children to come back to him; but the Compagnons du Beau Sanc will bring a new advent for the Church, a dispensation of universal peace for all creeds under the wise guidance of a fraternity of scholars, philosophers, and warrior monks. The Roman empire will again be under the aegis of the Church; the House of God will be put in order and administered properly; strife will be overcome. But we will need men like you."

"You will never overcome strife," said the boy, surprising himself with a bit of an epiphany, "for it is out of strife that all things proceed and progress in this world."

"You may well be right," added the knight, "but if there would be balance, it will be only as long as the opposites are locked in a relentless war. That is why the Knight Templar never surrenders on the battlefield, even if it means certain death. So, it matters not whether we succeed or fail as long as we know on which side we stand. And by my reckoning, the scales are unfairly tilted toward evil, which justifies our persistence."

"Persist as you may," rejoined the boy with a conciliatory tone, "you could conceivably defeat evil, but you will never destroy it." Jérôme's teachings on duality had indeed left their imprint on Fèlyx.

"Ah— yes my little scholar, of course: Apophis!" said the knight after a pause and with a knowing smile. The oblate did not understand the reference but left it at that.

The two servants of God fell silent again. Fèlyx dozed off a little. Soon they arrived at the abbey. They would walk different paths; but their friendship was sealed and sanctified in a shared, mystical fervor. The oblate admired the knight's spirit and determination; the knight loved the oblate's soul because it would always be untethered. Yet, the two riders had separate means and ends; and Saint Amant's was to establish an everlasting clerical order and frame a benevolent synarchy to replace both the papacy and the secular rulers.

19

Alkedoron nearly regretted having taken his foster son to the shrine in the hills. He felt responsible for the inauspicious turn their quiet life had taken since. Hymnoneos had become strangely aloof. Agdomenis had called upon him to visit her far more frequently, and the old warrior feared she would take the boy away from his care and supervision. After all, he was growing fast, and the priestess likely had other ambitions for the youth than to remain a goatherd. His trips to the city increased in number and length, and with each return home, he looked more sluggish and distracted, as if he had left behind an alter ego who was draining him of his thymos. Hymnoneos for his part resented being pulled away from his animals, the pastoral grounds he cherished, and his friends, on whims. Still, everything that made him happy he owed to Agdomenis' largesse, and he did not want to be ungrateful. The High Priestess' demands frustrated him though, and he figured that the secrecy surrounding their activities did not augur well for his future. Agdomenis' possessiveness and equivocal cosseting had the sickly sweetness of the beverages she made him drink at the temple. Those strange mixtures of wine, leaves, and berries sent him into trances, after which he could never remember what had taken place during those lapses. He sensed himself increasingly isolated and no longer had the time or energy to join the other students for class with Xenoastares. Instead, he was expected to spend more days and nights at the temple, rehearsing his role in a complex ceremonial procession and sacred dance that left him pleasantly intoxicated but empty. On his sporadic homecomings, the relief of being back to familiar grounds eroded his willingness to answer any enquiries, and

Alkedoron's barrage of questions was met with vague and evasive answers.

20 John propped himself comfortably with the pillows on his bed and began reading for the third time Sicard's translation of the manuscript the professor had dubbed, in a last jest to his friend, "the Secret Gospel of John." The new owner of the alleged gospel preferred to call it *The Revelation of the Beloved Disciple.*

At the end of the day of unleavened bread, after the disciples partook of the bread and drank of the new wine in a single cup, the teacher took the beloved disciple who followed him in all places, and also his brother, whom they called Didymus, to the house of Salome. And the other disciples spoke disapprovingly, but he said: "If a dog eats more than the portion of food he can take, he vomits that which he already had and goes empty. It is the children who need constant feeding. Therefore, be like children and you will receive the keys that have been lost by the professors of the law."

We abided for the night, and the paraclete revealed to us the mysteries of the true and holy name before we passed through the veil < ... > when he spoke unto us as with the voice of a spirit saying:

"In the beginning was the breath. The breath was captured in the flesh and became word, and the word sought the image hidden in the light. In the similitude of the image all things are made except the darkness that proceeds out of the nihil and is the adversary of the light." < ... >

"I am the beginning and the end in that which has neither beginning nor end. I am without beginning or end above all that which begins and ends. I am the primal light in the darkness; the light found a dwelling place in the irreproachable heart. I

am movement against stasis, the being and the becoming. I am the image hidden in the light of the unfathomable father and the word in the mouth of the children. I am the seed in everything. I am in you, and you are in me. Split a log of wood or lift the stone, I am there wherever you are. And when you gather me, you gather yourself. Open a door, and you will find me; lift a curtain, I am there, and my name is eternal."

John interrogated the paraclete: "My Lord, how can I be in the highest heaven with you, where the angels reign?"

And the spirit spoke unto us saying: "On the day you were one, you were precipitated from the light and you became two. On the day you become like a child, you will know the word, and you will see your image in the bosom of the father. When the image—which is in the light and is the light—and the word are made into one, you will be free from the world."

I asked the teacher: "What is the fate of the first seed that was cast from heaven?"

He said: "The Morning Star was the first light to come down. He saw the reflection of his own glory on the face of the waters below, and when he came closer, he fell. A great glow rose from the sea that attracted down a third of the lights < ... >

"Blessed is the lion man has tamed, and it becomes human; but cursed is the human who is devoured by the lion because the lion would be man.

"Behold, I have cast the seeds of the fire upon the world, and I am guarding them until it blazes. For in that time, the soul old in days will question a divine child about the place of life, and that soul will live."

And a vision of the kingdom of heaven opened to my inner eye, and I saw all the human souls that have dwelled in the flesh

since the days of Adam, and all those that have yet to come. They
were the chosen, the called, and the captive.

And the spirit spoke unto me again thus: "Because of the
seed of the heirs of the unfathomable father, the seeds fallen
outside the fertile soil may yet be saved."

John now was the sole heir of a liberating inner vision and the few haunting words ripped by time from the pages of a mysterious book, although he had yet to learn what to do with the sum of that metaphysical legacy. He did not feel special or worthy in any way, only aware that necessity had traced his path on the warp and weft of possibilities and led him to this exact moment: he, lying in bed with a medieval manuscript in his hands, and in his heart a singular desire to be free burning through the walls of the flesh. Never had he felt closer to the threshold of his true home.

21 Amaury Seurat was jubilant with the holy hatred he could now savor as he was about to right the wrongs that had been done to him. *This must be how Jehu had felt when he ordered Jezebel to be defenestrated by the eunuchs*, thought he. En route to La Vaur where his family once lived, the King's appointee had the leisure to reconsider the strange turns of destiny that dispossessed him of everything he had held dear only to bring him back to his native soil with a sevenfold restitution of blessings. God indeed works in mysterious ways and rewards the faithful servant. In his youth, Amaury was in the service of the Trencavels and groomed to become a knight. When his future shined at the brightest though, his fortunes changed for the worse. Foolishly, he had fallen in love with the bewitching Aurèlia, and once ennobled, he could have married her. But she rejected his advances, favoring her prospects with a much older man. After his naive indiscretion was uncovered, Seurat fell out of grace with the Trencavels. Their pride was at the root of his plight. Forlorn and dejected, he was at his most vulnerable when another temptress seduced him—one who traded carnal sins for a pittance. God knows what unholy sorcery the forest witch used to ensnare him in the coils of her flesh. She was a Cagot whom the locals regarded as a midwife and a healer. She gathered herbs to cure the ills of the superstitious peasants and well-born alike who did not have enough faith to be healed by God. Their liaison was short-lived; but she had spawned a bastard whose existence Seurat would discover years later. Although he had done right for the child who he could not even be sure was his, pernicious rumors continued to taint his prospects. When he petitioned the Grand Master of the poor fellow-soldiers of Jesus Christ and the

temple of Solomon for admission in their order, his request was denied. Fortunately, Amaury Seurat could now see that it was for the best because the Templars were a nest of vipers scarcely worthier than the heretics themselves. His own pious devotion and perseverance had earned him respect at the court of France, and for his diligent services and loyalty he was knighted by king Louis VII. At last, Seurat had become a powerful man, delegated by Louis' successor to join the secular arm of Cardinal de Marcy's mission against the heresy of the bons hommes. Flanked by two mounted sergeants, over twenty foot-soldiers, and a dozen mercenaries recruited along the way he was soon to bring the sword of divine retribution to the land of his enemies and the Felician abbey where everything connected: heretical beliefs, Templar money, and the boy who had repaid his benevolence with treachery. Seurat once wanted to believe the monks could save the bastard's soul, and to that end he had given generous stipends for the youngster's care and education. Sadly, the Cagot maggot displayed the same contumacious streak as his mother's. If the informants were correct, Fèlyx consorted with the Manicheans and committed sinful abominations.

22

A moon passed without interruption to their routine, but the serene and idyllic life Alkedoron and his young charge once relished together had not returned. Surely, Hymnoneos had always exhibited a taciturn personality and a tendency to withdraw, but he now lapsed into frequent spells of utter oblivion. Alkedoron hoped the priestess was planning to give her ward an administrative position or important function. Her reach into the ruling body was unhampered, and Hymnoneos was both intelligent and capable. The old warrior caught himself daydreaming about the man of means and influence he could visit one day to reminisce about the simpler, happy times they once shared away from the city. It would be very rewarding to see the child he had raised mature and assume major responsibilities. He could still be a part of his life in small measure, and that was satisfying enough. The reality, however, signaled different developments that worried Alkedoron. He suspected the mind of his young friend was being poisoned, and he knew who was distilling the poison. Suspicion and concern congealed into alarm when two attendants of the temple arrived one early morning to fetch Hymnoneos and escort him once more to the city. He had always traveled alone before, and this new arrangement was downright sinister. The boy did not protest or say anything and followed the envoys with apathetic compliance. But Alkedoron would resign neither his conscience nor his duty: though he could not act alone, he could ask others to intervene. He would not rest until satisfied that Hymnoneos was safe. The warrior set out to find the Wise.

23 John would not see his friend alive again. Following their get-together at the café, they kept in touch through emails that became sparser over the weeks. At the end of a one-month lapse, John received an announcement card informing him of the passing of Professor Davy Sicard.

The ceremony was anything but ceremonious because Sicard had opted for a "green funeral" and no fuss. John let everyone leave to stand by himself a while longer before the anonymous marker, an unpolished stone engraved with an epitaph. At Sicard's own request, John had chosen the words:

> *Arise O my soul, when this mortal body dies,*
> *In the dwellings of light the plenitude provides.*
> *By its own chatter the unyielding mind is tied*
> *But the soul is silent; a daimon is her guide*
> *And he who, worthily, with this angel abides*
> *Will confound even the wisest among the wise.*

"I trust you to find something sufficiently original and cryptic," Davy had e-mailed him with expected humor. "Not for me—I won't need it anymore—but for the passersby: give them something on which to reflect."

24 "And the boy?" asked Father Ricaud.

"Ah— the boy," echoed Father Gilbèrt pensively.

The fate of Fèlyx was one messy ink blot on a costly vellum the abbot wished a miracle could make disappear. For a moment, he remained suspended in a mystified contemplation of doom, as if hesitating to cross the threshold of realization and acceptance that all was lost. Prior Ricaud pressed the issue as if it were key to the whole crisis. He certainly never liked the brat who he thought was lacking the moral fiber for a monastic vocation, prone as he was to dangerous flights of the senses and a dislike of manual labor. And his predilection for probing the works of dead pagan philosophers was no substitute for piety, opined the prior. He suggested the boy should be sent away immediately under any pretext, and that the devilish books could be released to the young Templar who persistently bargained for their acquisition. The abbot objected that the plan was unworkable because there was not nearly enough time: Seurat and his troops had already been spotted down the hill, just four leagues away north-east, halted for encampment. The prior's mild optimism was not contagious. In the mind of the father superior was now creeping the nagging consideration that, in all probability, the only thing left to be salvaged from the incoming devastation was his own skin.

On the heels of the grim news that had reached them, the two ecclesiastics had convened the urgent meeting and spent the last two hours trying to decide what steps could be quickly taken to forestall the imminent impact of the storm about to engulf them. The decrees of the Lateran council had hung over the region like a sword of Damocles, and yet, foolishly, they had felt safe under the aegis of the House of Trencavel. They had failed to foresee how Raymond V of Toulouse would use the heretics as a pawn in his political game. Now Marciac was at the gates of La Vaur, and Seurat at the foot of the hill. Their concern for the souls of the heretics might have been more genuine than that of the Count of Toulouse but the Felician Fathers had no illusion: Seurat was here principally to settle old scores. His hatred for the Trancavels was an open secret, and the monks knew the man well: no matter how successful he had become at the court of France, he was the same ill-tempered son of a drunkard, who had left the Vicomté twelve years gone, penniless. He came from a wealthy house of leather craftsmen who owned shops, but his father dilapidated the family fortune, and his mother was affected by melancholy. God knows what other tares the young Amaury might have inherited. His fortunes could have improved considerably under the wing of Trencavel but he had thrown all his chances to the wind for an ill-conceived indiscretion involving the young Lady de Caraman. His return to the region after years of exile did not bode well for the Felicians, but his precise intentions were still unclear. The main problem for the abbot and his prior was to figure the extent to which the order could be implicated through a perceived association with the Manichean heresy. They knew with certainty Seurat would attempt to exact revenge on Aurèlia de Caraman and, by implication, her Trencavel relatives. But the Lady and her entourage had already fled to some unknown location, and without her, the Trencavels could not be hurt either. That left the heretic Jérôme and those of his followers who had declined to escape, the Felician monks, and Fèlyx.

The abbot bitterly regretted having been so naive. From the coffers of the Mistress of Les Martels, he had carelessly accepted generous donations to lavish on renovations and embellishments for the church. And there was also the matter of mutually beneficial arrangements he had negotiated with her Templar connections. What once appeared to make good business sense was now coming back to haunt Father Gilbèrt like a revenant howling the name *de Caraman*. Against the advice of his prior, he had turned a blind eye to Aurèlia's sins, knowing full well that, behind her shows of piety and devotion to the true Church, she consorted with the Manicheans and shared her dining table with the worshipers at the synagogue of Satan. On her own land she had allowed a house for women heretics who called themselves bonnes chrétiennes and brashly claimed rights that were given to men only, making a mockery of the teachings of Saint Paul. But the worst offense was the manner the chatelaine had corrupted the soul of the young Fèlyx with her seductive wiles, drawing him away from his duties and the abbot's loving concern.

25 A breezeless night could not dissipate the heat of the day. The pale nimbus of a gibbous moon underlaid the haze, and long, slender shadows tailed the drums of the colonnades on the temple grounds. Torches were lit. The supplicants were few. They drank the brew that opens the gates of the ancient gods' abode. A solemn melody rose from a lone player's flute, evoking with its melancholy notes the olden days when the laws of men were different and the deathless walked much closer to the mortals. It was soon accompanied by the percussive motions of cymbals and tambourines.

Followed closely by Hymnoneos, Agdomenis took the lead of the procession, and they headed down the coast toward a secluded cove. The marchers had reached a light trance by the time they arrived at their destination where they worked themselves into delirium. Hymnoneos danced, not of his own will, but under the sway of a hidden choreographer. His oiled limbs responded not to the mind but to the primal call of the music and the sea. His movements became feverish, frenetic, lascivious. The surface world was melting into a blur erasing all distinctions: no longer a night or a day; neither pain nor delight; no more discord and harmony, sadness and joy, hatred and love. The young dancer slid deeper toward the great center of gravity, into the moist embrace of the Great Mother. He saw her: her serpentine arms and legs around the earth; her curves like the hills and valleys. She wanted him forever, and he did not have a will to spurn her. Like the dreamer who feels himself obeying the whims of the dream, he let his awareness flow and dissolve into the awareness of the chthonic matriarch to become one with water, air, and soil; to sleep the sleep of the impenetrable forest.

Agdomenis was restoring religion of yore to replace the official cult that had grown stale and dwindled to mere formality. The latter gods had consigned to oblivion the primeval rulers. From the mud they had made the lowly man, and the soil of the dispossessed was trodden haughtily by the unworthy creatures. The tellurian, cavernous depths howled the rage of the antediluvian deities, and now the priestess of Poseidon could free one of them from their plight, unbinding at last the chains of bitterness that had restrained her. The blood, breath, and thymos of a human child would quench the chthonic entity's terrible thirst; the sacrifice of an irreproachable heart would appease her ire. The newest gods always take and rarely give. They yearn for the blood of men shed in perpetual battles to satisfy their vainglory. The Ancient One yearned for the blood that nourished her for she always gave back in equal measure to what she took. The wrath and love of the Tauric Goddess was the power Agdomenis would yield once the old dominion had been recovered and she had been rewarded as the instrument of the restoration. The priestess' devotions had led her to uncover the greatest secret of godhood: the gods awakened by the desires of men are immensely more powerful than those who create men in their image. Agdomenis looked intently on the perfect fruit of her loins. She gazed hungrily at the disturbing beauty that could tame and compel an unfathomable force to do her bidding through a sublime oblation—the sacrifice of a son by his own mother.

Hymnoneos was losing the awareness of his own body into the body of the Great Mother; his consciousness was being gormandized by her primal consciousness. But the moment his memories were to deliquesce into an amorphous oneness, the spell of the Mother was broken: he saw himself snatched from her grip and spirited away swiftly on the wings of a swan.

The boy never felt the worshippers tearing into an empty vessel of flesh, devouring the genitals and the entrails. Sweat, tears, and blood mixed as a single stream glistering metallically under the nocturnal lights. The night moaned. Elemental spirits arose from Chaos; Typhon raised its heads; Tartarus released its captives. Agdomenis was taking back into herself what she once delivered into the world. Yet, when she slit the corpse's thorax, there was no palpitating organ to be found. And the priestess' intoxicating frenzy suddenly turned into an eerie, numbing perplexity.

26 Fèlyx sat on the empty bench and let the thick silence play with his senses. Inasmuch as his leisure permitted, he liked to pray in the choir during the rare hours of the day when no one else was around. He often thought he could be a mystic if the appeal of the books wasn't exerting so great a draw on him. It was like being split between two enticing, solitary destinations: the exhilarating peaks of mysticism, or the peaceful vales of scholarship. He wondered if there could be such a thing as a scholar mystic, an ideal situation that would reconcile the seemingly opposite aspirations vying for his attention. Presently, the mystic tug had the upper hand. Fèlyx let the religious sentiment carry his soul upward toward the lambent corona of the stained-glass windows as if a part of him were to pass through an empyreal gate of colors and surrender to the vibrant melody of the angels' rainbow wings. Yet, the instant he was expecting his very soul to elope with a divine envoy, the analytical mind regained control, snatching the lad out of his anagogic reveries, and the oblate's interest turned to the church's frescoes. The magnificent images had been created by the best illuminator from the abbey and two artists especially appointed by the Lady de Caraman. It was awfully expensive, but la Dame des Martels had generously offered to cover the cost with her own money. A collaboration that was enthusiastically embraced by the Abbot. Currently, only two new artworks had been completed—one on each side of the nave—but six of them in total were planned.

Fèlyx began to scrutinize the details of the numinous scene transfixed on the wall. The representation would have been a rather conventional one if not for the particulars that surely escaped the awareness of the common congregant but not the curiosity of an inquisitive oblate. The fresco depicted the crucifixion in an unusual way: a single woman was portrayed prostrated at the foot of the cross, and, even from a distance, Fèlyx was certain that the mourner (whom he understood to be Marry Magdalene) was in the likeness of Aurèlia. Indeed, on the right bottom corner, one could make out the emblem of the de Caramans: a single rose pinned on a serpent biting its tail. A lone angel hovered behind Jesus, his feet leveled with the Savior's waist, his arms extended sideways, duplicating the outstretched arms of the crucified Son of God. Intriguingly, the Lord himself did not appear dead or dying. His eyes were open, fixating the viewer with a strange, undefinable gaze: serene; longing; gently mocking even. No blood dripped from the body; no thorn pierced the forehead; no nail crippled the hands; no wound gaped on the flank. This Savior was merely resting on the cross, and the boy who raised his eyes toward the enigmatic figure saw in it the God he desired to love and worship: not a redeemer tortured by men but a transcendent liberator, imperious to ugliness, suffering and death, calling his heir back to the realm of indescribable harmony.

Fèlyx was about to be enfolded by his god of eternal youth climbing down the cross, radiant and laughing, when men in arms burst through the doors, letting out terrifying war shouts.

27 Alkedoron never found the Wise despite a frantic search. Unbeknownst to him, Xenoastares had been knocking on the doors of many an official, soliciting audiences with powerful noblemen, consulting with friends, and working his influential connections in a last-minute attempt to disrupt the disastrous chain of events he mentally reconstructed. But his efforts remained unfruitful: he was unable to determine Hymnoneos' whereabouts, and none of his contacts were either willing or in a capacity to meddle in the priestess' intrigues. The Wise had been blind to the scheming fomented before his eyes by the one whose thirst for control he had underestimated. In the end, he was powerless to forestall the tragic developments he had been too slow to apprehend; he could only reproach himself. While the teacher was busy instilling in the boy an understanding of the subtle balance between logic and mystical cognizance, the young life of his student was steadily consumed by a nefarious, irrational, and fanatical determination.

When Xenoastares and Alkedoron met again, their reunion was marred not just by failure but also by the unbearable loss of their young charge and the crushing realization of a treachery they had not foreseen. At least, their pleadings for the return of Hymnoneos' remains were not ignored. The young goatherd's three friends cremated the mangled remnants of his body on the shore. They stood by when the tide washed over the pyre.

A cleft in the humongous billows of cumuli let the crescent moon shine through, and Poseidon reclaimed his own. Alkedoron waited until he was sure the ebb had taken the ghost of the child into the bosom of the sea; but he had preserved a lock of copper hair he swore to lay on the monolithic altar of the silent god high in the hills. Sparse droplets of rain fell like tears from a Sulphur colored cloud even as the sun rented the horizon.

28 The sergeants and their men were swift and efficient. Moving rapidly in the core of the night, acting on tips from Seurat's spies, they rounded up heretics and summoned witnesses. Most of the eighty prisoners were held in the church while the most valuable captives were thrown into the cellarium.

Fèlyx huddled against Jérôme in a cataleptic state of fear and befuddlement. For three days they had lacked basic necessities, suffering the underground cold and humidity with nothing to sustain their body save stale bread and water. Jérôme enfolded the boy's frail shoulders.

"My dear Fèlyx, we are going to be tortured, and it will be unbearable. Relent quickly and that too will pass, and you may live a little longer in this world so that you may choose to be consolated, and..." The Elder interrupted himself with the feeling, for the first time in his life, he might be pontificating. He resumed haltingly as if speaking to himself.

"Perhaps— perhaps the consolamentum is not everything after all."

"Listen. I want you to speak against me and anyone you will be asked to denounce. Renounce whatever they ask you to renounce. Let that which Seurat would extract from you by torture come out of your mouth willingly. It is better thus. Our fate is sealed. Your destiny is to become instrumental in bringing more souls to the knowledge of the good and true god. You will show them the escape from the artifices of matter and be a great teacher before we meet again in the place of light. You carry all my hopes. For now though, embrace what they want you to fear; repent from sins you never committed; admit errors you never made; and return to a faith that has let you down. Be cunning as the fox while you are among the wolves in sheep's clothes and be at peace with yourself. Do not let unwarranted guilt torment you: it takes more courage to live in this world than to leave it behind. I am weary of the schemes of men, the superficiality and pettiness of their lives. I am ripe for the sickle. I will stand boldly before death and step joyously into the life of a blessed angel.

"There is… There is a short prayer: it was taught to me when I was but a little older than you are by a man I followed on the roads. Certainly he was half-mad, but the prayer gave me great comfort in times of need." And Jérôme reminisced, whispering:

Savior angel of my soul, holy and merciful, I carry you with me; carry my soul with you to the place of light.

Fèlyx had fallen asleep in the arms of his spiritual father and dreamed dreams more pleasant than the nightmare of being alive.

Amaury Seurat was getting bored and slightly annoyed. In compliance with the wishes of the cardinal, he had taken along two Cistercians to take care of the administrative aspects of his mission. They were here to document the judicial proceedings against the heresy and ensure that the interrogation of the accused would not precipitate their death before they could be found guilty. Fathers Thaddeus and Dagobert were meek enough to recognize who was in charge and yet stubbornly insistent when it came to determining and recording with exactitude the beliefs of the heretics. The knight considered the theological finesses pointless, the administrative rigors tedious, and the extra work unnecessary. He saw himself as a forerunner, a model of efficiency to be emulated henceforth in the battle against all streams of heresy throughout the Roman Empire. He did not hold the Cistercians in high esteem: those priests were getting fat on wealth, and their order was quickly growing complacent. Come the end of his troubles with the Cathari, thought Seurat, he too might become a man of the cloth, which surely would heighten his prestige and authority at the court of France. There was a ferment in the Empire. Young, more militant mystics were making themselves known for their uncompromising stands, and before long new, stricter monastic bodies would rise to purge the Church of its complacency. Amaury could join one of them.

On the second day of the hearings, the abbot and his prior appeared before the judicial assembly. Neither were directly accused of heresy, but their testimony would be pivotal in finalizing the uprooting of Manicheism from the soil of Girocens. There was plenty of blame to go around. Father Gilbèrt admitted having been far too lenient in disciplining the monks, and especially the sole oblate. To his defense, he contended that no amount of ecclesiastical supervision could have compensated for the impious scheming of the Lady de Caraman who used her influence as patron of the abbey to win the heart of a helpless boy. As for the suspicious manuscripts that were aplenty on the shelves of the library, the Felician abbot explained he had put the prior in charge of the collections while he himself was busy supervising construction work for the renovation of the abbey. The prior blamed his own ignorance of scholarly matters, but mostly the deviousness of the brother librarian and a conspiracy of scholar monks who secretly traded books with the heretics. He also ascertained to the honorable inquirers that he, Prior Ricaud, had forewarned his superior about the lax discipline at the monastery and the moral deficiency of his pupil. The quarrelsome knots eventually entangled the two Felician Fathers in a shouting match that Seurat would have found comical had not piety forbidden him to be amused.

The dispute fizzled, and meekness prevailed when the pair consented to acknowledge the generous terms of the delegation's ruling: the congregation of the pious brethren of the Mother of God was to be dissolved immediately; Abbot Gilbert and Prior Ricaud would agree to be transferred in lower functions to the Cistercian order and were to be assigned to separate, unspecified monasteries at the discretion of the Cardinal de Marciac.

On the third day of the inquest into the heresy, Amaury Seurat was mostly satisfied that things were moving along swiftly and as planned. Trancavel was too busy in La Vaur negotiating acceptable terms in the dispute with his father-in-law to be preoccupied by the developments in Girocens. By the time the siege of La Vaur could be lifted, Seurat's mission would be fulfilled, and the knight would move on to grander designs for himself. His failure to snatch the biggest prize of course was a disappointment; but he found consolation in knowing that Aurèlia de Caraman would spend the rest of her life as an exile. There was nothing left to which she could return. At the very moment, Les Martels was engulfed in the fire; her estate would cease to be. Obviously, the Templars had helped the chatelaine flee with her entourage—like brigands in the night—and she was forced to take along in haste the bare essentials. The spoil that remained would go to Seurat's henchmen; the memory of her deeds would fade quickly; her legacy would evaporate. A true servant of God, Seurat was not interested in properties and material possessions, only the glory of the Father, his Son, and the sovereignty of the mother Church.

At the first hoist of the pulley, Fèlyx let out a horrific shriek that took the Cistercians by surprise. They were not keen on torture, but Seurat knew better. The oblate had already confessed all the sins his tormentor wanted him to reveal, and he had expressed a desire to repent and be reconciled with the mother Church. Still, the proper procedures of investigation needed validate his confession and sincerity. The boy was let down and subjected to further questioning. He could not utter a word; only his muffled sobs and low groaning were heard. He had fallen into the state where an intense pain becomes the whole of consciousness. Amaury looked dispassionately at the little half-breed he had never met before. The knight had wondered what it would feel like to face the Cagot witch's child. Could he be his own as well? Amaury was doubtful. He would not bring himself to sympathy. Was not the boy old enough to be responsible for his own deeds? The prior, too, had noted he was a rebellious soul, a seed of trouble. Why else would he squander his moderate intelligence in vain preoccupations with heresies repulsive to any sane mind? Why would he waste the opportunities he had been offered to make something of himself? Had he not admitted the vilest sins? Lust! The youth had succumbed to lust, Seurat concluded. Lust for the deceptions of the flesh, and for logic over the word of God.

On a nod of the inquirer principal, the small frame was lifted again. Fèlyx moaned pitifully and passed out. Amaury Seurat sighed. He looked anew at the strangely twisted body: there was nothing alike between him and the boy except the intense blackness of the hair with curious bluish reflections similar to the plumage of the raven. Could he be his blood? Plausibly, the child could have been conceived owing to the witchcraft his mother had used to tempt young Amaury. Abraham was willing to plunge the knife into the flesh of his only begotten son; he, Amaury Seurat, had been able to demonstrate the faith and resolve of Abraham. There was no need for the boy to die here and now, and nothing coherent could any longer be extracted from him. Presently, the inquirer turned his attention to the bigger fish caught in his net: Jérôme, the head of the heretics. When the head falls, the body would fall as well. More importantly, Jérôme had been a friend to Aurèlia de Caraman who had given him support and allowed him to spread his lies. That friendship was unpardonable. The ignominious death of the enemy of the cross would seal the knight's victory over the wretched woman who once had made his life miserable.

Jérôme was present at all the sessions of the inquiry. He witnessed his friends and followers being subjected to horrific tortures, but not a quiver, a twist or a wince did he let the investigators read on his impassive bearing. He took in the whole of a hell more terrifyingly real than the torments of afterlife promised by the priests to the sinners. The ghastly sight sent so violent a jolt to his soul that before being sentenced to death he was already dead to the world from which the good God is wholly absent. From tender childhood to his days at Les

Martels, his lifetime stretched before his mind's eye like a treacherous, winding road that ended at the threshold of a luminous realm wherein dwelled the invisible Father. Another day and he would cross that threshold into the place of light while the likes of Seurat would prolong their miserable existence in the place of darkness, the heinous world they perpetuate for themselves.

29 Father Dagobert was weary of the interrogations, the accusations and recriminations, the condemnations, and especially the tortures. He understood the necessity of severity for the heretics who make the Lord suffer anew, but, in his ecclesiastical opinion, justice should be tempered with mercy. He did not agree with Seurat's methods. There was no arguing though; the knight had behind him the authority of the edict of Lateran. Thankfully, the awful business had come to an end, and the two Cistercians had been summoned to rejoin Henri de Marciac the next day. La Vaur had surrendered; the Cardinal had obtained the terms he sought from Rogièr Trancavel and subdued the Manichean bishops. More important affairs were now calling him elsewhere.

Dagobert had a few hours before him to complete his own personal mission under the cover of night. He was a scholar too, torn between a hunger for knowledge and a need for certitude. In theory, the two went hand in hand: truth leads to certainty, and certitudes must be about the truth. From his years of study though, the Cistercian knew things were painfully otherwise: while absolute truth presupposed unlimited knowledge, certitude often requires knowledge to be restricted by faith. In other words, the certainty of absolute truth effloresces only beyond the limits of certitudes. With that dilemma in mind, night after night, the cleric had set about perusing the many unorthodox books that had found their way to the abbey of Girocens. A direct insight into the workings of the heretics' mind, he reasoned, could be gained by studying their written discursions, which in turn would help the Church in rectifying their error. Such an approach was more valuable than extracting dubious claims under the threat of torture. Armed with a few sheets of vellum, a quilt, and a vial of ink, the scholar monk worked methodically, taking notes and copying relevant samples of select manuscripts. Absorbed in his task, he could forget his part in the latest atrocities that had been committed for the glory of God.

In the morning, the inquirer principal for the heretic question in Girocens bade the two Cistercians farewell with barely concealed relief. The last thing he needed was another fresh batch of their same timid but annoyingly numerous procedural objections as he was tying up loose ends on the final day of his campaign. Time was running short. With de Marciac and his troops on the way out, Seurat feared the Vicomte Trancavel might take a detour by Girocens on his way back to Albi.

Only the influential, unrepentant, professed enemies of the cross had been processed and found guilty. Among the rest of the prisoners, it remained uncertain who were truly intruders, accomplices, or sympathizers. But Amaury Seurat would not run the risk of letting one tainted soul go free, however remotely associated with the heresy she might be. His intentions were definitive. He remembered that God the Father had sent down the great flood to drown all the inhabitants of the earth when the land was ripe with iniquity. Surely, the youngest children in those days could not possibly have been responsible for the sins of their parents or be cognizant of the same, and yet they had been made to perish as well. Was it not far better for them to be received in Limbo than grow up among sinners and lose their souls to an eternal inferno? As for the baptized who had kept true to the faith, the Lord himself had said that not one sparrow could fall without the Father's consent. Surely, then, the master would recognize his own among the dead and separate the sheep from the goats—a task that the servant did not have the leisure to see carried through.

In an early summer evening, mighty flames were seen leagues away rising from the abbey of Girocens. The knight and his men fled under the cover of darkness. Amaury Seurat had been the arm of the Almighty to yield the sword of divine retribution. His *opus dei* was a baptism of fire that left no stone unturned and purified the area from the stain of heresy once and for all.

30 With the promise of their fair share in the booty from Les Martels for sole motivation, the small party was advancing North at the slow pace of those who have been assigned an unenviable task. The outcome of the ambush was ineluctable: the single sergeant and the eight hirelings fell under a volley of arrows before being dispatched expeditiously into hell (or out of it, depending on one's theological frame) with a jab to the subclavian artery. Saint Amant jumped onto the chariot and lifted from the straw bedding the emaciated, dirty body that would have felt weightless if not for the irons fastened on the ankles and the wrists.

When Fèlyx awoke and his senses recovered their acuteness, he was relieved to find Saint Amant sitting by his bedside, looking at him. The knight Templar often observed the boy with that same gaze at once impassioned and reserved since the day they had met at the river. He smiled and laughed lightly.

"Well, look who has come back from the underworld. Were you too poor, or too stingy to pay the ferryman?"

Fèlyx smiled faintly. He tried to prop himself up but fell back on the traversin with a heavy flop. Saint Amant arranged pillows under the neck and shoulders of the ailing youth. Presently, Fèlyx could not wait to hear everything about his rescue and the whereabouts of those he loved. With his characteristic sober detachment, the warrior monk accounted for the terminal developments at Girocens as if speaking of an old wives' tale.

"Seurat ran out of time. The last of the prisoners—forty of them—men, women and children were rounded up in the library. The doors were sealed, and the entire compound was

119

set ablaze. The fire engulfed the monks, the heretics, and those who were neither, altogether with the books. You could hear canticles sung from within the furnace. The bonnes gens died with great courage. Even under torture, Jérôme never spoke a word to his accusers and did not give Seurat the satisfaction of being acknowledged."

Fèlyx grew sheepish at the mention of the Elder. Remembering the conversation they had in the cellar, he wished he had been blessed with the fiber to resist torture and remain impervious before death. He felt a crushing implosion in the center of his chest and would have broken into sobs if not for a childish refusal to appear weak in front of his protector.

"Father Gilbèrt betrayed you. Seurat planned to consign you to a monastic cell for the rest of your life with a Latin bible for sole companion—to give you a chance to reflect on your deeds and pray for the salvation of your soul. I had other plans for you."

Saint Amant thought it was time to reveal the secret to which everyone was privy except the boy at its center. Prudently though, he decided to leave it to the Lady of Caraman. She would know how; better than he did.

"Aurèlia is safe. She would never have abandoned you to your fate— Neither would I have. You have nothing to fear anymore, she will take care of you. It is her personal physician who is treating your injuries, you know. Even as we speak, she is waiting for you in Collioure, under the protection of the order. I'm afraid the Felicians have ceased to exist forever. The area is no longer safe for you: de Marciac and Seurat were the first of many to come with the same nefarious greed for control, and there is only so much the poor fellow-soldiers will be able or willing to do to help the Albigensians."

The knight unfastened his mantle and removed the brooch. He grasped Fèlyx's wrist, put the jewel in the open palm and closed the boy's finger over it.

"I have meant to give you a token for quite some time. If you ever need to find me, show the brooch at any commandery, and they will point the way to you."

Fèlyx had a hundred questions to ask, but Saint Amant was satisfied with the brief update. The knight made a sign, lifting his index finger to the lips.

"You need your rest now to prepare for your trip. I will see you again very soon. Fare well little lamb."

The young convalescent looked at the amber gem mounted in a silver frame, carved with the curious image of a mythical creature's head. He stroked the jewel a few times with his fingertips and put it under the traversin.

31

"I will tell you a tale that I heard when I was on a mission to the Byzantine Empire. It's the récit of a pagan boy about your age, whose heart was veritably taken by his god…"

Saint Amant was worried by Fèlyx's slow recovery. The boy was still feverish, and his mind often drifted away, threatening not to return.

A story is a remedy; it would anchor the youth's thoughts, conjectured the knight.

The last time the knight and the oblate saw one another was at the place of their first encounter by the abandoned mill on the bank of the Agot. In the distance, heavy black smoke still billowed above the cinders of the abbey.

"Three generations hence," remarked Saint Amant, "no one will remember what took place here. The peasants are already busy salvaging from the ruins whatever material they can reuse."

The knight was accompanied by his two most trusted cavalry sergeants and their mounts.

"You will ride alternately with each man, and they will not leave you out of eyeshot until you reach your destination."

The sergeants-at-arms were supposed to be in disguise; but no one would have dared stir up trouble at the sight of their countenance and the bulges of weaponry concealed under their cloaks.

The aspiring scholar mystic and the philosopher warrior sat once more on the sand discarded by the river to speed up its course toward the unknown. Fèlyx still had spikes of searing pain in his upper body and limited dexterity in his hands.

"I don't know if I can be a scholar. I don't know if I want to be anything anymore."

Saint Amant mentally reached for something he could say to rekindle the spirit of youth in the boy who had been plunged into the madness of men.

"I once heard a story from the very mouth of the sheikh who narrated it to the Berbers":

On a busy afternoon in an alley of Fès, the youngest daughter of a scholar picked off the ground an exhausted dragonfly to protect it from being trampled by the unmindful crowd. She carried the insect delicately in her cupped hand, but a strong gust of wind suddenly swept it off its shelter. The fragile dragonfly was flung against a wall with such violence that it tumbled down to the pavement and died. Who, then, was responsible for the death of the beautiful, winged creature: God, the devil, the maiden, or the wind?

The riddle had the intended effect of triggering Fèlyx's instincts of deduction, but he was not sure of the correct answer. Saint Amant smiled at him.

"I am still working out a solution myself."

He continued: "This will be your calling, to share your wisdom with those who are less capable of understanding. You will be the lamp on the nightstand everyone who comes and goes can see."

"What of the story about the boy whose heart was stolen by a god?" interjected Fèlyx.

"Nothing happens for a purpose," replied Saint Amant, "everything does happen by necessity. We are all linked in a chain of causal determinism, each of us playing a part in a design that escapes us: we are but a chapter in a story that has already been written; its beginning is also its ending— And whatever god we may worship, he is no farther than our minds and our hearts."

"And you," asked the boy, "where will your calling take you?"

Saint Amant paused, carefully framing his reply.

"I too have a long trip ahead of me. I will journey to the Valle del Silencio to report to my brothers, *sans* the books I promised them. They were reduced to ashes alongside the librarian."

"You never say much about the companionage to which you have wowed your loyalty," remarked Fèlyx, hinting at a question.

"We are bound to secrecy, and there is little I can tell you. My uncle rode with Hughes de Payen and his original knights. I followed in their steps, at first pursuing the same aims they put forth. I saw wonders forever cloaked to the ordinary man. I also walked the corridors where constantly shifting alliances are created and undone—a dangerous game, but one that is not without its rewards. The world is not black and white like our banner; our lives run on the thin gray line where the two opposite planes osculate. The order I served has become a monstrous marine creature with its head in the mother Church and its tentacles reaching far into the crevices of the world. Too many of us have lost sight of our founders' ideals and let themselves be poisoned by greed. We are eaten by the worms of rivalry, jealousy, and by the uncertainties of dominance and power plays. A few of the brethren set their sight on holier and loftier endeavors. I am with them now. A shrouded, mystical brotherhood within the order, we seek not to deviate from the tradition we have received and the mission we have imposed on ourselves and swore to carry on. That is where my calling is taking me."

The friends lingered together throughout the heat of noonday, retreating to the ruins of the mill where a cool draft bounced off the river and came twirling between the walls like a ghost. When the conversation stretched sparse, they let the silence bind their two souls. As the sun tired of shining and began to slouch, Saint Amant made preparations to leave. After giving his men last-minute instructions, he rejoined Fèlyx who was now standing on the riverbank as awkwardly as he stood before the Templar in the very same spot, on a like summer day nearly a year before. He did not speak. The knight's destrier nudged the boy's head with its muzzle, and Fèlyx laughed, trying to parry the head of the beast.

"I do not know if our paths will ever cross again..." started Saint Amant. He cradled the youth's cheek in the palm of his hand and gave him a kiss.

Fèlyx stood clasping in a tight fist the carved amber brooch the knight had given him two weeks before. There is always too much that remains unsaid for a timid scholar who knows only how to consign thoughts to the parchment. His knight protector; his Saint George! Before a sound could slice the knot in the boy's throat, the silhouettes of Saint Amant and Mithras were already disappearing in the mishmash of foliage and undergrowth. The Templar did not turn back to see his friend crying uninhibitedly: tears of joy and bitterness mixed in one salty flow. Now, a few words alighted on the oblate's mind as if they had drifted from a distant dream:

I carry you in me my savior; carry my soul with you.

Part Two

If I find in myself a desire which no experience in this world can satisfy, the most probable explanation is that I was made for another world.

—C. S. Lewis,
Mere Christianity

For he who could interpret would be dissolved and would become that which is interpreted.

—Solomon
Ode 26

THE WISDOM OF THE DOUBTER

A Passerby's Interpretation of the Gospel of
Thomas

Dear Dominique.

Even after so many years of silence, I had not lost confidence that news from you would come in time. Our bond is Sophia, and I always thought the wisdom you seek would lead you back to where your quest began. You were so willful to learn the things disdained by your elders who preferred to concern themselves with the distractions of the world. You are of an angelic mind, one who does not belong to this plane, whose destiny is to forgo all destinations. I believed you would appreciate my letters and use my words as a lamp on your solitary journey. Now, with much joy, I hear you keep a keen intellect in a healthy body, and I realize your erudition has exceeded my expectations. You unveiled wonders beyond the reach of the easy believers who are content to pay heed to the verbiage of self-appointed spiritual and religious authorities for as long as it assuages their fears, comforts them amid doubt, and distances them ever farther from facing their utter forlornness in a hostile universe. You learned more in your youth than I was able to garner in a lifetime. Yet, out of affectionate deference, or perhaps wondering if an old misanthrope might still be holding a handful of missing pieces to the puzzle of our existence, you ask me to articulate the inner mysteries of the savior-twin in light of the *Gospel of Thomas*. You are well aware my young friend that is a bait I could not resist.

* * *

Never in millennia past has there been a dearth of religious imagination, a paucity of epiphanic relevance such as we experience nowadays. The rich metaphysical harvest of the ancients has been reduced to an adulterated crop of beliefs and creeds to feed the masses a heavy meal that causes their souls to sink into a slumber. The Abrahamic faiths on the whole have shed the aesthetic power they once had to embrace their extremes of either blandness or lunacy. The institutionalized religions have penetrated the wall of the secular sphere so thoroughly that their clergies' priestly garments are stained with the mud of materialism. The 1960s ignited a "New-Age" explosion that ripped through swaths of eager minds disillusioned by the surviving decrepit piety, but none the wiser. The democratization of western beliefs and a popular access to eastern thought and indigenous spirituality soon gave rise to the excesses of subcultures and the raving nonsense of undisciplined, indiscriminate, unsophisticated convictions. Then, unsurprisingly, the initially refreshing revolutionary streak of the metaphysical 60s sold out to corporate interests and mass consumption. A newly minted enlightenment and wellness industry took over, driven mostly by profit. The "New Thought" movement had already prepared the way to such developments when, arising simultaneously with the industrial revolution, it blurred the line that separated materialism from spirituality; there would no longer be a conflict between pursuing the kingdom of heaven and securing an earthly dominion.

Like its 19th century forebears in the European salons of a blasé aristocracy, the 21st century spiritual tourist has the means and time to spend on vanity metaphysical endeavors. Though the modern seekers are satiated with spiritual trends and fads, a veil of materialistic mysticality has fallen upon all of them, and through its diaphanous folds they perceive the deformed figures they take for the veritable gods. Those gods are only pretenders who hide behind the curtain; their intent is not to break the chains of matter, but to remove them from plain sight and sustain in the mind of the easy believer the illusion that he is free. Meanwhile, freedom holds no value for fundamentalists of all sorts who have succumbed to the lure of repressive utopian theocracies.

In the 4th century CE, a handful of far-sighted eremitic librarians buried a collection of manuscripts in the desert to spare them destruction in the hands of the Church's heresy hunters. The owners of the papyri had foreseen the day when truth would "spring out of the earth" (Psalm 85:11) to confound the masters of distortion and repression. When, at last, the hidden twelve leather-bound codices were discovered and unburied in 1945, the Coptic *Gospel of Thomas* proved to be perhaps the most potent sacred text that could free the mind from confusion, rouse the soul from her torpor, an revive angelic possession in our epoch. Yet, curiosity about the intriguing wisdom of Thomas steadily waned over the years after the initial burst of interest that always follows the release to the public of something out of the ordinary. Once the shadow of secrecy and conspiracy that enveloped the apocryphon dissipated, the appeal of the book vanished as well. And although the promises at the center of the logia are lofty, on close examination, the rewards demand more sacrifice than the many are willing to offer. Unsteady seekers prefer to fall back on the comfort of books that tell them what they want to hear or outline for them a step-by-step path to follow without head-scratching. The spiritual consumer professes to follow his "own path," but in that purported emancipation he is tricked by the engineers of the enlightenment industry.

Sadly, Thomas' insights are now tackled for the most part by academicians whose approach buries anew the spirit of the codex, or by an eclectic bunch of enthusiasts who are looking in all the wrong places. I am not one of the former, and I hope to do better than the latter.

Jesus, Thomas, and the Disciples

In the logia of Thomas, Jesus is a tenuous figure. The only place where he figures prominently is at the beginning of each saying in order to introduce them. If we remove the instances of "Jesus said" from the text (I have done so in most cases for the sake of getting to the substance of teachings that were never conveyed by either Jesus or Thomas), the content is not in any way weakened, and the logia can solidly stand on their own without reference to whomever might have spoken them. The sayings allegedly collected by Thomas were assembled from different traditions across time and edited to fit an arbitrary format and convey a somewhat unified philosophy. The last needed touch was to give the collection a seal of authority and an aura of holiness. If the canonical gospels draw their clout from the names of the prominent Apostles who supposedly wrote them from memory (reminiscing after many years the acts and words of their savior), the Gospel of Thomas raises the ante: it claims to be a direct and faithful transcript of Jesus' words as if spoken to the readers themselves. Thus, the actual author of Thomas' gospel places himself audaciously above the competition in terms of preeminence and validity.[1] Thomas' Jesus, however, is

---

[1] The clever contraption works so well that even some modern scholars tend to see the Gospel of Thomas as closer to the real deal (that is the words of Jesus mostly recorded as they fell from his own mouth) when compared to the canonical gospels.

not the solemn Son of God who dies on a cross and is resurrected, who performs miracles and redeems mankind from sin before coming back dramatically to life as the Christ. That mythic redeemer of the New Testament gospels was crafted by the instigators of Roman Christianity bent on propagating a new mystery cult throughout the Empire. Indeed, we can regard the Christic journey as the epitome of humankind's search for its god-like nature and ultimate ascension to godhood. The mythologist John Lash expressed this view:

> *Christ is the image of ideal humanity, even of human divinity: in other words, the transcendent double of humankind. Through the sacrificial act of incarnation Christ is transformed into a unique hybrid, a one-and-one only case of the ultimate twinning: divine/human, God/Man, Christ/Jesus.*[2]

Manly P. Hall advanced a step farther on the path of esoteric Christianity, bridging the gap with the inner savior motif in Thomas:

> *This god-man, thus endowed with all the qualities of Deity, signifies the latent divinity in every man. Mortal man achieves deification only through at-one-ment with his divine Self. Union with the immortal Self constitutes immortality, and he who finds his true Self is therefore "saved." This Christos, or divine man in man, is man real hope of salvation—the living Mediator between abstract Deity and mortal humankind.*[3]

In the Gospel of Thomas, two Jesus personae abide side by side. To understand the dichotomy, one has to be mindful of the

---

[2] John Lash, *Twins and the Double*, 1993
[3] Manly P. Hall, *Mystic Christianity*, 1928

two basic factions of early Christianity, the Jewish and Roman movements.

The elusive inaugurator of Jewish Christianity could have been any of the many holy prophets, doomsayers, agitators, and ascetic teachers who roamed the dusty roads of Palestine at the turn of the current era, possibly a zealous Essene named Jesus (Yeshua/Jesus was a popular name in first-century Galilee) with a bold claim to a messianic mandate. This Jesus is to be understood as a flesh and blood individual.

The Hellenistic, Platonic Christ, on the other hand, was the creation of Paul and the Roman intelligentsia, subsequently refined by the anonymous authors of the canonical gospels. The miracle worker and resurrected Jesus fashioned after the savior gods of the ancient mystery cults can only be allegorical. Even if we allow for a historical "gospel Jesus"—perhaps an adept of the Egyptian mysteries—by the time such a mysterious figure appeared in the scriptural canon, he would have become a fully mythicized composite character, and his teachings would have been considerably emended.

The Gospel of Thomas stands at the crossroad of these two original Christian impetuses with its unique, hybrid Jesus who must be taken at once literally and figuratively. This is perhaps the main obstacle for one tasked with unveiling the message of Thomas—a hurdle that continues to steer the modern examiners in either direction when they should see the two roads conjoined as in a circle. In our exploration, we will have to exercise the flexibility of keeping this circular concept in mind instead of following one of the two linear, opposite roads. In a pertinent paper published on self-deification in Gnosticism, David Litwa explains:

In gnostic myths, the mediate deity is often represented as external to the self. But the mediate deity is in fact the higher self. The externality of this higher self is only a necessity of the lower self's embodied, historical existence.[4]

In Thomas, Jesus is the in-person philosopher-teacher, but he is also our higher, or divine self. The two possibilities unfold concurrently, and the coadunation of this double persona results before Thomas' eyes [5][91] in the transcendent, inner presence of a hierophant-savior, at once revealer and liberator—the numinous self [α][3]. Thomas calls him "Jesus who lives" because he is the "son of the living father" [37], and he is spiritually alive amidst a humanity who is mostly spiritually asleep or dead. It is also a subtle way to distinguish the radiant, joyous revealer of liberating cognizance from the grim cult figure who must suffer and die ignominiously on a cross in order to save his followers. Thomas' Jesus, unlike the sun God of the roman cult, doesn't die to be reborn; he is eternally alive.

Jesus the hierophant shares his knowledge and wisdom with a few select disciples as opposed to the throngs in the canonical gospels. But even among this smaller circle, only a handful seem to understand the deeper meaning of their teacher's words. Thomas stands out as the most promising of the lot and is chosen to pass on the teachings of his master. Or so the background narrative goes.

The formula of the master who imparts his knowledge to a favorite insider and entrusts him to write it down for posterity

---

[4] David Litwa, *Gnostic Self Deification: The Case of Simon of Samaria*, Gnosis: Journal of Gnostic Studies 1 (2016) 157-176

is a well-worn trope of religious mythmaking. The device preemptively and efficiently foils would-be critiques of the message and confers credibility on the messenger's claims of authenticity.[5] Thus, we should keep in mind that the "veiled words" are not as much what "Jesus said" as they are, more accurately, what Thomas (or whoever impersonated him) said Jesus said. The Gospel of Thomas is Thomas' gospel. The name Thomas itself is used as a pseudonym by the unknown writer or writers of the tractate who chose to withdraw behind their writings. Authorship was then attributed to a legendary figure who would be remembered for the ages. Much like Plato exposes the teachings of Socrates to his students in a series of "dialogues," it is the anonymous author of the gospel according to Thomas, and not Jesus, who speaks to us from the remote past.

The selection of Thomas as the alleged writer of a gospel was not random. Tradition describes him as someone who is not easily convinced and demands evidence (John 20: 24-29); he embodies the searcher's choice of a personal experiential approach over blind faith in the experiences of others. There exists in fact a mystical and philosophical tradition of doubt that is largely forgotten in our age that pits absolute convictions one against another. In the 11ᵗʰ century, the Sunni scholar and theologian Abu Hamid al-Ghazālī wrote:

> Doubt transports [you] to the truth. Who does not doubt fails to inquire. Who does not inquire fails to gain

---

[5] The same works for claims of revelations received directly from God or an angel and recorded by a prophet, medium, or channeler.

insight. Without insight, you remain blind and perplexed.[6]

René Descartes subsequently proposed:

If you would be a real seeker after truth, it is necessary that at least once in your life you doubt, as far as possible, all things.[7]

And in the 20th century, the philosopher mystic Jiddu Krishnamurti reformulated that essential proposition:

This very desire to be certain, to be secure, is the beginning of bondage. It's only when the mind is not caught in the net of certainty, and is not seeking certainty, that it is in a state of discovery.[8]

Thomas, familiarly known as "Doubting Thomas," epitomizes the profoundly pensive individual. He stands in contrast to the other disciples who are easily impressed by earthly, charismatic teachers whom they invest with an authority to tell them how to think.

The wisdom of the Doubter gives us a choice: we can be the disciples who heed second hand, human knowledge from the lips of whomever they decide to "like and follow" on a whim; or we can be Thomas the Skeptic who opens himself to the transcendent awareness streaming from its pellucid, numinous source.

Thomas is also the twin of Jesus [α], which again is to be taken both literally and metaphorically. This will take us to the unfolding of a Liberator/Savior myth that mirrors actual,

---

[6] Quoted in Ebrahim Moosa's *Ghazali and the Poetics of Imagination*; University of North Carolina Press, 2005

[7] René Descartes, *Principles of Philosophy*, 1644

[8] From *Commentaries on Living, Series III, Chapter 29*g

mystical developments in the core of our own being: "he who lives"[9] within us is recognized by Thomas his twin (the soul), while the obtuse disciples (the natural and lower selves, or mind) remain oblivious to inner savior [59].

Thomas' Gospel

No one ever sat at the feet of Jesus, transcribing faithfully every utterance that fell from his mouth. Scholars suggest that the "authentic," mostly moralistic words of one or more rabbis named Jesus (or of variant thereof) must have been circulated orally for quite some time before being laid down in writing. In the process, they were complemented by a primer of imaginative postulations from pagan, Hellenistic, Jewish esoteric, and gnostic circles. The coherence of Thomas' Gospel hinges on the thread of meaning successive redactor-copyists essayed to superimpose on each other's compilation. Unlike latter-day scholars, the erudite of a bygone era did not solely strive to preserve and explain the ideas of his predecessors; he had no qualm reshaping the material at his disposition to illustrate and support his own agenda. For instance, the Coptic text mentions the "kingdom" as being "within you," and "outside of you" [3] whereas the equivalent, earlier Greek logion speaks of the kingdom as "within" only. The difference cannot be passed as a clerical error. Clearly, the last copyist of the Coptic version interpolated the additional words in order to alter the meaning

---

[9] The recuring expression "he who lives" in Thomas is somewhat confusing because it may stand for the living father (of which the god-beings are individual aspects or faces) [37], the inner savior [59], or the heir of the divine [111]. In essence, it refers to a God-Spirit-Heir lineage [15 & 101], the back and forth between the divinely human and the humanly divine.

of the statement. Therein lies the problem: when most analysts talk or write about the Gospel of Thomas, they really concern themselves with the extant Coptic manuscript (together with a smattering of Greek fragments); all they say can only apply to that specific collection of the logia. We know nothing of an elusive, original text composed by Thomas, shorter or longer, in Greek or in Aramean, Christian or Gnostic. Moreover, dating[10] the phantom gospel has devolved into a contentious and vain attempt at validating an "authentic" form of Christianity, which does not interest us here—you do not validate a myth. Myths concern themselves not with empirical truths or historical facts but with the greater truth. They are ahistorical and timeless, and that is precisely why they are valuable.

The New Testament gospels were redacted to present a more or less coherent narrative that would anchor the redeemer god on the sands of history. For the past 2000 years, the gospels have been read as the story of Jesus, the son of the Jewish god, who is born miraculously, performs prodigies of his own, preaches to the throngs, takes upon himself the sins of the world, dies on the cross, and is resurrected as the savior of mankind. Such a tale is absent from Thomas' gospel in which the "historical" Jesus is merely the mouthpiece for clusters of assertions taken from overlapping traditions.

Nothing in Thomas' gospel is explained or interpreted; everything is enounced without a philosophical structure, a catechistic frame, or a clear and evident theme to connect all the logia. Portions of the papyrus are damaged, and the text is

---

[10] Even without an actual date, we can confidently assert that the oral composition of the logia preceded by decades or even centuries their latter compilation in Coptic.

sometimes illegible. The earliest logia must have been cryptic enough, but at the end of their journey through the hands of multiple redactor-copyists, they exhibit all the lacunae, interpolations, emending, mangling, deliberate omissions, and involuntary errors we could expect from subsequent translations, replications, and modifications.[11] If we may arguably benefit from what has been added, who knows what has been discarded and lost forever? The final amalgamation of the logia is a big ink blot onto which, as with the Rorschach test, anyone can project what he or she wants to see. It cannot be stressed enough that the Thomas manuscript consists in a long string of letters without spacing, indentation, paragraph, numbering, or any kind of punctuation, All the aforementioned are modern conventions, and their appearance in contemporary renditions of the Gospel of Thomas is not a matter of translation but of pure speculation. A single coma can entirely change the meaning of the text. Even if one could break through the linguistic barriers and come up with a "true" translation of the Coptic Gospel of Thomas, a modern interpretation has little chance to recover the intended meaning of an untouched version in a different language two or three centuries older. The initial

---

[11] R. McL. Wilson summarizes the issue we are facing:

> It must be remembered that our present Coptic text is probably a translation of a translation, and that in both versions it has been subjected to the vagaries of the scribe; moreover, the sayings have passed through a process of oral tradition, whether or not they are derived from our Gospels, and were originally uttered neither in Greek nor in Coptic, but in Aramaic. When we add the probability of redaction at the hands of one or more editors, who had ends of their own in view, the difficulties in the path of the investigator are manifest. (R. McL. Wilson, *Studies in the Gospel of Thomas*, 1960)

intent of that *hieros logos* is lost to us together with the remembrance of its first compilator. Yet, the same spirit that quickened the intellect of the antecedent thinker dwells in their modern counterparts as well, should they choose to draw from the inexhaustible, unmediated source of inspiration. It is through the workings of such numen that the truths of the sacred text will be intuited. Our purpose then should not be to recapture the original author's frame of mind—an impossible task—but to approach the legacy of long forgotten mystic philosophers as a template to retrace their contemplative steps. Thomas' words were never written in stone, and his gospel will forever remain fluid. We can safely leave to the scholar the endless pursuit of a perfect translation. As for us, we owe it to ourselves to adapt and rewrite the narrative in light of our own transcendent awareness, which is exactly what the ancient Gnostics did for themselves. Using the thoughts ascribed to Thomas as a ladder, we can climb the innermost heights of our own being where truth gushes out. I do not profess to speak for Thomas; I do not claim to have cracked a code or to reveal a momentous secret. Instead, I narrow my focus to a specific cluster of logia to distill the inner mysteries that liberate the soul.

With Thomas' veiled words for road signs, we will now wander beyond the rigor of dry academic examinations and the discursive speculations of spiritual thrill-mongers into the more fruitful, intuitive field of transcendent awareness. With each step, we will further the mapping of a wondrous journey from our origins in a realm of aethereal Life through our sojourn in the vale of matter. Most importantly, we will discover the keys to our ultimate return to the place of numinosity and harmony as a god-being.

For he who could interpret would be dissolved and would become that which is interpreted.[12]

✓ When relevant to my approach, the subsequent rendition of the Coptic Gospel of Thomas takes into consideration elements from the Greek Oxyrhynchus fragments.

✓ I have numbered each logion using the current standard of most published editions of the Gospel of Thomas. The numbers between brackets refer to the logia and/or the commentaries that follow them.

---

[12] James Rendel Harris, *The Odes And Psalms Of Solomon Published From The Syriac Version*, 1911

THE LOGIA

The Spirit and the Soul - α

These are the veiled words spoken by Jesus who lives and put down in writing by Judas Thomas, known as the twin.

Whence do we come? What are we? Whither are we bound? The pithy logia of Thomas answer for us questions that are nearly as old as our first steps when we descended from the great trees to start our unique adventure on Earth. Logion α introduces us to two interlocutors: Jesus and Thomas. Whether these individuals ever existed is irrelevant; the esoteric import of this gospel is drawn from an understanding that Thomas, Jesus, and the disciples can be regarded as allegorical figures: they stand for our own selves, representing aspects and layers of what we are.

In the canonical Gospel of John, Thomas is a doubter (John 20:24-29). Unlike Peter though, he is not unsteady or wavering; he must doubt everything and question all things before the truth can be manifested through him. Elaborating on Descartes' original thought, Antoine-Léonard Thomas reformulated the *cogito* as "since I doubt, I think; since I think, I exist," which suggests that the path to indubitable realization does not begin merely with thinking but precisely by doubting. Likewise, it is always doubt, not faith, that is at the origin of genuine spiritual insight. Faith is the relinquishing of knowledge, whereas doubt is the threshold of knowing. The person of faith decides what God is not and finds it unnecessary to dwell on what He might be; the searcher [9] seeks to know himself [3] in order to comprehend the nature of his god. In *The Book of Thomas the Contender*, Thomas is the "contender," an aspirant or seeker in the divine mysteries, that is a *mystes*. Figuratively, though, he personifies the soul searching for the spirit as her savior-twin. And at this juncture, we need to take a detour to explain what I mean by the soul.

The problem with "soul," is that everybody talks about it, how it feels, what it does, where it goes, but without the clearest idea of <u>what it is</u>. Indeed, in our days, we prefer to understand the soul in the vaguest terms possible so as not to bother ourselves with too much abstract, metaphysical thinking. To make matters worse, "soul" is often amalgamated with "spirit" in one amorphous, semantic blob. But the two were never the same. Furthermore, while there are endless debates about the provenance and post-death whereabouts of soul and Spirit, the question will never be adequately answered until we first understand their precise nature. In other words, the "what" must precede the "whence" and the "whither."

The soul is a cluster of information, specifically our memories, a unique sum of experiences, consciously remembered or not, factual or imaginary. Information must be formulated and cannot circulate without a medium or be processed without a receiver. In other words, information does not exist unless it is attached to something. The memories stored in our living tissues (nobody knows how and for sure) are processed by the mind attached to matter and shape self-awareness along with our perception of the world. The physical body, then, holds our soul together, which brings about our sense of individuality.[1] When the physical body dies and disintegrates, the memories disperse, and the individuality vanishes unless the information is transferred to a new medium that will carry it beyond the grave. With the decay of matter, the earthly mind disappears, and all forces previously exerted on our persona by the material world are void. The souls of the heirs who have attached themselves to the aethereal body [22] of their savior-twin can safely transit to a new, trans-material plane of existence. And just as the mind selects what memories to keep at any given time to frame our mortal, discordant, ever-changing individuality,[2] only certain memories will be retained by the sovereign self [3] to frame an eternal, harmonious individuality. There and then, those memories will become the personal story the heirs of the divine take away through death. They will no longer be experienced by the mind but sealed to the undivided divine as the meta-individualities of god-beings. Thus, the soul is liminal, functioning both in reality and aethereality as the marker of individuality in earthlings and the maker of meta-individualities in aethereal beings.

The interconnection between soul, memory, individuality, and liberation is suggested in remnants of the orphic mysteries. They speak of a pool by a poplar and a river by a cypress in Hades from which the souls of the departed could choose to drink. Those who drank from the river of Lethe would forget

---

[1] Since the soul gives us our sense of individuality, by extension "a soul" can also refer to the actual, individual person.
[2] The essential I, the lone observer that remains when we do not think of or about anything, is constant and unchanged through life. Our individuality however mutates from minute to minute. The fact is, we are not the same thinking person we are now as we were 10, 20, 40 years ago, or when we were a child. This is due to the perpetual flow of changing memories that come into and leave our consciousness.

who they are and incarnate again. The initiates who drank from the pool of Mnemosyne, however, would remember who they are and thereupon be released from the cycles of incarnation.

In contrast to ill-defined "soul," "spirit" has acquired so many definitions that its true meaning is now diluted and obfuscated. Originally, "spirit" (Latin *spiritus*, Greek *pneûma*) meant breath, or air in motion. In Judeo-Christian mythology, it became the fiery, powerful, divine breath. Conceptually, it is the primordial, uncreated generative Desire of the undivided divine by which all moving things in reality or aethereality are brought into manifestation [10]. It triggers physical creation, biological evolution, and underlies metaphysical transformations. The ancient Greeks thought of it as the Protogenos subsequently personified as the god Eros. The Stoics internalized the descending god as an indwelling guardian divinity, a guardian daimon or sacred spirit. The idea was co-opted in Gnosticism. The philosopher and theologian Henry Corbin explained that...

> *a fundamental gnostic intuition ... individualizes the Holy Spirit into an individual Spirit, who is the celestial paredros of the human being, its guardian angel, guide and companion, helper and savior.*[3]

This savior, adds Art historian and researcher Lynda Harris,

> *may appear to be a separate entity, but he is actually the soul's own spirit. He descends from the world of*

[3] Henry Corbin, *Avicenna and the Visionary Recital*, translated from the French by Willard R. Trask, Bollingen Series, 1960

light into the darkness of matter in order to help the fallen soul.[4]

It wouldn't be long before some Gnostic thinkers determined the divine inner presence to be none other than one's higher or true self, thereupon engaging in a "technology of the self"[5] to attain deification. Hence the accent on reflexivity and self-knowing that run as leitmotifs in Thomas' gospel. It is essential though to differentiate between self-glorification, elevating one's common self [3] to the status of a god, and self-divinization: the surrender of the soul to the numinous self [3] in order to enable the "individual Spirit" to regain his previous divine glory. The former is a delusion of grandeur; the latter is an understanding of mankind's divine descent and the humans' rightful claim to their empyrean inheritance.

The uncreated generative Desire flows in all beings. But the ineffable presence and numinous determination are felt only by the heirs of the divine [9]. They are the theurgists of the inner mysteries who recognize the stirrings of an angelic power. Eventually, the abstract living breath is actualized and individualized into the manifestation of a trans-physical being whom the heirs will know to be the mystical embodiment of their numinous self.

The word "spirit" is sparsely used in Thomas' gospel [14][29][44][5][114] and always refers to the living, though immaterial entity personified by Jesus. In other words, Jesus in Thomas is the outer projection of an inner savior [4][70], the indwelling guide and liberator of those who seek his influence and familiarize themselves with his voice.

---

[4] Lynda Harris, *The Secret Heresy of Hieronymus Bosch*, 2002
[5] Litwa 2016

The Eastern Christian tradition presents Thomas as a twin[6] brother of Jesus. Their twinship serves as a metaphor to show that the soul and her savior are eternally bound [12] as exemplified by the classical myth of the Dioscuri.[7]

The twins Castor and Pollux were the sons of God, one mortal, the other immortal. The latter nevertheless managed to have immortality bestowed on the former so that they would remain together forever. Soul and spirit then, are mystical twins, divine children, the dioscuric siblings who can only be free when they are bound to one another.

Henry Corbin remarks that the motif of the Heavenly Twin (*Taw'am*) is central to the soteriology of Manichaeism. He further comments:

> *Christos Angelos is the same in relation to Mani ... as is the taw'am, the "Heavenly Twin," in relation to each of the Elect respectively and individually. It is the Form of light which the Elect receive when they enter the Manichean community through the act of solemn renunciation of the powers of this world. At the passing away of one of the Elect, a psalm is sung in praise of "thy heavenly Partner who faileth not." In Catharism it is he who is called the Spiritus sanctus or angelicus of the particular soul.*[8]

---

[6] *to'am* (twin), the Hebrew transliteration of the Aramaic from which the name Thomas is derived, was not a given name in the time of Jesus. Its use to designate a specific individual as "the twin" is yet another indication that the subject matter of the logia is not historical but figurative.

[7] From the Greek *dios* (god) + *kouroi* (boys)

[8] Henry Corbin, *The Man of Light in Iranian Sufism*. Translated by Nancy Pearson. Shambhala Publications, Inc: Boulder, Colorado. 1978

Thomas refers to Jesus as he "who lives" to distinguish the living presence of the savior-twin in the heart of the heirs (esoteric) from the crucified god of mythological Christianity (exoteric).

In this book, I clarify the meaning of "Spirit" by referring more specifically to the three aspects of its evolution:

1. Uncreated generative Desire (divine force)
2. Numen, angelic or daimonic power (divine presence)
3. Numinous self (divine will)
4. Inner savior or "savior-twin" (divine manifestation).

The difference between our numinous self and the savior-twin is that the former is experienced abstractly as an inherent, psychological component of ourselves while the latter is revealed as the manifest "personal other," a distinct, transcendent aspect of oneself.

Words of Life - 1

And he said: "Whosoever stumbles upon the interpretation of these words will not taste death."

Truth be told, Thomas' gospel was never intended for the general public. It reached worldwide notoriety through a series of fortunate accidents, and its fame grew proportionally to a rumor it would turn the Christian world on its head and revolutionize religion. Interest was at the highest when the papyri were fraught with sensationalism and at the center of conspiracy theories. Now, the Gospel of Thomas is available for the mass market without having fulfilled its most dramatic expectations. The established Christian world hasn't suffered. The customary religious business goes on as usual. The controversies have been relegated to the academics' own hermetic world or the hardcore circles of esoteric thrill-mongers. The spiritual tourist has moved on to uncover the latest metaphysical "secret." The logia stand as inscrutable as ever, unadorned, unthreatening, silent. They are no longer shrouded in mystery; they are the mystery. Yet there is hope with a caveat. The meaning of the veiled words can be uncovered but it won't be through efforts of the mind; it is the gift of transcendent awareness bestowed on the heirs and accompanied with the promise of divinization in the realm of aethereal Life.

Thomas' first saying is profoundly gnostic and suggests why this gospel is largely misunderstood: the logia were never intended to be introduced to the world so that everyone could have a shot at interpreting them; they were sealed, and their significance preserved and reserved for those whose destiny is to receive it.

> So also can you yourselves receive the kingdom of heaven; unless you receive this through knowledge, you will not be able to find it.[9] (Parentheses are mine)

The kingdom of heaven, as we will see, is not a physical residence for the afterlife, but a special kind of knowledge, a divergent perception attainable not through the senses but through familiarity with one's numinous self [3]. This cognizance is liberating because it confers a superlative state of awareness in this life and guarantees a new form of consciousness for the life beyond. However, we must be willing to search the innermost silence with a heart-rending yearning for our savior-twin, which is the price of sovereignty. Credulous

---

[9] *The Apocryphon of James* translated by Francis E. Williams

seekers jump from one book to the next, unwilling to do persistent inner work, but always hungry for exclusive revelations. Obliging and savvy writers understand the marketing power of framing their allegations as secret, hidden, or suppressed knowledge. Thus do the gullible feel privileged for knowing something others don't. But they do not understand that books are treasure maps, not the treasure itself. Maps can only give pointers; they can also mislead. That is the extent and limit of their function. The treasure is the personal liberating cognizance that comes strictly from within.

Unlike the traditional gospels that disingenuously give away the meaning of its parables, or the rambling, explicating, and expounding letters of Paul, Thomas' gospel does not explain anything. The logia are symbols on a map and will yield meaning though contemplative learning, self-knowledge, and inner transformation; essaying to make sense of them through the analytical mind alone is an exercise in futility.

In the tale *Hayy Ibn Yaqzan*, we find a concluding statement that could just as well be about the Gospel of Thomas:

> *I have not left the secrets set down in these pages entirely without a veil—a sheer one, easily pierced by those fit to do so, but capable of growing so thick to those unworthy of passing beyond that they will never breach it.*[10]

Those fit to pierce the veil of secrets are the theurgists of the inner mysteries. The veil refers to a threshold to which the initiates in the ancient mystery cults were sometimes led.

---

[10] *Ibn Tufayl's Hayy Ibn Yaqzan: A Philosophical Tale*; Translated by Lenn E. Goodman; University of Chicago Press, 2003

Alternatively, the *mystai* themselves were veiled. In either case, the prop was meant to suggest another reality invisible to the human eye. We will find several other allusions to secret rituals in Thomas' gospel [2][13][28][33][50][62]. In the beginning, the mysteries appear to have been mainly concerned with pragmatic results such as securing a plentiful harvest or receiving protection at sea. Progressively though, they became more allegorized, culminating in the salvific rituals of Late Antiquity with their promise of rebirth into a blessed eternity beyond death. The mysteries were characterized by a high level of secrecy, yet they were open to all, including slaves. The worthiness of the candidate was not determined by his status but by his degree of preparedness and willingness. Thomas' gospel marks a new development in the tradition of the sacred mysteries by transposing the nocturnal, in-person ritual from secluded chambers, grottoes, and underground crypts to the privacy of one's heart. And the secretive element essential for the emotional impact of the antecedent initiations is now replaced by the intimacy of the soul with her savior-twin. Yet, through the "veiled words" of Thomas, the modern initiate still follows the same steps as the *mystai* who once symbolically passed from mortality to rebirth as denizens of an eternal world. An intuition for the new inner mysteries is demonstrated by Clement of Alexandria who had the ancient pagan, secret cults in mind when he proudly proclaimed:

> *O truly sacred Mysteries! O stainless light! My way is lighted with torches, and I contemplate the heavens and God; I become holy whilst I am initiated, but **the Lord is the hierophant**, and marks his initiate with the seal while illuminating him, and presents to the Father him*

who believes, to be kept safe for ever. Such are the
Bacchic rituals of my Mysteries.[11] (Emphasis is mine.)

Logion 17 also underscores the role of Jesus as the hierophant-savior of the inner mysteries (see *Jesus, Thomas, and the Disciples* in introduction):

I will give you the one upon whom no eye has looked, whom no ear has heard and no hand has touched, and who did not rise in the heart of man.[12]

I suggest that the Gospel of Thomas is not a book for everyone but the chosen few who understand [49] the new, inner mysteries of the savior-twin. The logia deserve more than the scanty paragraph accorded to each of them in most popular commentaries. That is why the "interpretation of these words" carries such power. A contemplative mystic will not just analyze the text but become its meaning in order to be immersed in the very source of the words. To receive such an interpretation is to become a "person of understanding" [21]—that is one "who lives" [α], a theurgist of the inner mysteries who becomes heir of the divine when the rest of mankind remain mere earthly humans. A simulacre of death was often ritualistically performed in the ancient mystery cults, and the *mystai* were

---

[11] Cited in Jan N. Bremmer's *Initiation into the Mysteries of the Ancient World*, 2014

[12] Logion 17 is traditionally translated in the neutral gender, i. e. "that upon which ... and which did not rise." However, it should be clear from Isaiah 64:4—*From ancient times no one has heard, no ear has perceived, no eye has seen any God besides You* (Berean Standard Bible)—that the logion is indeed referring to a divine being who cannot be found in the heart of the common man but will be born and rise in the heart of the heirs [70]. See also *The Prayer of the Apostle Paul* cited with [5].

said to be reborn not just because of the promise of an afterlife, but because they acquired the kind of knowledge that marked them as the truly living ones among the spiritually dead. So too does the sovereign self [2] triumph over the three deaths: the death of the body [22], the spiritual death [11], and the death of individuality [61].

Sovereign over the Entirety - 2

Nothing should deter the searcher; they search until they find. And whenever they should find, they will be disturbed. And should they be disturbed, they will be made to marvel and will be made sovereign over the entirety. And should they be sovereign, they will find restfulness.

Look about you: everyone claims to want the truth; but who is truly disposed to let go of his dearly held beliefs? A genuine pursuit of the truth can only be relentless and uncompromising. And if the truth is to set us free from the world, it ought to be unlike the things of the world; it must break the shackles of mind and matter, shatter the maze of our carnival mirrors, and wake us from our psycho-spiritual slumber, the outcome of which likely would be disturbing. Disturbing it is indeed to find out that one's soul is trapped in matter and that we must renounce everything earthly without exception if she is to be free. The searcher is troubled when his ordinary logic can no longer impose sense on what he is experiencing. The theurgist of the inner mysteries too is troubled when he realizes his prior perception of reality was based essentially on conditioning factors—mere habits of the mind. Even more disturbing perhaps is for the heirs to know they must continue to endure the burden of a painful mortal existence until the appointed time of their return to the company of the god-beings.

How to live in a world with which you disagree? How to live with mankind while not owing either their torments or their joys? When you cannot be one of them?[13]

There is nowadays an entire industry based on convincing the Western man that he can have the perfect career, perfect relationships, perfect health, and enlightenment on top of it all. The trappings of modern society constantly force us to evaluate what we have relatively to what we have not. The Americans even made up neat euphemisms for what is essentially a rat race. They call it "the pursuit of happiness," or the "American dream." In contrast, the mystics in all ages have remarked on that which, with a little honesty, we can all observe on a daily basis: physical existence is mostly suffering, punctuated with horrors and the brief, fleeting moments of genuine contentment or joy. But instead of working together to alleviate our ills, we continue to fight over impossible ways to cure them forever. Some propose that a spiritual awakening of mankind would usher in a paradise on Earth. But to awaken spiritually is to undergo a purging process that requires us to empty ourselves of all that which we hold dear before facing emptiness, silence, and the realization of what is. In that terrifying silent chasm one can finally see that the physical world is not our true home. We have a built-in capacity to readily accept suggestions that conform to our expectations, yet, to understand the nature of physical existence, we must be ready to see it as it is, not as we'd like it to be.

---

[13] Milan Kundera, *L'Immortalité*, 1990

The passerby [42] who feels alien to the terrestrial world cannot be satisfied with the nebulous soup of today's pop spirituality or the fossilized dogma of institutionalized religions; he ought to dedicate the rest of his days to finding a way out of material existence. Everyone has, hidden in the core of his being, a unique key to escape the prison of matter and enter—not as a subject but as a sovereign—the hitherto unseen wonders of the aethereality that borders on reality.[14] The lofty promise is expressed most beautifully in *The Book of Thomas the Contender*[15]:

> *Watch and pray that you not come to be in the flesh, but rather that you come forth from the bondage of the bitterness of this life. ... For when you come forth from the sufferings and passions of the body, you will receive rest from the good one, and you will reign with the king, you joined with him and he with you, from now on, for ever and ever.*

The sequence of "finding, being disturbed, being amazed, and being sovereign," is strongly suggestive of an initiation into the ancient mystery cults. "Prospective initiates would have been introduced into the secret teachings of the Mysteries by so-called mystagogues," explains Jan N. Bremmer. Then,

> *before the high point of the ritual occurred, the initiated were first subjected to a <u>terrifying experience</u>... As Plutarch notes: 'subsequently, before the climax ...*

---

[14] The nature of the "entirety" that encompasses both "reality" and "aethereality" will be explored in [18].
[15] Translation by John D. Turner

[come] all the terrors – shuddering ... and amazement.[16] (Emphases are mine.)

All authentic mystical initiations are purposely disorienting because they are not meant to lead the prospective initiate on a straight path but to break the patterns to which we are so easily attached. It is only when there is no artificial roadways left to pursue that we can contemplate the imaginal Orient[17] and find ourselves at the threshold of our true home at last.

The Gate to the Empyreal Sovereignty - 3

If your leaders tell you, "Behold, the kingdom is in the sky," then the birds of the sky will be there before you. If they tell you, "It is in the sea," then the fish will be there before you. Instead, the empyreal sovereignty is within you, and it is in the eye of the beholder. When you know yourselves, you will know this, and you will realize that you are the sons (children) of the living father. If however you do not know yourselves, then you exist in spiritual poverty, and you are the spiritual poverty.

There is a widespread consensus that the kingdom promoted in the scriptures by the mystical Jesus has nothing to do with physical boundaries but refers to an otherworldly reign. Additionally, we discovered in logion 2 that the spiritual apotheosis is tantamount to being "sovereign over the entirety." For this reason, I have elected to use "empyreal sovereignty" in lieu of the traditional "kingdom" found in standard translations. However, I have preserved the word "kingdom" when found in

---

[16] Bremmer 2014
[17] For the symbolism of the Orient, see [55]

the disciples' discourse. As we will see, the followers of Jesus who question him in the logia do not appear to grasp the concept of a transcendent reign and retain instead their utopian expectations of a concrete kingdom and a divine rule over the Earth.

The empyreal sovereignty is not a location where the swimming fishes, the flying birds, or the souls of the departed can go. It isn't a destination at the end of a path, or a transformation of anything material; it is a state of life and perceptions that transcends physical reality. There and then, the undivided divine is conscious of living in aethereality through the god-beings while also existing in physical reality through the mortal beings. Hence, the true "kingdom" is said to be "spread out upon the earth" [113] ("outside") while being carried potentially, or embryonically, in the innermost of all human beings ("within"), waiting to be manifested. However, the fulness of that kingdom is invisible to the physical eye of the nescient mortal and can only be seen through trans-physical eyes [22].

That which you are looking for out there has come, but you do not know it. Logion - 51

Hence, the sovereignty is manifest only for the liberated soul who has deserted the body of flesh at death to be taken into the aethereal body of her Liberator. Nothing material can be made spiritual. Matter simply cannot transform or evolve, let alone be purified into Spirit. The former must be discarded; the latter must be acquired by the soul. If matter and spirit can commingle like water and ink, they however remain distinct and separate elements. "The soul," wrote Iamblichus,

...has a proper principle of circumduction to the intelligible, and of a separation from generated natures; and also of a contact with real being, and that which is divine.

This "principle of the soul"

...is superior to all nature and generation, and through which we are capable of being united to the Gods, of transcending the mundane order, and of participating eternal life, and the energy of the supercelestial Gods. Through this principle, therefore, we are able to liberate ourselves from fate. For when the more excellent parts of us energize, and the soul is elevated to natures better than itself, then it is entirely separated from things which detain it in generation, departs from subordinate natures, exchanges the present for another life, and gives itself to another order of things, entirely abandoning the former order with which it was connected.[18]

The sea symbolizes matter,[19] and the sky stands for the cosmic. Soul emerged when the mind finally could process

---

[18] *Iamblichus on The Mysteries of the Egyptians, Chaldeans, and Assyrians*, Section 8, Chapter vii; translated from the Greek by Thomas Taylor, 1821

[19] Though our planet is called Earth, 71% of its surface is water. And if all the ice were to melt, there wouldn't be much visible land left. Genesis 1:2 informs us that at the moment of the creation, with the earth still "waste and void, ... the Spirit of God [was] fluttering on the face of the waters." Thus a contrast is drawn between spirit and matter/water when the former had yet to penetrate the latter. The baptism by immersion as it was practiced in the waters of the Jordan river represented the descent and entombment of the spirit into matter and its eventual release (rebirth) from it. For this reason, the Cathars and other dualists sects who abhorred matter above all else

information at the end of a long biological evolution that began in our planet's oceans[20]; spirit is of heavenly descent [α]. The heirs who know this lineage are the children of Heaven and Earth.

From the distant past comes to us this echo of the Orphic mysteries:

I am a child of Earth and of Starry Heaven;
But my race is of Heaven.[21]

And from classical antiquity we also received the delightful myth of Eros and Psyche. Psyche, the soul—figuratively feminine—is spellbound by the ever-youthful Eros. He is the "protogenos,"—figuratively masculine—the cosmic, winged (the wings symbolize his coming from the heavens) child. In Plato's dialogue between Socrates and Phaedrus, we are told that the soul once dwelled in a realm of absolute harmony which she all but forgot upon being imprisoned in matter. Yet, the sight of beauty in the world reminds the soul of her origins and fills her with longings for the divine. Eros then is the bridge between the earthly and the heavenly, a mediator through whom the desires of the soul to merge with the numinous can be satisfied.

Night after night, Eros and Psyche meet in the obscurity of a palatial bridal chamber. Eventually the couple elopes, and Psyche is granted immortality by Zeus when she is wedded to Eros on Mount Olympus. The lovers become undivided,

---

rejected the baptism of water and performed only a baptism of the Spirit.

[20] Interestingly (and perhaps not coincidentally), the English word "soul" may have originated from Proto-Germanic *saiwaz,* meaning "from the sea."

[21] Inscription from The Petelia Tablet, Found in excavations near Petelia, South Italy, now in the British Museum; translated by Jane Ellen Harrison, *Prolegomena to the Study of Greek Religion*, 1908

sovereigns over the entirety; the sacred peak represents their empyreal sovereignty. "Empyreal" derives from the Greek *empyros*, meaning "fire" (*pyr*) "within" (*em-*). The empyrean therefore is not a paradise-like place in the cosmos, but a commingling with the fire [10] of Desire. When we turn to the uncreated generative Desire (Eros) within us, our numinous self is born as a savior-twin. When we nurture the holy child [46], he becomes the liberator of our soul [70]. When the two are unified, they leave the physical world behind and rise as one in aethereality. These views on the origins and destination of soul and spirit are encapsulated by the author of the *Gospel of Philip*:

> The soul and the spirit have come forth [in] water and fire with light, which pertain to the son of the Bridal-Chamber. The fire is the Chrism, the light is the fire. I do not speak of this fire that has no form, but rather the other one—whose form is white, which is made of beautiful light and which bestows splendor.[22]

Another relevant myth, albeit not as elaborate as that of Eros and Psyche, is the story of Dionysos and Ariadne.

Having been abandoned by her ex-lover Theseus on the island of Naxos, Ariadne is rescued by Dionysos, another child-god (now grown-up) whose name associates him directly with a divine origin. Dionysus takes Ariadne for a wife, and again, the two end up happily ever-after in a realm of eternal delights.

Once more, then, we have the motif of soul (Ariadne) liberated from her earthly bounds (Theseus) and taken up by the love of a god. Thus, in the initiatic climax of the Dionysian

---

[22] *The Gospel of Philip*, translated by Thomas Paterson Brown

mysteries, women would identify with Ariadne, being ritually wedded to the god in order to be granted everlasting life. The practice of a ritualistic sacred marriage persists among the Catholic nuns who, upon taking their vows (in more restrained fashion than their pagan counterparts, surely), become the brides of Christ.

Earth is the Naxos Island of the mystics. Their heart is no longer with Theseus, but their soul is not yet with Dionysos. They only have longings for the god and the patience to wait until he takes them away from the dreary world of the mortals.

Because of their common role in saving the soul and shared attribute as mediator between reality and aethereality, both Eros and Dionysos were given the epithet of "Liberator" (*Eleutherios*).

Now for the rest of the logion:

The teachings of religious "leaders" past and present are influenced to a great extent by the scheming of the archons to whom we will return later.[23] Suffice to say those entities guard the gates of the cosmos, and their survival rests on keeping us trapped in matter. To that effect, they covertly promote the hegemony of cosmic (father sky) and Gaian (mother Earth) theologies and creeds. But the liberation of soul from the physical world, and the release of spirit from the bonds of matter cannot be effected through the parental religion, only through the religion of the twin children: a *religare* of the

---

[23] Logia 9, 21, 50. Especially, see Excursus; *The Archons*.

164

siblings—the Beloved and the lover[24]; a wedding of the groom to his bride symbolized respectively by the sun and the moon. Institutionalized religions have deservedly garnered a bad reputation in recent decades to the effect that an abundance of disappointed easy believers have now turned to non-denominational, eclectic, syncretic, and exotic spiritualities. They are however none the wiser for making the switch because "spirituality" means so many things nowadays that it no longer stands for anything. A more fruitful solution is to reclaim the meaning of "religion" that has fallen in disuse. Religion is derived from the Latin *religio*, but the etymology of the latter is still debated. One possibility is that it derives itself from *religare*, which means "binding anew." In that case, the inner religion, as I see it, would be a return to a state of "undividedness" through an unbreakable bond between spirit and soul. The outward religion is so pervasive however, that few escape its grasp. Most fail to hear the call springing from the source of liberating cognizance within. Hence, we find the disciples inquiring about a date for the establishment of a kingdom on Earth. They await a hypothetical, theocratic new world, when the departed are back to mingle with the living.

> *His disciples asked him: "On what day will the repose of the dead be, and on what day will the new world come?" He replied: "That which you are looking for out there has come, but you do not know it."* Logion - 51

No matter the clarification, we find the disciples once again asking the same question in the penultimate logion of Thomas'

---

[24] In ancient myths, siblings were frequently lovers as well: the Egyptian couple Isis and Osiris, or the Inca moon Goddess Mama Quilla and her brother the sun God Inti, for instance.

165

gospel. They could not shake off the hold that the conventional and long-standing teachings of the religious "leaders" had on them:

His disciples asked him: "What day is the kingdom coming?"

"It is not coming to be seen out there. It won't be said behold there or behold that. Instead, the empyreal sovereignty of the father is spread out upon the earth, and men do not see it." Logion – 113

Obviously, the disciples haven't learned anything, and the logion reiterates what they should already know: the empyreal sovereignty is not coming at a certain point in time or from any direction; it is eternally everywhere and nowhere because it is the bridging of a divided state and one of "undividedness," a two-way crossing between physical reality and aethereality that exists by virtue of the uncreated generative Desire of the undivided divine.

The many canonical scriptures and apocryphal texts in circulation have a foremost characteristic in common: they tell us a lot about the mindset of those who wrote them but not so much about us. The revelations of Thomas, on the other hand, are about the reader whom they directly involve.

We constantly hear that a big part of our malaise and troubles in life is due to a lack of self-esteem. It has become imperative, we are told, to rebuild our fragile, damaged sense of worth, and help our children develop pride in themselves. However, all that we appear to develop is self-preoccupation at best, arrogance at worst. Self-esteem has entirely replaced self-discipline, and our great failure is in gratifying the lower self when we should be nurturing instead a numinous self beyond the mind as a savior born in us to guide us [70]. Part of the problem lies in how the "self" is being used as an umbrella word tossed around indiscriminately with little meaning left attached to it. To clarify, throughout this book I distinguish between four selves:

1. the primal self (nature) is our evolutionary legacy of emotions and instincts. Our genetically inherited character is also part of it.

2. the lower or common self (nurtured) is our personality: the mind conscious of itself; our feelings; our frame of self-reference.

3. the numinous self (transcendent) is the guide of the soul. Once united outside the bounds of physicality, the pair becomes...

4. the sovereign self, an aspect or face of the undivided divine in aethereality.

Together, the primal and common selves are responsible for our ordinary perception of the world. They pertain to physical existence and constitute the mind. The numinous self pertains to the transcendent and seeks emancipation from mind and matter in which it is trapped.

In a foreword to F. W. H. Myers' *Human Personality and Its Survival of Bodily Death*, Aldous Huxley compares the consciousness models offered respectively by Freud, Jung, and Myers, and asks:

> *Is the house of the soul a mere bungalow with a cellar? Or does it have an upstairs above the ground floor of consciousness as well as a garbage-littered basement beneath?*

I have remodeled Huxley's clever metaphor here to house my own model of consciousness.

The primal self thrives in the dark and musty basement. Some people love to go down there and retrieve what had been discarded for good reasons, but it's also where the archons [21] spend most of their time. It might do us good from time to time to clear up and clean up the underground space, but that is a task for the mythical Danaïdes: in no time, the place is just as overrun by junk and fungi as it was before. The time we spend in the basement is time we miss in the attic; the glimmer that some believe they can find deep in the darkness always saturates the place of numinosity.

The living quarters is where we find the lower, everyday self, loafing and overstuffing.

And then, there is an attic bathed in soft, aethereal luminosity, where treasures untold are hidden. There is awaiting our numinous self.

The sovereign self has left the house altogether.

We have determined that the soul and the inner savior are personified respectively by Thomas and Jesus who themselves are twin siblings [α]. This proposition, implicit in the logion's exhortation to know oneself, is further suggested in *The Book of Thomas the Contender*:[25]

> Now, since it has been said that you are my twin and true companion, examine yourself, and learn who you are, in what way you exist, and how you will come to be. Since you will be called my brother, it is not fitting that

---

[25] Translation by John D. Turner

you be ignorant of yourself. And I know that you have understood, because you had already understood that I am the knowledge of the truth. So while you accompany me, although you are uncomprehending, you have (in fact) already come to know, and you will be called 'the one who knows himself'. For he who has not known himself has known nothing, but he who has known himself has at the same time already achieved knowledge about the depth of the all.

We now have all the elements needed to clarify logion 3.

When we heed our numinous self who is "the knowledge of the truth" (transcendent awareness), the soul is drawn to her meta-physical sibling. Spirit is known by soul and soul by Spirit. They realize they are the children of the undivided divine whom they know as "the living father" because he dwells in the realm of aethereal life (as opposed to the physical world, the realm of death).

The *Book of Lambspring* is a 16th century treatise on spiritual alchemy wherein soul is called "the Son" and spirit "the Guide." It is based on a series of 15 vignettes, each accompanied with a title, a caption, and a commentary. In a remarkable engraving (fig. 1) from a 17th century edition of the book, the spirit is easily recognized on account of his wings, his association with the sun (upper left corner), and the Phrygian cap he wears (which in allegorical art denotes a link to the antecedent mystery religions). Though the soul in the manuscript is represented by a man, her symbol is still the "feminine" moon (right upper corner). The soul is crowned to signal the empyreal sovereignty she will enter following her consort, guide, guardian, and king, the savior-twin. The peak

on which they stand represent the metaphysical heights to
which they ascend together above the material world at the
bottom of the mountain, free from the carnal body and matter
signified by the sea[26] in the background.

Figure 1

---

[26] The first vignette in the *Book of Lambspring* shows two fish
swimming in the sea. The caption reads: *The Sea is the Body, the two
Fishes are Soul and Spirit.*

The coadunation of soul and spirit is understood in inner alchemy as the realization of the philosopher stone through a twinning and a fusion (see fig. 2), and the apostle James (also purported to be another brother of Jesus) plainly wrote that "the soul is not saved without the spirit.[27]"

Figure 2. Detail of illustration from *Hermaphroditisches Sonn- und Monds-Kind, 1752.*

When we know ourselves, we discover our dyadic[28] god-seed—part soul, part Spirit—ensconced in the mortal body. Furthermore, we understand that immortality in the aethereal realm of Life is offered to those who surrender their soul to the inner savior. But those who remain in nescience will know only the poverty of the physical world and the mortal flesh to which

---

[27] *The Apocryphon of James,* translated by Francis E. Williams.
[28] In this book, I use the terms "dyad, dyadic, and dyadicity" when referring to the soul-spirit twinning aspects of the god-seed in us. The words "dual, dualist, dualistic, duality," on the other hand, refer to the double, opposite aspects underlying the entirety: materiality and trans-materiality; entropy and negentropy; reality and aethereality; becoming and being; stasis and movement; death and permanence.

they are attached [56]; they are spiritually poor, and no material riches, worldly successes, talents, skills, or "inner beauty" can ever make up for their loss. The Knowledge of *one's self* is the gate to the empyreal sovereignty. That last part of the Logion seems to contradict the first of the Beatitudes in Matthew who praises the condition of being "poor in spirit." This is understandable; by the time the Gospel of Matthew was written late in the first century, the object of Christianity was well established as reliance on an external savior. The "poor in spirit" therefore were those most likely to depend on a systematic religion that offered hope and a vicarious spirituality. The followers of Thomas on the other hand had all the spiritual richness they needed within themselves.

The Inner Guide - 4

The elder will not hesitate to inquire from the younger seven-day old concerning the place of life, and they will live. For many of the first will be last and the last first, and they will become undivided.[29]

It is doubtful an actual child seven days old would answer metaphysical questions except in the wonderland of religious scriptures where the imaginative miraculous abounds. We must look elsewhere for an interpretation of this allegory.

---

[29] I use the term "undivided," and sometimes the cumbersome but telling "undividedness" for this recurring, misunderstood, key metaphysical concept, the rendition of which varies wildly among translators of the Gospel of Thomas (e.g., "one and the same," "a single one," "a single thing," "one alone," "solitary," "a single unity," etc.). The "undividedness" is the indissoluble two-as-one, both unique and alike, a totality dyadic in structure, very much like the yin-yang of Taoism, the two parts of which are bound, interconnected, and reciprocally dependent, but separately distinguishable.

"Seven" is the number attached to the physical and cosmic plane.[30] It symbolizes the beginning, being the number of days in the biblical account of the creation. And by looking into the beginning—metaphorically questioning a child—we can best understand the end and our destiny [18].

The seven-day old child is the savior-twin, the god-to-be trapped in matter who often figures in mythologies as a youthful god born in our world and representative of the inner guide (e.g., Attis,[31] Dionysos, Apollo, Horus, or the young Jesus

---

[30] According to Genesis, 7 is the number of days the god of matter (demiurge) needed to create the world and rest. It is also the number of planets the ancients could distinguish as part of the cosmos. Thus, 7 is directly associated with the creation of the cosmic plane of matter.

[31] The legend of Attis is remarkable for narrating under the veil of metaphors the descent of an undivided god-seed (the androgynous form) into matter where it becomes divided (the metaphorical castration) before returning to a state of wholeness (the divinization). According to one account by Pausanias,

> Zeus [i.e. the Phrygian sky-god identified with Zeus], it is said, let fall in his sleep seed upon the ground, which in course of time sent up a Daimon, with two sexual organs, male and female. They call the Daimon Agdistis. But the gods, fearing Agdistis, cut off the male organ. There grew up from it an almond-tree with its fruit ripe, and a daughter of the river Saggarios (Sangarius), they say, took of the fruit and laid it in her bosom, when it at once disappeared, but she was with child. A boy was born, and exposed, but was tended by a he-goat. As he grew up his beauty was more than human, and Agdistis [now the goddess Kybele] fell in love with him. When he had grown up, Attis was sent by his relatives to Pessinos, that he might wed the king's daughter. The marriage-song was being sung, when Agdistis appeared, and Attis went mad and cut off his genitals, as also did he who was giving him his daughter in marriage. But Agdistis repented of what he had done to Attis, and persuaded Zeus to grant that the body of Attis should neither rot at all nor decay.
>
> (Pausanias, Description of Greece, translated by W. H. S. Jones)

who was questioned by the Elders in the temple). Logion 4 is telling us to seek a transcendent awareness of and from our numinous self, the daimon (in the platonic sense) or angel whose growth is commensurate to the attention we are giving him. The holy child who has been nurtured becomes the savior within who will give the soul a new, aethereal life. This idea appears in the so-called Naassene sermon cited by Hippolytus of Rome:

> *These (heretics) ... having ascertained ... that a child of seven years old is half of a father, say that in fourteen years, according to Thomas, he is manifested. This, with them, is the ineffable and mystical Logos.*[32]

(Emphasis is mine.)

In gnostic myth-making and apocryphal literature, the revealer and savior ("the ineffable and mystical Logos") is sometimes represented as a child or a youth. For instance, in the *Act of John*, Jesus appears to James as a child calling him from the seashore while the other disciples can only see their lord as an adult. Even more striking is the apparition of the child Christ in an episode from the *Pistis Sophia* we will soon examine [5]. A well-known prototype of the divine savior-child is the Egyptian Heru pa Khered whom the Greeks adopted as Harpocrates, and who was further amalgamated into Eros-Harpocrates.

Hippolytus again refers to the metaphysical child in Thomas' gospel:

> *Concerning this (nature) they hand down an explicit passage, occurring in the Gospel inscribed according to*

---

[32] Hippolytus, *Refutation of All Heresies*, Book 5, Chapter 2, translated by J.H. MacMahon.

Thomas, expressing themselves thus: "He who seeks me, will find me in children from seven years old; for there concealed, I shall in the fourteenth age be made manifest."

Note that the child in the quotation above is no longer seven days but seven years old and maturing. It emphasizes the growth of our numinous self as an independent metaphysical entity and also confirms that the number 7 is used here symbolically.

The parallel structure of the logion allows us to associate the elder with the first and the child with the last. In order of manifestation, the soul is born before the savior-twin [15 & 101]. But in order of preeminence, the inner savior comes first because he preserves the soul beyond death, leading her out of the world of matter and into the aethereal realm. Hence, the elder who came first is last while the child who came later is first.

There are yet two more interpretations we can derive from this same logion:

1. Those who are first in the affairs of the world may find themselves last to reach the empyreal sovereignty because mundane preoccupations keep them from nurturing their numinous self. They are absentee parents, so to speak, who miss their chance to create the necessary everlasting bond for the survival of the soul. Materialistic absorption is clearly the context given by the Evangelist Matthew as an obstacle to salvation, and for the idea that "the last will be first, and the first will be last" (Matthew 19:30 and 20:16 BSB). But the

aphorism could also suggest the next, far more esoteric proposition:

2. Assuming some recent scientific hypotheses are correct, there may not be just one plane of physical existence but myriad parallel universes on which perhaps the destinies of men could unfold differently to answer necessity. In other words, the souls last (or lost) on one plane may be first (and saved) on the other. We are not speaking here of reincarnation but of poly-incarnation, the descent and scattering of the uncreated generative Desire on multiple, co-occurring universes arranged like beads on a bracelet—each opening where the other end. We can further visualize the bracelet twisted to form an eight shape (infinity symbol or lemniscate) with a single bead at the cross junction. That locus would be the one universe where everything comes together for the soul who awakes to her own divinity and unites with her savior-twin.

The Veiled Savior - 5

Know him who is staring you in the face, and he who is veiled from your view will be unveiled. Indeed, there is nothing concealed that will not be revealed.

In the allegorical setting of Thomas' gospel, Jesus is speaking in front of the disciples. However, this Jesus, as we proposed, is but a figure for the manifestation of the numinous self.[33] To *know him who is staring us in the face* is to recognize oneself as a son/daughter of the living father [3] and to

---

[33] See logia α, 91, and the introduction: *Jesus, Thomas, and the disciples.*

understand that our dyadic god-seed is constituted of a soul and her twin sibling the inner savior. In a gnostic prayer allegedly offered by Paul, the Apostle tellingly identifies Jesus as an angelic spirit and asks for this inmost being to be manifested:

> Give me your gifts ... through the Son of Man, the Spirit, the Paraclete of truth ... and redeem my eternal light soul and my spirit.
>
> Grant what no angel eye has seen and no archon ear (has) heard, and what has not entered into the human heart which came to be angelic and (modelled) after the image[34] of the psychic God when it was formed in the beginning, ... And place upon me your beloved, elect, and blessed greatness, the First-born, the First-begotten, and the wonderful mystery of your house.[35]

The mystical encounter of the soul and her savior-twin is imaginatively recounted in a striking anecdote from the Gnostic work *Pistis Sophia*. The soul here is personified by the mortal boy Jesus who is united with his immortal likeness:

> When thou wert little, ... the spirit came out of the height and came to me in my house, <u>like unto thee;</u> and ... <u>I thought that thou wast he.</u> And the spirit said unto me: "Where is Jesus, my brother, that I meet with him?" And when he had said this unto me, I was at a loss and thought it was a phantom to try me. ... I went forth to you, to thee and Joseph in the field, ... when thou didst hear me speak the word unto Joseph, that thou didst understand the word, wert joyful and saidest: "Where is he, that I may see him; else I await him in this place."

---

[34] See *The Image of the Divinity* [83 & 84]
[35] *The Prayer of the Apostle Paul*, translated by Dieter Mueller.

… And we went down together, entered the house … And we looked on thee and him and found thee like unto him. … he took thee in his arms and kissed thee, and thou also didst kiss him. Ye became one.[36] (Emphases are mine.)

The resemblance between the savior-twin and the soul is reaffirmed in logion 108 and meant to emphasize their kinship:

Jesus said: "He who drinks out of my mouth will come to resemble me. Likewise, I myself will come to be as he is.

The soul and her savior—the two halves of the dyadic god-seed in us—are alike because they are imprinted with the image of the divinity [83 & 84]. They mirror one another and save each other [46]. The youth who narrates *The Hymn of the Robe of Glory,* another prominent Gnostic text traditionally, and significantly, also attributed to Thomas, describes the extraordinary correspondence in poetical fashion:

The Glory looked like my own self
I saw it in all of me,
And saw me all in [all of] it, –
That we were twain in distinction,
And yet again one in one likeness.[37] (Emphases are mine)

The ascendancy and triumph of the mystical siblings who have found each other is symbiotic. The revealer of that which is veiled [13] is the savior-twin to whom we have given birth

---

[36] *Pistis Sophia,* translated by G. R. S. Mead
[37] G.R.S. Mead, *The Hymn of the Robe of Glory; Echoes from the Gnosis. Vol. X,* 1908

[70] thus ensuring the liberation of the dyadic god-seed from matter. Through him, the heirs will know all things.

The perfect Savior said: "I came from the Infinite that I might tell you all things." [38]

But the only knowledge we need to free the soul is an understanding of our true essence.

He who finds himself, of him the world is not worthy.

Logion - 111

Together, the soul and her savior can break the chains of physicality and find restfulness in the empyreal sovereignty.

The Primal Duality in Man - 7

Blessed is the lion who is consumed by the man and becomes a human being; cursed is the man who is consumed by the lion who becomes a human being.

There are fewer than 30.000 lions alive in the wild nowadays, but in the old world, they were one of the most ubiquitous species; so much so that they figure in the art of many ancient cultures. The lion was once an emblem of spirituality, divinity, and royalty. For instance, Apedemak, "Lord of Royal Power," was the lion-headed war god of the redoubtable Kushites warriors, while the neo-Assyrian king Ashurnasirpal II referred to himself as a lion. Those mythological references often emphasized the lions' ferocity, but also its protective power, signifying a tremendous force that must be mastered. Both Herakles and Samson strangled a lion. In addition, it is not uncommonly believed that one can slay an animal to assimilate its essence and power by eating its organs. Likely though, the slaying mentioned by Thomas is allegorical.

---

[38] *The Sophia of Jesus Christ*, translated by Douglas M. Parrott.

The lion in this case refers to the primordial, intrinsic duality in physical man who was created (along with the whole of material reality) at the juncture and as a consequence of two diverging, opposite forces: an uncreated generative Desire (negentropy), and the pull of stasis (entropy) [10].

Hence, Thomas' bewildering saying gets clearer when the lion is understood as the zoomorphic embodiment of a dual creational tide at the origin of physical existence. That is how the "lion becomes man." When recognized, and properly channeled ("consumed," or absorbed), the uncreated generative Desire of the undivided divine that begot us emerges as a numinous self and the physical man becomes divinely human. That is why the lion is "blessed." A tide, however, always implies an ebbing: the waters that move beyond the main body and over the land also withdraw to their unmoved core. If the primal flow is ignored and untamed, the physical man is "cursed" by being drawn back deeper ("consumed by the lion") into the origination of matter until he can no longer tear himself free, and he loses the means of his liberation. A somewhat similar idea was expressed in the gnostic Naassene sermon:

> *This, he says, is ocean, "generation of gods and generation of men" ever whirled round by the eddies of water, at one time upwards, at another time downwards. But he says there ensues a generation of men when the ocean flows downwards; but when upwards ..., a generation of gods takes place. This, he asserts, is that which has been written: "I said, Ye are gods, and all children of the highest.[39]"*

---

[39] Hippolytus

Hence, the generation of immortal god-beings is in the upward flow (toward aethereality) of the dormant sea of *protoeidoi* [10], while the ebbing carries the man who cannot escape his mortal condition.

Man would be ruled by his primal, destructive instincts and the uncontrollable forces of nature until he learns to ride astride the beast within and without.

> *Be sober-minded and alert. Your adversary the devil prowls around like a roaring lion, seeking someone to devour.* (1 Peter 5:8 Berean Standard Bible)

In light of logion 7, this "devil" is not the imaginative evil entity of Christian lore but the very tidal force of creation that can either serve or destroy us. The Christian devil of course is also associated in the New Testament with the serpent (Revelation 20:2). But the serpent more universally represents the cosmic (demiurgic) forces of chaos and destruction, as well as generation, incarnation, fertility, and sexuality. Hence it is combined with the lion in gnostic iconography to form the potent allegorical image of Samael (fig. 3), the hybrid creature in the center of the cosmos, creator of

Figure 3.

mankind, who must be overwhelmed by the theurgist of the inner mysteries.

> *You will tread on the lion and cobra; you will trample the young lion and serpent.* (Psalm 91:13 BSB)

Thomas' curious allegory of the ferocious feline and the human resurfaces in symbolic and alchemical imagery. A 16ᵗʰ century illustration depicts the "lion of matter" devouring an anthropomorphic "sun of spirit" (fig. 4).

Figure 4.   Figure 5.

When the man is swallowed by the entropic aspect of creation, spirit cannot escape matter. Another illustration[40] from the same time period shows a woman subduing a lion (fig. 5)—a vivid rendition of the soul (figuratively feminine in the Western mystical tradition) given victory over the raw animality of the flesh and the decaying of the physical body. The

---

[40] From the *Tarot de Marseille*, a symbolic card deck often linked by scholars to alchemy and hermeticism. Note that "La Force," translated as "Strength" on English versions of the Tarot deck, also means "the force." Hence the card doesn't necessarily speak of physical might but possibly of the cause of motion or change (becoming). Interestingly, the number XI (11, or 1 and 1) attributed to the card suggests duality and opposition.

woman holding the lion's jaws wide open also suggests the role of the soul in liberating the spirit engulfed in matter [46]. The triumph of the sovereign self, then, could be imagined as a god-being riding a lion, and that is exactly how both Eros and Dionysos [3] often figure in the art of classical antiquity. The depiction of Eros taming a lion, or Amor's triumph over force, was also favored by painters and sculptors of the Renaissance and throughout the 19th century.

In the Western hermetic tradition, the lion is associated with the fire element, and fire is itself a symbol of desire and spirit [10]. Fire, as we well know, can benefit us greatly and just as well destroy us.

As long as we remain a slave to the primal duality that carries us throughout our earthly sojourn, it threatens us unto death. When we navigate skillfully the turbulent, unseen current, it takes us safely to the felicitous shore.

The Three Orientations of the Soul - 9

Behold, a sower came and threw a handful of seeds. Some fell onto the road; the birds came to pick them. Others fell onto the rock; they did not take root down into the earth, and they did not produce ears toward heavens. Yet others fell among the thorns that choked them, and the worm ate them. Still others fell upon good soil and produced good fruits toward heavens, yielding sixty per measure and a hundred and twenty per measure.

Prior to the unearthing of the Gospel of Thomas, the *Parable of the Sower* was already known from the synoptic gospels together with a conveniently detailed interpretation of its meaning. The clever redactor-copyist(s) writing as Matthew, Mark, or Luke made Jesus clarify his own words and show how the scattered seeds represented hearers in various stages of understanding and acceptance. In effect, the explanation turns the text into a cautionary tale about the perils of not heeding the priests and the preachers and neglecting to obey their writ to the letter. In Thomas however, the parable is free from the added commentary and lets the reader discover his own answer to the riddle of the Sower and the seeds.

The Sower is the undivided divine spilling and dispersing their uncreated generative Desire [1] upon the world. And the seeds are indeed a gnostic illustration for spirit scattered onto the physical plane: the god-seed present in each of us. The parable does not highlight the need to listen to creeds, it speaks of our essence reaching its destiny. That destiny is threefold in keeping with the three orientations of the soul:

1. The materialists who rely entirely on the mind or do not rise above material concerns never kindle their numinous self. They embrace neither Gaian nor cosmic mysticality (symbolized by being rooted into the earth and producing ears toward heaven). Instead of building bridges to aethereal realms, they erect dense walls that cannot be penetrated by the uncreated generative Desire. The numen in them remains dormant. Figuratively, their god-seed is "picked" by the birds (or "consumed by the lion," as we saw in logion 7) if not left to dry and wither "onto the rock" of matter.

2. The faithful and the easy believers strive to distance themselves from the grasp of the material world but fall under the sway of charismatic or influential religious leaders and peddlers of spiritual roadmaps to nowhere. The god-seed in

them is choked by treacherous dogma (the thorns) and eaten by the parasitic archons (the worm) who bore through unsuspecting minds [21].

3. Only the heirs are fertile ground (good soil) for the god-seed. They take part in the Sower's mystical masterwork of bringing about the coadunation of soul with spirit and strengthening their bond into an "undividedness" [57].

> *I came here, that they might be joined with that Spirit and Breath, and might from two become one, ... that you might yield much fruit and go up to Him Who Is from the Beginning, in ineffable joy and glory.* [41]

The second-third century Christian author Hippolytus documented the beliefs of the Naassene Gnostics who evidently knew of the angelic power in us and the three orientations of souls:

> *There are three kinds of all existent things — angelic, psychical, earthly; and there are three churches — angelic, psychical, earthly; and the names of these are elect, called, captive.* [42]

Among the Valentinians, the three orientations of the soul were known as *pneumatici* ("those of Spirit"), *psychici* ("those of soul"), and *hylici* ("those of matter"). As for the proponents of such views, they were nicknamed derogatorily *gnostici*, the "know-it-all," by their detractors. Thomas calls them the "persons of understanding" [21]. They are the theurgists of the inner mysteries, searchers of

---

[41] *The Sophia of Jesus Christ* Translated by Douglas M. Parrott
[42] Hippolytus of Rome, *Refutation of All Heresies*, Book V - Chapter 2, translated by J.H. MacMahon, 1886; revised and edited for newadvent.org by Kevin Knight.

the innermost silence, mystic lovers of the beloved savior-twin.

The Fiery Trail of Desire - 10

I have cast the fire upon the world, and behold, I watch over it until it blazes.

The "fire" is a metaphor for spirit (see for instance Acts 2: 3-4 or Luke 3:16), and that spirit is the uncreated generative Desire of the undivided divine. Unsurprisingly, desire (especially that of a sexual nature) is often characterized as a fire. Uncreated generative Desire is the substance of the entirety, the sustenance of aethereality, and the trigger of reality. Played by Desire, aethereality and reality, the two components of the entirety, meet, touch, overlap, and perpetually re-create one another not unlike the Yin and Yang of Taoism. Each carrying the seed of the other, the two are indispensable to one another. Yet, the totality they form is always dyadic: not two aspects of the same, but the dual, complementary parts of the whole. Such is the case too with the notions of discontinuous and continuous infinity or eternal recurrence and eternal sameness expressed by the hieroglyphs *neheh* (cyclical time as experienced by mortal beings and symbolized by the rebirth of Ra, the sun god) and *djet* (the flow of time as experienced by divine beings and personified as Osiris) in ancient Egypt. Together, they are the interdependent perceptions of time that form the dynamic permanence of the entirety.

Desire gives rise to movement, and its trajectory is like a fiery trail that makes the entirety pulsate. When Desire stirs the dormant sea of *protoeidoi*,[43] the inexhaustible reservoir of essences and possibilities in which the entirety is suspended, ripples form on its surface. But the aggregation of myriad ripples sets a tide in motion.[44] The generative Desire carried in the movement forward is then matched by the pull of stasis, and in the interplay of the two antithetical forces [7], a universe is born. There is no plan, no design, only Necessity. With several hundred billion galaxies, billions of stars and their orbiting planets in each galaxy, and an incalculable number of chemical reactions on all these worlds, life is bound to arise by necessity where and when the circumstances eventually manage to be just right. From the primeval furnace to the microbes, the uncreated generative Desire is there all along, accompanying matter on its journey. As cyclical life develops and evolves, so does Desire in us until it coalesces into a meta-physical indwelling. And when we nurture the indwelling Desire, it blooms into an angelic power.

When the soul aligns herself with that numen, the numinous self is ignited and set ablaze by the soul's yearnings to rise with her savior-twin in aethereality. It is the blaze that illumines the heart of the searchers:

---

[43] The *protoeidoi* are the substance of ideas from which everything physical and metaphysical is ultimately derived. The dormant sea of *protoeidoi* is the field containing such substance, which the ancient philosophers called Apeiron, where everything is generated, returned, and dissolved in agreement with the demands of necessity.

[44] This idea is also implied in Genesis when land appears after the withdrawal of a great sea (see Genesis 1:9). And when the god of the Bible wanted to re-create man, he flooded the land again (Genesis 6:17).

He who is close to me is close to the fire, and he who is far from me is far from the empyreal sovereignty. Logion - 82

The crowning glory of Desire is aethereal Life. Cyclical life is only incidental: an unpleasant but necessary step on the way. The ancient dualists regarded mere physical existence as a corruption at best. The uncreated generative Desire does not sustain cyclical life; it is only its trigger. Nor does it guide evolution; Necessity does. Desire accompanies physical life so that aethereal Life can follow material existence.

The dynamics and operation of Desire as the prime source of existence and renewal were considered magic by the 17th century German mystic Jakob Böhme:

Magic is the mother of eternity, of the being of all beings; for it creates itself, and is understood in desire. It is in itself nothing but a will, and this will is the great mystery of all wonders and secrets, but brings itself by the imagination of the desireful hunger into being. It is the original state of Nature. Its desire makes an imagination (Einbildung), and imagination or figuration is only the will of desire. But desire makes in the will such a being as the will in itself is. True Magic is not a being, but the desiring spirit of the being. It is a matrix without substance, but manifests itself in the substantial being.[45]

---

[45] Jakob Böhme, *Sex Puncta Mystica: or a short explanation of six mystical points*, translated by John Rollestone Earle, 1920

From Mater to Trans-materiality - 11

This heaven and the one above it will pass; and those who are dead are not alive while those who live will not die. In the days you ate that which is dead, you made it what is alive; when you exist in the light, what will you do? On the day you were one, you made the two; when, then, you come into being as two, what will you do?

Logion 11 makes a series of propositions we need to examine individually before we synthesize the whole.

The Heavens that Will Pass:

In the ancient world, Gnostics, Pagans, and Christians shared a preponderant view of the universe as a succession of heavens (their numbers and exact natures vary in keeping with differing traditions) or layers above (or around) the earth. At the lowest level stood our physical world while God dwelled in the highest heaven. Until at least the 10th century, Christians believed, as did Paul (see 2 Corinthians 12:2-4), that the souls of the righteous departed awaited resurrection in a paradise situated in the third heaven. In the 1st century Slavonic *Book of the Secrets of Enoch*, we learn of a wiseman (Enoch) who was taken by two angels to visit the various heavens that separated the lowest creation from aethereality.

The first heaven corresponds roughly to the visible day sky. The second heaven is a realm of "darkness greater than earthly darkness." There reside the fallen angels who watch over the boundaries of the cosmos. They are the Archons who stand guard before the prison of matter [50]. Beyond that, in the third heaven, Enoch is shown an Eden-like dwelling "between corruptibility and incorruptibility ... prepared for the righteous." For the Gnostics in general, various degrees of "weightiness," from gross matter to the aethereal, constituted the echelons between Earth and the plenitude of supernal light and harmony. The point in Thomas is that no heaven attached to the physical cosmos can endure eternally without being re-created. Only the most exalted realm that is the empyreal sovereignty will not pass because it is not a place in time or space, but the perception of the entirety [3].

Semantics of Life:

The mystical logic of the logia recurrently plays with the semantics of life and death. For the gnostic, the only true life was that which came before and comes after physical existence; in between is only dust and death [56].

> I want you to know that all men born from the foundation of the world until now are dust.[46]

And amid Earth's "living death," some are even "deader" than others. Those who are deaf to the call of the angelic power in their core being are alive "in person," but not "in spirit" because they lack in themselves what would save them [70]. Hence the words of Jesus as reported by Matthew:

> Follow Me, and let the dead bury their own dead.
> (Matthew 8:22 BSB)

The heirs of the divine alone are spiritually alive, having renounced the physical world and spurned the perception of reality on which mankind is transfixed. Their sights are set on the aethereal realm of the god-beings while their primal and lover selves are steadily dissolving into the numinous self [3].

---

[46] *Eugnostos, the Blessed*, translated by Douglas M. Parrott

Food for Thought:
On the physical plane, the living creatures must eat what is dead—the flesh of slayed animals—to sustain their physical existence. Even the most dedicated vegan unknowingly ingests massive amounts of dead bugs trapped in fresh produce and processed food alike. We may abstain from meat, but the decay and rotting of all things still makes up the ground that yields our aliment. As soon as we remove our nutriment from its source, it oxidizes and spoils unless we can preserve it. Corruptibility literally nourishes us: what is dead that we eat we make alive as our bodies convert it into energy and extract the necessary nutrients for biological life to continue. Experimentations on animals made possible the health and safety we enjoy; the price is the piles of their cadavers. And modern convenience comes at the cost of environmental destruction.

In the realm of aethereal life, the heirs of the divine will have no need for the decaying food of the dead. Having become an aspect of the undivided divine, they will live as god-beings "out of *he who lives*."

> *The heavens will be rolled up, and the earth (too) before you, and he who lives* [the heir of the divine] *out of 'he who lives'* [the savior-twin] *will not see death. Not only that, but Jesus also says: "He who finds himself, of him the world is not worthy."* Logion - 111

Separation and Reunion:
We originate in the uncreated generative Desire of the undivided divine. From its projection onto the material plane of

191

existence, we acquired our dyadic essence of soul and spirit. The two however are divided under the same roof [48] and must recover a state of "undividedness" before returning to the empyreal sovereignty.

Synthesis:

The cosmos will not last, nor will any dimension between here and aethereality. But for the heirs of the divine, death is not the end. They have found themselves—that is the numinous self in whose embrace lies a promise of deification. Being a god is our past and our future in the circular nature of the entirety [18]. The undivided divine is perpetually projected in reality to sustain god-beings eternally in aethereality.

> *For the Father is the beginning (or principle) of what is visible. For he (the Lord) is the beginningless Forefather. He sees himself within himself, like a mirror, having appeared in his likeness as Self-Father, that is, Self-Begetter ... And the whole multitude of the place over which there is no kingdom is called 'Sons of Unbegotten Father.*[47]

Holding the Heel of the Twin - 12

The disciples said to Jesus: "We know that you will depart from us. Who (then) will be our superior?" Jesus told them: "In the place you have come you will go to

---

[47] *Eugnostos, the Blessed.* Compare to *The Sophia of Jesus Christ:* "And afterward was revealed a whole multitude ... and that whole multitude over which there is no kingdom is called 'Sons of Unbegotten Father, God, Savior, Son of God,' whose likeness is with you."

James the Just for the sake of whom the sky and the earth came into being."

The historicity, identity, and presumed deeds of James the Just are interesting subjects from a scholarly perspective but of no import with regard to the liberation of our soul. The gospels, canonical or not, will always lead astray the literalist and the academic alike down the endlessly meandering paths of conjectures. But the theurgist of the inner mysteries looks behind the veil of the scriptures.

"James" is etymologically *Ya'aqov* or "holder of the heel," referring to Jacob the son of Isaac who was born holding the heel of his twin Esau (Genesis 25:25-6). James is likened to Jacob, "the younger" who is served by "the elder," his twin brother Esau (Genesis 25:23 and 27:37). Thomas claims that "the sky and the earth"—that is the cosmos—"came into being" for James. This unparalleled and mysterious pronouncement behooving a god more than a mortal suggests a figure of speech. James stands for something much loftier than the office of leadership in a branch of the obscure Jesus movement.[48] The twinning of Jacob and Esau once again points to the mystical pairing of the soul with her savior-twin. Esau, as the earthiest and first born of the two brothers is the soul; the more powerful of the twin siblings, Jacob, "comes on his heels."

The esoteric meaning of the logion communicates the exact opposite of its exoteric meaning: the heirs of the divine do not need anyone in the physical world to guide them; they will meet

---

[48] Had the logion truly been referring so approvingly to the historical James, Jesus could not have denigrated, as he did the Jewish custom of circumcision [53], which was most certainly venerated by the leader of the faction of Christianity closest traditionally to Judaism. (See Galatians 2:11-12)

"the Just,"[49] their savior-twin who is with them wherever they are. They go to him not by traveling physically but inwardly. This explains the rather awkward literal phrasing of the logion: "The place you have come there you will go to James." It is for this divine heir that the cosmos became a cradle. Yet, as Jacob once held the heel of his sibling, the savior-twin must seize the soul to be freed with her from the bonds of matter. James the Just is for the disciples what *Christos angelos* is for Thomas [α]. And when Jesus tells Thomas "Cleave wood, I myself am there; lift up the stone and there you shall find me" [77], it means that wherever Thomas is, whatever he might be doing—from cleaving wood to lifting stones (common occupations in his time)—his *Christos angelos*, or savior-twin is always with him.

Secret Knowledge - 13

Compare me and tell me whom I resemble." Simon Peter said to him: "You resemble a just angel." Matthew said to him: "You resemble a thoughtful philosopher." Thomas said to him: "Oh Teacher, I am altogether speechless as to whom you resemble." Jesus said: "I am not your teacher. Because you drank, you became intoxicated from the bubbling spring I measured." And he took him, withdrew, and told him three words. After that, when Thomas went to his comrades, they asked him: "What did Jesus tell you?" Thomas said to them: "I tell you one of the words he said to me, you will pick stones to throw at me, and out of the stones will come a fire that will burn you.

---

[49] Simon Peter calls Jesus "a just angel" in the next logion [13].

When people think of a historical Jesus, they usually regard him as either a supernal being or a sage. Similarly, at the time the logion was formulated—when the doctrine of a redeemer suffering for the sins of mankind had yet to be invented—the disciples saw their teacher as "a righteous angel" or "a thoughtful philosopher." Neither Peter's nor Matthew's answer is wrong, only partial. Thomas' *cri de coeur*, on the other hand, reflects the inner gospel in which the nature of one's savior is not determined by the creed of a church.[50] Because the ineffable presence is in the core of one's being, it is given to everyone to find for themselves their savior-twin. This journey of discovery however inevitably starts not with knowing but with "unknowing." When we get rid of the metaphysical clutter and leave behind all dogmata, beliefs, and preconceptions, we reach a blank state in which we can no longer utter a single word with regard to the nature of spiritual realities. (A rare thing indeed nowadays, especially on the internet.) There and then, all that remains are the utmost longings of the soul for divine passion, harmony, and light, and we are ready to fill the void with the new wine of ecstasy.

The motif of drinking carried an important symbolic significance as suggested by the following passages:

> *I have eaten from the timbrel; I have drunk from the cymbal; I am become an initiate of Attis.* (Secret password uttered by the Galli in the mysteries of Attis.) *I fasted; I drank the kykeon.* (Declaration of the initiate in the Eleusinian Mysteries.)

---

[50] Note how Peter's spontaneous answer in the Gospel of Thomas evolved into a contrived reply (Matthew 16:16) that was plainly customized to lay the foundation of a creed.

Ganymede—generally thought to represent the soul—was taken by the gods to become the "wine-pourer" or cup-bearer of Zeus. And the worshippers of Dionysus who ritually drank the wine said to have been a symbol of the god's blood were promised eternal life.[51] Wine of course figures extensively in the synoptic gospels, which is not surprising since they are largely an adaptation of Greco-Roman and Egyptian mystery cults. In the context of the mystery religions, then, drinking, and in particular the consumption of an intoxicating beverage was linked to communion with the gods. And communing with a god warrants a divine knowledge. Thomas drank from the divine fount, the "bubbling spring." He is now "intoxicated" with a perception of his numinous self [28] and ready to receive the secret cognizance reserved for the theurgist of the inner mysteries. That sacred revelation doesn't come from an earthly "spiritual teacher" though. "I am not your teacher" insists Jesus; he is the revealer within, the savior-twin who imparts the inner gospel. The allegory continues with the hierophant-Jesus taking Thomas apart to tell him "three words" no one else will hear. Understandably, the other disciples are a bit jealous and want to know what was disclosed to Thomas exclusively. He tells his companions that if he were to share with them his personal revelation, they would cast stones at him. Those stones are not ordinary: a fire would come out of them to burn the disciples. Remember that the fire is spirit [10]. In other words, the stones have spiritual powers; they are the sacred words revealed to Thomas, and those who cast them are the builders

---

[51] James Hall, *Illustrated Dictionary of Symbols in Eastern and Western Art*

who would reject the cornerstone for lack of understanding.[52] Like many modern seekers, Thomas' companions were eager for secrets, but only insofar as those would not compromise their belief structures or offend their creed.

The stones reappear in logion 19:

> *Blessed is he who existed in the beginning before he became.[53]*
>
> *Should you become my disciples and listen to my words, these stones will bear fruit to serve you.*

Here, there is a direct correlation between "my words" and "these stones." A paraphrase of the logion then would read as follows: *When you are initiated in my mysteries and receive the secret words, these words will bear fruit to serve you.* The secret cognizance serves those who receive it humbly and respectfully, immersing themselves in its source and power. But whoever would receive this gift only to reject it would be spiritually consumed [61] because they did not have what could save them [70]. Those who cannot touch the fire should not play with it. Hence a warning not to

> *give that which is holy to the dogs lest they throw it onto the dung heap. Do not throw pearls to the swine, lest they shatter them.* Logion – 93

And for that reason, dear reader, the secret words cannot be written in a book; they are written on the wall of your heart, if you can read them.

---

[52] *Show me the one stone those who build rejected; it is the cornerstone.* Logion - 66

[53] For an understanding of this first part, see logion 18.

Our Metaphysical Lineage - 15 & 101

When you behold him who was not born of the woman, prostrate yourselves on your faces and worship him. That one is your father.

...

They who do not hate their father and their mother as I do cannot become a disciple of mine; and they who do not love their father and their mother as I do cannot become a disciple of mine. For my mother {...}, yet my true mother gave me the Life.

There are many references to mothers and fathers in Thomas' gospel, some literal, others metaphorical, all thrown in together, causing a great deal of confusion. The physical family ties will be examined in [55] and [99]. But in [15] and [101], it is our metaphysical lineage that we will uncover, from the "living father," down to Earth, and back again to the empyreal sovereignty as god-beings. That lineage is one of the main tenets of the metaphysics of the sovereign self [10][11][18][49][50].

Thomas distinguishes between the institutionalized, earthly family we must renounce and our figurative, metaphysical parents we ought to love.

"Him who was not born of the woman" is not born physically and does not come from the flesh. He is the "living father," the undivided divine from which the soul and her savior-twin are the descendant children [3], and to whom they return as a god-being. Thus, the living father stands eternally and undivided in the beginning and at the end [18] [49]. In this context, the epithet "living" refers to his immortality as opposed to the mortality of earthly fathers.

The true mother of our numinous self is the soul who draws so near the angelic power within, it transmutes into an inner savior. The statute of the soul as true mother of the savior-twin is confirmed in perhaps the most puzzling of Thomas pronouncements:

He who will know the father and the mother will be referred to as the son of a harlot. Logion - 105

"He who will know the [true] father (the undivided divine) and the [true] mother (the soul)" is the savior-twin. To understand why his mother is called "a harlot," we need to turn to a gnostic allegory. In some gnostic circles, the soul is indeed compared to a prostitute because of her entanglements in the material world as described in *The Exegesis of the Soul*:

And in her body, she prostituted herself and gave herself to one and all, considering each one she was about to embrace to be her husband. When she had given herself to wanton, unfaithful adulterers, so that they might make use of her, then she sighed deeply and repented. But even when she turns her face from those adulterers, she runs to others and they compel her to live with them and render service to them upon their bed, as if they were her masters. Out of shame she no longer dares to leave them, whereas they deceive her for a long time, pretending to be faithful, true husbands, as if they greatly respected her. And after all this they abandon her and go.[54]

---

[54] *The Exegesis of the Soul*, translated by William C. Robinson Jr.

We can see how the soul is easily led away from her legitimate companion (her "son") and degraded by her wandering and interests in the physical world. She is deceived by the archons [21] who are the "adulterers" and "masters" who "make use of her." The "Exegesis" continues:

> From heaven the father sent her her man, who is her brother, the firstborn. ... But then the bridegroom, according to the father's will, came down to her into the bridal chamber, which was prepared. And he decorated the bridal chamber.

Because of the flesh, the soul is debased; but with regard to her role as mother, sibling, and bride of the savior-twin, she is holy in the sight of "her brother, the firstborn." She gives up her prostitution and cleanses herself of the pollution of the adulterers in "the bridal chamber" [75]. She then takes her place next to her husband-brother in the empyreal sovereignty. This is the end of the soul's captivity; this is the final, upward portion of her journey, the ascent to heaven. A verse from *The Thunder, Perfect Mind* sums-up the painful wandering of the soul through corruption and whoredom all the while preserving her divine quality:

> I am the whore and the holy one.
> I am the wife and the virgin.[55]

The "living father" then is both the origin and the completion of our metaphysical lineage as well as the highest expression of a cycle in eternal recurrence

---

[55] *The Thunder, Perfect Mind*, translated by George W. MacRae

[10][18]. The soul is at once the mother of our numinous self, and the twin sibling-bride of the inner savior. This, in effect, reinforces the notion of how inextricably the two are bound to each other. *The Thunder, Perfect Mind* affirms that seemingly paradoxical multiplicity of the soul's roles:

> *I am the bride and the bridegroom,*
>
> *...*
>
> *and the sister of my husband*
> *and he is my offspring.*
>
> *...*
>
> *I am the staff of his power in his youth,*
> *and he is the rod of my old age.*

The Circular Nature of the Entirety - 18

The disciples said to Jesus: "Tell us, in what way our end will come to be?" Jesus told them: "Have you then unveiled the beginning that you would inquire after the end? For in the place where the beginning is, there will the end be (as well). Blessed are they who would stand upright in the beginning; they will know the end, and they will not experience death."

Why is there something rather than nothing? If God created us, who created God? Before the birth of the universe, was there a creator all alone and self-existing? Those are some of the most baffling questions that continue to occupy the thoughts of philosopher mystics. But most people, such as the disciples who figure in Thomas' narrative, have a single, more persistent, pragmatic concern in mind: they want answers to the enigma of death. Indeed, one of the strangest facts of existence is that nature built an organism designed to last forever only to rig it with an auto-destruct mechanism. In reply, Logion 18 reveals that the secret of immortality is found in the circular and reflective qualities of the entirety.

The central assertion of the logion is that the place of the beginning is also the place of the end. In other words, the heirs of the divine come from the empyreal sovereignty to which they will return. The entirety is like a circle without beginning or end, perpetually revolving: a sempiternity reflecting simultaneously the infinite return of cosmic cycles in reality, and the infinite continuation of aethereality [10].

"They who would stand upright" are the theurgists of the inner mysteries. They are truly alive because they are familiar with their inner savior [11][59]. They are the same individual old in age (symbolizing the end) who, in Logion 4, asked a child (symbolizing the beginning) about the place of life. To "stand upright" is to be awake and alive. In contrast, those who lie down are no longer standing on their feet because they are dead or asleep. That is not just physically, but especially metaphorically.[56] "They who would stand upright" are exemplified by Jesus himself (see *Jesus, Thomas, and the Disciples* in the introduction).

Jesus' answer to the disciples suggests we cannot understand the end without linking it to the beginning. The god-beings are sustained in aethereality through the projection of the undivided divine into reality, the seeding of the uncreated generative Desire onto the physical plane (descent), the

---

[56] Ancient rites still practiced by some contemporary occult societies required an initiate to be symbolically buried in order to rise anew and stand among those who are truly alive in this life.

nurturing of the numen by the theurgist of the inner mysteries, and finally, the transcendent ascent of the inner savior. When the soul embraces her savior-twin, the two are reborn into aethereality as a god-being, a unique aspect of the undivided divine.

"I have said, 'You are gods; you are all sons of the Most High," sang the psalmist (Psalm 82:6 BSB). God is both one and many. The "Most High" is the undivided divine whose children are his many faces. This "living father" is the reservoir of all the memories of the creation and all the god-beings' combined desire that forces Necessity to sally forth.

God has been poetically likened to an infinite sphere whose center is everywhere, and whose circumference is nowhere. The extraordinary thing about this proposition (apart from the fact that it is perpetually mis-attributed) is that no one sees its most glaring implication: God is undivided but dyadic, both the creator and his own creation. Some think of the divine as a remote sovereign ruling over the creation; others find God in "the All." The unknown author of the aforementioned axiom indirectly affirms the paradoxical dichotomy of the entirety, part center and part circumference, the undivided and the divided, aethereality and reality, being and becoming. Because we are in the image of God, the nature of the earthly man is dyadic too: we have a soul and a spirit. Within the heirs of the divine, the god-seed becomes the soul and her savior-twin, distinct and yet unconceivable separately, searching for one another, merging and withdrawing, coming together undivided to free each other from the world of matter.

There never was a genesis per se, let alone a creation "ex nihilo," because everything that can be is and has always been; only, we are looking at it from one of two windows: the center or the circumference. Once the curtain of ignorance is lifted from the stage of reality, we will discover we are both the audience and the actors.

Hypothetically, we can ascribe the existence of things to a creator, but to understand existence—being and becoming as opposed to nihil—we have to assume the entirety is self-sustained: two mirrors facing each other to generate infinity; an endless loop on which we see through the god who sees through us; a window of apprehension that faces reality and aethereality from its two opposite sides. Thus are the god-beings perpetually reborn through the projection of the undivided divine. (See also *synthesis* of Logion 11)

To sum up, it is because reality and aethereality complement and engender one another through the uncreated generative Desire of the undivided divine that existence has no beginning or end—it is eternal—and nothingness is illusory. Central to *A Book to Free the Soul* is the idea that the human soul is the agent of perpetuation of the entirety by recurrently giving birth to an aethereality as a counterpoise to reality.

"Nothingness" is a relative notion since it can only be conceived relatively to existence. Nothingness is a concept created from the standpoint of being not the other way around. Without somethingness, the idea of nothingness is irrelevant, absurdist even. The question of why there is something and not nothing can only stand as long as we give the nothing a reality it does not have. Once we understand nothingness as an abstraction to put existence in relief, the question answers itself: being is eternal; there was never a time, space, field, or condition of nothingness. The closest we can reach to an absolute "nothing" is the absence of matter as an aggregation of energy particles. Nihil then, is only the endless decline toward non-existence, the receding value that never reaches the absolute zero. And the cypher exists solely in the mind of the mathematician.

The Enemies Within - 21

Mary said to Jesus: "Whom do your disciples resemble?"
He replied: "They resemble young children sojourning in a field that is not theirs. When the lords of the field come, they will say: 'Give us our field back.' To give it back to them, they strip naked in their presence and let them have their field. Therefore, I say: If the owner of the house knew that the thief is coming, he would keep watch before he comes and would not permit him to tunnel into the house of his domain to take his possessions. You, then, keep watch from the beginning of the world, gird your loins with great power lest the thieves find a way to come up to you; for the help you seek from the outside, they will find. Let there be in your midst a person of understanding. When the fruit split, they came quickly, sickle in hand and reaped it. They who have an ear to lend, let them listen."

Mary's question is formulated in such a way as to elicit an allegory. The answer comes in an elaborate mosaic, with elements that have their counterpart in the traditional canon but are here reworked and imbued with esoteric meaning.

The two children are the soul and her savior-twin, the dioscuric siblings trapped in the field (the world of matter) that does not belong to them. Indeed, the physical plane is the domain of the archons, the supernatural entities who lord over the cosmos. The children give back the field and strip naked. Metaphorically, they shed their carnal envelope—the garment of flesh that is the physical body—to recover their god-like nature.

Throughout history, the motif of the child in sacred art and literature has been recurrently used to signify either the soul or the spirit. To be "turned and become as the children" and "enter into the reign of the heavens" (Matthew 18:3 - Young's Literal Translation), then, is to facilitate the reunion of the divine siblings—soul and spirit—within us.

In his "Red Book," the famed founder of analytical psychology Carl Jung states:

> I had to recognize and accept that my soul is a child and that my God in my soul is a child.[57]

That is not only because the attributes of godhood closely match those of childhood and youth, but also because our numinous self is born and grows in us as a child would [70].

If the field does not belong to the children, the physical body is to some extent their own because it is the dwelling place of soul and spirit on earth; it is their home. That house, however, isn't safe. The lords of the field are also thieves: like a landlord who would break into your apartment when you are not home to

---

[57] Carl G. Jung, *The Red Book – Liber Novus*, A Reader's Edition; edited by Sonu Shamdasani; translated by Mark Kyburz, John Peck, and Sonu Shamdasani, 2009.

steal your things, they are interested in what you have which they lack.

From the beginning of the world, the heirs of the divine have kept watch lest the thieving archons wormed through their psychic barriers and took control of their possessions. Those possessions are the thymos and the memories that the archons need to survive. What those enemies want is made clear from the *First Apocalypse of James:*

> *they ... sit as toll collectors. Not only do they demand toll, but they also take away souls by theft.*[58]

Thymos (an ancient Greek word with no equivalent in modern languages) is a concept of great antiquity symbolically associated with the blood once thought to carry the emotions. It is defined not just by the emotional life and the drives of an individual but by his inherent traits of character as well, some benignant and uplifting, others deleterious. The virtuous thymos is alimented by an uncorrupted desire and manifests itself through empathy, joy, generosity, compassion, the sense of friendship, the love of harmony, a sensual enthusiasm, a mystical eroticism, and a divine passion. On the other hand, an imbalanced thymos degenerates into selfishness, vainness, greed, hate, cruelty, paranoia, a propensity for destruction, and toxic sexual proclivities that are shackled to the worst impulses of the flesh.

The importance of the thymos is that, depending on its drift, it nourishes either the angelic or the archonic power. Our thymos is also intricately intertwined with our soul, that is the

---

[58] *First Apocalypse of James*, translated by William R. Schoedel

memories. Even an amnesiac has a modicum of recently formed memories, but imagine a hypothetical absolute inability to form memories—not remembering the past two minutes of your life; what would be left of emotions and desires then? The archons covet only the weak form of thymos (because it weighs down the soul and draws it into matter) from which they derive their strength. And from the thymos they can access our memories from which they derive a sense of identity (see Excursus; *The Archons*). To protect our soul from being "taken by theft" then, we need to stabilize the thymos' volatility by strengthening our reliance on the numinous self.

In the battle for the literal spirit and soul of the house, we cannot find help among outsiders or with external means because all earthly institutions, religious or secular, are already under the control of archonic influences (see Excursus; *The Archons*). Therefore, the theurgist of the inner mysteries must "gird [their] loins with [the] great power" that is the angelic power. Figuratively, the loins are the center of Desire from which the numen rises toward the heart. The head (presumably where the memories are held) is the dwelling the soul must leave for the vaulted chamber of the heart where she meets her savior-twin in the same way the lovers met in the myth of Eros and Psyche [3] [75].

The archons' looting strategies are many, and Thomas shares an insight on how we should prepare against their relentless assaults:

> *No one has the capacity to go into a strong (person's) house and take it by force unless they bind his hands; then they will turn his house (into theirs).* Logion - 35

The task of our enemy is easier when our "hands are tied," a metaphor for our attachments to worldly matters. More than ever, we live in a state of perpetual distraction: on top of the traditional concentric world of family, work, societal obligations, church, hobbies, and entertainment, we are now ensnared in the new digital world. The little time we once had to rest the mind is now relinquished to an intrusive artificial intelligence that continually commands our attention. With our awareness effectively redirected away from our inner center and toward the center of the digital sphere, we do not notice the intruders lurking in a dark corner of our psyche. The hidden masters of physical dimensions have bound us to do as they please in our own home. Only sustained vigilance and persistence in nurturing our numinous self can ensure the soul will eventually bond with her savior-twin and escape the clutches of materiality. But when the strong person relaxes her guard, the archons immediately intrude.

When the fruit splits in two (meaning that the dyadic god-seed is matured) concludes the logion, the "person of understanding" (the theurgist of the inner mysteries) is struck by a sense of urgency to reap it,[59] ensuring that the destinies of the soul and her savior-twin are shared and sealed in aethereality.

The Aethereal Body - 22

Jesus saw little ones taking milk. He told his disciples: "These little ones taking milk can be compared to those who enter the empyreal sovereignty." They said to him:

---

[59] Remember logion 11: "when you come into being as two, what will you do?"

"Well then, by being little ones we will enter the kingdom?" Jesus told them: "When you make the two undivided, the inside like the outside and the outside like the inside, and the above like the below, thus making the male and the female such an undividedness that the male will not be male nor the female female; when you make eyes in the place of an eye, and a hand in the place of a hand, and a foot in the place of a foot, (and) an image in the place of an image, then you will enter the empyreal sovereignty."

The two young children from the previous logion are now mere infants taking milk from the same mother, a motif known in antiquity as the *kourotrophos*. The suckling twins personify the soul and her savior nourished by Magna Mater. Like breast-feeding children, the dioscuric siblings are in a state of dependency from the world of matter until they are able to form an "undividedness" by relying exclusively on each other and set themselves free.

In similitude to Psyche and Eros' marriage, the soul and her savior-twin must be sealed unto one another before the dyad collapses into a mystical "undividedness" whereupon the lover and the Beloved coadunate, and their respective, symbolic attributes mix.

The mystical attributes of the inner savior are:

- the "inside"—non-physical; introvertive
- the "above"—independent from the material sphere; transcendent; empyreal
- maleness; knowledge.

Those of the soul are:

- the "outside"—the memories of which the soul is made come from our experience in and of the physical world
- the "below"—appendant to the material sphere
- femaleness; wisdom.

Because the human soul is formed by our unsubstantial memories [α], it cannot be preserved unless it is attached to a medium. Remember, the soul is just a cluster of information. What gives her form is the vessel that holds her just like the information on a script is not a movie until it is framed on celluloid. In a way, the soul can never be completely free; what is free is the eternal meta-individuality compounded from a soul and the parcel of spirit to which she attached herself. A soul cannot hold herself together on her own; she must be transferred from her prison of matter to an incorruptible, aethereal body if she is to survive.

The freeing of the soul then is not mere escapism: it has nothing to do with astral travel, out of body experience (OBE), or shamanic journey, which do not anchor the soul and therefore make her easy prey to the archons [21]. The theurgy of the savior-twin is essentially twofold:

1. to give birth to our inner savior and nourish him/her [70]
2. to transfer the memories from the flesh to the aethereal body of the savior-twin.

It is the nascency of this trans-physical body that the rest of the logion depicts. Thus, an aethereal eye, hand, and foot are substituted for the physical eye, hand, and foot.

If the rotting body of flesh and bones that once covered the soul can be compared to an old, discarded garment [21] [37], then the new, aethereal body can be likened to a resplendent mantle, an illustration of which is given in *The Hymn of the Robe of Glory*:

> *My love urged forward*
> *To run for to meet it, to take it.*
> *And I stretched myself forth to receive it;*
> *With its beauty of colour I decked me,*
> *And my Mantle of sparkling colours*
> *I wrapped entirely all o'er me.*
> *I clothed me therewith, and ascended*
> *To the Gate of Greeting and Homage.*

The theurgist of the inner mysteries does not fear the end of the physical body or seek to preserve it at any cost. To the contrary, they look forward to trading the mortal envelope for an incorruptible robe of glory in a triumph over death.

The Person of Light – 24 & 33

His disciples said: "Give us instruction regarding the place where you are because it is a necessity for us to seek it." He told them: "They who have an ear to lend, let them listen. Light exists within a person of light, and they become light to the entire world. If they do not become light, there is darkness.

"That to which you will listen in one of your ears, preach upon your housetops. No one lights a lamp and puts it under (a bushel) *nor do they put it in a hidden place; instead, they put it on the stand so that anyone who comes in and goes out may behold their light."*

A careful reading of logion 24 gives us another hint that Thomas' gospel is not relating actual events taking place in the physical world. If Jesus was a historical being chatting with the disciples, there would be no need for them to look for the place where he is. We determined that for Thomas, the hierophant Jesus is the revealer within (see *Jesus, Thomas, and the disciples* in introduction). The place where the savior is that we need to seek is the innermost of our being, the hidden place where he has made his dwelling. Indeed, Jesus' reply immediately refers to an inner state.

The spark of light in us that comes from the divine fire [10] is ensconced in matter [83 & 84], invisible to the eye. The "person of light" is also the "person of understanding" [21], and the light in them issues from the numinous self. That brighter light diffused by the theurgist of the inner mysteries can shine on the entire world, like the beam cast from a lighthouse, to gather the heirs who have yet to recognize themselves [33]. Conversely,

> *If a blind man leads a blind man, they both fall into a pit.* [34]

The blind man metaphor refers to those who lack the epiphanic, illumined discernment derived from the numinous self and nevertheless make a vocation of luring fellow travelers to their train of thought.

One should learn to recognize the inner light and be wary of the physical light that precedes, surrounds, or accompanies religious and paranormal events (see Excursus; *The Archons*). The uncorrupted, uncreated light experienced by the theurgist of the inner mysteries is always a numinosity within because all things perceived in the sensible world are corrupted by matter.

Light and darkness coexist relatively to each other. Darkness is rest, passive, receptive. Light is movement, active, creative. The darkness can never overtake the light; it can only fill the space that light has left vacant. The light can never replace the darkness, only push it back. The association of darkness and light with evil and good in popular consciousness is misleading. Good and evil are not active, actual forces, but abstractions and perceptions that result from the opposite pulls of the two primal forces inherent to the dormant sea of *protoeidoi*.

From the outset, logion 33 is again suggestive of a mystical, initiation-like process at work in Thomas' writings [1]. To "listen in one of your ears" is to receive confidential information as if whispered by a mystagogue. Thus, the recurring scriptural expression "They who have an ear to lend, let them listen" means the communication of arcane instruction. *Preaching upon our housetops* seems to go against that context of secrecy, but only because we misunderstand what it means. The same words are used in the New Testament (Matthew 10: 27) and are at the origin of the idiom "to preach over the rooftops," which means to proclaim something to whomever can hear. However, if Jesus taught his closest disciples in confidence, there is no rationale for them to preach the "veiled words" [α] to the whole wide world. There is a semantic difference between "over the rooftops" and "on" or "upon the rooftops." At the time of Jesus in Palestine, rooftops were typically converted into terraces (as they still are nowadays in many Mediterranean and eastern countries) as an extension to the living quarters for the family, and for occasional social gatherings. Even nowadays, people from around the Mediterranean Basin continue to sleep on the terrace-like roof of their houses during the hottest nights of the year (note the reference to "the darkness" in Matthew 10:27, which could suggest the intimate discussions extended late into the hours of the night, as did the initiations into the ancient mystery cults). It is unlikely then that Thomas meant we should harangue the crowds. This is confirmed by the last part of the logion which enjoins us to be like a lamp on a stand: only the guest of the house "who comes in and goes out may see" the light of the "person of light." A comment by Rudolf Steiner encapsulates the idea:

> Let your work be the shadow that your I casts when it is shone upon by the flame of your higher self.[60]

Contrary to the New Testament's great commission "Therefore go and make disciples of all nations, … teaching them to obey all that I have commanded you" (Matthew 28:19-20 BSB), Thomas does not promulgate such a missionary grand design. There is no mandate to squander precious pearls throughout the world: the liberating cognizance should be shared not broadly but prudently and economically, only with those who demonstrate the readiness and willingness of an open heart.

Who Is Your Brother? - 25

> Love your brother like your soul; guard him like the pupil of your eye.

This logion has such an obvious moral implication, it is hard to see how its meaning could be anything but literal. From Mark 3:35, we could imply that our brother is "whoever does the will of God," yet, by peeling away that surface layer, we can uncover an esoteric metaphor.

---

[60] Rudolf Steiner, *Mantric Sayings Meditations 1903-1925*, translated by Dana Fleming

From the *Pistis Sophia*, has come to us the strange, mystical anecdote of an angel who, appearing to Mary, asks: "Where is Jesus *my brother*, that I may meet him?" [5] We also established that the soul and the inner savior are twin siblings, forming together the god-seed in the heart of the heirs. Thus, the brother of the soul is her savior-twin, the one we must *love like our soul*. We must *guard him like the pupil of our eye* because he is the source of the numinosity within [24].

The choice of the pupil as the worthiest part of the body to guard may not be random. Jacques Lacarriere wrote the following beautiful insight:

> *The eye is also an aperture. But it is the only one in the entire body whose exchanges with the external world escape corruption, as well as the law of entropy. It is the only one which lives on light while the rest of the body is sustained entirely by filth. ... There is the central circle of the pupil, the abyss of shadows wherein one may glimpse the depths of the soul and the reflection of that luminous emulsion which is the matrical trace of the divine light.*[61]

Hence, the numinous self personified as the inner savior bears comparison to the eye as the uncorrupted agent that allows us to see beyond physical light and peer into the divine light.

Divine Intoxication - 28 & 108

I took my place in the midst of the world, and I was manifest to them in the flesh. I found them all drunk; I found none thirsting among them. And my soul was

---

[61] Jacques Lacarriere, *The Gnostics*, translated by Nina Rootes, 1977

grieved over the children of mankind because blind they
are in their hearts. And they do not see because empty
they have come to the world. Empty still, they seek to
come out of the world. But now, they are drunk. When
they shake off their wine, then they will repent.
They who drink out of my mouth will come to resemble
me. Likewise, I myself will come to be as they are, and
that which is veiled will be unveiled to them.

We already touched on the significance of drinking in the mystery religions [13]. And although having too much to drink generally carried the same stigma in ancient times as it does in the modern world, intoxication could also be looked upon favorably in the context of an initiation. Joscelyn Godwin comments:

Some of the Mysteries went further to anticipate the
ambience of heaven by inducing unworldly states. Wine
probably affected the ancients far more powerfully than
it does us (they seldom drank it unmixed with water) ...
In the Mysteries, all five senses might be elevated
through wine, music, lights, incense and sexuality, to
say nothing of drugs, in order to create an unforgettable
experience and encourage hopes of heavenly bliss.[62]

In Thomas' gospel, a distinction is made between drunkenness and divine intoxication as it transpires from the juxtaposition of logia 28 and 108.

Spirit incarnates on Earth in search of the souls with which it can pair up. But the souls are imprisoned in the mind of the humans who for the most part are metaphorically (when not

---

[62] Joscelyn Godwin, *Mystery Religions in the Ancient World*, 1981

actually) drunk. The wine mankind drinks is the beverage of forgetfulness and ignorance that leaves their heart and mind empty when they recover their senses. We all carry in us the spark of the divine as a seed when we come to the world. But the seed doesn't mean much unless it takes roots and grows [9] in the hearts of the "children of mankind." The heart remains empty and dark until it is illumined by the presence of our savior-twin grown out of the divine seed [70] [75]. What fills the "person of light" [24] is the light of the numinous self that the theurgist of the inner mysteries kindles within themselves. Without that light in their heart and mind to guide them, most of the children of mankind are destined to seek their exit from the world with a knowledge borrowed from the world.

For all its drawbacks though, inebriety has one advantage: it often reveals the real self. When we are drunk, our inhibitions fall, and we speak our thoughts as they are or act on the impulses we work so hard to mask while sober. We stand naked (sometimes literally) for all to see that which we would not otherwise reveal. If it is highly inadvisable to learn about oneself in such a manner, it does make for an enlightening metaphor: just as having too much wine is a weakness that unmasks the self we would rather hide, divine intoxication is a madness that unveils the numinous self we cannot otherwise find. That is why both Eros and Dionysos [3] were thought to save the souls of men through a divine madness that distilled the eternal self from oneself: the madness of love through Eros, and that of ecstasy through Dionysos. Attis too was driven mad to the point of castrating himself. Yet that allegorical castration—a complete surrender to the divine [53]—made him a divine being. When we drink from the mouth of our inner savior, their word intoxicates us to such an extent that we are seized by heavenly rapture, transported in ecstasy, and illumined by numinosity and divine passion. It is the state of hallowed inspiration and possession called *enthousiasmós* in ancient Greek religion.

To be drunk with earthy wine is to descend to sloth and the lowest sort of ephemeral euphoria; to be drunk with the wine of the gods is to ascend [13] to their eternal, aethereal abode as Ganymede once did. There appears to be a possible word play in the logion whereas the Coptic string of letters "ta6e" could be read as "being drunk," or as "my manner" ("ta.6e"). Thus, the logion may alternatively mean "Whoever drinks out of my mouth will be in my manner"—that is *will come to resemble me*—or, possibly, "Whoever drinks out of my mouth will come to be drunk"—that is divinely intoxicated. In the latter case, the inner savior is said to be like the adept because they share the same divine intoxication that brings transcendent awareness to the forefront. This interpretation is supported by logion 13 in which Jesus ask the disciples "compare me and tell me whom I resemble." The riddle of course is answered in logion 108. The numinous self resembles the one who recognizes him as his dioscuric sibling, or savior-twin. The disciples do not come close to the right answer. Only Thomas' answer is looked upon favorably by Jesus because they are spiritual kin.

In the ancient mysteries, a trance-like state—possibly induced by wine or other intoxicating beverages—often preceded secret revelations. Similarly, a divine intoxication is the prerequisite for the most sacred and highest cognizance bestowed on the heirs of the divine by their numinous self. Upon receiving his epiphany of the "bubbling spring," Thomas is taken apart to be granted the secrets of which the other disciples are not privy [13].

Descent & Ascension - 29

If the flesh has come into being because of spirit, that is a marvel; Yet, if spirit (comes into being) because of the body, that would be an amazing wonder. But I myself am amazed at this: how this great richness was placed in this poverty.

From Logion 18, we have gained an understanding of the circular nature of the entirety: the divine is our past and our future, the Alpha and the Omega, both a parent and our offspring. That is also the substance of Logion 22.

All the Abrahamic religions acknowledge that God created man ("the flesh has come into being because of spirit"), which they regard as a great wonder, the more so because they have no idea why the supreme being would do such a thing. The theurgist of the inner mysteries recognizes the origin of man not as an act of love (honestly, plunging the souls in misery and suffering?) or a selfish endeavor (the lonely God needed company) but as a deed of necessity: the undivided divine projects itself into matter to be perpetually reborn in aethereality. It becomes human so that the heirs of the divine would recreate it as a god-being. In other words, "spirit (comes into being) because of the body." That is the mystery of God's eternal nature.

"God is Spirit, and His worshipers must worship Him in spirit and in truth" (John 4: 24 BSB), proclaims John the Evangelist. The uncreated generative Desire of the undivided divine reaches into the poverty of the flesh as the dyadic god-seed formed by the soul and the numinous self. When the soul is sealed to her savior-twin, an "undividedness" is re-formed in aethereality. The object of Thomas' amazement is the fall of the divine seeds into matter, a descent of richness into poverty [56].

There Is No Savior outside of Yourself - 37

His disciples said: "On what day will you appear to us, and on what day will we behold you?" Jesus said: "When you strip yourselves naked without being ashamed, taking your clothes and laying them under your feet like those young children, and you trample them, then you will look upon the child of 'he who lives', and you will not be afraid."

"The child of *he who lives*" is our savior-twin [15 & 101]. But the disciples would rather await a messiah who must be feared because of the great retribution he will bring down on the unbeliever when he imposes his rule on Earth. That fear of retribution combined with the hope of reward is what in no small measure makes the faithful walk the line, not the love they profess to have for their lord. But Thomas is reminding us that our savior must be born within [75], not in the world. He will not arrive out there on a cloud and appear on an appointed day. Just as all predictions to the contrary have failed over the past centuries, prophecies of an advent and a rapture will continue to remain unfulfilled. When the disciples remark that "twenty-four prophets proclaimed in Israel, and they all spoke through you," Jesus replies:

You have dismissed in your presence 'he who lives,' and you have spoken of they who are dead. [52]

In Logion 21, we already met "those young children" who "strip naked." They are the dioscuric siblings, the sons of God who trample the garment of flesh under their feet to free themselves from the cast of matter, an image similar to that found in the Gnostic *Hymn of the Robe of Glory*:

> *Their filthy and unclean garments*
> *I stripped off and left in their country* [Egypt, which is an allegory for the physical world].

The Keys of Gnosis - 39

The Pharisees and the scribes took the keys of gnosis and hid them. They did not go in, and those who desire to go in they did not permit. You, however, be wise like serpents and innocent like doves."

The dogmatists of our time are the Pharisees, and the modern literalists are the scribes described by Thomas. They preach a creed they can control and hinder the faithful from thinking for themselves. You cannot receive a transcendent awareness (gnosis) unless you are able to think about gnosis and pursue Self-inquiry or "going in." Those are the keys to liberating cognizance. Logion 21 warned that "the help we seek from the outside" is not to be trusted, but that is the only form of help the scribes and Pharisees have to offer. They do not question their belief system and seek to impose their creed on others. Why they would do such a thing is as understandable as human nature is predictable: the surest way to convince oneself of something is to work tirelessly at convincing someone else of the same. The keys of gnosis are taken when what should be validated internally and individually is transformed into dogmatic schemes and behavioral rules to which one is bound to adhere rigidly. They are hidden when what should be understood allegorically is taught as literal. There are also individuals who are in disbelief, but for weakness or misplaced pride would not change course. In twisted fashion, those lost souls would not go down the road of error alone and perversely point to their own culs-de-sac when asked for spiritual direction. Thomas describes them too in Logion 102:

> Woe to the Pharisees, because they resemble a dog sleeping in the manger of the oxen; neither does it eat, nor does it permit the oxen to eat.

Dogs are the epitome of loyalty and do what their masters command. It is harrowing to watch deranged individuals ill-treating pets who remain loyal to their abusers. Yet, that is a fitting allegory for the human condition: the hand that feeds us is also the hand that tyrannizes us, and we take the crumbs offered by the elite who gorge themselves with luxuries while other people suffer in poverty. Thus, the wealth of the world is concentrated within a few nations, and the wealth of a nation is in the hands of a few individuals. But beyond the world of injustice, the allegory points to a tragic paradox: those who willfully participate in the enslavement of their kind are slaves themselves. Indeed, tyrants understand that the most efficiently run prisons are those where a few inmates collaborate with the warders to keep the other prisoners in line like dogs who do not eat and do not let the cattle eat either. Such is the case of the Pharisees and the scribes who perpetuate the imprisonment of the soul (including their own) while touting dubious paths of liberation, and spiritual dead ends. Of them it can be say that

The dearest ambition of a slave is not liberty but to have a slave of his own.[63]

The theurgist of the inner mysteries however is to be wise like a serpent and innocent like a dove. Although the simile appears self-evident enough to satisfy a superficial interpretation, there is a lot more to discover about the analogy beyond a mere skimming of the surface.

The Serpent and the Dove

The pair is yet another set of symbols associated with soul and Spirit.

The dove, with its capacity to fly, relates to the wind and consequently the spirit. The *Acts of the Apostles* reports that while assembled for Pentecost they suddenly heard:

> *a sound like a mighty rushing wind* [that] *came from heaven and filled the whole house where they were sitting. ... And they were all filled with the Holy Spirit and began to speak in other tongues as the Spirit enabled them.* (Acts 2:1-4; BSB)

The paraclete embodied by the dove is a widespread icon in Christian art. "And the Holy Spirit descended upon Him in a bodily form as a dove," records Luke (Luke 3: 22 BSB). Their power and presence manifest in the heirs' innermost where they coalesce as an inner savior. The dove's whiteness represents innocence: the savior-twin is innocent because it has unfathomable knowledge but not the wisdom that comes from experiencing physical life. Although they are often used interchangeably in literary compositions, knowledge and wisdom are two different things. The former is information

---

[63] Richard Francis Burton in a footnote to *The Book of The Thousand Nights And A Night*, 1885

while the latter is the capacity acquired by experience to validate and apply the information.

Perhaps no other creature has had greater variety of symbolic and allegorical meanings (often contradictory, sometimes complementary) than the serpent, at once worshiped and reviled, benignant or destructive. In the context of logion 39, the serpent's significance comes from its association with the dove. Unlike the dove who soars in the sky and represents the heavenly descent of Spirit—child of heavens—the serpent is cursed to crawl on the earthly surface. That is also the fate of the soul born on the physical plane and bound to matter; she is a child of the earth. Wisdom is attached to the soul because the soul is memories [a], and whatever wisdom we hold is contingent on remembering. Because our memories are often unreliable, partial, subjective, or locked away, our wisdom is usually weak. But the wisdom of the heirs will be perfected when their memories are safely transferred and preserved into the aethereal body [22] of their savior-twin. The marriage of perfect wisdom and perfect knowledge will then yield the perfect consciousness of a god-being.

Life Is a Bridge - 42

Come into being as you pass away [alternatively: *Become passersby*].

Logion 42 is a good example of the ambiguity of the text and how distance through time and language makes it impossible to recover the original mind of the author.[64] There are at least two possible translations here, but scholars disagree as to which is more likely. One, almost always chosen over the other, enjoins

---

[64] See *Thomas' Gospel* in the introduction.

the reader to be a passerby. This Zen-like admonition appeals to all but the most hardened materialist. It is the persistent reminder of the transience of life, that we all die, and that nothing of this world can be taken into the next, save perhaps the memories. For all the original esoteric acumen of their mysteries, the devout mysticism of the ancient Egyptians degenerated over the millennia into an onerous (not to mention costly) obsession with manipulating the afterlife and an inordinate compulsion to fix this life with magical spells. The passerby, on the other hand, is careless of transferring to the beyond their earthly possessions and worldly positions. They prefer to travel light and shun the strings and entanglements of materiality. They know their existence is a short crossing. Yet, the mystic passerby is no tourist. Although there is much beauty they can appreciate in the cosmos, his longing for the sovereignty to come far exceeds any remaining attachment to the physical world. Many indeed are drawn to a better world, but who in fact dedicates this life to preparing for the next? Most people are too busy looking for a purpose in life or, worse even, searching for life's purpose, the great illusion that there is in this existence something momentous or meaningful to achieve. But truly, though we may not see it, all that is needed is a surrender to the uncreated generative Desire of the undivided divine. This takes us to the other translation of the logion and the interpretation I favor: We must die to the world of becoming to be reborn in the world of being.

The Sovereign Child - 46

Among those born of women, from Adam to John the Baptist, none is so more exalted than John the Baptist that their eye would not be clouded.[65] *Nonetheless I said: he who comes into being within you as a child will know the empyreal sovereignty and be more exalted than John.*

There is in the Gospel of Thomas an emphasis on twinning dynamics as is clearly the case between Jesus and Thomas [α] as well as between James the Just and a hypothetical disciple [12]. Those allegorical twinnings are meant to suggest the interdependence of the soul and her savior in the process of liberation. This observation holds too for Jesus and John the Baptist[66] whom Renaissance artists frequently represented as two nearly identical babes sometimes in an embrace, not unlike the Gemini.

John the Baptist is regarded as a great prophet and precursor of the "word made flesh" (John 1:14 and 3:28), or he who came to prepare the way before Jesus (John 1:6-8). Similarly, the soul is the precursor of the inner savior allegorized as a child [4] and who may appear as such to the inner eye [21]. The undivided divine sows the seed of soul and spirit, but without the soul reflecting the image of the "living father," [83 & 84] there would be no holy child [70]. And yet, as pivotal the role of the soul is, *he who comes into being as a child*

---

[65] Literally "that his eyes will not be broken," an expression that has baffled scholars and hasn't been satisfactorily explained. The text here is probably corrupted, and I based my own interpretation on Mathew 6:22. Accordingly, if someone was superior to John the Baptist, their eye—the lamp of their body—would be good, and they would be full of light (see also Logia 24 & 33). For the corruption of the text, see *Thomas' gospel* in the introduction.

[66] We could point to the mystical twinning of Jesus and John in Luke 1:41 when Mary visits her cousin Elizabeth, and the unborn baby John leaps in the womb of his mother.

within us, meaning the savior-twin [70] is "more exalted" than her because upon him rests the power of liberation from the material world. So, although soul and spirit are reliant on each other on the journey from "becoming" to "being," there is a hierarchy of being: the sovereign self is lord of the soul. Logion 46 gives new meaning to the words of John the Baptist as reported in the Gospel of John:

> *The bride* (John the Baptist's soul) *belongs to the bridegroom* (her savior-twin). *The friend of the bridegroom* (John as an individual) *stands (at the door of the bridal chamber; see Logion 75) and listens for him, and is overjoyed to hear the bridegroom's voice. That joy is mine* (John's), *and it is now complete. He (the savior-twin) must increase; I* (John the Baptist speaking as an individual) *must decrease. The One who comes from above* (the spirit) *is above all. The one who is from the earth* (the soul; see Logion 39) *belongs to the earth and speaks as one from the earth. The One who comes from heaven is above all.* (John 3: 29-31 BSB)

The bride-soul belongs to the groom-savior, her legitimate heir, while the friend (the Baptist in person) "becomes less" because of the surrendering of his soul, which is the circumcision in spirit [53].

The Two Gods - 47

No one has the power to mount two horses and stretch two bows. And no servant has the ability to serve two masters, or else he would honor one, and the other he would despise. No one drinks aged wine and within the hour wants to drink new wine. And new wine is not poured into old wineskins lest they split; nor does anyone pour aged wine into a new wineskin lest it be wasted. Old patches are not sewn onto new garments because a tear would appear.

We have examined the primal duality in man and determined it parallels the two opposite forces that shape physical existence [7]. In the Middle Ages, the dualist Cathars called those forces the two principles, a dual function they saw as embodied in a good god, father of all the Spirit-angels, and an evil one who entraps those same Spirits in the human body. Objectively, however, and despite what religious propagandists past and present maintain, the moral dichotomy of good and evil has no reality outside of our mind. The real opposition is between the generative current of the uncreated Desire and the entropic, destructive pull of stasis. The good god of the Cathars and his nemesis represent the aethereal and the material respectively. They are a balancing act by the two halves of the entirety [18]. The two primordial forces inherent to the dormant sea of *protoeidoi* reach onto the physical plane and right into the breast of mankind. Thomas lists a series of short, vivid examples to illustrate the disastrous consequences of attempting to reconcile two mutually exclusive possibilities (try mounting two horses at once while stretching two bows!) as summed up in that other famous assertion: "You are not able to serve God and mammon" (Matthew 6:24 BSB).

We live in an illusory world seen through carefully crafted lenses. Conceptual fabrications make us feel endowed with the responsibility to defend a benevolent natural order against an imaginary nefarious entity. Our fight becomes moral, and we seek to promote what we perceive as good and thwart what we believe is evil. But evil is simply that which causes entropy. We are blindsided by a purpose-driven life where we believe we ought to be the agents of the ultimate triumph of goodness. But the struggle never was between good and evil, and we are not combatants in the battle that unfolds on its own; we are the battlefield. We are the center of the titanic divergence that is at the origin of matter. It gave us birth, and now it is tearing us apart. Thus, we spend our existence striving *to mount two horses, stretch two bows, and serve two masters.* The struggle however must end one way or the other: "If a house is divided against itself, it cannot stand" (Mark 3:25 BSB), and we are bound to destruction and death. Rescue from the grim outcome rests on the liberation of our soul through the agency of the savior-twin, the master chosen by the heirs of the divine over the others. Until then, we must bear the strain of the struggle between the uncreated generative Desire and its opposite the pull of stasis. They are like two taunt bows, and we are not the archer but the single arrow. Inevitably, only one bow can shoot a single arrow.

Can We Move Mountains? – 48 & 106

Should two make peace with each other in this one house, they will tell the mountain "move away!" and it will move.

Should you make the two undivided, you will become the sons of man, and if you tell this mountain "move away!" it will move.

Ever since the fantastical notion of moving mountains by the power of faith or belief appeared in the New Testament, it has been a favorite reference for the inveterate hopeful and the unshakable proponents of mind over matter. Has anything even remotely like that happened in the past 2000 years? For those who are not holding their breath, we will approach Logia 48 and 106 from a different angle. To begin with, the house mentioned here by Thomas isn't an edifice of stone and wood, but the physical body.[67] And when Jesus speaks of "this one house," we can picture him pointing not at a man-made structure but at his own body of flesh that shelters the soul, and the spirit. This home of ours is profoundly divided: on the one hand, our mind and our body are torn by two great opposite forces [7][47]; on the other hand, the soul and the spirit are kept separated in the labyrinthine corridors of our inner being until the soul turns to the numinous self. When the separation has vanished and death arrives at last, the mystical siblings can enter the empyreal sovereignty and inhabit their new home [22]. In aethereality, they will have the leisure to shape the landscape and rearrange their domain at will (see Excursus; *Aethereality and the Beyond*). The mountain can also symbolize the physical world. If such is the case, a command to move mountains away would be an to remove oneself from physicality.

When we juxtapose Logia 48 and 106, we see that the two who make peace become undivided. In other words, our soul and inner savior must dwell in harmony, closeness, and complete mutual dependency in the core of our being before they can abide together eternally, having repudiated the physical world.

The use of the expression "Son of Man" in the New Testament is confusing and its meaning highly debated, but

---

[67] In Matthew 12:43-45, an unclean spirit says: "I will turn back to my house whence I came." It is clear from the parable that he is referring to someone's body.

231

Jesus is the only person to have ever claimed the title. "Son of Man," then, is synonymous with "Son of God." The "sons of man," the humanly divine descended in the flesh to become divinely human. Therefore, the "sons of God" are the dioscuric siblings [3][50], the soul and her savior-twin (the god-seed), the two who ought to dwell in peace in the same house.

Determinism - 49

Blessed are those who are undivided and chosen for you will find the empyreal sovereignty, so that having come out of it, you will return there once again.

The circular nature of the entirety [18] implies an element of determinism. Our existence that seems to unfold in time is already lived out of time. It is only one of untold possibilities, all present at once in the dormant sea of *protoeidoi* and awakened only by the Desire of the undivided divine.

The chosen are heirs of the divine, theurgists of the inner mysteries, lovers of the beloved savior-twin. Their path is the best possible outcome in which all the other possible outcomes merge, the thread of existence by which spirit is set free. We can compare the entirety to an eternal maze with one path ending where it begins while the others are dead ends. The chosen is the path of return, and the divine stands at the beginning and the end of that path. Desire flows through all the paths, and ultimately it does not matter if our mortal eyes are open to one path of existence or the other, whether we are looking through one window or the other; they are all versions of a story that has already been written.

To be one of the heirs is not a matter of self-righteousness or aggrandizement; the theurgist of the inner mysteries knows themselves because of their yearning above all else to be free from the bonds of matter and physicality. In their heart, the soul and her savior-twin find a place to dwell, an altar at which to be joined, and a gate to the empyreal sovereignty. The chosen and the heirs then are not a race or an elite. It is their adherence to a set of fundamentals that distinguishes them from the others:

- They recognize the duality of spirit and matter and the superiority of the former over the latter.
- They carry within themselves the same divine seed as everyone but, unlike everyone, they are aware of its presence and nature. Moreover, they know they can nurture their numinous self into becoming an inner savior.
- Hence, they understand there is no universal salvation or world savior and that an individual is the sole artisan of their own salvation and creator of their own heaven (see Excursus: *The Beyond*).

The Return to the Light - 50

Should they say to you, "Whence have you come to be?" tell them this: "We came from the light, the place where the light is self-sustained, projecting itself in their (the chosen's) *image." Should they say to you, "Are you him* (the living Father)*?" say this: "We are his sons* (children)*, and we are the chosen of the living father." Should they ask you, "What is in you the sign of your father?" tell them this: "It is movement and restfulness."*

This spoken exchange bears the hallmarks of an initiation into a mystery cult. Note how the postulants are instructed to give a specific answer to a set of questions. In the ancient mysteries, often at a threshold of some sort, the initiates would recite formulas in answer to key questions before being admitted symbolically to the other side of reality. The ritual prefigured the passage of the heirs of the divine from the physical world to a veiled place of supernal light. On the way, they will figuratively have to face the archons and foil their last attempt at preventing the release of the god-seed from the shackles of materiality. But the custodians of the cosmos find themselves powerless against the heirs. The transcendent awareness developed by the theurgist of the inner mysteries transpires from the replies they give to the occult rulers soon to be defeated.

The reply to the archons' first query was examined in [49]: we came from the empyreal sovereignty, from an aethereal realm of numinosity and harmony, the dwelling of the undivided divine who projects itself into the world; and we are returning there as god-beings with lucent bodies [22].

Are you the living father? ask the archons. To which the heirs of the divine answer that they are his sons [3].

The archons then ask a third and last question to test the Dioscuri: What proof do they have of being the sons of the living father? The heirs' answer shows they know to whom they are returning because he is the one from whom they came. In the *First Apocalypse of James*, Jesus expounds on the oppositional power of the archons in words that are remarkable similar to Logion 50:

> *When you come into their (the archon's) power, one of them who is their guard will say to you, 'Who are you or where are you from?' You are to say to him, 'I am a son,*

and I am from the Father.' He will say to you, 'What sort
of son are you, and to what father do you belong?' You
are to say to him, 'I am from the Pre-existent Father,
and a son in the Pre-existent One ... When he also says
to you, 'Where will you go?', you are to say to him, 'To
the place from which I have come, there shall I return.'
And if you say these things, you will escape their
attacks.

The sons of God can describe the sign of the living father in them because it is the empyreal sovereignty [2] where eternal restfulness balances the movement stemming from the uncreated generative Desire.

Transcendent awareness defeats the archons.

Circumcision in Spirit - 53

His disciples said to him: "Is circumcision beneficial to us, or not?" He told them: "If it were beneficial, their father would beget them (the sons) *circumcised from their mother. Instead, one has found profit in the true, complete, spiritual circumcision."*

The heirs of the undivided divine can look forward to their promised release from the cocoon of the physical world, but they also strive to free themselves from the follies of men. One such folly is the subject of logion 53.

Wherever we seek the origin of, or a justification for the custom of circumcision, the barbaric practice means only one thing: subservience. In ancient times, male slaves and defeated enemies were humiliated and branded by the removal of their prepuce. Conversely, at some point it must have been thought a mark of bravery to endure the ordeal. Indeed, in some parts of Africa, the tradition of circumcising boys signals their passage into the status of a warrior. We also read in the Old Testament that Joshua institutionalized the severing of the prepuce for the Israelite male population just before enrolling them for war into the conquest of Canaan (Joshua 5). The earliest and most frequent references to ritualized circumcision appear in the context of initiation: adolescents entering a hieratic or aristocratic order would bear a mark that set them apart from the inferior castes. The neighboring Semites got the idea from Egypt, and the Jews made it the mark of allegiance to a blood-thirsty god. Going two steps farther than their predecessors, the boys would now be circumcised at an earlier age, and the more gruesome *peri'ah* (laying bare the glans by stripping away the skin) would replace cutting only the tip of the prepuce. Astonishingly in our 21st century, the very same aberrant practice under the guise of misguided claims of health and hygiene (a case of weird science) still has proponents within the medical establishment of countries with a bias for conformity. But from its questionable, distant origins up to its modern practice, circumcision has meant only one thing: a repulsive sacrifice of flesh and blood.

In Thomas' time, circumcision of the flesh was despised by the more enlightened Hellenists whose mental, abstract acuity could not fathom the crude, ritualistic mutilation for the sake of pleasing a vulgar god. Self-maiming is a sign of subservience that epitomizes a slave culture. The sacrifice of the flesh stands in sharp contrast to the surrender of the soul, which is the *true circumcision in spirit*.

Surrender is a word that has acquired a bad connotation as it conjures the image of waving a white flag and giving up out of weakness or cowardice. Etymologically, it is based on the Old French *sur-* (over, on), and *rendre* (give back, render). To surrender is to turn over something that does not belong to us in the first place, a meaning best exemplified in the admonition to "render therefore the things of Caesar to Caesar, and the things of God to God" (Matthew 22:21). Modern individuals have an irrational fear of relinquishing control over things and persons (including their own), not realizing they themselves are controlled by forces to which they are blind. Our mindset is all about hoarding and controlling but we would be well advised to get rid of the extra baggage instead of our prepuce. Let go of the superfluous; turn over that which isn't for you to keep; yield to the uncorrupted will and Desire of the inner savior who does not claim a bit of flesh but the whole soul. The surrender of the soul is her drifting away from matter and toward Spirit, her replacing the body of decaying flesh with an aethereal one that is immortal [22].

And speaking of giving up, one of our most unhealthy attachments, despite our conditioned beliefs to the contrary, is the value we put on the modern household, the aberration we call the nuclear family, to which we now turn.

Family Ties - 55

Whosoever does not hate his father and his mother cannot become my disciple, and if he does not hate his brothers and his sisters and does not take up his cross like me, he will not be deserving of me.

At the outset, we must remark that the point of the logion is not to hate father, mother, and siblings as persons but to hate ties and arrangements aimed at fostering an artificial order in society. The structure of the modern family optimally serves the interests of the rulers and archons;

- ensuring the perpetuation of our species in captivity
- keeping humans in a state of subservience to institutions
- controlling the development of children
- strengthening the hold of the physical world over the god-seed trapped in matter.

Thomas' stance presents a challenge to 21st century ideals that emphasize the two-parent family unit as the building block of civilization and attach moral, psychological, and social values to what is in fact a religiously biased, reactionary construct. The extended family, small tribe, or clan is the natural and original organization for the community of men.

Thomas' exhortation closely follows verses of the traditional gospels (Luke 14:26, Matthew 10:37) that leave the conservative Christians in a quandary and at pains to explain why their family-oriented Jesus would say such a thing. They often circumvent the dilemma in the same way we excuse a politician's outlandish claims: "He was exaggerating to make a point." But these words attributed to Jesus are for once devoid of any ambiguity: earthly family ties are an impediment to transcendence and liberation. The Gnostics in particular loathed any worldly scheme imposed on individuals to subjugate them to a material order and, in particular, to foster procreation. It is indeed in the heart of the household system that the rules and rationales of the social order are initially inculcated and promulgated by the lawgivers. Our masters know that a rejection of the smallest social component would tear apart the cohesive structure of control they have established over us in the human superorganism. Meanwhile, vocal, Evangelical Christian detractors of Thomas are quick to point out the anti-marriage, anti-family stand of his gospel as if it were an affront to human dignity. The truth however is that there is nothing morally superior in being pro-marriage or pro-family. The mystic Jiddu Krishnamurti did not shy away from exposing the function of our beloved institutions:

> *Your parents are frightened, your educators are frightened, the governments and religions are frightened of your becoming a total individual, because they all want you to remain safely within the prison of environmental and cultural influences. But it is only the individuals who break through the social pattern by understanding it, and who are therefore not bound by the conditioning of their own minds - it is only such people who can bring about a new civilization, not the people who merely conform, or who resist one particular pattern because they are shaped by another. The search for God or truth does not lie within the prison, but rather in understanding the prison and breaking through its walls.[68]*

The earthly family is a mechanism of conformity that hinders the emancipation of the soul and prevents the realization of the transcendentally sovereign individual. The fundamental unit of society as understood in the industrialized world is but an incubator for neuroses. In tribal communities, infants typically have several "mothers" who share the burden of raising anyone's progeny. Children form bands with minimal supervision, unhampered to roam and play on their own,

---

[68] Jiddu Krishnamurti, *Think on these Things*

learning together the patterns and cycles of their environment.[69] They discover the elements and skills of life by observing and imitating the adults of the tribe, not just their parents, and certainly not through programming. They had no need for contrived, ever shifting, tendentious sex education[70] since the sexual activities of the parents are in plain view of the children, whose own sex plays are unhampered and forthright. For that matter, pornography is an inexistant concept. Subsequently, the elders and the wisest teach the adolescents the specific myths and ways of the tribe and reveal to them the mysteries of the phenomenal and supersensible worlds. Thus, the members of the tribe are spared most of the derangement of "civilized" nations.[71]

---

[69] These facts I personally observed when the remnants of traditional Tahitian society (which had a strong matriarchal bent) were still perceptible. Kids were frequently *faa'amu*, that is fostered, by the grandmother or an older woman unrelated to biological parents. Children were given broad latitude to spend time in groups of their own away from adult circles.

[70] Sex education has nothing to do with imparting a knowledge the kids may need and is all about controlling that knowledge to serve specific aims. Modern education, in fact, never aims at fulfilling the needs of the child to know but satisfies instead the aims of the system. This line of argument can easily be substantiated by referring to the well-documented saga of Søren Hansen and Jesper Jensen's radical (at the time) *Little Red Schoolbook*. The publication eventually was banned in most Western countries in an extraordinary case of a book's premises being confirmed by the book's own fate. To quote from the authors themselves,

> The system is controlled by the people who have the money (or influence, I would add - Y.C.), and directly or indirectly these people decide what you should be taught and how.

[71] It should be noted that I do not subscribe to the myth of the "noble savage," and I do not necessarily advocate a return to archaic social structures; I only argue that, if not a panacea, the ancient ways were often more practical and less detrimental than our modern entanglements. The trouble is that, once we left the animal state, we

In logion 99, Thomas pushes his ideas on the family even further:

The disciples said to him: "Your brothers and your mother are standing outside." He replied: "Those in these places here who do the will of my father, these are my brothers and my mother; they are the ones who will enter the mystical sovereignty of my father." (See also Mark 3:32-35)

This suggests a spiritual family as opposed to the earthly one:

a family of beings of light who draw it [the soul] toward a clime beyond all hitherto known climes. Thus there rises on its horizon an Orient.[72]

The Orient, explains Corbin, is "the world of the Angel" (the empyreal sovereignty) as opposed to the "world of Exile" signified by the Occident. And the return to the "Orient" implies

a kinship with the divinity, with celestial beings, forms of light and beauty, which for the gnostic are his true family.[73]

The liberated soul will naturally be drawn to other souls on the basis of a shared affinity. But the soul's next of kin is her brother the savior-twin. With him we will dwell in our true home.

---

entered an insolvable human social dilemma. I maintain that the only exit for us is the liberation of the soul through a surrender to the uncorrupted, individuality-affirming Desire that ushers an aethereality as opposed to the complex bonds that inextricably tie mortal beings together. Man can only do evil in relation to his fellow earthlings; free from the web of physical life, he can do no evil because there is no evil to be done.

[72] Henry Corbin, *Avicenna and the Visionary Recital*
[73] Ibid.

And with thy Brother ...

Shalt thou be Heir in our Kingdom.

But he can also be our intimate companion and guide throughout our earthly journey for as long as we listen to his counsel:

Lone was I there, yea, all lonely;

To my fellow-lodgers a stranger.

However I saw there a noble,

From out of the Dawn-land my kinsman,

A young man fair and well favoured,

Son of Grandees; he came and he joined me.

I made him my chosen companion

...

He warned me against the Egyptians,

'Gainst mixing with the unclean ones.

Here, *The Hymn of the Robe of Glory* shows how the soul in her forlornness can turn to her spiritual kin, an angel from the Orient, who will guide her out of the material world (Egypt, metaphorically).

The World of the Dead - 56

Whosoever has known the world has stumbled upon a corpse, and whosoever has stumbled upon a corpse, the world is not worthy of him.

Our universe and our planet are dead even as they harbor life. The whole cosmos is in a perpetual state of decay, and Earth is a tomb for the infinite life of which cyclical life is a mere by-product. The uncreated generative Desire pervades the earthy shell, but only when the god-seed breaks out of its carapace will it develop as aethereal Life. The soul is in the world to find her angelic counterpart, but the world that holds them both captive is as perishable and transitory as a corpse.

Logia 56 and 80 are identical save for the word "body" substituted for "corpse." Both versions play on the ambiguous, twofold nature of our corporal envelope and, by extension, of the world. The earthy abide is like an old cathedral with slowly crumbling, musty stones and rotting wood, and a damp, dark crypt where a reliquary keeps our god-like essence prisoner. But the once glorious, hallowed edifice is also the birth home of the soul and a temple for the inner savior. This is why we must take care of the body of flesh and bones and the planet even if, paradoxically, the world of matter hampers the flowering of the uncreated generative Desire. Matter and flesh are not evil, they are the paradox of necessity. The theurgist of the inner mysteries realizes there is nothing of truer, higher value in earthly life than the soul and her angelic companion. What we call our home is a field that does not belong to us [21], and our fleshy skin quickly degrades into an old garment fit to be trampled under one's feet [3]. The physical world inevitably decomposes like a rotting cadaver while the aethereality abides eternally. Our universe is but cosmic poverty when compared to the richness of the empyreal sovereignty. *Suffer the dead to bury their own dead*, declares the Evangelist (Luke 9:60), signifying that those who bury their dead are metaphorically no more alive than the departed for as long as they belong to the world.

What do people mean when they say unreflectively "it's good to be alive?" Did they just have a brush with death that triggered their inborn instinct to survive at any cost? Did they enjoy a turn of luck from which they derive benefits? Did they find themselves suddenly in such happy circumstances that they can forget the horror they witnessed a while before or ignore the despair that could still invade them any moment? Was their brain flooded with the feel-good neurochemicals our body is able to produce to fog reason? Or was the unfathomable circuity of the mind suddenly selecting their most satisfying memories while eliding the unpleasant ones? If it is good to be alive at this instant, will the feeling persist tomorrow when hardship, affliction, or disaster strikes randomly? Have you ever heard a child claiming that it is good to be alive? (Unless, obviously, he is parroting.) Children cannot think of something so ridiculous to say: when they are jubilant, they delight in the experience without making pronouncements of dubious validity; when they hurt, they suffer without asking why misfortune befell them. Furthermore, if life is a school, as so many maintain, why are the tutorials mostly painful? Don't we learn far better and faster with positive reinforcement than through punishing means? Only adults who do not pause an instant to think about what they are saying (or otherwise have a vested interest in making us believe the contrary to that which we can plainly observe) would describe the physical plane in glowing terms. And they do it without a care for the evidence that our days are more distressful than blissful (as Gautama Buddha discovered as soon as he escaped his golden cage). Where is the goodness in aliveness? Life is not a gift (from whom exactly?), it is a burden. It has no meaning because it does not need one; it has no purpose, but a *raison d'être* born of necessity.

When we are fortunate enough to glimpse for a passing moment a parcel of preternatural beauty trapped in the world;

when we are overwhelmed by incomprehensible joy, awe, or compassion, we are in harmony with the uncreated, uncorrupted Desire that streams through the cosmos in a rush to escape its confines. It has never been good to be alive physically, it is good to be alive spiritually [18]. And whosoever wants a part in aethereality must forgo her stake in the world of physicality.

The God-Seed in the World - 57

The empyreal sovereignty of the father can be compared to a man who had good seed. His enemy came in the night and sowed weeds over the good seed. The man did not let anyone pull out the weeds, "lest you go to pull out the weeds and end up pulling up the grain with it," he said to them. On the day of the harvest, when the weeds are discernible, they will be plucked and burned.

To understand this parable, we need to refer to [9], from which we determined that the (good) seed is the god-seed, the dyadic essence formed by the soul and her savior-twin. As for the enemy, they are the archons whose essential aim is to prevent the seed from growing and keep it confined to matter ("the rock"). The most efficient means at their disposal to perpetrate their designs is to spread so much falsehood that the seeds of liberating cognizance are dissimulated [39] and choked. Attempting to pull out all the lies, however, is not the best option. Not only does the enormous amount of deception render the task impossible to carry out, but wherever one weedy falsehood is unrooted, another quickly sprouts out (as is plainly observable in the media of the digital information age). Moreover, there may be a kernel of truth even in the most damning lie. The best solution therefore rests not in a quixotic quest to battle windmills, but in taking care of the god-seed by strengthening the bond between the soul and our numinous self.

The tiniest seed that falls "on tilled ground" (that is the good soil prepared by the theurgist of the inner mysteries; see logion 9) will grow larger and stronger than the weeds until the grain can be harvested or the fruit reaped [21]. It will produce a "large branch" (the inner savior) for the support, shelter, and protection of the soul:

> *The disciples asked Jesus: "Tell us, to what the empyreal sovereignty can be compared?" He replied: "It can be compared to a grain of mustard, smallest among all the seeds. However, when it falls on tilled ground, it sends out a large branch and becomes a shelter (for) the birds of the sky.* [20]

Thus, if a fertile ground is necessary for the development of our numinous self, it is also essential for the survival of the soul beyond death. That is the subject of yet another of Thomas' metaphors:

> *A vine of grapes planted outside of the father did not grow strong. It will be pulled up by its root and destroyed.* [40]

The "father" stands for the undivided divine from which the soul and her dioscuric sibling descend [15 & 101]. The soul that is not firmly and deeply rooted in "undividedness" with her savior-twin cannot survive beyond the death of the physical body [61] [112]. The "vine of grapes" is a symbol associated with both Dionysos and Christ (the serpent is another symbol they have in common), who share many other similarities. Their respective myths have been interpreted in esoteric circles as allegories for the soul's journey, her sojourn in the realm of matter, her ascent to the empyrean, and her apotheosis. Christ is the son of God, the word made flesh (John 1:14) who was killed by the Roman soldiers and rose again immortal. Dionysos was the son of Zeus, part divine, part mortal from his (second) mother's side. He was killed by the Titans but reborn from the loins of Zeus. Both Christ and Dionysos were thus saved by their father, that is by virtue of the undivided divine.

Undiluted Gnosticism - 58

Blessed is the man who has been disturbed; he has found life.

There are those who think we can relax our way to nirvana or paradise. Some pseudo-mystical systems having made their peace with crass materialism maintain that the path to God is paved with prosperity and accomplishments in the world. Uncounted pop spirituality currents bypass the long and difficult struggle to transcendent awareness by promoting instead an array of feel-good shortcuts to "awakening" and "enlightenment." But the message of Thomas is clear: approaching the aethereal is commensurate with one's disdain for the physical plane, and finding infinite life is inextricable from a sense of forlornness in the universe, alienness in the physical world [2]. The heirs of the divine realize we live in a place that is not ours [21], of which we are the prisoners. They cannot find joy in the prison, no matter how gilded, and are strengthened only by the promise of their escape and union with their inner savior. Whereas the goal of the many is enlightenment, awakening, or salvation, the theurgist of the inner mysteries seeks liberation from the bonds of matter through their savior-twin. Nowadays, some are comfortable with a spirituality of compromises that makes enough room for earthly attachments. The ancient dualistic philosophies are frequently deformed to accommodate non-dual perspectives. Cosmic or Gaian theologies and creeds flourish. We just cannot leave the corpse behind [56]. But when the soul is in the thrall of her savior-twin, she can only manifest contempt for the realm of the dead of which she is still a captive. She cannot serve two lords without honoring one and despising the other [47].

The Pressing Matter of the Living - 59

Look after 'he who lives' while you are living, lest you die and have no power to see him when you try.

We have already covered the semantics of life and death in gnostic thought [11] [56]. The heirs of the divine who are spiritually alive among the dead have found the true life. But it is one thing to find infinite life and another to enter it. The liberating cognizance must be immediately followed by an absolute surrender of the soul to her dioscuric companion and savior. Failure to respond pressingly and appropriately to the revelation and call of our numinous self puts us at risk of being choked by the thorns [9] or overwhelmed by the weeds [57]. Sifting through the precepts of the world and the teachings of those who have taken and hidden the keys to transcendent awareness [39], he who dies spiritually is unable to "see" his inner savior ("he who lives") or feel his presence within himself [59].

The sense of urgency transpiring from Thomas' gospel is all but lost to modern sensitivities. By and large we seek to satisfy both our spiritual needs and our material appetite in an attempt to have our cake and eat it too.

The time for the bridegroom (the savior-twin) and the bride (the soul) to know each other is now [75]. At death, Spirit, and soul drift apart [61] [112] unless preparations for their wedding in aethereality have already been made while existing in physical reality. In other words, we do not face God when we die physically; and we become one only if we were spiritually alive during our earthly existence.

The Choice between Life and Death - 61

Of two lying on a bed, one will die, the other will live. Salome said: "Who are you Sir that, coming out of undividedness, you would climb onto my bed and eat at my table." Jesus said to her: "I am he who exists out of he who is equal. I partake of my father."

"I am your disciple" (replies Salome).

"Because of this, I say, when he comes to be equal, he will be filled with light; when, however, he comes to be divided, he will be full of darkness."

We have determined that the most pressing matter in life has nothing to do with our earthly existence but with the liberation of the soul from physicality, a notion that appears to escape most of the children of Earth [59]. This understanding is reaffirmed in the curious exchange between Jesus and Salome to which we now turn our attention.

The two lying on the bed are implicitly Salome and Jesus who just climbed next to her on the same couch. There is a sexual element in the encounter that is reminiscent of the myth of Eros and Psyche, which we have already visited [3] [22].

Jesus here would be Eros, the angelic embodiment of the uncreated generative Desire [α]. His origins are in the divine who is undivided and equal. Salome is Psyche, the soul.

The soul of an individual is the sum of his memories (including those dormant and unprocessed) at the moment of death. One's individuality, however, is how the memories are processed and blended with the thoughts, emotions, moods, and feelings. Thus, although I have the memories of childhood, I am not the same individual I was as a child. The individuality of the child I once was has all but disappeared. The mind is the agent that works with and on the memories while we are in the body of flesh. Once our memories are transferred to the aethereal body of the savior-twin, through him we will receive our eternal sense of individuality. The discrete memories of mankind can never vanish, but they will disperse when the flesh decomposes. [α] In other words, unless our memories are gathered in an aethereal body, our individuality perishes.

The soul and the numinous self form the god-seed, the projection of the undivided divine on the physical plane [11] [22]. Only when the soul and the inner savior become "equal" (twins) and undivided (sealed unto each other) can they be "filled with light." If they remain "divided" (separate), and "unequal," they will be "full of darkness." A very similar idea to that expressed by Thomas is found in a snippet of Valentinian metaphysics:

> Now they say that our Angels were put forth in unity, and are one, in that they came out from One. Now since we existed in separation, Jesus was baptised that the undivided should be divided until he should unite us with them in the Pleroma that we "the many" having

become "one," might all be mingled in in the One which was divided for our sakes.[74]

Hence, the heirs of the divine will receive an aethereal body when they die [22], while, as we have seen in the previous logion, those who are physically alive but spiritually divided continue to abide in the darkness of nescience. If they die in such an unchanged state of darkness, their memories (the soul) disperse, and their spirit (the angelic power) starts anew from scratch elsewhere.

The soul Salome is given a choice. If she surrenders to the savior-twin next to her, she will partake in the immortality of her dioscuric sibling. Salome's affirmation "I am your disciple" shows she has made the right choice. This allegorical reading of the logion is further supported by the etymology of the Greek name "Salome," which is most likely derived from the Hebrew *shalem,* meaning "complete," "whole" or "unbroken."

The inner mysteries of Jesus the hierophant - 62

I tell my mysteries to [those who are worthy of my] mysteries. Do not let your left hand know that which your right hand will do.

As we have previously determined (in *Jesus, Thomas, and the Disciples*; see introduction), "Jesus who lives" is the personification of the numinous self who imparts the liberating cognizance. This transcendent awareness proceeds from an inner initiation [1], a mystery unfolding within the vaulted chamber of one's own heart, and not between the walls of churches, temples, mosques, or synagogues.

---

[74] Robert Pierce Casey, *The Excerpta ex Theodoto of Clement of Alexandria* (Studies and Documents 1; London: Christophers, 1934)

Various explanations have been offered for the reference to the right hand, but the context clearly leans again toward the ancient mystery cults. For instance, the right-hand gesture of the *benedictio Latina* was borrowed by the early Christians from the pagan mysteries where it represented the knowledge acquired through initiation. The famed "hand of Sabazios" was a sacred artifact in the cult of the mysterious god who is thought to have been a fusion of several deities, especially Zeus (the father above; see logia 3, 15 & 101, 50) and Dionysos (the soul below; see logion 57). The lack of understanding we have regarding its function and significance is a testimony to the element of secrecy that characterized the ancient mysteries. *Not to let our left hand know that which our right hand does* is a fancy way of saying not to mix the sacred with the mundane. The sacred knowledge revealed to "those who are worthy" should not be shared with those who are unworthy. Our next logion will have more to say about this subject.

The Birth of the Holy Child - 70

When you give birth to the one in yourselves, he who is in you will save you. If you do not have him in you, his absence will kill you.

Logion 70 sums up the mysteries of self-salvation: we literally, if not physically, give birth to our own savior.

The uncreated generative Desire flows in all humans, but only in the core of the most religiously[75] minded does it manifest as an angelic power and a guiding light from which will be born a savior-twin in the heart of the heirs. Like the infant Jesus

---

[75] Again, in the sense of *religio* [3], not necessarily by adhering to any religion.

born in the grotto, his growth henceforth is commensurate to the care and attention he is given. If the grotto is empty, man is already dead before death strikes.

In a way, Evangelical Christians are right: salvation is easy in that it consists in accepting a mythic being as our savior. Only, that savior did not walk the earth and does not come from the sky; we can only be born-again in him if he is first born within us.

The Bridal Chamber - 75

There are many standing at the door, but only those who are undivided will enter the place of wedding.

In light of all we have learned so far, logion 75 is self-explanatory. But it gives us a chance to revisit the beautiful myth of Eros and Psyche. The two protagonists respectively personify Desire (Eros) and the soul (Psyche). Desire is the primal cause at the origin of creation and existence. Thus, in remote antiquity, Eros was recognized as *Protogenos,* who existed before the beginning and in whom all things originate. Desire is the everlasting, moving force of the entirety. The myth tells us how Eros and Psyche were fated to an overwhelming, reciprocal passion. They begin their liaison by meeting every night in the darkened bedchamber of a beautiful palace. At first Psyche cannot see who her beloved is, but she uncovers his identity by lighting up the alcove where they lie with her lamp (figuratively the guiding light of transcendent awareness). Psyche must undergo many tribulations before her perseverance is rewarded with immortality and an eternal Life with Eros. The child of their love is Hedone, meaning pleasure and delight.

The myth of Eros and Psyche has a counterpart, albeit a less elaborated one, in the story of Dyonisos and Adriadne

The classical theme of the lover and the beloved is at the core of a Western mysticism that allegorized the angelic henosis of the human soul with her savior. It is also a pervasive, hidden motif in the imagery of Thomas' gospel.

Many are standing outside the bridal chamber. They cannot open the door because they do not have the key [39]. But the heirs of the divine are admitted inside to offer their soul as a bride. She has received the keys of liberating cognizance that open the door to the sacred room where the inner savior is waiting. In the vaulted chamber of the heart, the soul and her betrothed consummate the passion that will carry them into aethereality.

The Pearl that Never Perishes - 76

The empyreal sovereignty of the father can be compared to a trader who had merchandise and stumbled upon a pearl. The trader who was wise gave his merchandise back and bought that single pearl for himself. "You, yourselves, seek his treasure that does not perish, but endures where no moth comes to eat, and no worm destroys."

The traders are those who concern themselves with material instead of spiritual wealth. A wiser one among them soon recognizes the folly of his ways and abandons what he owns in favor of a single pearl. The pearl is another symbol for the undivided (single) god-seed, shining and beautiful, but prisoner of its shell. It is the only prize that matters, the same treasure the princely youth in *The Hymn of the Robe of Glory* (also called *Hymn of the Pearl*) was sent to recover.

I bethought me again of the Pearl,
For which I was sent down to Egypt.
And I began [then] to charm him,
The terrible loud-breathing Serpent.[76]
I lulled him to sleep and to slumber, ...
And [thereon] I snatched up the Pearl,
And turned to the House of my Father.

Once the youth finds the pearl, he is empowered to return to the house of the living father, the realm of harmony and numinosity. The dyadic god-seed formed by the soul sealed to her savior-twin becomes a god-being who abides eternally in a place where the archons—"the moths" and "the worms"[77]—no longer have no power.

Detachment - 80 & 87

Whosoever has known the world has stumbled upon a corpse, and whosoever has stumbled upon a corpse, the world is not worthy of him.

...

Miserable is the body that clings to a body, and miserable is the soul that clings to both.

We have already analyzed [80] in the context of [56] to which it is nearly identical. Now, it provides us with the key to understand a pun used for a rhetorical purpose. In that light,

---

[76] Because the youth's quest earlier in the hymn is located in Egypt, the serpent here is Apophis, the embodiment of destruction, enemy of the sun-god Ra who is giver of life. See also logion 7.
[77] We saw in logion 9 that the worms specifically represent the archons.

"the body that clings to a body" is the man who is incapable of renouncing the appeal of the material world. His "miserable" body perishes and decays in the world with which it shares the same material substance. The "miserable" soul of the materialists who "clings to both" is not liberated from her carnal envelope when death strikes and dissipates with the corpse onto the physical plane. By now we should be fully cognizant of how Thomas views physicality [22][29][47][56]. Logion 11 in particular alludes to the horrifying condition of man on earth, forced to sustain his life by eating the flesh of carcasses. Life on Earth—cyclical life—feeds on death. Everything that lives depends for nourishment on something that dies. It is the immutable law of the physical universe, and our biological existence is no more than a recycling process. In addition, our kind has the woeful distinction of having secured scientific advances and material comfort on the back of other species. From cruel experimentations using feeling, intelligent animals to the degradation of the environment, our earthly presence comes at a deadly cost to everything non-human. Yet there is an escape from this morbid condition: if we can lift our eternal essence to sovereignty, we can become an immortal, aethereal being. The heirs' true home is the place of light where their soul will be transported to find restfulness [50].

Decay is what makes biological life possible. The curse on Adam was not a condemnation to die but a sentencing to exist in a state conditioned by death. Hence, a modified version of [87] reads as follow:

> Woe to the flesh that clings to the soul; woe to the soul that clings to the flesh. [112]

When Adam and Eve discovered they were naked in the garden of Eden, they sewed together fig leaves to make loincloths. Admittedly, their tailoring skills may not have been well developed, but with the help of a god they could have learned to use cotton or other natural fibers, you would think. The Rex Mundi[78] had other plans though: he preferred to cover "his children" with the flayed skin of dead animals. (Of particular interest is the contrast between the skin of animals covering our mortal souls on Earth and the robe of glory promised to the immortal soul described in the *Hymn of Thomas*; see logion 84) Thenceforth, the souls of our first parents, and ours, would be enveloped in death. (See Genesis 3:21). Next, the god of decay demanded blood sacrifices. Fruits and grains would not suffice, it had to be a lamb sliced alive on an altar (see Genesis 4:4). How "miserable" indeed is the soul for depending on the body in the realm of death.

"The flesh that clings to the soul" then is the matter that cradles the soul during her short terrestrial sojourn. The soul is contingent on a physical body only for as long as the memories arise and are stored in the living tissues. This necessary constraint, however, is lifted when she is taken into a new, aethereal body [22]. After that, the flesh has no function in aethereality. It was cursed from the beginning, doomed to be

---

[78] The Rex Mundi (King of the World) is a conceptual entity that represents the totality of the archonic powers, or the ruler of the archons. In Cathar theology, he was the demiurge, an inferior emanation often assimilated with the Judeo-Christian Yahweh, the jealous and false god of the Old Testament who fancied himself as sovereign over the All. In esoteric thinking, that demiurge is the personification of the blind forces of creation, the embodiment of matter, and the mythological dominion of the cosmos or physical plane.

trampled upon and crushed under the heel of the savior-twin [37]. But the soul is also cursed for those individuals who do not hear or heed the call [91] and refuse to concede the necessity and urgency of abandoning material pursuits and materialistic concerns to turn without delay to the pressing matter of liberation from the bonds of the physical world [59]. A failure to care in this existence for the next is a condemnation for one's individuality to perish [61]. The woes of the soul are compounded when her glorious liberation and destiny are obfuscated by beliefs that envision the afterlife as little more than an improved version of earthly existence. In many faiths ancient and modern, there is no concept of a higher state in human existence other than the recovery of the same body—albeit minus the flaws—one had at the moment of death. From that perspective, the soul forever "clings to the flesh."

Renouncement - 81 & 110

Whoever has become rich let him become king, and he who has power let him renounce it.

...

Whoever has found the world and become rich let him renounce the world.

The Gospel of Thomas loves ambiguity and paradox. Just as there two kinds of life—the true Life in aethereality and the death-like life of reality [11][56]—we can have two kinds of wealth: the richness of the spirit (intimated in logion 81), or the material possessions of the world (mentioned in logion 110). To find the world, is to find a corpse [56]; to be involved in the world is to live in poverty of Spirit, no matter how materially wealthy we might be [3] [29]. Consequently, *he who has become materially rich in the world* must learn to be detached from his earthly treasure and ought to renounce the world before he can become a theurgist of the inner mysteries. The heirs of the divine who have become spiritually rich, on the other hand, will be made "kings" because they "will be sovereign over the entirety" [2] and hold the empyreal power. The worldly powers of earthly existence are not compatible with such trans-material sovereignty; they are the arena of the archons. Lest they be controlled by the archons, those whose individual destinies are to become leaders should lead in the spirit of the *Tao Te Ching*:

> *I will do nothing (of purpose), and the people will be transformed of themselves; I will be fond of keeping still, and the people will of themselves become correct. I will take no trouble about it, and the people will of themselves become rich; I will manifest no ambition, and the people will of themselves attain to the primitive simplicity.*[79]

The theurgist of the inner mysteries knows how to take care of themselves; they also understand the delicate balance between making one's sojourn on Earth bearable, or even pleasant, while renouncing a crass pursuit of material gains and profits to avoid the pitfall of mundane entanglements. The material plane has nothing of authentic value to offer the mystic passerby [42]. Before all else, she seeks not the rewards of the world but those of heavens through a knowledge of herself [3].

We built an industrialized civilization only to be turned into the powerless consumers and slaves of the dystopian system we

---

[79] *Tao Te Ching, Laozi,* translated by James Legge, 1890

created. We keep generating unnecessary needs only to find ourselves worrying all day long about fulfilling them. When our mind is obsessed with acquisitiveness, our numinous self atrophies; when the mind is unconcerned with having and possessing, the inner savior gains strength and grows.

There is no reason the poor should not apply themselves to seeking the means of escaping indigence, but they must do so without jeopardizing what should be the cardinal enterprise of life: the liberation of the soul and the release of the god-seed from physicality. Goods, properties, and money are the bricks in the walls of materialism that enclose the soul in a donjon. The legitimate efforts to improve one's lot can just as easily turn into greed and materialistic fixations.

The rich enjoy circumstances of comfort and ease that afford them the leisure of loftier endeavors, but they rarely have an interest in metaphysical concerns. The poor who must strain and struggle to make ends meet and survive are left with the hopes that keep them subservient to the system. Thus, a class-oriented society is inherently not conducive to mystical aspirations. Instead, such a society fosters adherence to collective creeds and *prêt-à-porter* religions that do not require independent thinking and barely allay spiritual thirst. The leading denominations ensure the status quo is preserved because they receive the monetary support of the wealthy and the protection of the powerful. The lower classes at the base of the system are offered dubious hope and reassurance that obedience, faith, and hard work will ultimately be rewarded in this life or the next.

We are not blessed when forced into misery by an absurd, unfair, and elitist economic rationale, but when we acquire the presence of mind to stop following institutionalized rapacity, chasing after ever greater profits, and hoarding goods. A decreased involvement in materialistic aims fosters the attention we give to the welfare of our soul. As the philosopher Georges Bernanos puts it,

> *Spiritual values will never be restored as long as profit is honored, whereas it should only be tolerated and controlled.*

Frugality may not be a guaranty of piety but, unsurprisingly, tribal societies without a class structure based on ownership and the accumulation of property demonstrate a keener interest in the supersensible realm, and a greater satisfaction in life than does the modern man in his daily "pursuit of happiness" (the most inventive euphemism ever concocted for our obsession with property and the accumulation of the useless). They show no need for industrialization, economic theories, and capital, implementing communal stewardship and plucking off the land only that which they need to share fairly. Without economic class distinction, they see no rationale for upward mobility. Without attributing meaning to material wealth, they find more significance in their connection to fellow humans, nature, and a transcendent realm. In our industrial societies our "needs" are constantly pushed farther so that there is no possibility of ever fulfilling them, and we rush headlong in a greedy chase after persistently receding aims. Oblivious to its annihilating power, we revel in the insatiability that devours us.

The Image of Divinity - 83 & 84

The images appear to man, and the light within them is hidden. It will be revealed by the image of the father's light, though his (the living father's) *image is hidden in his* (the living father's) *light.*

When you see your likeness, you rejoice. However, if you were to behold your images that came into being in your beginning—which do not die and are not revealed—how much would you bear?

In order to understand this complex pair of logia, we need to establish several elements:

• The material world is not an illusion; it is reality penetrated by uncreated generative Desire.

• The uncreated generative Desire is the fire that comes from aethereality, the realm of light itself, and is invisible to the physical eye.

• The heirs of the divine are a "person of light": in them, the angelic power which is a spark of the divine fire becomes the numinous self, the guiding light who is "the father's light."

• There are two sorts of images according to Thomas: on the one hand we have the images we perceive in the world under the physical light; on the other hand, there exists an image of divinity that is veiled in the spiritual light.

• The image of divinity, or image of the living father's light, is an imprint projected from the undivided divine and carried through the uncreated generative Desire like the parental genes passed on to the children; a "spiritual DNA," so to speak, that instructs the development and growth of our own being before it is reflected by the soul to be finally passed onto the numinous self henceforth becoming our savior-twin. Men are made in the image of a god-being for the god-beings to be reborn in the image of man; thus is *an image made in the place of an image* [22].

We saw how Thomas and the author of *The Hymn of the Robe of Glory* likened the mortal body to a filthy garment [22]. The Hymn then endeavors to describe with flourish the aethereal body it compares to a glorious robe emblazoned with the image of the divinity.

> *The Glorious Robe all-bespangled*
> *With sparkling splendour of colours ...*
> *the King of Kings' Image*
> *Was depicted entirely all o'er it.*

We can now see more clearly into the meaning of logia 83 and 84:

The images of objects (our "likeness," in the case of the human being) are visible to us in the physical realm, but the spiritual light that penetrates them is concealed from our view. The spiritual light will be revealed to the theurgist of the inner mysteries by their numinous self, but the image of divinity is an unseen spiritual marker that contributes to our physical appearance and determines the forms of the aethereal body [22]. Unlike physical images, the image of the divinity cannot die and was always with us since the beginning; if it were possible to behold such an image, it would defy our understanding.

The Yoke of the Living - 90

Come to me, because my yoke is easy and my sovereignty
is gentle, and you will find restfulness.

A yoke is an apparatus by which two draft animals are
joined together. The yoke of the inner savior therefore is that
which binds the soul and her liberator into an "undividedness."
Far from being a burden as suggested in the Gospel of Matthew
(11:29-30), the bond described by Thomas is pleasant and leads
the heirs who accept it to restfulness and sovereignty over the
entirety [2].

The Call - 91

They said to him: "Tell us who you are so that we may
believe in you." He said to them: "You read the face of
the sky and the earth, and he who is in your presence
you do not know, and you do not know how to read this
moment."

The disciples again are characteristically obtuse. They ask
for a figurehead with impressive credentials to tell them what
to do and what to think. They want someone in whom to believe,
who will promise them earthly blessings and heavenly rewards.
The disciples want a flesh-and-blood Jesus to lead them; they
are unable to develop their numinous self as a constant
companion in their presence. They read the face of the sky and
the earth (this describes an attachment to cosmic or Gaian
theologies and creeds as well as a yearning for supernatural
phenomena), but they fail to understand that anyone, at any
moment can rejoice in the proximity and guidance of an inner
savior. The words of John the Baptist speaking of Jesus (John
1:26) are traditionally rendered as "among you"—that is *among*

the crowd—"stands one you do not know" (BSB). But literal translations of the bible allow for an alternate meaning: "in the midst of you"—that is *in the middle of each of you, your very center*—"stands One whom you do not know" (Berean Literal Bible). When the disciples refer to the prophets in Israel, Jesus tells them:

> *You have omitted the one who lives in your presence,*
> *and you have spoken of those who are dead.* [52]

In typical, similar fashion, we have a disposition to validate and justify our beliefs by weighing them against traditions and the voices (real or imagined) of those who have spoken before. It is a dubious exercise but one that is so ingrained in common piety that modern spiritual movements often produce mythic lineages of authority to enhance their credibility.

To read the earth and the sky is to stick with the traditions of man. To read the moment is to hear the call from the innermost of our being. Heeding the call is much more than awakening. When we awaken, we purge ourselves of everything we have assimilated as when we shake off the memories of a bad dream at the end of the night. Awakening requires the courage to face emptiness; it is the coming to a blank page in the middle of the great book of life expectations; it is the edge of the abyss, the point at which we are forced to ask ourselves: *now what?* That is when we are most ready to hear the call that answers our question and triggers a radical change in our perception. It is the memory, diffuse at first, of our origins and what we were. It is also an invitation to return. The call is a hierophany and the best way to describe it is in the form of an allegory. We thus return to *The Hymn of the Robe of Glory* and the mystical journey of its princely, youthful hero before he could recover the god-seed entrapped in matter [76]. We find him in a spiritual torpor, forlorn in the land of Egypt (a gnostic image for the physical world), a slave of matter and of the archons:

I forgot that I was a King's son,
And became a slave to their king.
I forgot all concerning the Pearl
For which my Parents had sent me;
And from the weight of their victuals
I sank down into a deep sleep.

In the allegory, the call comes in magical ways as a missive taking the form of an eagle who changes itself into a letter:

It flew and alighted beside me,
And turned into speech altogether.
At its voice and the sound of its winging,
I waked and arose from my deep sleep.

The youth unseals the letter and reads:

"Up an arise from thy sleep,
Give ear to the words of Our Letter!
"Remember that thou art a King's son;
See whom thou hast served in thy slavedom.
Bethink thyself of the Pearl
For which thou didst journey to Egypt.
"Remember thy Glorious Robe,
Thy Splendid Mantle remember,
"To put on and wear as adornment,
When thy Name may be read in the Book of the Heroes,
"And with Our Successor, thy Brother,
Thou mayest be Heir in Our Kingdom."

The youth then reflects on the transformation that occurred:

> E'en as it stood in my heart writ,
> The words of my Letter were written.
> I remembered that I was a King's son,
> And my rank did long for its nature.

The Prophecy - 97

The empyreal sovereignty of the father can be compared to a woman carrying a jar full of meal. She was walking down a distant road when the jar's handle broke; the meal spilled out behind her on the road. She did not know it since she had not seen it happen. When she arrived home, she put the jar down and found it to be empty.

Logion 97 stands apart from the other parables of Thomas as it may well present a prophecy written nearly 2000 years before its fulfillment in our century.

In this allegory, the liberating cognizance is represented by the meal that is the spiritual nourishment spread over the world to guide the souls of the heirs everywhere until they reach the empyreal sovereignty of the father. Having traveled through the long road of time, Fate—who is the blind agency represented by the woman carrying the meal—arrives at her destination and sees that the gnosis from the jar had "spilled out behind her on the road." Here is a cue to understand the parable: whereas everyone keeps wondering about the meaning of the empty jar, nobody asks what happened to the meal.

In 1945, an Egyptian farmer and his brothers found the Gospel of Thomas and other manuscripts sealed in an earthenware jar hidden in a cave. The farmer broke the container and removed its contents, leaving the broken jar empty. Subsequently, the tractates were dispersed and sold on the black market before being painstakingly gathered again. In this manner, just as related in the parable, the sacred writings were spread around the entire world for the benefits of genuine seekers.

We know that around the time the manuscripts were buried by the monks of a nearby monastery, the freshly minted Christian Church was actively engaged in a violent campaign to suppress dissentience among themselves and eradicate the pagan and gnostic beliefs of others. The new "Christian Pharisees" were proactively taking away the "keys of gnosis" [39]. In order to spare the treasures of written wisdom they had collected a grim end, the desert eremites chose to entrust them to divine providence. Without such prescience, all that would be left nowadays of the precious Gospel of Thomas would be a handful of fragments in Greek. It is possible that the writer of logion 97 foresaw such an extraordinary turn of events. In any case, the complot against gnosis was foiled.

Because they were not intended for the general public but only for the chosen [50], gnostic texts have a tradition of being sealed and hidden either literally or metaphorically. For instance, Simon Magus spoke of a work entitled the *Revelation of a Voice and of a Name*:

> *This writing comes from the Great Power, the Infinite Power. That is why it will be sealed, hidden, veiled and*

deposited in the dwelling where the Root of All Things has its beginnings.[80]

This invaluable work that could shed so much light on the mysteries of the Simonians has yet to be given a second chance with mankind.

The Sethian *Holy Book of the Great Invisible Spirit* however was unburied at Nag Hammadi together with the *Gospel of Thomas*. At the conclusion of the manuscript, we read:

This is the book which the great Seth wrote, and placed in high mountains on which the sun has not risen ... And since the days of the prophets and the apostles and the preachers, the name has not at all risen upon their hearts ... And their ear has not heard it.

... He placed it in the mountain that is called 'Charaxio,' in order that, at the end of the times and the eras, by the will of the divine Autogenes and the whole pleroma, through the gift of the untraceable, unthinkable, fatherly love, it may come forth and reveal this incorruptible, holy race of the great savior ... and the great, invisible, eternal Spirit, and his only-begotten Son, and the eternal light.[81]

Escape from the flesh - 98

The empyreal sovereignty of the father can be compared to a man who wanted to kill a powerful man. He drew his sword in his house and drove it into the wall so that

---

[80] Lacarriere
[81] *The Gospel of the Egyptians*, Translated by Alexander Bohlig and Frederik Wisse

he might know for himself his hand would be strong.
Then he slew the powerful one.

A murdering plot seems like an odd comparison to describe the empyreal sovereignty, unless salvific liberation did depend on the death of a powerful entity. The powerful one is the Rex Mundi, the epitome of the archons taken in their entirety [80][87]. This single entity personifies the guardians of the physical world [50] and rulers of the cosmos we call the Archons. To kill him is to get rid of all the forces that keep us ensnared in physicality and to be victorious over matter.

If the "powerful man" stands for the ruling power of the cosmos, the sword is the power of the inner savior. To thrust a sword into the wall of the house (recall that the house represents the physical body; see logion 48) is metaphorically to breach the wall of the flesh, thus releasing the spirit and liberating the soul.

Shepherd of the Soul - 107

The empyreal sovereignty can be compared to a shepherd who had a hundred sheep. The largest one strayed (from the flock), and he left the ninety-nine (sheep to) go after that one until he found it. Having gone to such trouble, he said to the sheep: "I desire you more than the ninety-nine (others)."

As soon as the uncreated generative Desire has entered reality, it is ruled by one imperative only: to engender the souls that will facilitate its return to aethereality. The shepherd is the inner savior. Note that his search is motivated by Desire (*I desire you more than the others*). Also, unlike its counterpart in Luke (15:1-7), the sheep in Thomas is not lost because of her sins, having wandered away from the folk of the faithful; she has separated herself from the herd of the materialists and the easy believers. This sheep is a non-conformist and stands for the heirs of the divine ready to leave the world behind. That is why the shepherd loves her and needs her. An individual soul is unique to a single lifetime whereas the uncreated generative Desire journeys through myriad simultaneous cycles of time to shepherd an unimaginable number of souls: they are "the ninety-nine" the inner savior leaves behind for the only one with whom he can be released from the fetters of matter. That is also the meaning of logion 23:

> *I will choose you, one out of a thousand and two out of ten thousand, and they will stand upright, being undivided.*

The Treasure Within - 109

> *The empyreal sovereignty can be compared to a man who unknowingly had a treasure [hidden] in his field and, [after] his death, left it to his [son]. The son did not know (either). He took over the field (and) gave it [away]; [and] whoever bought it went plowing and [stumbled upon] the treasure. He began to give money at interest to whom he loved.*

Logion 109 alludes again, metaphorically, to the three orientations of the souls [9]. The parable speaks of the owner of a field, his son who inherits the field, and a buyer to whom the heir gives the field away. They are respectively the materialist (the first owner), the easy believer (the second owner), and the true heir (the last owner).

The materialist is incognizant of the inner spiritual dimension. The easy believers have an inner spiritual life but do not probe its depths. They prefer to relinquish analytical thinking and surrender their mind to the purveyors of spirituality who will map for them the territory within. Only the theurgist of the inner mysteries invests completely in the field within where they find the hidden treasure, the liberating cognizance revealed by the savior-twin. They then share what they know (metaphorically "the money," because of its value) with those who are closest to them [33] and reap the benefits (interests) of passing on what they have learnt. Indeed, the reward of shared wisdom is even greater wisdom. For, in the process of explaining profound matters, we never fail to deepen our understanding.

Male Spirit, Female Soul - 114

Simon Peter said to them: "Let Mary leave us, for women are not worthy of the life." Jesus replied: "Behold, I myself will lead her so that I might make her male, so she might also come to be a living spirit in your male likeness. For any woman making herself male will enter the empyreal sovereignty."

It is one thing to find in the Gospel of Thomas a veiled mystery that fulfills one's loftiest aspirations; it is an entirely different thing to make the entire text of Thomas' gospel fit neatly into one's modern expectations. For those who want to see Jesus as a proto-feminist goody guru, logion 114 is a letdown. Even scholars make excuses, telling us this is a late, unfortunate addition, and reject these final words as unauthentic. They make the same mistake as the purists who are still looking for an unadulterated Gospel of Jesus, fallen from his lips and couched intact on the papyrus as if it were not the product of many imaginations. Everything in Thomas' gospel is subsequent additions redacted through time into a syncretic tractate. It is precisely that crowning, combined effort of mystics and philosophers that interests us, not the hypothetical moralistic (and likely tedious) thoughts and precepts of a half-raving itinerant preacher.

It is Peter the bumbling disciple who is making the inept remark. Unsurprisingly, he is that same Apostle whose hieratic lineage would give rise to the Roman Catholic Church, the reformation, and the latter-day, disparate factions of neo-Christianity. Peter thinks that women are not worthy of "the (aethereal) life," but women and men alike are led by an inner savior into the empyreal sovereignty.

Femaleness and maleness are mystical, metaphorical attributes of the soul and her savior-twin respectively [22]. All humans have a "female" soul who must leave the flesh to follow her counterpart "male" spirit. This is the esoteric meaning of the first creation of man and woman in the Bible (Genesis 1:26-27). The "masculine" numinous self must lead the "feminine" soul in his likeness to the undivided divine. The confluence of the soul and her savior-twin is allegorized throughout the logia as the wedding of a bride with her bridegroom. Thus, their ecstatic union is the unstated consummation of a meta-physical sexual act. The soul loses herself in the embrace of her mystical companion, thereon she coalesces with him to form an androgynous, numinous "undividedness."

EXCURSUS

The Archons

Before mankind rose, the archons did not exist. Yet, they are as eternal as we are in the circular nature of the entirety [18], being born out of our chaotic primeval mind. Whereas the uncreated generative Desire engenders the human species, humankind engenders the archons through involuntary, exacerbated emotional states. We unwittingly create them during our earthly sojourn with the powerful emotions that clog our psyche as a part of the deep-seated legacy of our primal, dual disposition [7]. The more we tamper with those emotions (as for example when we strive to suppress anger, attract happiness, or deny and repress "improper" desires), the stronger they grow until they trickle or discharge violently out of our minds. Just as the mind has many psychological defense and coping mechanisms in ordinary life, it can also have recourse to psychical mechanisms in more extreme situations. Instead of examining internally that which we wish would disappear, we exteriorize our fears, dread, and uncertainty. Instead of calling on our numinous self for help, we expect help in external means of salvation.[82] Whereupon arise into matter

---

[82] "The help you seek from the outside, they will find" [21].
Be they space visitors, supernatural beings, religious apparitions, or mythical and mythological figures, the archons take the forms in the world of whatever we expect to bring change to our conditions or the fate of mankind. Here is the simple fact: nothing trans-physical can manifest in the universe because the material plane comes out of transcendent dimensions, not the other way around. Everything appearing in the cosmos or material world, notwithstanding how "spiritual-looking," is fettered to matter.

projections driven by an imperative to self-actualize and endure. If the soul's dioscuric sibling is the inner savior—the preserving and illuminating agent within us—the archons can be thought of as the deceptive part of ourselves, our "demons," the angels and servants of the Rex Mundi who himself personifies matter and the physical world. Emotions are biochemical and electrical responses that affect our body, and it is not inconceivable that they can affect and alter the continuity of matter in which the body moves. Once the archons escape the confines of the mind, they take a life on their own in the supersubstantial regions that border the hard physical plane and start vying for our attention. The most evolved of the archons have the ability to assume the shapes of our experiential expectations and form a rough identity based on individual and collective memories. Once outside the mind, they abide as purely material albeit fluid entities, without much if any self-awareness, and lacking the meta-physical thrust, the uncreated generative Desire, that links the rest of the creation to the divine. Yet, they possess a collective cognizance and a propensity for organizational, colony-type structure derived from the primeval mind that is the earliest aspect of our evolutionary makeup.

The archons are fascinated by the human soul they lack, and their existence becomes parasitic, sustained by our own psychic life on which they prey. They feed on our *thymos*, seeking to permanently occupy our consciousness as a platform to multiply, gain strength, and make our memories their own [21]. They strive to forestall the birth of the inner savior [70] as they know it would usher the liberation of the god-seed from matter, which would precipitate their end.

The entire domain of the archons is the cosmos, Earth, and the whole of the physical plane, over which they rule and of which they are de facto guardians. Their mastery of matter allows them to shift appearances, materialize swiftly, and disappear just as fast in elusive fashion. The archonic powers are the hierarchy of all paranormal phenomena, including most religious and spiritual apparitions. To what degree those mental manifestations are truly independent is difficult to say. It is safe to compare the phenomenon to the multiple personalities of patients afflicted with dissociative identity disorder. Those personae exhibit remarkable individuality and, in some extreme cases, can appear in the perception of the sufferer, moving about freely and interfering in his existence without ever being detached from his psyche. In that sense, and with regard to the paranormal, we are all victims of our disorderly mind, producing without awareness individualized and collective phantasms that invade sensible perception. Yet, the strongest archons seem to survive the death of their originator.

The rulers and warders of the cosmos are also the ambassadors of the Magna Mater—alternately generous or cruel, often possessive, jealous and deceptive, occasionally nefarious, always self-serving and dominated by a drive to endure she shares with the archons. In the same mythological vein, Yahweh, the mountain god of the Old Testament can be considered the leader of the archons.

Without us there would be no them, and their interest lies in keeping us ensnared in matter. To that end, they control the gates that lead to freedom for the god-seed, and they work tirelessly to influence the societal, cultural, and religious developments that serve their aims more effectively. Benjamin Franklin wrote that the longer he lived, "the more convincing Proofs" he saw of "this Truth — That God governs in the Affairs of Men."[83] Well, there's no doubt about that! The problem is that it is the demiurge indeed, the supreme archon or Rex Mundi who is the god so involved in the material world that is certainly his.

The archons inevitably come into conflict with the uncreated generative Desire that seeks the coadunating apotheosis of soul and spirit in aethereality that isn't of this world. In effect, the archons are the thieves of the soul who compete with the angelic power in us for hegemony. Yet, to fear them is to strengthen them. They are an integral part of ourselves, and, as we silence our mind and open our heart to our numinous self, they progressively fade and will vanish in the end, yielding to the triumph of the sovereign Self.

The notion of archons overlaps with that of the "egregores," of occult lore. The latter can be understood as a phase of development in the growth of the former.

Egregores start with a concept such as that of a Saint, a demon, or the spirit of a nation, and are consciously developed in the mind before being released. Subsequently, they are imbued with emotional mass energies such as devotion, fear, or patriotism. At that stage, they turn into thought-forms with a powerful hold on the psyche but no capacity for self-preservation: when the idea dies, its attendant egregore dies as well. If egregores have any perceivable forms, they are those of

---

[83] Words often quoted by politicians who dream to see all distinctions erased between the kingdom of God and an ideal form of government. To them, the best society is a theocratic society.

symbols, allegories, or hallucinations, and their impact may be negative, positive, or neutral. But when an egregore is endowed with a purpose to meddle in the fortunes of mankind or to alter the world, it evolves into an archon empowered with an instinct for self-preservation and self-perpetuation, sustained and fortified by our hysteria, fanaticism, obsession, greed, idolization, and other forceful impulses.

The following examples will be useful in understanding the nature and reach of egregores and archons.

Poltergeists have been widely documented and observed with scientific rigor. They frequently appear in conjunction with outbursts of the ultra-potent psycho-sexual and emotional energy of pubescent children and adolescents. Poltergeists unfold as disturbing noises, strange light effects, and telekinesis. If, as is most often the case, a postulate is attached to the paranormal event—usually that of a spirit or a ghost—an egregore is born that will have a psychic hold on all who share the belief. Now, when the believers decide the supernatural entities are eager to communicate, or have significant knowledge to impart, an aim is ascribed to the egregore who will henceforth act on its own volition as an archon. An identical scenario occurs in the case of random lights and elusive fast-moving objects with multifarious shapes (physical manifestations of collective emotional projections) that are attributed to alien visitors (the egregore). When the ETs are thought to be on a mission—nefarious or redemptive—they morph into the archons responsible for cases of "alien" abductions. One can see the same pattern replicated with Marian and sensible angelic visitations, crop circles, cryptids, and other paranormal phenomena.

In short, egregores are pervasive, mostly collective, mental structures that influence us all to some degree, positively or negatively, and result from our various psychical investments: sport enthusiasm, political ideologies, fad diets, holistic lifestyle, conspiracy theories, religious beliefs, nationalism are all fertile ground for mild to overwhelming egregores. The archons, on the other hand, are willful supernatural, semi-autonomous entities with a physical, if elusive presence, essentiated and sustained by the raw emotions of the primeval mind, who intrude on our psychic space and interfere with our destinies.

Men of the world may scoff at the idea of parasitic, supersubstantial creatures coveting our memories. Yet, the fingerprints of the archons can be detected in the greatest danger facing us in our time: the rise of transhumanism and our unconditional surrender to the technology that serves the cloaked designs of our enemies. Virtual reality is rewiring our brains to adapt to a new, fabricated universe within the created universe while disengaging our faculty to apprehend the sensible world and blurring the distinction between natural environment and fantasy. The onslaught of AI-generated fake videos and images on social media have brought us to the defining point past which we will no longer distinguish the real from the unreal. CGI further pulls us away from natural and artistic harmony down into the mind of the machine. Trapped in a prison within a prison, our inability to escape the world of matter will be all but ensured. In the nightmarish visions they pass for the ultimate path of freedom and well-being, the prophets of the singularity aim at digitalizing the mind and uploading consciousness. Transformed into electronic bits, the minds of the posthumans would be captured in machines, and (whatever may remain of) their soul cut off from the angelic power within to face an uncertain fate worse than roaming the corridors of the house of Hades. The words of Lewis Mumford come to mind:

> *Western society has accepted as unquestionable a technological imperative that is quite as arbitrary as the most primitive taboo: not merely the duty to foster invention and constantly to create technological novelties, but equally the duty to surrender to these novelties unconditionally, just because they are offered, without respect to their human consequences.*

Time, Memory, Incarnation, and Liberation

All perception is the end of a process that lies in the past. That which we call the present has no existence because everything we perceive has already occurred before it reaches our consciousness. Therefore our reality is our memories.

The idea of reincarnation is inextricably linked to the passing of time, but time is a beautiful trick the god-beings experience by necessity or use for their merriment. Time is sealed: its beginning is also its end. Nothing can exit time and reenter it; everything must be at once in and out of time or must not be. Therefore, a "soul" cannot reincarnate or progress from a lower sphere to a superior one because what exists eternally cannot be altered. Moreover, if souls reincarnate to balance Karma, why would the first souls with no Karma incarnate? And if souls incarnate to gain experience and learn, then we should see a decrease in population numbers as the most advanced souls exit the wheel of reincarnation; but just the opposite is true.

No amount of limpid, "past-lives" memories is proof of a former life. That is because memories are not remembrance of the past, but the retrieval of information, and information circulates freely from one medium to the next. Thus, there is no false memory *per se*: we constantly direct our attention to parcels of reality that are not necessarily sequential and can be experienced in alternate or simultaneous ways; or else, we capture someone else's experience as our own.

The mortals' outlook is unidirectional. Their morphology predisposes them to gaze at what's happening in front of them and consider an illusory present. If they see a forked road, they believe the choice is theirs only. The immortals see in all directions and remember both the past and the future, the two directional arrows on a circle. For an eternal being, the present has no reality, and neither does the notion of choice because the past not only affects future events but is also affected by them. The god-beings are in the image of the two-faced Janus: the child looking into the future, the man looking into the past, like the two towers of a pylon flanking the gate through which flows eternity.

The soul does not reincarnate because she is the cluster of memories attached to our one lifetime [α]. The spirit does not reincarnate because it is perpetually incarnated in time and space on multiple planes [4] [18]. Once the release of spirit from the bonds of matter is facilitated by a theurgist of the inner mysteries, the two become a god-being who preserves the individuality of that particular god-seed combination. Because incarnation is driven by necessity and our life conditioned by determinism, there is no such thing as moral sin. What separates the heirs of the divine from the rest is not moral superiority, but an advantage in understanding, options, and providential turns of events. Is there a mechanism then to ensure that more, if not all the souls, may be rescued? I did not explore the question because ultimately it is incumbent upon each individual to find their own salvation. I believe that once a god is reborn in aethereality, any cluster of human or animal memories (souls) can be liberated and drawn into this divine being through Desire. The liberated souls could be gathered by affinities and a common disposition for looking through the same window of apprehension while being cognizant of their own uniqueness. Was this trajectory perhaps suggested in the words of the Illuminationist philosopher Shihab al-Din al-Suhrawardi?

> For each individual soul, <u>or perhaps for several together</u>
> <u>having the same nature and affinity</u>, there is a being in
> the spiritual world which throughout their existence
> watches over this soul <u>and group of souls</u> with especial
> solicitude and tenderness, leads them to knowledge,
> protects, guides, defends, comforts them, leads them to
> victory; and this being is what they called Perfect
> Nature (the numinous self); This friend, defender and
> protector is what in religious terminology is called the
> Angel.[84] (Emphases and parentheses are mine)

Such is the marvel of necessity and the triumph of the sovereign Self: because of the heirs born out of the variations and multiplicity of existence, the rest of the creation may not be wasted. It is a design that would warrant the liberation of most souls.

---

[84] Henry Corbin, *The Man of Light in Iranian Sufism*, 1994

The Beyond

Who can claim knowing what lies beyond death? Many will try for dubious purposes, but no one has ever truly died to document the afterlife and come back to report on it. To be sure, near-death experiencers, visionary mystics, spiritualists, modern prophets, and those with an alleged direct line to "ascended masters" won't stop expounding on the heavenly landscape, but all in differing ways that suspiciously reflect their own time, mores, expectations, culture, religion, or preexisting notions. So, we cannot take their accounts at face value. There are as many conceptual variations on the Heavens as there are belief systems. Yet, the anticipation of an afterlife generally falls under two broad categories[85]:

1. The heavenly plane is a spectacular improvement on the lower plane (often with a hellish counterpart); a sumptuous replica of earthly existence, minus the aging, suffering, and evil but plus the moral exigencies and peculiars whims of one's god(s).

2. The beyond is a dissolution of the "ego" and a merging of one's consciousness with a supreme, non-dual consciousness frozen in eternal present—a return to amorphous oneness with an undefined, desireless, blissful absolute.

Frankly, none of the above holds any appeal to me. Both models beg the question of why it was necessary to fall from or leave a state of wholeness and perfection in the first place, but the answers they provide are half-baked and never conclusive.

---

[85] I do not mention reincarnation here because it is only a process of cyclical lives meant to lead to either one of the two basic models of afterlife.

The metaphysics of the sovereign self suggests an alternative: The god-beings (the coadunation of the soul (our memories) with her savior-twin (our numinous self) are the creators of their own realm. On the physical plane, the consciousness of matter perceives a world that conforms to our perception; the consciousness of aether will perceive a kingdom shaped by the sovereign Self's uncorrupted desires out of the dormant sea of *protoeidoi*. From that perspective, no two individuals can ever have the same experience of the beyond; it is as unique as each individuality. As Carl G. Jung puts it in his personal writings:

> *What is to come will be created in you and from you. Hence look into yourself. Do not compare, do not measure. No other way is like yours. All other ways deceive and tempt you. You must fulfill the way that is in you.* (The Red Book)

The self triumphant is truly sovereign.

If we posit any sort of afterlife, we must assume a consciousness, an enduring agency, and information. Like a computer program that can create anything we command on a screen from mere binary digits, the beyond then is information projected by the agent on the screen of consciousness. Hence, in gnostic lore the promised destination of the chosen is described in terms of reigning over one's own kingdom—a promising way to spend an eternity. Who isn't aware of the scriptural saying:

> *Truly I tell you ... unless you change and become like little children, you will never enter the kingdom of heaven.* (Matthew 18:3 BSB)

Children create the stories they want to be true and evoke their own fluid, endless myths in which they are the heroes, at once creators, actors, and audience. This remarkable ability is mostly lost in the adult who, as already stated, prefers to trust overly abstract concepts they do not even fathom, or else retreat into unimaginative and predictable expectations of an afterlife. To change and become like a child is to uncover one's spontaneity and earnestness and recover the eternal individuality that is sovereign over a unique, never-ending aethereality. Thus, according to the presocratic philosopher Heraclitus, eternity can be compared to a child at play (Heraclitus, fragment 52).

Jesus and the Bird Seller: an examination of C. Bloch's painting in view of the inner mystery of the savior-twin

Once familiarized with the mysteries of the inner savior as articulated in this book, one will be able to recognize patterns and elements in works of art and literature that reflect its tenets. In art as in literature, the original purpose of the author is often supplanted by a determination beyond his own mind. Artists are not always aware of the concealed meaning that infiltrates their creations from an autonomous creative impulse. For that reason, the creator is rarely the best interpreter of his own work. The task of uncovering a subtext, of unveiling the hidden, and of bringing to awareness buried motives and motifs falls to the esotericist. Such is the case for the particular piece we will now examine.

It is unlikely Bloch's intent was anything more than the artistic rendering of a classic, beloved episode of Christian lore. The scene shows Jesus at age 12 being questioned by rabbis in the temple of Jerusalem and is based on an incident from the Gospel of Luke:

> And it came to pass, that after three days they found him in the temple, sitting in the midst of the doctors, both hearing them, and asking them questions. And all that heard him were astonished at his understanding and answers. (2:46 KJV)

The subject is not remarkable, but the composition reveals some noteworthy details that illustrate the dynamics between the soul and her savior-twin personified by Jesus.

On the canvas, the boy Jesus is seen conversing with learned men in the temple that represents the human body (see John 2:19-21 and 1 Corinthians 6:19) and houses both soul and Spirit. The caged pigeon or dove in the bottom left corner is the only creature of the tableau to look directly at the viewer: it is our invitation to step into the painting and explore the secrets it might conceal. From the bird's cage, we follow a string on the floor to its end in the hand of a young bird seller sitting at a left angle at the bottom of a stairs. The boy's rather-suspicious gaze directs us to Joseph and Mary (recognizable by her iconic blue mantle) who, with her extended hands, leads us toward Jesus. Joseph and Mary are the largest figures on the canvas, representing the reach, power, and authority of the established Church as mediator between humankind and its redeemer. But they turn their back to the audience and move away from the viewer. This suggests that the mediation of the exoteric church has become obsolete. We must look for a less conspicuous, direct, esoteric link between the soul and her savior. Such a link is indeed manifest in the painting. The intensity of the light falls on the bird seller, confirming him as the central character to whom we ought to give our attention in the overall composition. He stands for the soul and, as child of the earth [3], his feet are firmly planted on the floor. There is an invisible axis we can trace from his spinal cord to that of Jesus who is sitting roughly at the same angle but to the right, on top of the stairs. Thus, the steps take us symbolically[86] from the earthly soul to her spiritual liberator. Indeed, Jesus here appears

---

[86] Stairways, ladders and trees recur in mystical imagery to symbolize the means to ascend to the god(s), or alternatively the conduit for god(s) and angels to enter the material realm.

nothing like a physical being, but as a somewhat frail, ghostly figure in semi-obscurity. He is precariously seated on the edge of his chair, as if suspended in air. With his feet hidden behind the diaphanous helm of his robe, he does not seem to be touching the ground. Jesus preaching in the physical temple is an allegory for the spiritual hierophant (see *Jesus, Thomas, and the disciples* in introduction) dispensing an inner initiation in the temple of the soul. From his lofty seat, he reaches down into the depths of matter. Hence, his presence is symbolically duplicated by the dove next to the child-soul (recall that the dove is a symbol for the Spirit; see logion 39). The dove is caged, signifying the imprisonment of the numinous self in the physical world. Yet, the soul has the keys to the release of her Liberator and Savior [46]. Thus, the bird seller holds in his hand a string to pull the hatch of the cage and let the bird out.

In conclusion, the unique episode captured by Bloch from the mythical childhood of Jesus portrays that moment in the soul's initiatic journey when she comes into the presence of her savior-twin (note that Jesus and the bird seller appear roughly of the same age; see also logia α and 5). I started my exploration of Bloch's painting with the white dove who in Christian iconography stands for the Holy Spirit. In some Gnostic and Cathar circles, that Holy Spirit was the guardian angel or spiritual twin of the soul, as well as her liberator. This Heavenly Twin however must first be awakened by the soul in order to liberate her. Through these metaphysical dynamics the soul and spirit become saviors unto each other. But until such liberating time arises, and the spiritual siblings can soar together to a higher realm, they remain caged birds, prisoners of the material world.

Eros and Christ: an iconographic correspondence

One of the main ideas I hope to have successfully developed in this book is that there cannot be any event physical or metaphysical without desire. Eros, the protogenos at the origin of all things [α], the uncreated generative Desire that pervades matter, is an esoteric variant of Christ, the word incarnate by whom all things are made (John 1:3 & Colossians 1:16). Both stand for the projection of the undivided divine in physicality, the numinous impetus in all human beings that manifests as the bestower of transcendent awareness, and the savior-to-be of the soul. Whereas many see Dionysos as a type of antecedent for Christ, a similar connection between the Christian savior and Eros has yet to be acknowledged.

In the art of classical antiquity dolphins and tortoises frequently appeared. They were associated with various gods and goddesses of the Mediterranean world. Dionysos and Eros are often represented riding a dolphin, the king of the fish (not until the 18th century would cetaceans be recognized as mammals, aquatic animals in a class on their own, apart from fish) that would turn into an enduring symbol of the Christian faith often in conjunction with the anchor or the cross. In the 1st century CE, the Roman emperor Titus (of the Flavian aristocratic family) chose as an emblem a dolphin twisted round an anchor, and that is where things get even more interesting. As they did with so many other pagan images, the early Christians appropriated the dolphin (or fish) and anchor (fig. 6) for a new symbolic purpose: to signify the divine presence. It is easy to see how the shape of the anchor would yield the two intersecting lines of the cross.

Figure 6.   **Figure 7.**
Illustration from *Nucleus*
emblematum selectissimorum
by Gabriel Rollenhagen, 1611.

Just as the anchor is lowered in the depth of water, the cross represents the seeding of the spirit (vertical axis) into matter (horizontal axis); at the intersection is the savior of the souls. Remarkably, a Roman marble from the 2nd century CE (fig. 7) shows Eros plunging into the sea, dragged by a serpentine dolphin (water symbolizes matter, and a serpentine creature stands for incarnation) entwined around his body. Thus is Christ the exoteric savior who descends into the world, whereas Eros is the esoteric Liberator ensconced in the depth of matter. Desire is the spiritual anchor of mankind.

Part Three

Be thine own Deus: Make self free,
    Liberal as the circling air:
Thy Thought to thee an Empire be;
    Break every prisoning lock and bar.

—Sir Richard Francis Burton,
Stanzas from the *Kasidah*

I must Create a System, or be enslav'd by another Mans
I will not Reason & Compare: my business is to Create

—William Blake,
Jerusalem: The Emanation of the Giant Albion

THE LEGACY OF THE WINDESWAISEN

Occult and Metaphysical Explorations

*S*o much the night unveils that is veiled by the glare of the day.

In the faint, metallic shine of the nocturnal lights, the child conjures ghostly forms out of the faded patterns of the window curtains and the arabesques on the tattered wallpaper: mythic heroes, chimeric monsters, giant insects, sailboats, hills and castles. She rises and tiptoes through the dormitory, following a moth who had detached itself from the fabric like a diminutive fairy flying off a leaf. All the other students are asleep. The child hears her name called thrice by the silence and ventures further down the unlit corridors of the boarding school to enter the deserted classroom. Sitting on the teacher's chair, facing the row of large awning windows, she stretches her legs and crosses her feet atop the desk to let the moonbeams play with her toes. Her gaze penetrates the improbable shapes in the schoolyard and pursues the scurrying, night-loving creatures until they vanish into their hidden sanctuaries. She befriends the silence, and the silence loves her.

* * *

My name is Theresa Klerr. I was born in Belgium from a Walloon mother and a German father. Following mom's premature death, we returned to Germany. I went from boarding school to boarding school until Father gave up his custodial rights entirely and handed me over to the care of the Rauhes Haus institution. At 16, I joined a movement under the guidance of a man whose ideas I will touch upon. His name was Jörg Theuderic Henny Wiencken, but for us he was always "Henny." We called ourselves the Windeswaisen.

At the time of my arrival, our little society was still very much an all-boys club, but our founder had already begun a shift to a mixed following. Our early focus was on youth *randonnées*, esoteric instruction, and a lifestyle modelled after turn-of-the-century Lebensreform.

The Windeswaisen eventually ran afoul of the East-German authorities who saw Wiencken's educational ideas as a threat to the Marxist aims. Henny was prosecuted on trumped-up charges and imprisoned after a sham trial. His early writings were destroyed by the Stasi. Thanks to his old connections in the party's establishment though, he was able to secure his release and leave the country. He changed his legal name and moved to Corsica where he established a small, transient community. Following the rhythm of the seasons, we would spend four months respectively on the South-East coast, in the mountains, and on the South-West coast. In those years the spiritual father of our small tribe also adopted the nom de plume Sen Nefer Ka Ra (hereafter abbreviated as S.N.K.R.), which he used for the rest of his life in his self-published pamphlets and brochures and in his personal correspondences. Our group survived until Henny's death. By then, we had already become an oddity for a system that was no longer interested in communal experiments. Never again will there be a community of the Windeswaisen. The bond we shared quickly dissolved into internecine strife and petty rivalries. Human nature regained its own. There were only a handful of us left anyway, and each went his or her own way. I alone remain a little longer to pass on the true legacy of the Windeswaisen to whomever I please.

I never had visions, never spoke in tongues, communicated with angels, let alone channeled a mythic "ascended master."

Perhaps the most significant transformative experience I had in my life occurred when I was about 10 or 11—a sort of dream wide awake (or else a mini psychotic episode):

Upon waking up one morning, I thought it necessary to thank my roommates for helping me find the solution to a math problem the day before. I was very happy that the teacher had validated a job well done. The real problem though wasn't mathematical, it was that none of that which I recalled ever took place (or maybe it did for me but not for the others). Yet, my conviction was absolute, and the consternation of my entourage was met with mine. I couldn't understand why they would not remember anything I knew they knew, and vehemently protested their worries and insistent inquiries about my wellbeing. I wasn't ill; I felt great, in fact. Nevertheless, I was persuaded to rest more, and when I awoke anew, the entire illusion had vanished. I did my best to reassure my friends who were somewhat agitated, telling them that everything was normal now, even if I didn't know what had gotten into me. They soon dismissed and forgot the incident with the amazing faculty children have to quickly brush away that which would have triggered a longer state of panic in hardened adults. The memory of that curious matter stayed with me however, and I often wondered how a bit of my life could appear so solid when it had no reality. Our lives are but strands of memories; which ones are real? Could an entire life be but a dream?

I gained a lot from this unusual occurrence that would shape my understanding of the world and our existence: we only cognize our perceptions, which controls what we are and what we "see." And if I never again trusted my eyes or my recollections completely, it gave me all the more reason not to swallow whole the perceptions others sought to impose on me. Throughout my long association with S.N.K.R., I held him in high esteem because he never dealt in rigid belief systems, naïve faith, or absolute convictions. Neither did he ever say or suggest that we should accept what he told us uncritically. Instead, he emphasized the value of a personal myth, and what he called "inner evocation":

"We and the universe are constantly evoked and remembered," he told us, "and through the evocation and the remembering, we can fathom the entirety. Make it your effort daily to call forth from your center that which no one before has ever beheld within or without. Your liberation lies in the inner evocation of the means of liberation and the manifestation of your liberator. All religions without exception originated as a myth in someone's head. All civilizations were built on true fallacies. Religion shapes cultures, and cultures shape societies. No society was ever formed in a vacuum of beliefs. The societal beliefs we accept collectively are stamped on our individual psyche to ensure our compliance and conformity. Doesn't it stand to reason that one should know himself through his own myth rather than that of others?" Fears, guilt, shame, responsibilities, duties, obligations; the myths imposed on us are reflected in the dreaming. No wonder our dreams are so chaotic, eerie, and threatening. When that which you dream in the night harmonizes with the myth you have created for yourself in the day, you will know you have crossed the threshold of true freedom."

ESOTERIC PRAXIS & MODALITIES

S.N.K.R. did not think much of the various systems of enlightenment that seem to multiply with each passing generation. Nor did he have kind words for their promulgators and followers alike:

"Puffed-up frauds relish the spotlight not to clarify but to mystify and dazzle with their pretense. As for their admirers who are being fed crumbs, when they develop psychosomatic symptoms, they think they are enlightened. Fools everywhere expect they can speak of the genuine stuff that has taken saints a lifetime of unpublicized abnegation to barely glimpse. They go around flaunting their nouveau spiritual status, but their conceited speech betrays that far from being enlightened, they are overtaken by a devotional delusion of grandeur. When they see themselves climbing the ladder of God-realization and consciousness expansion, I see them stepping further down the stairs of self-absorption. They may feel blissful but can never grow the soul of the virtuous mystic who has learned more from life's suffering than from tricks of the mind."

"The inexpressible will always seek you more intently than you can ever seek the inexpressible," he taught, "and everything you might do to commune with your god is inevitably marred by the flaws and perils inherent to that which is manmade. The primal field of creation is amorphous and impersonal, but the divinity is polymorphous and personal. Fundamentally, there is no imperative for anyone to strive for the numinous as there isn't a need for the fish to find the sea that has already found the fish. We are parts of the unsoundable ocean. Like the creatures yielding to the powerful marine currents or the lover abandoning himself to the passion of the beloved, the empyreal destiny of man lies in surrendering himself entirely to the supernal breath, the divine pneuma that is at the origin of all things existing."

Still, humans have a compulsion for the assurance of being guided in the right direction. Moreover, the souls most touched by the divinity in turn thirst most for the divine, yearning to fling open the doors that seemingly separate them from the object of their affection. S.N.K.R. showed us a safe, adaptable praxis to center our pious longings and devotions properly. At the same time, he constantly warned against the politics of beliefs and the dangers of falling for profound sounding, but empty rhetoric.

"The caveats," he reminded us, "are first to be mindful that there is no perfect spiritual discipline, and then to avoid mistaking the means for the ends. Do not pick mind-body practices because of their popularity or trumpeted superiority. Follow the affinities of your heart; listen to the god-becoming in the center of your being. It is tedious to hear enthusiasts haughtily lauding their particular methods like door-to-door salesmen touting their ware with a daunting, specialized jargon. Unlike the salesman though, they take themselves very seriously, not realizing they have become prisoners of that which was meant to set them free. There will always be individuals who unconsciously make themselves feel superior by making others feel inferior."

The Shield & the Sword

> *O people saved by the Lord, the shield of thy help,*
> *and ... the sword of thy excellency!*

Two symbols were reoccurring significantly in the esoteric knowledge S.N.K.R. passed on to his students over the nearly eighty years he taught and inspired with the same lucidity that was his gift to the end:

"A warrior needs both a sword and a shield to triumph in the battle. Used singly, they are lacking; together, they work in harmony. The two artifacts—one offensive, the other defensive—complete one another. There was a time when armament was more than an impersonal, bland means for destruction and murderous aims. Some weapons were once considered an extension of the human body and of the mind; they could also be ascribed magical properties or mystical qualities. Rigorous and aesthetic disciplines were developed based on the use of the javelin, the sword, and the bow that were efficacious training in times of war but also mental and spiritual exercises during peaceful days."

The Sword

The blade of the sword is phallic and masculine. The hilt, however, came to assume the shape of the ovary (the cross-guard being in the similitude of the fallopian tubes) coincidentally with the growth of Marian devotion, and later, the development of courtly love, when the religious consciousness of the West was enriched anew by the feminine mystical attributes. The masculine and feminine thrusts must come together to perpetuate man's meta-physical evolution. Hence, the hilt of the sword is also an image of the phallus (represented by the grip of the sword designed to be hand-held) penetrating the vulva (the sword's pommel).

When the sword pointing upward is superimposed to the human figure, the hilt overlays the genitals while the blade matches the rising of the divine pneuma, of which the sexual impulse is a physical expression. On many medieval sarcophagi, the knight's sword figures resting on his body in the reverse position—pointing downward—to indicate the return of the supernal breath to the earth.

The Shield

The round shield represents the integration of masculine and feminine aspects (sun and earth), wholeness, and endlessness. On the forearm of Abrasax (the quintessential, liminal god of the Basilidians, who personifies at once the sky and earth forms of the divinity), the shield stands for the sun. Athena, the manifestation of divine wisdom, is shown carrying a shield on her own to signify the power of her protection. Throughout the bible, the same device symbolizes God's presence and protection: "Fear not, I am thy shield," was told Abraham in a vision.

The Breathing Light Contemplation

Every day at dawn, and before physical culture, the Windeswaisen greeted the reborn sun by performing twelve times (outdoors if weather permitted) the *Opening of the Rose*, a practice based on the first three poses of the *Sūrya Namaskār*. Since nothing among us was mandatory except chores and thoughtful etiquette, the participants were often limited to the early birds.

S.N.K.R. also showed those of us who were interested an esoteric, contemplative practice he would supervise. He told us it was in usage among the adherents of a medieval mystical brotherhood.

We did the breathing light contemplation generally in the morning (when we were alert and less likely to fall asleep), lying on our back. We placed our hands to rest lightly on each side of the groin, palms flat, fingertips just over the inguinal ligaments. Each of our arms thus formed an arc to enclose a roughly circular space above the torso and abdomen. Next, we would imagine our body sinking in the ground and concentrate on its being progressively overtaken by numbness as if it were petrified. Then, directing our attention to the sole of the feet, we made ourselves feel a dull tingling coursing upward through the legs to create a psychosomatic sensation of the divine pneuma drawn from the earth, penetrating our body through the feet. The supernal breath infused the planet at the moment of creation and subsequently rose in all living things like the morning dew. "Therefore God give thee of the dew of heaven," we read in the book of Genesis. The supernal breath is especially concentrated in water and the bodily fluids and finds expression both in the sexual impulse and a transformative thrust toward godhood. (Hence it is often allegorized in myths as a great river of life, from which one tributary runs in every earthling.) In the loins, it turns into a dynamic center that we would visualize as a swirling vortex between our two hands, brushing the fingertips.

Now we visualized a fiery sword with its hilt superimposed on the loins to represent the creative energy flowing higher up toward the breast. The glowing blade is the path taken by the supernal breath as an elevation of the sex drive into a longing for the god-becoming in us. The strange experience of emptiness and forlornness following an orgasm is the result of a sudden drop of the divine pneuma, a diminution of the *devenir dans l'être* [1] that translates into a feeling of remoteness from the beloved.

The book of Genesis describes how God "placed at the east of the garden of Eden Cherubims, and a flaming sword which turned every way, to keep the way of the tree of life." The metaphor tells how Adam who was made in the image of God (His projection on Earth) is bound to follow the flaming sword (the path of the divine pneuma) to reach the tree of life (immortality) in the garden (the heart) where he will be joined to Eve (the soul). The soul Eve came out of Adam (Genesis 2:23), and to Adam she must return to be whole again (Genesis 2:24). S. N. K. R. explained that the figurative dwelling of the soul is the head from which she descends to the heart—the metaphorical garden—while the supernal breath ascends to it.

The double arcs formed by the participant's arms opened two pathways to draw up the divine pneuma from the pelvic nexus and move it around the direct path of the flaming sword. Thus, we created a larger dynamic center in the shape of a blazing shield poised above the thorax, abdomen, and pelvis, increasing the flow of the supernal breath drawn through the body. "The Lord is my strength and my shield; my heart trusted in him, and I am helped," sang the Psalmist.

---

[1] "Becoming into being." But the English translation somewhat fails to convey the subtle nuance of the French in this case.

The luminous shield is the ingress to the kingdom within.[2] In our contemplation, we imagined ourselves collapsing inwardly and falling through this portal as if swallowed by a gaping chasm of shimmering hues of blue light to meet the god-becoming in the innermost. This is the inhaling of the soul associated with the color blue: the ground stratum of the practice, the purpose of which was to fix in our mind the idea that the actualization of the god-like is an inner process.

The higher stratum of the contemplation consisted in the reverse process by mentally observing a mist of living amber hues egressing through the shield like the rays of the rising sun. This is the exhaling (releasing) of the god-like. If the diaphanous effusion were to take the form that most inflames the passion of the soul, we had to remember that the god-like should always be apprehended internally (the reason we kept our eyes closed). Any manifestation, no matter how glorious, apprehended on the physical plane and through the senses is bound to be the projection of an involuntary, emotional, and potentially highly deceptive construct.

Having followed Henny and the Windeswaisen for the longest time, I knew he oversaw among us a smaller, secretive group of like-minded fellows to which I was never invited. Over the years I felt increasingly frustrated he never mentioned anything to me even though he considered me his closest associate. Eventually, I confronted him. His answer was illuminating if

---

[2] One of the most striking, visual renditions of this mystical portal appears in Hieronymus Bosch's famous *Ascent of the Blessed into the Empyrean*.

not completely satisfying. He said there were many gates and doors to the same mansion:

"I opened the front door to everyone, and what I showed openly is sufficient for all of us. But not everybody is the same, and a few may prefer to enter through the garden door. They know who they are, and it isn't a question of elitism. Furthermore, I can only speak of what I know, and women have mysteries of their own which can only be explicated among themselves."

As far as the *compagnons du beau sang* (as they called themselves) were concerned, there wasn't much I could extract from Henny's silence.

They had had a polytheistic outlook and six grades of initiation. The first and second were performed respectively under the aegis of Pan and Dionysus, the breakers of worldly rules and conventions. The third centered around a curious artifact called the Priapus gallinaceus, a bronze bust that shows a rooster's head supported by the neck and shoulders of a man and inscribed at the bottom with the words "Savior of the world" in Greek. The oddity of this strange idol is in having an erect human penis substituted for the bird's beak. S.N.K.R. insisted the object was an original and that the same was once used ritualistically by a secretive faction of the Knights Templar. Hence the accusations leveled against the mystic warrior monks of worshiping an idol's head and of sexual proclivities. Henny explained to me that the phallus represented the penetration of Earth by the masculine principle, and that the rooster signified the rise of the sun of salvation.

Rituals in the fourth grade called on the triad of Serapis as the father, Isis as the mother, and Harpocrates as the divine child. Henny explained to me that Serapis the sun is an embodiment of the numinous impulse, the creative and vital force; Isis the moon represents the soul. They are the two inseparable aspects of divinity that are utterly dependent on each other and cannot remain alone. Together, they are represented by a single aspect, the child born of their union: heru pa khered who was further amalgamated as Eros-Harpocrates, the guiding principle or daimon.

The final fifth and sixth grades featured the rites of Attis. They distinguished between Attis-Mên and Attis-Christ: the former humanly divine and lunar; the latter divinely human and solar. Thus, they seemed to have taught a way of self-divinization. Henny mentioned that many ancient gods, such as Isis and Osiris started as daimons in the consciousness of men before they were regarded as gods, which suggested a theurgical path to deification for the humans through the agency of one's personal daimon.

A couple of months before he was taken from us, and perhaps sensing the impending demise of the Windeswaisen, Henny finally revealed to me the secrets of the *compagnons*. However, he insisted that his efforts to revive the antecedent order would die with him and that the said order was no longer on Earth but had been "spiritualized." On the other hand, he promised to refer me to an acquaintance of his, the leader of an all-woman order on the southern coast of France that harked back to the High Middle Ages and preserved an even older gnostic tradition.

* * *

Dear Dominique.

By the time my mentor and I reconnected, she was performing the "Opening of the Rose" (also called "the Shield and the Vessel") facing the moon. It doesn't matter though whether you undertake your practice facing any of the luminaries or cardinal directions. (Ms. Clare associated herself with the cult of the Black Madona, a permutation of Isis whose symbols were both the sun and the moon.) What is important is that you understand its significance in relation to everything I have transmitted to you so far. If you can do so, then you will know how and why the "Opening of the Rose" can be beneficial to you. It is an oversimplification to say that this holy invocation is based on the *Sūrya Namaskār*. Yes, the poses are roughly similar, but they are found in many ancient cultures worldwide as physical expressions of worship and theurgy. I will go into detail the next time I see you in person. What follows is a brief outline of the essential steps on how to proceed.

You begin standing with your feet slightly apart, your chest expanded, your shoulders relaxed, and your palms pressed together in a praying gesture just above the solar plexus, your thumbs aligned with the sternum. You will recognize the similarity to the praying hands of medieval knight's effigy tombs as the posture is one of piety, imploration, and protection, marking the gateway to the heart.

Call on your *shield* (mentally or in a whisper).

Next, raise your hands above your head, opening your arms to form roughly a U or V like the shape of a vessel—the Holy Grail. Your back will arch naturally, but there is no need to bend backward exaggeratedly. It is the posture of the famed "Praying Boy" (the exquisite bronze sculpture from ancient Rhodes), associated with prayer in pagan antiquity and transformed into a sacramental gesture by early Christians. You will also see it depicted by turn-of-the-century Germanic pagan revival artists.

Call on your *vessel*.

Then, lower your arms again, bend downward from the waist, and reach for the ground with your hands. There is no need to lock your knees. From there unfold your body, rolling your spine up, to return to step one and two. Simply return to step one when finishing the series. All movements should be done slowly, in a relaxed, comfortable way. Breathe naturally throughout. Let your breathing find its rhythm. You can repeat the movements as many times as you like (I do the series twelve times). Step three represents the descent of spirit into matter while step two symbolizes the soul transported to the empyrean. Further symbolism you will discover on your own with practice, as well as the magical import of the invocation.

The Garden of Silence

The point in contemplation is not to empty the mind as much as to replace the useless with what's beneficent and, patiently, let the god-presence fill the heart and longings, indeed one's whole being, with a holy thrust—the *devenir dans l'être*. Only monks and nuns have the benefit of spending most of their time lost in uplifting contemplation; the rest of us must contend with the perpetual assaults of the material world in which we move, often at a hectic pace. The bulk of our thoughts is useless chatter that keeps us distracted and immersed in the lower plane of existence. But we can build a bridge over the river of mental noise to reach the god-becoming. That bridge is also a garden.

A "numinous absorption," said S.N.K.R., "can be developed wherever you are and even throughout the multiple exigencies of everyday life. You would remember from the book of genesis that the god of the world created a garden where he placed Adam. That garden was a place of artifice to lure the soul in the same way abyssal creatures lure their prey with a bioluminescent appendage. You however have the ability to grow and cultivate an inner garden of silence, where your god will walk as the demiurge once walked in the physical Eden. The silence of the mind is not emptiness but the luxuriance that replaces invasive thoughts. The god-becoming lives in the center of your being, and to hear the god-becoming, the within must be silent. The silence is both the missive that carries the weight of our longings and a vessel that pours in your veins a new, spiritual blood like the life-giving rain released from the cloud to penetrate the parched soil. It underprops your bond to the *devenir dans l'être* until the fullness of the god-presence is manifested. You can evoke that fullness with an image, a word, or a pithy prayer. When you are overwhelmed with thoughts, just seeing the image in your mind, or saying the word(s) mentally will vanquish the distraction and take you back to the angelic presence in the garden. Those are tools only that must not interfere with the natural growth of the garden. The tools are primarily to tend the good seed and get rid of the bad. Sometimes, you will hear the word spontaneously, or an inner vision may appear on its own to call you back to the garden of silence, and with practice, you will be able to spend more time in that holy place.

"Few if any spiritual seekers or worshipers understand that the intent of all religious exercises is not to take in but to give in. In his misguided endeavors, many a spiritually minded individual will attempt to obtain a godly favor, a blessing, a healing, a message, or an acknowledgement of some sort. The irreproachable heart knows that by giving himself entirely to the god-becoming within, that holy presence will become his savior, and all else that is expedient will flow accordingly without having to ask. Such is the hidden meaning for the legend of the three wise kings who offered their most precious gifts to the Holy Infant.

"When we tend the garden of silence, our attention shifts from mundane preoccupations to an awareness of the holy presence. The expanding, rising awareness in turn brings progressive peace and solace to the mind while heightening the communion of the soul with the god-becoming. The decisions and choices we make are gradually taken over by the unclouded will of the god-like instead of being the mere product of a conditioned mind's automatic processes. In that heightened state, there is no longer a necessity or the worry to live one's life, because the true life is lived through you, and becoming yields to being.

"The garden of silence is a gift to your god and the place of your liberation."

Numinous Absorption

S.N.K.R. did not like to speak of techniques, methods, or systems. He thought the terms were restrictive and binding and carried the risk of turning spiritual practices into ends in themselves. He did not want to have us bound to any discipline and miss the forest for the trees. His purpose was to help us develop our own ways to connect with the god-presence within ourselves. Because everyone is different, he showed us alternative forms of contemplations to suit everyone's preferences.

"Prayers, yoga, meditation are only tools to open a channel of transference with the numinous and to keep in good condition a pathway of symbiosis."

He always encouraged us to be creative on our personal journey to theosis.

"All religious rituals, spiritual paths, mystical practices, and philosophies without exception started with one individual before spreading to others. There is no reason you could not or should not be that person at the origin of your own means of inner discovery and transformation."

Often, we would just lie on the grass, peering at the tips of the highest branches of trees. The gently waiving of the upmost parts of a foliage crown on the background of the vast sky induces a near-hypnotic trance that ought to be experienced, and a feeling of being detached from physical reality.

S.N.K.R. thought trees were in the likeness of the soul striving to know a higher world.

"From the moment a sapling pierces the earthly crust of the forest, it is governed by one imperative only: to search for the source of light and reach the vastness of the sky; to defy gravity and extend its limbs away from the material surface. Such should be the strivings of human beings, instead of being content to crawl on the ground of materialism."

For me, the most pleasant and revealing experiences occurred while doing the "mirror contemplation." We had built a small room entirely walled with mirrors, including ceiling and floor. Only one person could be admitted inside at a time. The spare furnishing consisted of a chair and a source of light. The procedure was straightforward: we just sat and gazed in absolute silence into the multiplicity of one's reflections duplicating themselves without ends, repeating the central image infinitely. The powerful effect it had on me was to reveal the breaking of reality into a myriad of coexisting, alternate planes of existence and the opening of a passageway into timelessness and nonlocality. With repetition, I acquired the otherworldly perception of simultaneous lives with versions and variations of myself.

S.N.K.R.'s Views on Psychedelics

Having lived through the heydays of experimentation with psychedelics, S.N.K.R. had many reservations concerning the use of so-called mind-altering substances. He looked favorably on their promising therapeutic benefits and was well disposed toward the occasional creative boost they could provide. He was also highly critical of their usage to induce alternate states he thought would become ends in themselves and might be misleading. "Once the 'doors of perception,' are open" he commented, "one eventually finds himself into hallucinogenic cul-de-sacs."

"Far from awakening the subject to a 'truer reality,' psychoactive substances open a pandora box of highly subjective imprints that can make almost anything pass for universal truth though it is marred by spiritual baggage and a preexisting framework. Indeed, subjects who experiment in the exact same circumstances have vastly different takeaways, which suggests that the mind is still actively tailoring their experience.

"The use of psychoactive substances has its origin in shamanism and the ancient priesthoods. Shamanism did not originate in a search for the god of light, harmony, and love; its roots are in the worship of the violent sky gods, the chthonic deities, and the untrustworthy denizen of the spirit world. The Shamans and the priests were once intercessors between the suppliants and supernatural beings; they were the ones who ingested or inhaled substances, not those for whom they interceded. But the modern man no longer has an appetite for intercessors; he wants the shamanic experience for himself. Without the excruciating years of preparation—often involving pain rituals—endured by those whose calling was to reach the other world for the benefit of the living, the spiritual tourists casually open a gate to outcomes they do not have the capability to discriminate or modulate. Don't they know that the same powers from which they are seeking guidance and elation were also raised in cultures that favored human sacrifices (including children) or worked their warriors into hallucinogenic frenzy to make them formidable killing machines?

"No chemicals can ever liberate the soul from matter since they are a product of matter. You will not taste the numinosity of the eternal world by eating the fruits of the ephemeral one. The blissful oneness and cosmic epiphanies experienced under the influence of mind-altering stimulants do not loose the bonds of the cosmos; they tighten them.

"Psychedelics have never, in no instance, provided a coherent answer to a profound metaphysical question; they only offer sensations and muddled, banal notions of infinite love or oneness. The solutions to the riddles of existence, until now, are still the exclusive domain of philosophy and mysticism. The province of the psychedelics is the un-processing mind. But there is a reason that corner of the mind is hiding things from us: it is nature's way to protect our psyche. Nature does not do anything haphazardly, and to undo her mechanisms is to play with fire. Not everything should be brought into full awareness. For all the publicized, cheery reports of 'mind-blowing trips,' there is an equal number of hushed 'bad trips,' and many, mostly unreported psychotic incidents of terrifying delirium and dangerously amplified emotions.

"A theurgic pharmacology is nearly always introduced in the decadent phase of a cult when external circumstances— social or environmental—had made it more difficult to reach sacred epiphanies by other means. In time, intoxicants became the preferred method of inducing visionary and auditory hallucinations for the ease and speed with which they trigger intense experiences. Unsurprisingly, some individuals hooked on the psychical gratification seek to renew its effects frequently. Psychedelics are quickly becoming a shortcut for the spiritual thrill-seekers and those too lazy to tread the long road of numinous illumination.

"Every generation it seems 'discovers' a choice drug thought to be a transformative philosopher's stone. In the 19th century, Théophile Gautier founded the *club des hachichins*, opening a venue for a circle of artists and intellectual luminaries to experiment with opium and hashish. The results were underwhelming, and Gautier was no fool. He soon renounced his forays into mind-altering substances and announced:

317

*Le vrai littérateur n'a besoin que de ses rêves naturels,
et il n'aime pas que sa pensée subisse l'influence d'un
agent quelconque.*[3]

The same truth, I say, applies to the authentic spiritual
searcher.

---

[3] *The genuine creator of literature only needs his natural dreams, and
he does not like his mind to be under the influence of any other agent.*

ESOTERIC PRECEPTS & PRINCIPLES

Axioms

1. because the dreamer dreams, the observer observes and the thinker thinks there is something and not nothing.
2. because no thing can proceed without a mover there was always something and never nothing.
3. because the nothing has no reality, the thingness does not proceed from nothingness, and therefore the primal mover must proceed from itself.
4. because the primal mover proceeds from itself, the beginning and end of thingness is in the primal mover.
5. because there is no beginning, and no end apart from the primal mover, everything has always been, and everything that happens has already happened.
6. because everything has already happened, the dreamer, the observer, and the thinker are not self-willed, nor were they ever created. They are only moving shapes in the juggling of necessity.

Hate & Love

The underlying cause of the hate so conspicuous in human nature is the survival instinct that adapted to operate underground, so to speak, when it was no longer needed on the surface. Therefore is humankind more hate than love although we remain blind to the fact and continue to stick to the illusion that we can always choose love over hate. To say so, however, is tantamount to claiming we have successfully excised the reptilian brain from our biological makeup, and it doesn't take a scientist to know it isn't so. Automatic responses almost always overpower the rational mind. Hate is real, easy to fathom; love is a human abstraction, a concept so vague we need to expound it ad infinitum. There is only one valid way to elide hate and relate appropriately to our fellow humans and this temporary world: in surrendering our soul to the god-presence in the center of our being we loosen the grip of the mind's automatic processes and let the divine self take over our functions and individuality.

The Metaphysical Eros

There was considerable latitude and laissez faire among the Windeswaisen with regard to sexual mores. Henny thought that the less we tinker with a natural process, the less we risk derailing it, and that the danger of too much control over individual sexualities far exceeds the risk of too little oversight. He was especially disdainful of taboos, religious strictures, and legislated morality. By and large, the fewer the rules, the more harmonious life was for our group, and I daresay we fared much better than similar communities before and during our days. Perhaps it was because our mentor did not just admit anyone among us and was characteristically prudent in his selection of new members. Still, he was well *au fait* with issues inherent to human nature whenever and wherever sex is involved. Instead of focusing exaggeratedly on the sexuality of the flesh though, he constantly sought to bring back our attention to what he called the metaphysical Eros.

"At all times and in all things, you ought to hold in your mind the realization that everything you perceive and feel is experienced behind the bars of an invisible prison. This is true for what's pleasurable as well. Always remind yourself that you are a vagabond spirit temporarily trapped in a human being. You must tend to the needs of the vagabond before you tend his prison."

Henny said it was a great mistake to pair sex with romantic attachment on the physical plane of becoming because love as a romantic ideal to which humankind aspire is not attainable in this world but in the divine abode, the realm of true being: a love that is only delight and vibrancy, unburden by human nature and frailty—the grail sung by the medieval troubadours.

Friendship in Henny's views is the basis of the best relationships and the most natural outlet for human erotic impulses here on Earth, while abstract notions about love and no practical consideration only lead to failure, great disappointments, or heartaches. He liked to misquote Goethe deliberately with a wordplay, quipping that "Marriage is the beginning and end of civilization." He also conceded that often, one must adapt *bon gré, mal gré* to the circumstances and demands of society and remain discreet, judicious, and wise if endeavoring to do something that isn't culturally tolerated.

In the last few decades of his life, Henny himself seemed to have been abstinent. He explained to me that he had ample opportunities in his youth to experiment playfully and joyfully, and that he had now moved to something larger. He furthered his view by suggesting that there are two sexual currents stemming from the tide of creation: one that gratifies the flesh and fulfill the demands of reproduction but never seems to satisfy the longings of the soul, the other that never cloys and leads the soul to the heights of creativity and ecstasy. The latter, he added, is the metaphysical Eros. The more we strive to elevate the soul through our sexuality, the less likely we are to fall for toxic, destructive forms of sexual behaviors. And the closer we come to emulate the metaphysical Eros, the more harmonious will the bents of our libido become regardless of societal conventions. He remarked that mystics in all ages struggled to transcend the sexual impulse only to end up expressing the inexpressible with erotically charged metaphors and that the height of religious bliss is an erotic apprehension.

"The most sublime side of sexuality can never be attained in the flesh," he said, and "only those who spare their most intense longings for the numinous presence in their heart will be bound to their god by an infinite Desire. It is that passion that enables the seeing and feeling of that which was hitherto invisible."

Henny was a firm believer in panspermia, the idea that the cosmos came about through an act of a sexual nature and that the diversity and multiplicity of physical creations are the result of dispersed divine *spermata*. Under his pseudonym Sen Nefer Ka Ra, he wrote that the ubiquitous, antecedent phallic worships were at the foundation of all mythologies and theologies as well as the source of most religious symbolism.

"Apotropaic, exaggerated representations of sexual organs were once widespread and continued to appear inconspicuously on the stone motifs of Gothic architecture; the basic shapes of genitals are preserved in the Christian symbols of the cross (masculine) and the fish (the *vesica piscis*—feminine). The rose and the heart, which both represent desire and passion, are especially prevalent in mystical and esoteric symbology. Indeed, 'rose' is an anagram or 'eros' in German, French, and English. The serpent, the omnipresent creature that slithers through religious lore worldwide, suggests the powers of generation, and regeneration, the forces of desire and destruction.

"The divine is the source, its desire the thrust, its seed the flowing brook. The same proto-Indo-European root *sper-* (meaning 'to strew') is found both in *speak* and *sperm*. In Christology, the divine utterance made all things visible and spurted on the physical plane as God incarnate. Likewise, the Egyptian creator gods scattered their seminal fluid to bring forth the cosmos, and the lesser divinities. They were imitated by the Pharaoh who publicly masturbated and ejaculated in the Nile River to perpetuate the bounties of its waters for the inhabitants of the land. The Egyptian ruler's performance was not solely a blessing upon the Earth though. Because the Nile was the terrestrial counterpart of the heavenly river of life, and because the Pharaoh was the embodiment of the divine, the seeding of the waters was the reenacting of a cosmic event. *As above, so below.* In different contexts, authentic Tantra practitioners and some Gnostics sects advocated the ingestion of sexual fluids as a mean to liberate the divine essence.

"The creation was never planned in the mind of a demiurge, never willed in the heart of heavens; it is the outgrowth of a seed, like the child born out of a night of passion between two lovers. The deep forlornness that consistently follows the pleasure we derive from carnal intimacy is an indication that what we desperately seek in romantic attachments we will inevitably fail to find with our mortal partners. No intensity of romance, amount of lovemaking, or diversity in erotic exploration can ever fulfill our most profound yearning. The same equal emptiness will always meet our constant return to the gratification of amorous games, promises, and relationships. The refusal to suffer the absence makes it impossible to know the presence. Tending to the spiritual fire within should supersede satisfying the earthly appetites, or else the latter should be a means to the former. Earthly sexuality is but a meager substitute and a tattered shroud for a transcendent erotic consummation more delightful than anything known in the physical world. The ecstatic rapture of the metaphysical Eros is found only by those who embrace the god-becoming in the center of their being."

Governing the Ungovernable

The first victim of history is the truth. History can never be objective because it always implies a projection of contemporary thinking onto our reading of a past we did not and will never experience. The more we probe the past, the less we learn from it; the more we interpret this and that moment in time, the less we notice the patterns that cripple humanity.

Whenever and wherever human beings assemble, a power structure immediately takes shape. Our polities, just like our religions, have been dominated since the dawn of time by the double parental influence of the archetypal sky-father and earth-mother. Small bands of hunter gatherers faced by a harsh, dangerous environment may have been led by the stronger male, following a structure not dissimilar to that of the wild packs of wolves they often encountered. Different forms of consensus and soft leadership probably suited clans whose need for collective and individual decisions were limited and mostly concerned with survival. Larger communities with more complex social and economic challenges developed hierarchies of power. Urban centers often necessitated a king at the head of a large administrative structure while feudalism functioned adequately for sparser populations. With each new circumstance the government adapted, evolved, or reinvented itself until the exponential growth of populations and industrialization far outpaced our ability to match the prodigious complexity of modern societies with effective forms of management. We simply ran out of ideas. Truth be told, the level of intricacy in our 20th century civilization is a juggernaut that can no longer be managed. The servant of the house has grown into a titan threatening to swallow us.

All organizations that make use of an enforcement agency are inherently oppressive. All political regimes are flawed and ultimately inefficient in fulfilling their stated aims because the nature of humans is to take advantage of human nature, and there are too many humans. Consensus is no longer possible because there will always be well-intentioned (or nefarious) voices rising louder than the others to muffle them, as we can observe plainly in the political discourse and praxis.

Anarchy never accounted for mankind's unsound disposition, relying instead on the dubious notion of man's innate goodness and goodwill. But we would not expect a pack of wolves to function without hierarchy, and we are not remotely different from wolves.[4]

---

[4] Unsurprisingly, the wolf was the first domesticated animal—perhaps as early as 40,000 years ago, and certainly because we have so much in common.

The power of belief has always been greater than that of logic. Our brain somehow is wired to respond to belief more readily than it would strive to use logic. That is why no measure of educating or re-educating (which more often than not amounts to brainwashing anyway) can make someone accept what he has decided not to believe.

Never has a revolution truly benefited the vulnerable and the powerless in the long run. They just substitute a new elite for the old one, sometimes with a short intercession of mob rule, the only merit of which is to settle accounts and repay violence with violence. Hannah Arendt said it well: "Revolutionaries do not make revolutions. The revolutionaries are those who know when power is lying in the street and then they can pick it up."

Democracies are ships of fools with each and every one attempting to steer the boat in a different direction. When the fools choose representatives among themselves to sort things out, they have a republic. Rare are the elected representatives who make their case on the naked strength of their ideas; most would sooner rely on populist, simplistic ideas, personal charisma, or the gifts they have for duplicity, the manipulation of mass consciousness, and the use of disinformation and propaganda.[5] In fact, the best way to subvert a democracy is to use the tools of democracy. Cesar, Napoleon, and Hitler rose to power by means of an electorate and the support of a majority of their people. Demagoguery has its roots in representational systems. Once in command, policymakers can hardly resist the compulsion of staying in a position of authority from which they

---

[5] Nowadays, the phenomenon is compounded by the pervasive impact of the internet with its ubiquitous forums and social media that cater to the unreflective mind, inflaming emotions instead of fostering logic.

frequently derive personal advantages. They make themselves easy prey to corruption and a sway of influences from powerful entities, all the while deluding themselves into thinking they represent the will of the people. The idea that the state should be constituted by the will of its people is simply anti-natural because:

1. such organizational formulation is never found among social animals.

2. the will of the people can never be one, and therefore a government by the people is doomed by virtue of its factionalism.

Democracies thrived in the industrial age, powered by the single idea of freedom with which it has deceptively become synonymous. But freedom is an illusion sold by those who stand to profit most from it. We have wished for myriad laws to protect us from ourselves, but now our soul is crushed under their weight. To our detriment, we have neglected the wisdom of the Tao:

> In the kingdom the multiplication of prohibitive enactments increases the poverty of the people; the more implements to add to their profit that the people have, the greater disorder is there in the state and clan; the more acts of crafty dexterity that men possess, the more do strange contrivances appear; the more display there is of legislation, the more thieves and robbers there are.

No one is ever free in this world. And if the ancient orders were not a paragon of fairness, at least their rules were understood by all, and all could have a realistic expectation of what was possible or not to achieve in one's life. The people then were conscious of participating in a grander, nobler, traditional, or divine hierarchy. Democracies purport to be governments of all the people, made by the people for all the people,[6] but in fact, their constituents have relinquished a decision-making ability to place it in the hands of an elite. It could well have been easier to topple a king in a bloody revolution than to reverse the course of a modern republic. Democratic systems inevitably veer toward a status quo that is relished by the wealthiest because the representative government relies on the dubious notion that anyone can be what he wishes to become. Yet the game is rigged. There is no longer enough space or resources in the land for everybody to live the lifestyle of the rich and the famous or even that of the nouveau bourgeoisie. So, those at the bottom are usually told the top is eluding them because they do not make a sufficient effort: theirs is the freedom to hope, dream, and work unceasingly to fatten those who stand on the highest echelons of the system. If it wasn't especially unusual to find poor nobles under ancient regimes, poor leaders in democratic orders are nonexistent. Western societies are like a ladder: in principle everyone can climb up, but there is only so much space on the rungs. Hopes and dreams have such a hold on our minds that we would rather stick to their fallacy and chant the mantras of democracy than change our perspectives on life and society. Thus the democratic train rolls on, powered by forces it no longer controls, carrying the cargo of its own disintegration.[7]

---

[6] Tellingly, this popular maxim did not originate in a secular address but with much earlier calls steeped in religious sentiment for a popular government "under the unchanging law of God."

[7] The relatively short-lived (on the scale of human history) Athenian democracy and Roman republic we took as models were plagued by wars, chaos, and despotism. In contrast, the stable, prosperous Egyptian kingdom, with its mostly contended people under the hieratic rule of the Pharaohs, lasted more than 3000 years with long

stretches of peace. In a sad paradox, it was undone by the dying republican power of Rome. But it gave us numerous elements of civilization (some of them were borrowed by the Hellenes) and, more curiously perhaps, a basis for many of the esoteric and mystical aspects of western religion. Let us not forget—though most people seem to—that Abraham, Joseph, Moses, Solomon, and Jesus all had ties to Egypt. Interestingly, though the Egyptians demonstrated a high level of scientific knowledge, they were never interested in the surfeits of industrialization.

Part Four

Take wing, my Soule, and mount up higher
For, Earth, fulfills not my Desire.

—George Wither

Some shoot at souls with transcendent arrows so that,
receiving the spiritual goads of desire, they may long to see
the fiery courts.

—Proclus, *Hymn to Aphrodite*

Qui que tu sois, voici ton maître
Il l'est, le fût, ou le doit être.

—Voltaire,
Verses engraved on Falconet's sculpture
L'Amour menaçant

WHISPERINGS OF THE PROTOGENOS

A Passerby's Spiritual Journey

The letters, essays, and vignettes that follow will shatter the carnival mirrors of your life and open a door to the backstage of your existence.

The bulk of mystical literature nowadays is either plagiarism or compromise. On the one hand, it parrots the voices who sung the redemptive values of a return to the Magna Mater and the "ancient" ways; on the other hand, it seeks to reconcile hope with the pervasive horror on Earth, insisting all you need is to "live in the now," send good thoughts to the universe, let go of the ego, or realize you are one with the All. Worse yet are the clamors to put your faith in a promised but elusive messiah, or a technological savior. But a third-party mediated salvation is not around the corner, and the nightmare is not going away.

Find your own Ariadne's thread out of the maze of falsehood and deceit. The hidden god you are seeking is calling you from the silence. Your response to his call will be the measure of how close or distant the uncreated, uncorrupted Desire within is to manifest its designs through your individual existence.

Listen to the words spoken in murmurs to the soul. Listen to the whisperings of the Protogenos. *Silentium deum cole; monas manet in se.*

GENESIS

A Novel Hymn

Down the plains of Passion's youth there comes a season for sweet sorrow,

When the Beloved knows the Lover and their seeds fall into the dormant waters of Life.

Now a ripple forms on the glassy surface of the boundless sea, and Desire is in the movement.

Stasis responds in kind with a pull until a great flood and an ebb lap the shores of the land they begat.

From his lofty dominion in the realm of delights, Desire has plunged into chaos and darkness,

And out of the fire of the first dawn, they exhale two sparks:

One grows to be the offspring of the memories; the other soars—he is Hylieros, the child of life.

Through unending cycles of destiny, "becoming" feeds on its own decay. And from the ashen world, our salvation arises,

At first sparse and diffuse like the spume on the sea, and then pointed and sharp as an arrow:

The first ray of the new sun piercing through the fog, darting heavenward in the amber morn.

Water, air, fire, and soil cradle the dioscuric siblings, but to the savior-twin matter is the first rung on the ladder.

Looking down below he contemplates the evanescent reflect of his own being.

When at last Soul embraces Spirit, the twy-formed god rises from their union, and lure of Nihil loses its hold.

Le Vainqueur

In the city hall of Limoges stands a sculpture by Adolphe-Martial Thabard depicting the allegorical victory of young Hannibal over an eagle. But, for one with ears to hear the silence of the stone, the marble caressed by the glow of a stained-glass window has another extraordinary story to tell.

The light brush of a coarse feather on the marble thigh brought the contender to his senses. As the rhythm of his breath quieted down to a gentler pace, he felt subdued by an unfathomable lassitude. He withdrew his hand from the beak of the beast and sat in silence, his whole body still tense, muscles tight with a hint of shaking.

The eagle lay motionless on his back, his head turned sideways, his eye locked on the young adolescent. Could anything be so intolerably beautiful that mere mortals would seek to destroy it? Is it not the foremost duty of the gods to guard beauty for themselves, away from the humans?

The bird had been acting too fast, he had to bide his time. It must have been in a moment of panic that the clash was triggered: an impulsive reaction from the boy who had been drawn to the animal; a defensive reflex from one who constantly must be alert to the dangers of the wilderness. Or else, the lad had sought to wrestle the winged creature into acquiescence as Jacob once did to win a blessing from the angel. Is it not the deepest wish of beauty trapped in matter to escape the physical world?

Presently, the gallery and the walls, stairways and windows faded in lambent effervescence, and the artist's dormant dream came to a new life. A stranger scenery imposed itself. What was then this awakening, and wherein? Shards of memories were assembling one at a time, with much effort, as when one regains consciousness after a faint and the blood flows back like the tide of a warm sea within.

"Where are we?" The youth asked.

"The place is called by many names through time. This is Arcadia, land of the shepherds and of the gods who are bound to them more than they are bound by their vows."

Now, the bird of prey was piecing together his purpose, uncertain whether it stemmed from anamnesis or the birth of a new myth. The moment before—if there was one—had vanished unshaped in a distance without time. Perhaps the gods too need forgetting if their delights are to be prolonged eternally.

The youth fell in a pleasant languor. Reclining on a smooth rock in the shade of an evergreen, his hands cradling the nape of his neck, he was assailed by soothing sensations. Mostly, the sounds captured his attention: the crickets, the cicadas and the songbirds mixing their melodies to an everlasting summer; and amid the festive chirrups of the choir, words calm, reassuring, soft as a lullaby. Had a wild animal descended from the sky to speak to him as the voice of heaven? The boy shut his eyes to the clouds and opened his heart to the innermost.

"Listen, listen to the echoes of our beginnings without end. Abandon the world. Abandon all earthly loves. Renounce your own will, and let the incorruptible Desire that thought you, essentiated you from Apeiron below be the determination lifting you to the empyreal above."

Eden

Such knowledge they had yet to gain, never to trade a garment of leaves for a garment of skin. Though it be the gift of a god, it is a treacherous offer in disguise: the weighty curse forever follows those who are deceived—not by a serpent but by their creator—until they understand the words of a doubter and, like children, trample under their feet the filth of Eden.

Companions of the Beau Sanc

Knights Templar, your seal was your undoing when those who accused without knowing (or knowing only too well) denounced it as a proof of debauchery. Perhaps it was an image for the vow of poverty, or a mere representation of the seasoned warriors' fighting tactic. But an echo of gnosis claims otherwise.

You sought the promise of the Holy Writ: "Wherever two or more of you are gathered in My name, there am I, in the midst of them." You carried in the battlefield the revered gonfalon that bore the black and white of the dualist visionaries. Defined by the twins, the cross and the fish, your effigy now stands esoterically on one of the loftiest, sacred edifices built by the mystic architects.

Knights of the temple of Solomon, the hermetic core of your order was shaped when you befriended the Cathar *perfecti*, the Sufi walis, and the Kabbalah scholars who gave the mystagogic undercurrents of your time their swell in the land you patrolled from border to horizon.

Compagnons du Beau Sanc on a single horse, you are Dioscuri, the mystic twins—one mortal soul and her immortal sibling, saviors unto each other, forever riding in an embrace on a white, regal equine.

THE LONGING AND THE FORGETTING

The Wildflower Child

For my 9th birthday, my father bought me a rugby ball. I had secretly wished for a brigantine model kit, a pocket knife, or a box of Lego, certainly not a ball. Though the boy's initiation into the mystery of man's infatuation with the bouncing plaything was inevitable, I would never understand what is intrinsically masculine, or so fascinating about it. But I was a good kid, I didn't want to disappoint, and I feigned joyful surprise. It is disconcerting to realize how much a child can convincingly pretend in order to meet family expectations. Parents raise their children to be miniatures of themselves, and the kids mostly comply and dance to their tune. I tried to toss and catch that ball artfully, but without much success. Truth is, it bored me then just as watching a ball game bores me now. Fortunately, away from adult stares, the oblong device managed to have some use. It became a *Jules-Vernesque* flying and amphibious vessel, on which tiny people sought protection when storm clouds with a watery luster of gray and sulfur hovered, almost touching the sea, threatening to drench our playground.

When I was a boy, I liked picking wild daisies to gather in small bouquets. If posies are for sissies, then catching balls is for puppies who obey and follow their masters' rules; the wildflower child follows his own.

With the Corsican heat weighing on summertime, my family pursued the cool moisture in altitude where it had retreated among the chestnut trees. There, my siblings and I sought a delicate flower with miter-like petals the liturgical shades of violaceus. To find a few stems nestled in the spongy humus was justification enough for the trip.

At the turn of the 21st century, the market economy with its unbridled manufacturing and commercialism has denatured the many symbols of a simpler, earthier time. With the dilution of these symbols has come the loss of meaning. With the loss of meaning we can no longer cross the bridge from the physical to the meta-physical. Now that everything is mass-produced, replicated, engineered, enhanced, standardized, and trademarked, the graceful flowerings from my youth have withdrawn into fading memories. They have found new, fertile grounds in the garden of the soul, away and protected from a world of greed.

Wild cyclamens are not fragile; they are sensitive to their environment but can withstand days in the elements that would kill a man. If youth, like a seasonal flower, passes ephemerally on the earthly plane, it never withers in the empyrean beyond. There is nothing beautiful in aging masculinity.

A Taste of Freedom

An afternoon of June 1970 delivered the omen of my childhood's end when I missed my classmate who had stopped by our apartment for a visit. I would never see him again, but he had left a parting gift: a biography of Captain James Cook; a present nice and proper as my school friend was. On the front pastedown lay a dedication in a few, well-chosen words of sympathy from an intelligent boy, not older but appreciably more mature and composed than I was. We had shared two years in friendship before my father died abruptly at 38. I had just turned 10.

Neither my mother nor my father had overly concerned themselves with my upbringing. They unwittingly espoused a laissez-faire approach with few and reasonable expectations, flexible rules, and lenient discipline. Dad was a thoughtful person who enjoyed spending leisurely moments with me. However, he would not be around often because of professional demands punctuated by considerable worries. He was also somewhat of a solitary soul himself. Mom seemed at her happiest with me out of her way to make room for her lifestyle. Many an off-school day, I was offered a mandatory release from home together with a sandwich and strict instruction not to return until early evening. I spent those gleeful hours roaming the town and its outskirts with other kids. There was no internet or video games at home back then to live one's boyhood vicariously. The adventurous, exciting world was still outdoors where the playgrounds for potential discoveries and mischief abounded. Nothing virtual or digital came in the way of our physical, or imaginary playtime activities.

Weekends of the sunny season were for family outings to the beach. Mother worked on her tan; Father went skin-diving and spearfishing. I would alone spend hours dawdling on long stretches of sand, gathering live bivalves to eat raw, collecting shells and colorful, sea-polished glass bits. I scoured the dunes and explored creeks and coves, making up heroic feats and confronting chimerical perils on my path. In those days, the sea was the constant background of my life. My father carved and assembled a schooner from the dry cuttlebones I had brought back from my excursions. My daydreams were filled with sailing ships bound for exotic lands by way of the blue expanse, and the exploits of pirates, corsairs, and filibusters. The lure of the sea is the call to freedom that fills the reveries of the boy until he becomes a man and forgets he is in chains.

Once a month, we would visit the grandparents who had agrarian lands by the Golu River in the hills of Corsica. On such occasion, I could disappear for half a day in the maquis. There, I followed the undergrowth tunnels bored in the dense clusters of evergreen shrubs by the frequent passing of wild boars. Rarely did my prolonged absences elicit concern and, in return, I never expected much from the grown-ups. My blessing was not to be spoiled, it was to be left alone. After sundown, while the grown-ups prolonged their conversations on the patio, I withdrew to our car and lay on the back seat. Dipping my eyes in the vast, pellucid sky, with no light but the stars, and the rhythmic return of the luminescent beam from a distant lighthouse, I let the inexpressible fill my soul. It felt as if all the answers to man's queries since the genesis of our kind were hidden in the obscured heights veiled by the scintillating canopy. (While being young in years, I had my own legitimate, existential concerns and burgeoning mystical yearnings.) It was a time of wonder, of raw sensing and intuiting, when existing seemed more veracious as it was still unhampered by the threads of lives that soon would be weaved in an inextricable, sticky web around me.

On the night my father died, I felt no sadness. My mother's dramatic embraces were awkward and embarrassing. Soon afterward, my maternal grandparents—young enough to be parents again—became my de facto guardians. There was the catch and the price to pay for consorting so early with the genius of Liberty. My grandfather was wholly unprepared for the role of a substitute father and was inconsistently thoughtful and lenient, distant and inscrutable, or demanding and intransigent, but never concerned with my own wishes. My grandmother's love was the smothering ardor that demands total reciprocal devotion and unequivocal affection. I was denied growth and movement, relieved of all control over my choices, and turned into an idealized hybrid surrogate, part despondent and compliant youngster, part sympathetic, miniature adult expected to fulfill the family vainglories and to be happy with my assigned role. The eldmother lived vicariously by directing my life completely in a sad, desperate attempt to compensate for the unspoken frustrations of her existence. Her conviction was absolute: she knew me as presumably I could not know myself, my wants, needs, and feelings. This was my very own "turn of the screw": a repressed bourgeoise haunted by egregores of propriety and respectability had transformed me into a fetish of perfection and purity, a fantasy of eroticized innocence who ought to be protected from contamination. Henceforth, I was shielded from anyone's influence but hers; I had fallen into a trap of love, and my own grandmother was the hunter. I had not realized how ambrosial the taste of freedom could be until I was robbed of my cup of the sweet nectar.

There was a time I relished the sunny sands of the island, the salty wind from the sea—memories now distant, shelved together with a bargain edition of the tales of a British explorer sailing the vast ocean. There came days when choosing my own death seemed the only option on my mind to avoid being suffocated; but destiny had other plans.

The Owl

I heard once, when I was a 12-year-old, that a farmer in our area had crucified a tawny owl on his door to ward off some imaginary evil, obscure remnant of ancient tales. On that day, I realized that fear and ignorance are reason enough for men to be cruel.

In those early years, I listened expectantly for your cry in the innermost of the night. I tracked you, inscrutable visitant of the silence, in the small dens of a stone barn. I even spotted you for a season in the cavity of a plane tree on the path of the schoolchildren. Did you give me your ageless blessing every morning as I walked to class? I found you at last on the high beam of a timeworn pigeon tower, side by side with one of your kind like Siamese siblings. Looking down from your lofty perch, you imparted a secret: I, too, had a mystical twin.

The Summer of Pan

The summers of the early 70s sent me gamboling throughout the countryside in search of the benevolent godlings and nature spirits in the hills and the woods, the fields and the brooks. I undressed under the towering oaks to feel with my skin the skin of the forest and was overwhelmed by a holy sensuality. Lying on a cover of moss over hoary roots, I breathed in the pungent moisture of the soil and invoked the potent god of the wild. It is he who, whispering unto me the primordial mysteries, told me to mistrust any guide except my mystical twin, to renege all masters but the wind. When the delusions of the adults' world wiped out the last mythic encounters of my childhood, the boy I was became a man. Yet, my soul would not relent and still awaits in the winters of my latter years the return of the eternal Pan.

The Winter of Mên

There was once a boy who fell in love with the moon. If that seems like a rather odd preoccupation, think of all the ridiculous things people over the ages have concerned and are still concerning themselves with to the point of obsession. Few were the nights the boy hadn't waited with arms crossed on the windowsill for the passage of the moon traversing the small space framed by rooftops, chimneys, and walls. This was the secret, sacred setting afforded by the boy's bedroom window where lover and beloved could meet, naked, unconcerned, unashamed, undisturbed by worldly impositions, rules, and conventions. Even in the cold, dark hours of winter, the window could be flung open, removing even a fragile, transparent barrier of glass to surrender the love mates to their plays. While the heat of the radiator inside kept the boy warm, the chill outside kept the atmosphere pellucid, seemingly shortening the distance between the luminous parchment-colored disk and the sublunar region. Then would the moon rays travel speedily, crossing the ether until they reach the human flesh to delicately lap with their tips the contours of the boy's body. Then would the boy feel raptured out of his mortal envelope, his aethereal frame lifted to the nimbus of the moon where the cool, lambent paleness of the luminary could melt on the warmth of his skin. And at last, the boy could yield languorously and completely to the embrace of the heavenly sphere. So ardent was his passion and constant demands that the moon relented and faded out of the night sky to rise one evening in the boy's heart. And when I opened my inner eyes, he was sitting on the chair facing me from across my bed, his knees drawn up under his crossed arms, his own eyes filled with liquid moonshine. My silent angel, my watching daimon who came into my dreams under the names of Michel, Aristakes, and Semyon. But he was Mên, the moon-god, the reflection of my own Self, the vessel of my desires and longings.

Life is a School

Prince Siddhartha, the Buddha-to-be, spent his youth shielded from the real world and surrounded by all the luxuries he could wish for, except the fresh air of freedom. So, at the first window of opportunity, young Sid sneaked out of his gilded cage in search of a better atmosphere. However, no sooner had the wind of freedom blown on his forehead than reality slapped him in the face. After being confronted with misery, disease, and death, young Sid received the foremost insight of his existence: Life is suffering! The once royalty went on to be a wanderer in rags driven by one imperative only: release from the shackles of the material world.

In high school, I lolled in the back row of the classroom next to the east windowpane. In the winter morning, a late, pale sun rose behind the mist, above the hill on the outskirts of town—a golden disk glowing softly on the tip where the road vanished in the sky. There was never anything desirable for me in formal education, everything invaluable was beyond the figurative academic walls and the literal fences of academies.

Life is a school indeed:

The curriculum is useless, and the Principal is a despot. The weak are bullied, and the strong are glorified. The teachers are ignorant of their own ignorance, and we are taught to learn and repeat the mistakes of our elders in new and original ways. That could be the point: transcendent awareness is not garnered through life but because and in spite of it.

When I was a senior student, I sat in the back row of the classroom, close to the windows, and plotted my escape. Life is a school, and only one thing mattered then as it matters now: to find the royal road out of it.

In the last days of spring just before summer recess, I skipped the languor of the classroom for the stretches of grass by the canal where I basked, indolent. In the light of the sun, my cigarette gave up ribbons of blue carrying my daydreams to pathless lands.

In the autumn of my life, I wonder if those messengers have found at last some distant, aetheric realm from which they sent a kindred spirit in return to guide me forth when winter comes.

Mirror

I am 15. Looking at myself in the mirror, I am not pleased. I want to look and feel adult, lose the child's figure and features that keep me tethered to other people's will: teachers, family, they all want to shape my destiny. As if their lives were so exemplary! I long for an escape to exotic lands accessible solely to the soldier of fortune and the explorer. I want to leave childish things behind; and yet, there is another child, incorporeal and unchanging, peering through my eyes, patiently waiting for the day he no longer sees through me but I through him.

I am 55, looking at my reflection in the mirror. I loathe what I see. Not a single corpuscle of the youth I used to be is present in me. Year after year, cell by cell, decrepitude crept in. And I see now how the institutions shaped my destiny; how they made me believe my choices were my own, my decisions were free. O Youth, your passions are so easily betrayed: you never gave me the time to even begin welcoming your ephemeral gifts, and then you took them away like a disenchanted, capricious friend. Why is the embodiment of juvenescence bound to degenerate? What absurd cosmic law devised the irreversible process to be worse than its inevitable end?

Now I hear a small, crystalline laughter like the tittering of the chime carried in the wind, piercing the silence before the memories. Now I see the morning sun rising out of the sea: heru pa khered, Lord of the two horizons; Eleutherios!

The Mormon

Ever since early childhood, I was plagued and blessed by the melancholy nature that beset me, and my farthest memories are colored somber except for the rare éclat of mysticality. The solitary path was most suited to me, and yet, as I began to traverse the treacherous years of adolescence, its strict exigencies and forlornness grew unbearable. The mixture of overwhelming yet unfulfilled sexual and mystical longings had a corrosive effect on my psyche. Death became increasingly attractive, and I would have succumbed to its siren song if not for lack of courage. Soon I was left wishing to lose myself in a fortress of solid structure, conformity, and conviction where relief from the goads of the imponderable would be assured. Within a year, I had dropped from high school, joined the military for what would turn to be but a brief stint, and converted to the Mormon faith. Had I been privy to the wisdom of the Bons Hommes, I would have realized the *Church is not made of stones or wood, nor of anything made by the hands of men.* Regrettably, at the onset of adulthood, when I was bereft of quietude and inner vision, I was deceived into believing the opposite.

An early morning of spring 1980, I was boring my way through a fresh cover of snow to reach the "House of God." The sun was already shining brightly; but the birth of the new decade was also the crepuscule of the daring, liberating socio-cultural experiments, the light of which had illuminated the past twenty years. A conservative tide, and waves of moral panics would soon usher a backlash and solidify a repressive culture that irreversibly altered the societal landscape of the nascent millennium. On a more personal level, the day I walked through the doors of the temple, a fog fell on the world inside me as well.

There was no natural light in the Mormons' most sacred edifice, no window to let the sun reach the "Celestial Room" where the murmurs of the faithful mingled with the perpetual, muffled whir of air conditioning before drowning in the synthetic carpeting and heavy draperies. The décor was as artificial as the ceremony. Nonetheless, I let myself be outfitted with the ridiculous ceremonial attire and seated in the front row of a theater. I was now ready to receive the "key words, the signs, and the tokens pertaining to the Holy Priesthood," indispensable to being admitted in the afterlife presence of "the Heavenly Father." I had reluctantly submitted to the preliminary "washing and anointing" of the morning with growing unease, and the unsettling feeling of being swallowed in an absurdist experiment with my life. Now, perspiring profusely beneath the nylon of the "garment," I strained to control a train of thoughts without a driver. The attempt would be short-lived. Out of the speakers hanging from the high ceiling of the "Telestial Room" came a voice stern and threatening: God would not be mocked, and whosoever was not willing to take the most exacting oaths should signal at once.

I wish dread had given me the nerve to run—never mind the embarrassment—but instead, it froze me in place until I rationalized my acquiescence through the gory "penalties" of the "endowment." I could not retreat. It had to be all true. I did not want the crucial decisions I had made to be in vain. I would not be plunged again in the void of my adolescence without the cherished certitudes and promises I had borrowed from the Mormon "prophets" to prop me.

A filmed presentation of the "Plan of Salvation" followed, and Elohim himself made a dramatic appearance. Presently, the god with "a body of flesh and bones as tangible as man's" (notably, he is bound to matter just as we are), who resides on a distant star in the cosmos, enlisted the help of his son Jehovah and the spirit Michael:

"Come, let us go down."

They had found "unorganized matter" and decided to turn it into a world similar to those they had already formed. Under further directions from the celestial boss, Jehovah and Michael create the earth, after which, the spirit Michael is dumped unceremoniously into the comatose body of the first man. He wakes up as Adam, the representative of humankind, and does not remember a thing. A poor reward for his earlier toil, he winds up trapped in physicality, and scarcely has he gained consciousness that the cosmic demiurge sends him back to slumber.

I, too, would sleep the sleep of indoctrination until the spell of the Latter-Day Saints' initiation weakened at last. It took 15 years for my psycho-spiritual camisole to ravel out thread by thread but, in the end, I was rewarded when I stumbled upon an ancient and mysterious little book. The *Hypostasis of the Archons* once and for all lifted for me the curtain that still obfuscates the true origins of the Mormon ritualistic dead end.

"Come, let us create a man that will be soil from the earth" said the archons.

"Come, let us cause a deep sleep to fall upon Adam."

"And he slept," continues the narrator: "Now, the deep sleep that they caused to fall upon him, and he slept, is Ignorance."

Joseph Smith never learned his secrets from the God of Light, but from Samael, the blind god, and his church was the visible, monumental edifice to the glory of the hidden archons.

Emptiness

Forgoing the Mormon Church thrust my soul into a psychical void. All that had hitherto given meaning to my life evaporated, and my state of mind turned into a blur.

The days of the faithful Mormon are ruled by the precepts of his church: sexual rules, dietary restrictions, career decisions, political affiliations, suitable entertainment choices, hardly any aspect of his day-to-day life is not affected, if not dictated, by the Mormon praxis. When the buttresses of my artificial existence collapsed, I understood my life compass had been surreptitiously tempered with. The ravine that opened under my feet surprisingly had a welcoming, liberating atmosphere. The toboggan descent was gut churning, but every pit is a bottom from which a fresh ascent can be considered. In the course of the next three weeks, the quotidian assumed an eeriness and remoteness that left me incapable of forming new perspectives beyond eating, working, washing up, and sleeping. So much the better; I was now free of concern. The constriction in my throat and the heaviness on my chest both abated. It was like returning from a month-long meditation and stress reduction retreat, except that I did not have to pay a fee. I had been baptized in hell and reborn from the ashes. As I navigated once more the waters of uncertainty, I swore to myself no one from Heaven or Earth would ever again commandeer my boat.

So desperate are we for purposeful directions we grab at anything to steer us away from doubt—patriotism, cultural pride, religion, or romance—while our involvements in careers, sports, hobbies, or trendy fads numb us to our uncertainties. Our dependency on purveyors of purpose is cunningly used by the human superorganism to lead us into acting and thinking in ways that are deemed acceptable and productive. Despite our deep-seated need for meaning, however, it remains elusive. The religiously inclined will find it in his faith (or in his hope, for the less fundamentalist), but convictions and hopes can abandon us. The secularly minded cultivates meaning in heroic endeavors, passionate missions, or a simple "pursuit of happiness," the consequences of which often betray our intents and expectations. Only wisdom through sustained lucidity fails none because it is not an accomplishment, nor an end, but a journey without harbor. If we reach insight, new questions arise. Thus does the theurgist of the inner mysteries make their way, taking doubt as their companion while advancing steadily in the night through the vagaries of life.

THE PASSERBY

Parenthood

Much consolation the distressed soul can find in the sweetness of an image: a mother gently rocking her infant to sleep in her embrace. In such a way, the mind is lulled and soothed by the semblance of beauty and harmony on the face of the world. Nevertheless, the man who refuses to sleep should ask:

Should a life be summoned because of a fanatical edict to multiply? What consolation is there in bringing a child to a servile existence? What is parental love but the demand for an object of affection, the craving for a caress or a touch to fill the emptiness within? What will the inheritance of the young ones be, but the delusions and ignorance nurtured by the elders? Will the offspring of selfish expectations grow up to be saints or monsters? Would they shine briefly, or burn quickly on earth before passing into oblivion and leaving no trace behind? Can we admit and carry the burden of our evident responsibility for the subsequent ills falling upon the generations we have called forth, the souls we have baited into physicality? Whatever measure of goodness we can give the child, her unequivocal well-being will always require much more than we can ever offer.

Biological procreancy is amoral; lying to ourselves is immoral: we can never give birth to a child for the sake of love. Our yearning only seeks to assuage a terrible sense of incompleteness and the dread of our unwholeness. It is the longing to compensate for the void and absence in the core of our being. And in seeking the proximity of childness for the loftier characterizations it reflects away from the sordid, we only project an idealized version of ourselves. At the root, the will to "replenish the earth" is a superlative act of selfishness. It is no wonder we regard procreation as having the sanction of God, for God, seeing himself alone, created man to satisfy his selfish needs.

Homo Sapiens

You are *not* beautiful exactly as you are, and no number of inspirational quotes, internet memes, or positive affirmations will change that. Not even children need such spurious nonsense to develop a healthy psyche. They need the truth, and the truth is that we all have qualities and flaws, appealing and repelling characteristics in various proportions. They need to understand and learn to cope with the facts of life pragmatically instead of being given pop psychology candies. And when at last they are able to contemplate unflinchingly the patterns of reality, they will behold the abhorrence of our species as a whole: we are ugly; we reek; we multiply like flies; we annihilate our own progeny; we are incurably greedy; we destroy everything.

At the root of the western social order stands Abraham who had more bearing on our laws and mores than the great classical philosophers themselves. A filicidal schizophrenic, callous slave owner, first capitalist, and land-grabber, his best-known legacy is the barbaric, primitive custom of circumcision, and the strange notion that killing is sanctioned by God. "Thou shalt not kill," later amended Moses, except when God or the Law demands it, which hardly makes any difference. The acquisitiveness of mankind can be traced at least as far back as the "father of a multitude" who was "exceedingly wealthy in cattle, in silver, and in gold," the Book of Genesis informs us. There too we find the Rex Mundi's glorification of material possessions. With the blessing of the one cosmic god, we banalized greed and called it profit thus turning a nasty inclination into a license to drive to poverty more than three quarters of the world population. We left in the distant past a legitimate yearning for comfort and rushed headlong in an acquisitive chase after persistently receding aims. Oblivious to its annihilating power, we revel in the insatiability that devours us. That alone is the primary force that shaped our modern time. Other civilizations sans Abraham did not fare better, except perhaps a few peaceful, forgotten Stone Age tribes. Overall, human nature is just as repugnant wherever we set foot.

If only I could be spared once and for all the persistent and ubiquitous lectures on us being beautiful inside and out. Whosoever holds the astonishing belief cannot possibly have been ensnared in crammed public transports and offered the leisure to scrutinize the daily commuters as a choice sample of the human genome. As for our so-called inner beauty, 10,000 years of prevalent wanton destruction, violence, and injustice are proof enough of the opposite. "Men are always murderers," said Leonid Nikolayevich Andreyev, "and their calmness and generosity is the calmness of a well-fed animal that knows itself out of danger." Even the saints harbor the disturbing impulses that are the legacy of our dual nature. Given the right circumstances, we are all capable of the worst, and the worst always has its roots within us. Our cruelty toward our own kind

358

knows no boundary and extends to defenseless animals as well, making us by far the most brutal and vicious species on Earth.

The only beauty of man is accidental and lasting but a season, when negentropy is at its highest. Once the charms of our youth are devoured by entropy, nothing admirable remains to behold. Thus is the allure of the young even more precious than art that is intentional and lasts far longer.

Were it not for our extensive use of deodorant, shampoo, soap, and mouthwash, our odor would reach the gods on Mount Olympus. No stench on the planet is worse than that of the man who does not bathe properly. Even my cat who runs from a bath faster than a demon before holy water does not smell bad. She licks herself through and through of course, which admittedly we cannot do. Earth made the flowers and the grass, the forest and the soil, the sand and the sea give off enticing, and varied scents to cover our stink, yet we chose to pack ourselves in sprawling cities surrounded by the fetor of our filth.

The hunter-gatherers had no desire for descendants. Necessity gave them the offspring they welcome in a tribe kept small by natural laws. With a shift to agricultural societies we sought an economic advantage in sizable populations. Status, and racial dominance soon were factored in as well. Nowadays, the Abrahamists continue to make good on the edict to "be fruitful and increase in number," while the poor and the uneducated cannot help having families they cannot assume. However, the medal for the most logic-defying procreating intent must be saved for those who spawn a progeny in order to love them, which essentially stems from the same psycho-emotional motivation as a fondness for having pets at home. If we loved children truly, we would adopt all those who are without a family and think twice before calling forth a human life into certain suffering. Something that does not exist does not need love or protection unless we bring it into existence. Curiously, "overpopulation" is no longer in the 21st century the buzz word it was in the 20th. Yet, the question is not how many more of us the planet can sustain, but at what cost will we be able to sustain all of us.

The bountiful expanse of the nomads and foraging tribes has disappeared: we populate a planet deforested, emptied from its fauna, its poisoned seas rising, its remaining livable land taken over by developers. Precious resources are concentrated for the benefit of a few and wasted by the privileged. Meantime, worldly leaders play musical chairs, and the winner gets to reformulate the same promise that, this time around, the future is going to look much brighter. We believe, and we breed.

Because we produce more children than we can handle, we kill them swiftly with wars, slowly with environmental poisons, surreptitiously with poverty, and cruelly with sweets. We also possess psychological weapons in our arsenal yielded by the schools, the churches, and the corporations to devour the mind of the child they bring into subservience. The coup de grâce is delivered by the institutionalized nuclear family who groom their young in its likeness before surrendering them to the superorganism.

I once visited a public aquarium featuring as stars of its undersea exhibits two graceful Leafy Sea-dragons. These extraordinary, fragile creatures are endangered in the wild, and no one then had bred them successfully in captivity. Yet, irresponsible marine biologists and administrators pushed forward with a display that turned into a fiasco. Visitors persistently ignored a prominent sign posted by the tank where the delicate animals were held. Day after day, a crowd of ignorant passersby activated the blinding flash of their smartphones to take the pictures their "friends" on Facebook could "like." The Sea-dragons lost their eyesight and died of stress soon thereafter.

In one of Yukio Mishima's nihilistic works of fiction, the main character sets a magnificent temple on fire because the unequaled beauty of the luminous edifice is unbearable to behold: "Let the darkness of my heart ... equal the darkness of the night which encloses those countless lights!"

There is nothing too sublime we create or discover that we do not eventually annihilate. We are the children taken by the rapturous urge to trample with frenzied pleasure the sandcastle they had shaped with passion the moment before. We are the boys feeding live lizards to the blades of a fan or burning ants with a magnifying glass for amusement. We are the Taliban using explosives to fell in a flash the majestic Buddhas that had kept vigil over the Bamyan valley for centuries. We are Botticelli destroying his own irreplaceable masterpieces under the watchful eye of a psychotic Dominican by the name of Savonarola.

If we do not destroy, we cannot keep up with the necessary maintenance of what we created. Hence the sorry state of our cities and the infrastructure worldwide: only what's new shines; the rest is but decay and filth. Time is devouring, but humanity is even more voracious!

Desire is the fountainhead of two streams, one flowing through the evocative, the other through the flesh. Desire fuels dreams, enflames our passions, and feeds the artistic thrust, forging experience into the memories that shape the soul. Whereas Desire thrives on harmony, greed is the insatiable acquisitiveness that leads to mayhem and destruction. Five mass extinctions befell Earth forcing biological life to switch to alternate forms until it spouted our kind. Humans were permitted to take center stage, but scientists propose a 6th mass extinction is underway—one of our own making, ironically. Our existence is a threat to our existence, and we will deservedly succeed where nothing else did in obliterating our species while striving to preserve it.

The three great stages in the march of civilization, the so-called agricultural, industrial, and digital revolutions, each came with the promise of subduing and co-opting the natural elements that impede the progress of the human species. All left in their trail the unnatural elements that have developed into our worst enemies. Technology itself is not causing our doom, but combined catastrophically with human nature, it becomes our downfall. And if technology can preserve us from going extinct, it will be at a terrible price to the human soul.

How can we satisfy Homo sapiens' voracious appetites and continue to pretend the plate will still be full tomorrow? Why are we so eager to heed the assurances of demagogues we place in positions of power and influence? Why, when the human race had everything needed to survive, did we inflate its needs? In sporadic contacts with our glorious, industrialized civilization, pre-industrial tribes scrutinize us with bewilderment and do not covet what we value most. Millennia-old traditional societies have no interest in our commodities until we appropriate their land and force our poison on them. What does that tell us about the miracle of industry and the wonders of progress? Yet we are incapable of reading the damnatory assessment, and those who embrace civilizing continue to outnumber those who resist it, which is the evidence of a mental deficiency and irrational flaw in man. We constantly vaunt our incomparable successes, yet we are blind to the obvious:

- Our professed major achievements are loaded with the seeds of disaster
- The truly worthy accomplishments of mankind are the deeds of a few who are not the representatives of humanity but the exceptional ones who rose above it.

Essentially, humankind concerns itself with four areas of focus:

1. The means to produce and destroy
2. A diet to palliate the intense labor involved in producing
3. An extension of life expectancy to consume that which we produce
4. Multiple forms of entertainment to distract us from our impending demise.

We invest considerable resources in combating the illnesses that originate in our abuses, but comparatively, little time and scarce energy are allotted to addressing the source of our pain and suffering.

Art stands apart as our unique contribution of worth because it is purposeless and a reflection of our inner life. The genuineness of artful pursuits is inversely proportional to our motivation in the vain "pursuit of happiness" framed by the work-family-country praxis that characterizes the human superorganism. Thus, the wandering German youths at the turn of the 20th century viewed their lives as a work of art and would declare proudly "our lack of purpose is our strength."

We have plundered the land and the seas; now we want to save the earth. Fashionably, we speak of a growing awareness for the plight of mother nature, yet our concern is laughable because so characteristically self-centered. We lament the vanishing of the trees, the orangutans, and the coral reef, but we continue to eradicate the life forms that thrive at our expense or compete too closely for our turf; we lavish attention on charismatic species to which we relate (think cuddly panda), or because of their usefulness to us (think honeybee), but we do not loosen the purse strings for those that aren't photogenic. Meanwhile, we do not curb the disruptive overabundance of domesticated animals. Man himself multiplies like parasites crawling on and under the skin of mother Earth who will be better off when her toxic children disappear. The Western nouveau bourgeois may assuage his guilt with a newfound planetary consciousness, recycling religiously and eating meat-alternative burgers, but humans will never stop multiplying, reduce their living space, curb their travels, freeze consumerism, and above all, give up the electronic entertainment that so easily divert us from our predicament. We purport to temper our ravages with a shift to soft exploitation dubbed ethical and sustainable; it is neither. We persist in treating the butchered victims with band aids while letting the serial killer roam at large. Mother Earth will pass away and us with, or long before her.

Happy Face

The Happy Face is the mirror reflection of the shallow and bland optimism spawned in the heyday of Capitalism: a beatific icon for the mirage of infinite increase based on finite resources. Soon, it imposed itself as the symbol of a new, motivational pop philosophy, and a mask for the countless laborers who toil in the superorganism. Over time, the exploitative economic strategy has considerably refined its means, moving from a mass of workers bereft of power and with little to lose to a rather contented workforce integrated in the market economy as its principal consumer. The former was an unstable, and ultimately unsustainable resource while the latter is self-motivated, self-sustainable, and self-perpetuating. This admirable improvement was accomplished by giving people the illusion they have a say in the system and, more importantly, that they will be rewarded unlimitedly for their productivity. The promise—magnificently dubbed "pursuit of happiness"—remarkably remains credible while always unattainable thus ensuring we'll keep the engine running.

From office receptionists to bus drivers, many have voluntarily enrolled in the cheerfulness police to officiate as the proud agents of a transformative idea for the common man. The flat yellow face is their badge, and they insist the ills of society could be remedied if only the disaffected and the disillusioned would hang a smile on their jaws and think happy thoughts. But show me a creative genius who wasn't morose or conflicted! You will find none. The most gifted individuals should be troubled because visionary solutions and inspired art can only leap from the mind capable of sounding the depths of the human experience. Intoxicating poetry demonstrates how nostalgia and melancholy attune the self to realities, sharpen the senses, refine the emotions, stimulate contemplation, and foster lucidity. The perpetual optimists for their part question nothing, being under the ruling imperative to curate happy faces and dispel any suspicious little cloud. Meanwhile, the leaders of the hive cultivate a methodical "shock-and-awe" strategy of merriment with mass entertainments, sweet demagogy, rampant consumerism, the promulgation of positive thinking, or the propagation of prosperity theology. The aim is to preserve the status quo combined with a state of blissful hope. We are not suffering from an epidemic of pessimism; we are infected with a recurrent virus of unhinged enthusiasm and confidence. Why else would we persist in trusting the same ideas and powers that historically failed us?

All forms of optimism unchecked by a lucid sense of logic have a potential for tragic results. Smiley is the noonday sun that promises light and delivers scorching heat. Our makeshift wings keep us afloat on the winds of elation, but as we near the zenith, the wax that holds the feathers is melting, and we are bound to be precipitated into the sea of uncertainty whence we came.

The Panacea Syndrome

Homo sapiens' history is the story of solutions born out of his creativity; his curse is the predicament that inevitably follows each of his solutions since the days he came down from the forest canopy. Nothing good has ever been created that soon would not be corrupted, and the corrective formulas of yesterday morph into the problems of tomorrow. When we embrace chaos, the chaos devours us; when we favor order, we are made slaves of a system. We are not advancing boldly into conscious evolution but dancing a one-step-forward, one-step-backward sad and predictable dance. Our natural instinct is for simplification, but our intuition is constantly thwarted by the human brain's preference for complexity. Thus we persist in adding structure where and when we should instead subtract what is fundamentally unnecessary. When it becomes limpid our success is twin to our doom, we may at last return to the remedies that would mitigate the sufferings of our unavoidable extinction and perhaps delay the end.

Fresh idealism is normal and coming together to make the planet a better place is commendable, but we shouldn't fool ourselves: the world is irredeemable. A radical reshaping of our sphere can never happen without two fundamentals: a transformation of human nature and an alteration of the natural laws, neither of which is possible. Entropy will always defeat life, and the cosmos will one day end. The world is intrinsically flawed, and we are inherently flawed because we are of the same substance and governed by the same principles as the world. Outer technological, spiritual, or societal solutions are but childish endeavors because, like the child, we never foresee the ultimate consequences of our fixes.

"Whosoever has known the world has stumbled upon a corpse," once claimed a dissentient Apostle, "and whosoever has stumbled upon a corpse, the world is not worthy of him."

Only the inner alchemy of the human soul absorbed by the angelic power in the core of one's being can effect a lasting measure of relief and favorable transformation in the world without. If we could look intently into the depths of Tartarus, we would see our reflection. If we sought the empyreal sovereignty of the uncreated, uncorrupted Desire within, we would rise above both the problem and the solution to live in balance and become harmony.

Dominion

That the children of Adam should have dominion over the creatures of Earth is one of the most enduring lies of Eden. When the nakedness of the fallen angels was covered with the skin of the flayed, they acquired a taste for the flesh of the dead. To seal the fate of the innocent animals, the cosmic God commanded Abel to shed the blood of a lamb in a ritual. But the hierophants we forsook once demonstrated to their pupils that the life feeding off death is without the breath of the eternal, and the souls feasting on the flesh of the dead will cling to the corpse and decay.

Anamnesis of the Trees

It is said a man could once travel from one corner of Europe to the other without stepping out of the primeval forest. Then came too many agricultural revolutions before the industrial final solution. Trees can outlive many generations of humans and only look better for it. Because of that, out of repressed jealousy, we tacitly decided to kill them all. Trees, however, are armed with long-suffering. When, in the not-so-distant future, the culture of the useless collapses, the silent denizens of the one peaceful kingdom will crush the rubbles of our noisy deeds in the tangles of their ancient roots.

The forest was the original home for our kind, and trees were both shelters and providers. When you sit at the foot of the venerable oak, the singing poplar, the fragrant linden, the vigilant chestnut, or the princely cedar, opening your senses to the feel of their bark, the scent of their sap, and the susurrated song of their crown tousled by the wind, you may learn something unique because trees remember in ways no electronic device can remember. If the last sapling on Earth were to vanish, the hidden memories of our species would vanish as well, leaving us ensnared in a virtual universe, addicted to a poisonous fantasy.

Companion of the Heretic

Cats can sleep up to 16 hours per day and have utter contempt for the curse of Eden that keeps man in chains. No fetching for them! They appreciate clean litter, fresh water, and a bowl filled with food, yet they are skilled at surviving on their own in the wild. Many a cat lover is a bit on the odd side, independent and ill-disposed toward obedience, much like his feline companion.

I love dogs, but cats possess a far more developed aesthetic sense and manage to extricate themselves from foolish situations with cool grace and remote nonchalance. Dogs display three basic modes of interaction—playful, cuddly, and menacing—easily understood for the homo sapiens with an affinity for predictability. In art, dogs take a supporting role for their masters and shine only as representations of loyalty and subservience to our kind. Our interest in canine companions, for the most part, is relative to what they can give us in return.

Cats, with their array of hermetic moods and esoteric behaviors, are a mystery. The exchange of affection with humans is always on their terms. They relish the outdoors and yet find delight in the comfort of hearth. The passing world offers the elements for their lengthy contemplations. In paintings, on a photograph, or in the corner of the living-room, they will not be upstaged. Their hypnotic detachment commands attention, transforming the banal scene into one of quiet reflection, solace, and mystique. They pose with the insouciance that makes them interesting subjects for the artist, seemingly observing us with trenchant curiosity and noble disdain.

Listens attentively to the purring of a cat, putting your ear to the beast's flank to feel the rumble in its lungs, letting the droning roll resonate and penetrate you; know that it is a primal sound emerging from preternatural distances to lap the shores of our plane of existence. Allow the feline friend in your bedchamber at night and it will recline sphinxlike against your body as if to stand guard, probing the obscurity with keen sight and hearing for unwanted intruders of the dark.

Syzygos

Scarcely have we come out of the womb that we look for the symbiosis we lost twice.

We yearn to drink from the aetheric life stream that flows through us and courses away leaving behind droplets that never quench our thirst.

We find comfort under the wings of the Erotes, seeking in vain to preserve the ever-fleeting mental and tactile sensations that pervade their being. We pursue them to the gates of their kingdom we are interdicted to enter. Tragically, we persist in our romantic endeavors, struggling to entangle in the world of matter what can never be possessed physically. What draws our passions inexplicably, forcefully, toward a visage or a countenance that occupies our thoughts and subdues our mind with pangs of disquietude?

We create God in our image—believing he has made us in his—and we follow him to the end of our days when we realize (if we are so fortunate) his voice to which we were listening was our very own.

We eat the crumbs dropped from the table of our masters (we are quick to recognize other people's masters but blind to our own, hidden in plain sight) who encroach on our existence like so many parasitic surrogates for he who speaks in murmurs in the vaulted chamber of the heart—we do not hear him.

We attempt to commune with nature for peace, unaware of an inner struggle to recapture the parcels of our essence that escape us—they have taken refuge among the trees and in the rivulets and turned into the elementals we call kami and djinn, sprites, elves, and fairies.

Who is this ephemeral Zephyr whose gentle caress we long for? Who is this Angel of Bethesda whose healing water we seek? He is our aethereal sibling, our genius born of the same primeval chaos as we are, the mirror reflection of our soul, hidden in the innermost.

THE SHIELD

Walls

Strong, impenetrable, defensive walls; the more the better; fresh enemies are made to justify building them. Erecting walls is an urge as old as survival itself: we surround ourselves with massive barriers severing our roots to nature, isolating our kind from what it perceives as undesirable. We build structures of steel and concrete casting over the heart of our cities an unwholesome shroud of dankness under which life, deprived of sunshine, wanes into anemia. We cower behind our ramparts like infants under a blanket to assuage our fears. When all our horizons are obfuscated with bricks and mortar, we raise fences in our own minds to keep doubt at bay. The ultimate separation having been achieved, we find ourselves in a prison of our own making and spend the rest of our lives thinking of ways we can escape the maze we have constructed.

Hoary, mossy walls whose stones are pregnant with the memories of the passersby; mysterious walls; craggy walls to clamber up; crumbly walls that offer great expectations of what may lie behind and beyond: in the eyes of the child, physical obstacles exist to be scaled, or to be pulverized, but always to reveal extraordinary possibilities. Walls become fortuitous challenges with the reward of standing high above the crowd, contemplating hitherto hidden horizons, and even, if one is so lucky, managing a getaway. The mystic himself is the child at heart who surmounts the limitations that separate reality from the aethereality he longs to contemplate.

In November 1979, the English rock band Pink Floyd released their album *The Wall,* an interesting, personal work about feelings of alienation morphing into the metaphorical walls of a psychic prison. It could have been a requiem for the death of an unfulfilled, two-decade quest for moral, psychological, and social liberation. In the 70s, as an exercise in imagination, it was a popular activity for kids in art class to draw a brick wall partially collapsed in its center that uncovered the vista of a beautiful, open landscape. In our reality, the hole in the wall was being rapidly cemented, and a dream was about to be drowned in the powerful reactionary waves that were engulfing the Western world.

In November 1989, the Berlin Wall was torn down. It gave the people a false sense of optimism and hope while conferring legitimacy upon the powers that surreptitiously were already laying the foundations of new walls, invisible to the eyes. Soon, the potent imagery of the collapsing wall mostly disappeared from our collective psyche until September 11, 2001, when the massive twin towers of the World Trade Center came tumbling down before all nations as disturbingly prefigured in the imagery of a tarot deck's 10th arcanum. The tragedy shook our comfortable assumptions but failed to make us re-appraise the structures that support our mental distortions and motivate our erroneous beliefs. Instead, we proceeded to patch, buttress, and expand our aged walls. It would not augur well for our future.

Permanence and Fragility

Youth is freedom, and the spirit of youth is a passion for being unconditionally free. Look not for the chimera of innocence or purity in the first age of man; its real worth is in the temporary absence of delusion and mental corruption, taboos and self-imposed, artificial limits, which all become neuroses of the adult. Childhood innocence is the myth that benefits the state and the state-sanctioned family to justify protection of that which doesn't exist by means of control, suppression, and repression. Place no hope into the young for human nature preys on them like an eagle preys on chicks, and they will grow up to be just like us. Our children must be taken at face value, not because of the dubious promises they hold. Their needs, desires, emotions, feelings are no different from those of their parents except for being in a constant state of fluctuation—as yet to be solidified—and amenable to being manipulated or used as the screen of self-serving, adult projections. For childhood is the raw state of humanity without its trompe l'oeil flourishes; its archetypal god is Dionysos, the child lost in plays who embodies all of nature's paradoxes, the soul of man at its most redeemable.

Youths can exhaust themselves in play but are naturally averse to hard work. Why wouldn't they? Hard work forges the character that will best serve the economic establishment. It has no intrinsic value until someone puts it in our mind differently. The structure of the economy-based social system rests on the necessity of a servile mass to fulfill the needs of a dominant class, and children are groomed to be assimilated in either one of the two. Only industrial civilizations encourage families to maintain near-absolute control over their progeny,

374

generating populations of neurotics out of touch with the cycles and rhythms of natural harmony. Children and adolescents reputedly enjoy long hours of sleep and napping, which modern society quickly endeavors to restrict. Lack of adequate sleep is one of the great, overlooked ills of the contemporary man, but an efficient tool of the system to keep him malleable and suggestible. With enough rest, we would be more clear-sighted and less prone to manipulation; with just the right balance of overwork and sleep deprivation (in which electronic devices now are a major factor), we remain productive but docile and submissive servants.

At the turn of the century, German youth loosely organized themselves in small wandering troops to assume a measure of self-determination away from parental influence and bourgeois governance. Encouraged by the revolutionary theories of brilliant educators and daring visionaries, the Wandervögel emancipated themselves from the political, religious, militaristic, and materialistic preoccupations of their elders to cultivate a utopian, romantic way of life and foster development through outdoor activities, physical culture, expressive arts, the appreciation of nature, and the respect of rural traditions. As always, however, the worst aspects of human nature prevailed and the Jugendbewegung was ripped by internecine strife before being tragically co-opted and retooled as an instrument of nefarious designs and mass control. Youthful ambitions of autonomy would be squashed by the fascist and Marxist states, and then dissolved by the new work-family-country scheme. This would be the triumph of a parental model vested with an assumed omniscience of what is best for the children. For generations to come, the young could be dragged on the path the forefathers themselves were conditioned to follow without deviance. The fresh idealism proffered in spring is blinded in summer, or gives way to fanaticism before being lost to complacence in fall, forgotten in winter. When the spontaneity of youth is elided, all the marvelous accomplishments of men are just credulous attempts to leave an imperishable mark in a perishable world. But the artifices of mankind too will crumble with age.

I wasted the latter part of my youth confronting the riddles of the soul, not realizing the answers were in the very youth I was about to betray. There is a numinous beauty in juvenescence that did not go unnoticed by the Renaissance artists and was contemplated by mystic philosophers, celebrated by romantic poets and writers. To love youth is to praise the ephemeral. To praise the ephemeral is to understand nothing can be retained. If nothing can be retained, everything must be surrendered, and in surrender we find permanence or the essence of youth.

There is in the life of man an arrow-slit window of time that lets through the fugitive impression of a hope that the human tragedy would not play out. During this privileged and generous spell, infantile dreams are progressively left behind but reality is harshly questioned and introspection reaches its peak. The skin affects a transparency that allows the soul to shine through before the body hardens as the shell that delimits her prison. The masculine and feminine tend toward each other—almost touching and approaching unison—exposing ambiguous mannerism and androgynous grace. The voice has a melodious timbre, the mind is supple, malleable and expectant; curiosity is at an unflinching height. Those are the days when Hylieros rises briefly above his entropic opposite, before being engulfed in the gravity of Nihil.

In the wondrous age on the common border of the childhood's realm of imagination and the introspective landscape of adolescence, tucked between an inquisitive awakening to the world and the doubting of everything in it is the leaving of a place of reassurance for the seeking of improbable certitudes. Were adults blessed with pure insight, they would seize the interval and prepare the souls of the incoming generation for the stifling constraints of the carnal envelope. Instead, we shield our young from the troubling realities of earthly existence, feed them the fallacies of the human superorganism, and strive to shape them in the semblance of what we are, or worse, what we wish we could be. A treacherous will soon lures the child forcibly into the seductive but deceptive promises of adulthood. Until then, the flaws of human nature could be palliated to some extent; after that, they are permanently fossilized. The degenerative results of maturation are disastrous, physically and spiritually. From the resilience of youth we pass into the rigidity of adulthood, and the system exploits that vulnerability to weed out those who cannot assimilate; they are cast in the sewers of the social and economic edifice. The rest successfully stumble into all the snares of growing up to join the ranks of the forgetful and the deluded.

In classical cultures, pubescence occupied a unique position: its quintessential domain was that of virtue and valor, vigor and grace, generosity and desire, deference and combativeness, spontaneity and resilience. As a substitute, adolescent rebellion enlivened the modern age, but its own heydays, too, soon slipped like all else into the bin of clichés to which is ascribed a commercial value. Youth's authentic voice has been replaced with that of the social media, the infotainment outlets, the political leaders, the religious figures, corporate marketing, and the ever-present cohorts of social scientists that accompany them all. Even countercultures are now managed by trendsetters and social engineers. The young used to be trained or forced to comply; now they are easily coaxed into compliance with the smooth, addictive artifices of a ravenous world.

Dear Dominique.

The *raison d'être* of your youth is to give you a sense of the freedom you will soon lose, and a vision of the possibilities the universe conspires to deny you. Even more desirable than the genius of youth is the goddess of wisdom. Unfortunately, mortals cannot pursue both lovers at once: they must leave the most ephemeral of the two to chase after a fugitive.

Children are possessed with a silent daimon, Eros-Harpocrates, guardian and companion of the soul, who loves her more than any mortal can love, preserving her with his passion into eternal Life.

At the crest of youth, man is transported in such proximity to aethereality, the gates of heavens reflect on his essence, appearance, and countenance. But no one abides there for long. When you find wisdom, you must recover youth in the rise of the Holy Child (allegorized by the boy Jesus at age 12 teaching the Elders in the Jerusalem Temple). And when wisdom and youth are united at last, you will reach the apotheosis of the mystical twins.

Common sense suggests that the older we get, the wiser we become. But too often, the exact opposite is true: once we enter adulthood, we start carrying extra baggage until our load is such that we can hardly move at all or direct our attention to anything except the unnecessary burden that defines our lives. Truly, if the souls of men can be saved, countless might be plucked in their youthful stage as they were before time, layer upon layer, enfolded the pearl in the shell. But when death strikes at last, the shell cracks and the pearl endures forever.

The Wisdom of Erotes

Ever since our earliest, clumsy attempts at comprehending sexuality, hardly anything has been gained except controversy, confusion, and a perpetually expanding nomenclature to pigeonhole that which we do not understand. In truth, we cannot slice the sexual thrust into convenient, discreet parts to put under the microscope and qualify as nature or nurture, normal or deviant, of the body or of the mind. That is because sexual behaviors are only points of reference with blurred contours, like the color bands of the light spectrum inextricably blended into each other. As for the "experts" and "authorities," they are utterly incapable of telling where the continuum of human eroticism begins and where it ends.

The bonobos—our closest extant relatives in the wild— never stop enjoying themselves and others to analyze or codify what they are doing. Their multifarious libidinous performances strengthen group cohesion, lessen conflicts within and between clans, cement relationships, and alleviate stress; reproduction is incidental. We, however, continue to classify and study our libidinal profiles like dead butterflies pinned on a board. The prevalent work-family-country praxis persistently spurs our libido with induced neuroses masked under sectarian double standards and hypocritical, inconsistent conventions. Normalcy is defined by the state; morality is a relic of institutionalized religions.

> *What is highly improper at one time may be both proper and religious at another. ... It is scarcely necessary to remind any one ... that man's conceptions of right and wrong have been constantly changing; that the standard of morality and religion has been different in each age; that the virtue of yesterday is the sin of to-day, and that what one race has regarded with reverence another has spurned with condemnation.*[1]

The codification of sex can be attributed almost entirely to religious influences[2] or traced back to archaic taboos. If you feel this isn't true, ask why, in modern, secular societies, nudity is deemed inappropriate, and sexual matters are treated through the filters of euphemisms, censorship,[3] or erratic and arbitrary legalities. Covert sexualization however is actively encouraged

---

[1] Clifford Howard, *Sex worship: an exposition of the Phallic origin of religion*, Chicago, Chicago Medical Book Co., 1899

[2] A remarkable reversal in view of the cogent argument made by the religious anthropologists of the "phallicist school" that all mythologies, theologies, religions, and creeds of the world originate directly or indirectly from the worship of the generative powers of nature (including human sexuality).

[3] I was astounded to find out that many popular writing and editing tools highlight or flag straightforward sexual vocabulary as potentially offensive to readers. Nudity is now prohibited on most social media, which have adopted a Disney-like approach to their content. Books that deal with controversial sexual topics are banned by some publishers or withdrawn from advertising.

with both genders at all ages for the sake of crass commercialism. Such curious perspectives would have been laughable in antecedent cultures that made a liberal use of overt and frank graphic imagery (largely expunged from contemporary media) in mundane as well as in sacred contexts. Nations that claim to have built a wall of separation between state and religion need only look at the sex laws on their books to see how they delude themselves. Institutionalized religions are all about controlling the human psyche, and there is perhaps no higher means of control than regulating and managing human sexuality. The sensual, amoral gods have been replaced by the asexual but moral Rex Mundi who condones sexual acts only within the strict limits that serve the aims of a repressive system more than they benefit human health and harmony.[4]

Having sought to direct the flow of the living waters on our planet, we will soon inherit a parched land. Similarly, we endeavor to regulate the libidinal tides (instead of letting them follow their natural rhythm), irremediably messing with the psyche in the process. Our species' sexuality is broken down to its biological, social, and psychological components that can be controlled by the engineers of morality. It isn't by accident that

---

[4] Homosexuality for instance has made tremendous inroads (a return, in fact) into societal acceptance, but not because tolerance for differences has increased. The homosexual subculture, once an expression of non-conformity (even subversion), and a fertile ground for talents, revolutionary ideas, and dares, has dissolved into the aspirations of the middle class—the paragon of conditioned, defined normalcy. And to look more like everyone else, the redefined "gay" has sanitized his history, moving from the closet to the tomb of oblivion the skeletons of pervasive intergenerational sex, and salient class inequalities.

cultures with less artificial, saner, and more logical mores often attribute a metaphysical dimension to sex. Here then is a prediction: we will continue to navigate the treacherous currents that shape the ever-changing landscape of accepted sexuality, and few will come out with their psyche unscathed. Even fewer will know the forgotten wisdom of the Erotes and let themselves be steered by their chant toward the tranquil, pastel waters of felicitous shores.

Necessity

Dear Dominique.

If you want to vex the Western man, there is a better way than insisting his religious beliefs are erroneous or his political views skewed: tell him he has no free will and see how swift and forceful the comeback will be. Whereas determinism can be demonstrated philosophically and proven empirically, free will is the convenient fantasy that aliments the mirages of the Western societal model.[5] The picture of a pre-determined existence disturbs (except when good things happen to us) because we fear it takes away our ability to decide our options. In truth, Ananke let us do all the choosing and deciding we crave, only our selections are shaped by factors entirely beyond our control and thrusts anterior to our own volition. This

---

[5] When anyone ascertains that we always have a choice, do they base their stand on science or mere belief? The author has yet to come across an empirical study that demonstrates we own our choices. To the contrary, genetics, the mapping of the brain, and recurrent, controlled social-science experiments, all show decision-making to be a conditioned process.

seeming paradox is best summed up in an aphorism attributed to Arthur Schopenhauer:

> *Man can do what he wills, but he cannot will what he wills.*

Our task then, is not to find our destiny, let alone to create it (an impossibility), but to unveil the hidden processes that direct the course of our existence. And this understanding is liberating.

I hear sometimes: "destiny is what you do with your fate." That is a misconstruction. You cannot rewrite or amend what is inevitable. Destiny is the channel fate has carved out for us, the storyline in a book that cannot be edited. Even the deities are fated: could the gods possibly not be god? They who forged our circumstances and live through us are bound to us as we are to them. Scrutinize your thinking, your impressions, perceptions, and emotions, your actions and behaviors. See how they emanate from a fount beyond your reach. We are but little paper boats folded from the pages of a book of necessity, adrift on the ocean of existence.

Determinism is the notion that our existential path and its outcome are unchangeably set from the start. Everything we do and think, all our minute choices and momentous decisions, is linked in a chain of cause and effect that stretches from before the beginning of time when we were just a ripple on the surface of the void. Our past unfolded inexorably, what lies before us is written with indelible ink. Yet, most individuals, religious or not, find this concept unpleasant (at least in cultures influenced by the West) and prefer to cling to the cherished fantasy of "free will" that gives them the illusion of control. It is interesting to note that the judicial systems worldwide in which we put our faith rest on the assumption that we have the implicit capacity (inherent or acquired) to choose between right and wrong in most instances. Yet, when faced with our own unexpected, deviant behaviors, we reflect with astonishing naivety: "What was I thinking? If only I knew then what I know now; I did not know any better; I know I did wrong, but it's not who I am." Ergo, if past mistakes demonstrate we were not in charge, there is no reason to expect our future to be undertaken freely. And yet, strangely, while we exhibit an extraordinary ability to blame previous errors on overwhelming factors, we remain confident we can fully master our next moves and impending decisions.

In what circumstances could we possibly attain a mental process so limpid, so exempt of biological and societal interference that we would be unequivocally responsible for our choices? A free will, by definition, would have to be objective, detached, unemotional, all-knowing, and unconditioned. Such faculties can only emanate from a machine. Paradoxically then, the machine is relatively free whereas our un-freeness makes us human: we are all subjective, emotion-prone, conditioned by attachments, with limited understanding and access to unmitigated information.

What is the sociopath child to do, who was born unable to develop empathy? Clearly, not all of us are sociopathic, but not seeing our limitations doesn't mean we do not have any. The truth is, every single one of our actions or thoughts falls predictably, precisely, in the pre-set momentum of an existential current. Still, the common man would have none of that, and the simple self-inquiry "am I truly free?" scares the bejesus out of him. Without going through the trouble of questioning their assumptions, many refute the arguments in favor of predetermination with a predictable answer—more an evasion than a refutation—that betrays our fear of losing control: "Then, might as well give up and go through the motions!" At that point, all logic has abandoned the free will enthusiast and, to avoid circular arguing, it is best not to remark that we already go through the motions despite our belief to the contrary. There is never a moment of life when we are not affected by our environment, social interactions, and biological dispositions, and giving up anything would be just another conditioned reaction. What we should seriously consider giving up, though, is our infantile, detrimental attachment to the myth of self-determination.

Our tenuous hold on self-determination is plainly in evidence during the one-third of our lifetime we spend dreaming. In our dreams, we frequently and "willingly" accept what we would reject in our waking state. We may even feel like we have two consciousness at once with the one powerless to keep the other in check. We are confident the tormenting puppeteer magically disappears when we awake—a naughty ghost receding in the night—but our primal impulses however deeply submerged they may be by the distractions of the day will burst at the surface in an instant given the right set of circumstances.

The dreamer not only yields to the dictates of a disassociated will, but he unquestionably takes the weirdness of the dream for his reality. Who then determines the landscape of the dreaming? When we awake to our everyday perception, how do we know our consciousness isn't just another sublevel of awareness? How can we be so sure our day-to-day reality isn't yet another illusion controlled by the same agent who made us swallow whole the "reality" of a dream? And, incidentally, which appeared first in human consciousness: the reality of the dreaming or that of the waking hours?

The recesses of the psyche are not alone in pulling strings discreetly: one's peculiar genetic make-up, the wiring of our brain, its neurochemicals proportions, even the food we ingest and the bacterial population in our guts affect the moods that influence the decisions we make. Body language, facial expressions, and gait, all affect our social interactions and can have unforeseen consequences. Ninety percent of what we do and feel is managed by the brain stem, the cerebellum, the limbic system, and the thalamus, which together process roughly 200,000 times more bits of information than does our conscious mind. The extent of our perceived volition is limited to the 10% of our conscious actions carried through the cerebral cortex, and even that is under the sway of skilled puppeteers: parents, educators, the media, marketers, politicians, motivational speakers, and religious leaders among many others know how to manipulate our cerebral processes. We are in fact so predictable that our weaknesses can be easily exploited in the various, practical fields of crowd movements, geographic profiling, neuropolitics, marketing, and PSYOP.

Compulsion, not "free will" is the distinctive characteristic of being human. Careful day-to-day observation of what takes place in and around us yields abundant proof that we are being conditioned. There is also evidence that few of our memories are completely accurate. What we think we remember objectively and impartially is emended by the automatic mind to fit a learned perception of others, our environment, and our persona.

Beyond mere propaganda, a whole science of influence has been developed to profit businesses, corporations, the social media, political leaders, social engineers, the military, law enforcement, and everyone with a vested interest in swaying our decisions the way they like. Thus, the philosopher and essayist Walter Benjamin could confidently claim:

> *People [who] have only the narrowest private interest in mind when they act ... are at the same time more than ever determined in their behavior by the instincts of the mass. ... The diversity of individual goals is immaterial in face of the identity of the determining forces.*[6]

There are no limits to what we can be made to think and do all the while believing we are free to choose. To say that we create our own path in life is to tell an elderly lady who has been scammed out of her life savings that she really had a choice not to give her money to con artists.

At the Nuremberg International Military Tribunal of 1947, Hitler's ex-minister of armaments said the following in his striking, final statement:

> *Through technical devices ... 80 million people were deprived of independent thought. It was thereby possible to subject them to the will of one man. ... Earlier dictators during their work of leadership needed highly qualified assistants, even at the lowest level, men who could think and act independently. The totalitarian system in the period of modern technical*

---

[6] Walter Benjamin, *Selected Writings: 1913-1926, Volume 1*; Belknap Press; First Edition (December 1, 1996)

development can dispense with them; the means of communication alone make it possible to mechanize the subordinate leadership. As a result of this there arises a new type: the uncritical recipient of orders. ... Today the danger of being terrorized by technocracy threatens every country in the world. In modern dictatorship this appears to me inevitable. ... The more technical the world becomes, the greater this danger will be.

Speer's words were remarkably prescient and remain an unsettling reminder for our time when we witness the rise of deepfakes and the artificial intelligence that mines the minds for vulnerabilities.

The broadly popular self-help trend has its roots in the "new thought" movement of 19th century America and thrived with a generation drawn to the mirage of material status and social influence. As it evolved to address the century's expanding array of emotional ills, it nevertheless conserved the same managerial vocabulary and methods it had originally developed. Overcoming, mastering, progressing, succeeding, achieving, empowering, setting goals, being productive, reaching dreams, conquering fears, thinking positively, are commonplace expressions in multiple combinations that masquerade as instruments of self-actualization when in truth they underlie a stifling praxis of individual and collective control. Far from paving an avenue to freedom, they lead to functional subservience to the demands of the human superorganism while hammering through our heads the illusory conviction we are the masters and makers of our destinies—a mindset that has brought our planet to the point of no return. More reasonably, the Taoist espouses *wu-wei*—action through non-action: a manner of living one's destiny through spontaneity; a disposition for "being" over "striving"; an inclination to conform one's path to the natural watercourse instead of the artificial asphalt road; an ability to adopt the pliability of the reed rather than the rigidity of the oak. The Western mentality typically strives to forge a destiny by being proactive (as if we were so skilled at predicting the consequences of our actions), and becoming a doer, a leader, a go-getter, an achiever, altogether going against naturalness. Astonishingly, in the paradoxical syncretism of 21st century pop spirituality, enthusiasts embrace the infeasible by extolling detachment and "letting go" while subscribing to a credo of absolute self-determination. However, outside puerile fantasies, there is no escape from the web of cause and effect that has its every strand keeping us securely within the bounds of necessity. Imagine the fabric of reality as countless neural circuits on which we are a thought shot through a discrete pathway. The peculiar combination of strands we are directed to travel is our existence. But who nowadays is content to just amble along? We insist we should be able to "hop circuit" on a whim in the same way we jump lanes on the freeway (only to find ourselves stuck again in the traffic). We call that "choosing our own destiny," which is a fatuous statement: a destiny is ours precisely because it cannot be chosen or changed.

The writers of classical epic myths would have scoffed at the suggestion that we are the shapers of our lives. Existence then was but a tragic play directed by the gods. Saul of Tarsus, the founder of Christianity, never spoke of free agency the way the Evangelical Christians and other factions of neo-

Christianity do. Paradoxically, his freedom lay in becoming a "prisoner of Christ." The scriptures and sacred texts of the world invariably show the supreme being steering people's heart and sense. And when the Muslim says "in sha'Allah" (if Allah wills), he acknowledges the inevitability of all things, that outcomes will forever be in accordance with God's plan.

The modern era was significantly shaped by Puritanism, a cast of mind that twisted and deformed the tenets of determinism when it added a Calvinist touch to the foundations of contemporary society. The Puritans perceived in the circumstances of those blessed with prosperity an assurance of God's favoritism: to be materially successful was to be predestined to salvation. They donned a unique ethic of hard work, thrift, and moral abnegation, applying themselves to fulfil the prophecy of material success with a bit of help from vast, open lands ready to be colonized and exploited. Calvinism became the strongest theological tradition in the American colonies.

Predestination was especially alluring to the wealthy man who saw himself as the elect of God. The little bourgeoisie, always envious of the upper class, soon followed a new line of reasoning: if the fortunate was foreordained to be on the good side of God, God should inevitably be on the side of the determined fortune seeker. Thus was born among Christians a thaumaturgy of wealth that developed unhindered, purging itself from troublesome fatalism, and ultimately embracing the flexible, manageable principle of "free agency." The updated paradigm would oversee the unconstrained advance of free-market economies, fueled by the inviting (yet erroneous) belief that everybody has a fair chance to prosper under the dome of a capitalist structure. The newest, quintessential American religions (Mormons, Evangelists, and, more recently, a plethora of pseudo non-denominational and other neo-Christian churches) made "free agency" a cornerstone of their dogma notwithstanding the fact that the Christian canon is replete with fatalistic metaphysics. At the same time, "free market economy" became a godly decree. The symbiosis of acquisitiveness and thaumaturgy reached its apotheosis in our days with bizarre schemes that conveniently allow for materialistic impulses to be preserved and fulfilled through a twisted perspective. The functional wall of dualism that once separated spirit from matter has been felled by the proponents of the so-called prosperity gospel, the followers of the "law of attraction," and the supporters of such other "health and wealth" fantasies. A new materialistic mysticality grows like a cancer, fueled by metaphysical gadgetry, spiritual consumerism, and the dubious knowledge shared on the Internet. Now, Jesus wants us to be rich. Now, when the spiritual consumers of the Aquarian age want something, "the universe conspires to make it happen!"

At the dawn of the 21st century, determinism has lost the preeminence it once had but persists in the back of our mind: many can see that the much-touted self-determination seems invariably to privilege a few over the masses. When people are told they fail only because they make poor choices, do not work hard enough, or have negative thoughts, they may buy the proposition for a time but will start to wonder. So, while we pay lip service to unconditional free will, we also relish contradictory, deterministic pop philosophical drivels: "everything in life happens for a reason; everyone has a special purpose; we need to find our mission on Earth; the Universe (or whatever) sends us the lessons we need to learn." The one-liners are such a staple of the contemporary individual's psychic diet that they easily pass for empirical knowledge. Underlying the spurious wisdom, though, are the undetected, subversive aspects of "determinism lite," suggesting that we want free agency provided some higher power compensates for our mistakes and we can rest assured that all will be fine in the end.

The genuine determinist is free from the imperative of looking for a purpose in or of life as if one had misplaced the home keys and needed to rummage through all the corners of the office and under the car seat to find them. There is even a whole lucrative industry bent on convincing us of the worth and urgency of such pursuit, also promising they can help us. This obsession with purpose only adds to the anxiety of people already plagued by a good deal of personal angst. I was there too for many years and squandered my energies seeking the mystifying beast until I realized it was with me all the time: there is no need to look for purpose because our being is reason unto itself. It is often the most zealous devotee to free will who more readily gives up on life. When his best efforts do not meet his expectations, he easily plunges into despair and fills his emptiness with all sorts of addictions. I spent my own "free-willed" stint in utter misery, but once I stopped trying to re-write my existential narrative, things fell naturally into place. Far from hampering my actions, my understanding of life's determining influences and factors has freed me to realize the true motives behind my decisions and helped me make more mindful choices.

At the root of most people's vehement rejection of determinism are the imperatives of human nature to control and hoard, and a refusal to admit we cannot always have what we want. Beware of all the popular talks about making your dreams come true, finding your own purpose, shaping your own destiny, attracting the life you deserve; they are popular because they offer the mind what is pleasingly sweet to the natural self. Who does not want to hear we can get everything we wish from life? But that is the lure pulling the unsuspecting fool into cooperating unwittingly with a cosmic plot designed to strengthen his own attachment to the material world.

When we relinquish the conviction that we are free and its appendant contradictions, we can appreciate the sober dynamism and simple elegance of necessity: we are a vessel of wonders following a distinctive trajectory through time, space, and sempiternity.

The channels of the great rivers and the small runnels alike are etched by the features of the landscape, not the will of the water. So is the course of your existence modulated by a resolve anterior to your volition. On the thrust of that resolve, and not by your free will, you were brought to read these lines today and perchance recognize the truth in them. Freedom lies in paradoxes: he who sees the strings that move us breaks the chains that restrain him; he who acknowledges the puppeteers fulfills his destiny without regret; he who surrenders his willpower to the power of the uncreated, uncorrupted Desire within is set free.

Once the dice are cast, nothing can be changed. Still, in the unending game of Desire and creation, the dice must roll a great many times: when a universe is created or re-created, when a spark of the fiery spirit falls anew on the physical plane, or when the foot of an angel grazes reality. Only the shooter of the dice knows with certainty.

The Thread

Hanging by a single thread of a spider's web, invisible to the eye, a pine needle hangs and sways as if moving of its own accord in the air. Haphazardly under a light breeze, the thread catches a ray of sunshine that makes it turn golden. Thus is the mystery of our life unveiled: believing we run to and fro of our own accord, we are incognizant of the unseen strand by which we hang. How many of those threads have been woven by a primal arachnidan determination, with mathematical certainty, into the daedal web of our fate? Our story does not unravel from past to future, it is entwined and held together in the fiber of a completed tapestry.

The Prisoner

Sitting behind his office desk, a warden revolves the sense and bends of his life: the unsatisfying job, the mortgage, his marriage, the antics of the kids, eight hours of work and one for the commute, and a home that isn't so sweet after all. His deeds define him. He believes he has a choice: life is a game to win by effort alone, and he must finish the race by the strength of his resolve.

Sitting in a corner of his cell, a prisoner ponders the silence. His mind is rocked gently by the distant chirping of the finches outside the walls when he falls into a gap of strange lucidity, his gaze trapped by a single leaf at the tip of its stem, peeking from outside through a little window high under the ceiling. Presently, he realizes that our actions and their consequences do not last forever, only the memory of them is eternal. The prisoner's fate is a game of patience, the prize is the deliverance of his soul to the desire of her Liberator.

A Mind on Its Own

Despite claims to the contrary, no one so far has been able to fully understand or adequately explain the workings of the mind. I will certainly not boast of a grand theory myself, but I will propose two simple metaphors I believe can go a long way in helping us understand the mental experience.

If we picture life as a plane trip, then the mind offers two modes to keep us on a trajectory: a pilot and an autopilot. Unlike the plane's pilot and auto-pilot though, the mind's functions are not alternate but work together. We already know that the body's vital operations are on autopilot. For instance, and thankfully, we do not have to think about or be reminded of breathing. The autopilot also takes effect by necessity when we narrow our mental focus. For example, as I write these lines, I need to concentrate on what I am saying, and that requires all my attention. This part of my mental and physical activity is in pilot mode. Yet, there are countless factors in my environment that continue to affect me and to which I am forced to respond. My cat who has been watching me may suddenly decide to jump on my desk and knock the monitor down. Subsequently, my reaction could be one of fear, anger, or amusement. In any case, my response would be conditioned by the autopilot. If I did not want to be surprised by the cat, I could have expanded the pilot mode to a broader sphere. I could have watched the little beast from the corner of my eye and been prepared for all eventualities, including how I would voluntarily respond to its misbehavior. However, by broadening my awareness, I risk being less efficient at my main task. In other words, everywhere we go in life we need to weigh how much we can handle in the pilot mode and what must be left to the autopilot. The more complex our existence tends to be, the more we are required to rely on the autopilot. Comparatively, our Neanderthal ancestors had less to care about to merely survive in their environment than we do to function in a modern industrial society. Our mind is constantly pulled apart in all directions. We can of course learn to be more mindful of our thoughts and actions. I could train myself to react with poise every time the cat startles me. Even so, we are bound to keep the largest part of our mental and physical lives on autopilot unless we are a hermit or a monk dedicated to mindfulness and pure awareness. There is no way around the inevitability of the autopilot. This isn't necessarily a bad thing. In some circumstances, it is preferable to let the autopilot do its job, and in many instances, it is more efficient than even the best pilot. Acquired skills such as riding a bike or playing the piano can rely almost entirely on the autopilot. Occasionally, the body is better prepared to respond to external factors by bypassing the reflective mind. In any event, we realize that the autopilot should never completely substitute for the pilot, although it often does. If we put critical decision making on autopilot (and most often than not, we do) our choices will be easily influenced by others whose minds are working to manipulate ours. In an era of "fake news" and "fact checks," propaganda claims and counterclaims, PSYOP and algorithms, we can never be too careful before letting the autopilot take over.

My pilot/autopilot metaphor may not be entirely new, but it is worth repeating and remembering while striving to know oneself. Still, it might be a little too close to the simplistic conscious/unconscious[7] dichotomy with its clearly defined boundaries. Hence a second metaphor.

Life is largely a process/response affair, and the world is entirely dark until we use our mind in the same way we use a flashlight to search the night. Our mind/flashlight has more than an on/off switch; it is equipped with a zoom function. The narrower the beam, the clearer the object or information to which we bring our attention appears. However, the narrow beam leaves everything else in the dark. The wider the beam, the more is brought into light. However, with less brightness, things tend to be blurry, information is more subjective and perception increasingly deceptive, leading to misinterpretations and misconceptions. To repeat, when we apply focused attention on information, it will be processed effectively by the pilot, but much will be left out to be processed by the autopilot. With a wider focus, a greater amount of information will be processed, but less effectively. Regardless of the zooming

---

[7] It is fashionable nowadays to regard the unconscious as a mysterious and mystical realm of darkness and chaos one needs to embrace and make conscious in order to become whole. That is rubbish. Before Freud and Jung the unconscious was left alone, and I dare say people then were no more unbalanced than we are now (quite the opposite possibly). The aforementioned "experts of the psyche" might have thought very highly of themselves, but their personal lives demonstrate they were far from being any saner than the rest of us. If there is an unconscious, it is as unstable as an old, abandoned gold mine. Is it worth taking the risk of being crushed for the unlikely chance of finding anything precious there? Our modern obsession with the unconscious has led to the aberrations of repressed memories with devastating consequences as exemplified by the 1980s' satanic panic.

capacity we use, the vast world remains dark to us while still affecting us remotely in more ways than we are able to anticipate. To compensate for the mind's limitations, people then rely on hypotheses, guesses, imagination, beliefs, or faith with wildly variable results.

Having said that, I trust there is a recourse to the shortcomings of the mind, one that motivated and inspired the book you are holding and figures as its leitmotif. A heavenly twin dwells in our innermost who will readily supplant both the pilot and the autopilot if you no longer interfere. The theorist of consciousness may scoff at the idea, nevertheless, many of the greatest minds the world has known indubitably relied on a daimon or numen for their inspiration.

The Seeker

Flying too close to the fiery sphere, Icarus burnt his wings. On the road to Damascus, Saul lost his eyesight to a flash of light from the sky—a fitting metaphor for the blind who would lead the blind. And in the woods of Manchester, a young magician was deceived by a cosmic entity descended from a glowing column "above the brightness of the sun." Men search for the truth in the brilliance of the zenith and are dazzled by the glare that conceals what they seek. Stare not at the light on high but at the glimmer in the core of your being.

There is no god but Desire. Neither Allah nor Jehovah, his name was not spat from the flames of a burning bush or the mouths of self-proclaimed prophets who legitimize the rules of the Rex Mundi. The rightful heir of the souls cannot be found in the spheres of the sky. Look not for a celestial kingdom above but for the empyreal sovereignty within!

Orantes

Long ago, it seems, on the path of the schoolchildren, there were dozens of things to investigate—things tempting and exciting to the imagination, the senses, and the heart. But that time has come to an end, and on the commuters' route nowadays there is only the glare of digital displays.

Seers augured our days and Ahriman's rise. Did they foresee the humans hunched over electronic devices, marching to the beat of a passive revolution? With their eyes cast down, they are mesmerized by digital fantasies; they sleep while awake, and they forget.

But the Orantes unfailingly remember; raising their eyes to the sky, they pray. Their arms outstretched heavenward, they see past the sun and the stars into their origin and end conjoined.

Secret Devotions

Though they hear in your murmurs the words pleasing to a cosmic deity, your soul is full of secret devotions, sung like the roll of the rivulets in summer that coalesce into a rushing chant and plunge down a chasm to vex with resonance the chthonic entities in their cavernous depths. With the crystalline trickling of a spring the melody ends, suddenly waking in your heart a little god by his holy name.

There is no loftier adoration than longing to become the god you worship: to let his will devour your will; to let your soul blend in lambent opalescence, merging and emerging, embracing and withdrawing like the tides lapping the shore—the everlasting rhythm of the two in one recreating one another through the pleroma of Desire.

The Image and the Word

Was the universe born of a verb or an image? Which surfaced first amidst our kind? In the golden age when the archetypes were still gods soon to be banished from their transcendent abode down to the depths of our psyche, every word was an image. The image and the word once were equal in power: the image told what the word could not express, and the word revealed what the image was hiding. In symbiosis, the two were the vehicle of archetypal evocation.

Our time is the crepuscule of the archetypes, the building blocks of psychic life.

The word has been sullied, debased, compromised, and engineered to manipulate the masses. Its real intent has abandoned us. Without words to express and understand our emotions (and incidentally to experience them properly), we use "emoticons" to represent our mental states, and the fresh metamorphosis of the dubious Smiley has become the one-face-fits-most symbol of an unreflecting generation. Fortunately, in the desolated lands we are leaving behind in search of an uncertain future, the word may thrive again one day, unconquered and relentless.

Images can be even more deceptive and easily manipulated than words. Hence, it is in the interest of the leaders to foster a culture of the image while de-emphasizing the need for words: a vocabulary reduced to the smallest common denominator is an efficient means of control. The new electronic images are so ravenous, they overtake the written and spoken languages, the virtue of which is increasingly diluted. The "emoji" now is supplanting the "emoticon," and the worst is yet to come. Soon, a digital likeness of this world will be on all our windows of perception to replace our natural apprehension of life.

When I was a child, I clipped beautiful hand-drawn illustrations from youth magazines and pasted them carefully— with veneration almost—onto the pages of a school notebook. The image was benign then. It was not instant and accompanied me in the silent, dreamy hours of the night. By day, it lingered and murmured from within. Because we are so permeable to the rushing overflow of images, we dispense with understanding their meaning. Because we are no longer interested in spending time with a picture to pierce its intent, it instantly overpowers us. Deprived of meaning, pictorial representations in any medium are mere triggers of emotions. Hooked on digital stimuli unmoderated by the intellect, we rapidly descend into the delusions of an electronic Nirvana.

Dear Dominique.

I was a precocious and voracious reader although the image enticed me the most. When I was a young boy, I kept a notebook in which I pasted pictures clipped from used periodicals and brochures. The illustrations spoke to me. Things of childhood rarely last, and this one did not either. I then read abundantly and exponentially, and I am indebted to a few books for unlocking mysteries, solving riddles, and mapping roads. Others injected a measure of dreamy relief into the ruthless reality. A lot of them yielded valuable information by virtue of their errors or what they never intended to say. Too many misled me. The written works that contributed notably to my edification are the ones that showed me how to read the image, taking me through a loop back to boyhood with the supplement of a little wisdom.

Perhaps all literature ever published is worth perusing without exception, but no one has so much time at disposition to read the incalculable number of circulated publications. A conscientious reader ought to be selective. When you study the books that help you understand that which you can observe on your own, you become an able reader of the patterns in art, history, the natural world, and human behaviors. This proficiency unveils the knowledge that matters most.

In a dream once, an unworldly friend appeared to me—this time in the guise of a princely Levantine youth. He took me by the arm to walk a few steps, though he would not go any farther. He then asked me with the naivety of the child if I could read. I did not fathom the point of the question until after I departed the land of the Oneiroi: not just the words must be examined, but the faces of people, the artifacts of men, the trees, the flowers, the landscapes, the portents, the symbols, and of course the dreams.

There are words so intensely meaningful they can stand singly without buttresses or foundations. But they do great wonders when paired with companions of voyage in the introvertive realms. Be still and let those visitors be habitual guests in the garden of your soul. Thus you will acquire the lucidity to discern the aethereality beyond and behind the known reality and pair the Logos with the Eidolon.

Arcana

The Mountebank

I am the Mountebank, master of illusions. My greatest deception was to pass myself for a Magus in the eyes of senseless occultists. So imbued with pretense were the presumptuous knowers of the unseen, they would not see the truth glaring before their eyes. I once scraped a living in the street, performing for a gullible crowd. Now I yield the wand of the transformer, dispenser of marvels, confident of the lawgivers. I have the confidence of the elite and prestige among the masses.

In a bygone century, an artist and a seer, a revealer of hidden things, painted me in the act of relieving the townspeople of their purse. With the changing times my skills have evolved and sharpened. Now I don the reversible coat of the sage and the savant. I have the credence and respectability to make you believe I can change your fate by the power of beliefs or the miracles of technology. My audience is multitude, my reach crosses the geographical barriers and penetrates the electronic frontier. I am everywhere, your false friend, your treacherous ally.

The Empress

I am nature's abundance and cruelty. I am the giver who does not forgive. I am the mother of the souls, and I suffer for the sake of my daughters. I offer myself wholly to the fruit of my womb, but I must possess whom I spawned. I am the freedom of the young and the crippling chains of the old ones. I am the delights and the excesses of the flesh, its life and its decay. I am joined in matrimony with the Emperor—a marriage of convenience for the sake of selfish interests, an alliance between Earth and the Rex Mundi.

The Hanged Man

I am the Hanged Man. I recall the days when hanging upside down was child's play. My composure is serene, my gaze intent and focused. I see the world from an inverted perspective to my advantage. I surrender to an unclouded will, and in unraveling I realize my potential. I am Wisdom—an expanding of the mind—welcoming novel ideas that run against mass conventions and defy popular norms.

I am the Hanged Man: acquisitiveness has condemned me to my precarious position. I struggle, and with each desperate attempt to set myself free the noose tightens around my ankle. I clutch my gold in fear of losing what is dearest to me. I am Materialism—a narrowing of the mind to mere intellect— falling prey to paradigms of my own I cannot escape.

The Fool

I am the Fool—the only unnumbered card in the set; I am the beginning and the end, the cipher and the whole. I am the curiosity of the child and the sovereign youth impervious to mathematical certainty. I was born with the moon and will pass with the sun. I travel through the 21 arcana, wearing masks. Unlike the great sphere journeying through the constellations of the sky, I chart my course haphazardly to the human eye, following the decrees of an unforeseeable volition. I learn wisdom through my folly, dispensing hierophanies to my *compagnons de voyage*. I am the truth coming out of the mouth of children; the heedlessness and impetuousness of adolescence; I am young at any age. I pluck memories out of the world and carry them in a bundle. My staff is the power of Desire coursing through me. My feet are bound to Earth, my mother, yet, by nature I am immortal, and divine from my father's side. I am Eleutherios—the liberator; I am the passerby.

Tales Sen Nefer Ka Ra Told by the Light of the Campfire and the Moon

The legend of the Orphan of the Wind

Long ago, in the foothills of Olympus, near the village Pimpleia, lived a youth who earned a living as a wizard. No one knew who his parents were, and some villagers spoke of him as an orphan of the wind. To most, he was known as Orpheus. The boy spent his days in the forest with the satyrs and the nymphs who gathered in the clearings to hear him singing. The orphan of the wind, you see, was such an extraordinary singer and musician that even the stones and the trees responded to his melodies. Unbeknownst to him, the gods themselves could hear the sweet musical voice softly rising from the woodlands until it brushed faintly the peak of Olympus. Apollo, the god of the Arts, was so ravished by the youth's charms and talent that he gifted him with a lyre. In gratitude, Orpheus became a lifelong worshipper of the sun-god while, out of consideration for his wilderness friends, he continued to follow the rituals of Dionysos.

Apollo taught Orpheus how to play the lyre he had given him; it was that very same instrument the mortal bard used to mellow the heart of Hades, according to the legend, in the same way the mythical David is said to have calmed the anxiety of King Saul.

Orpheus had taken a bride, Eurydice, who died from the bite of a viper, and he swore to deliver his beloved from the grip of the underworld. He descended into the realm of the dead, which none had attempted before, to face the ruler of the subterranean province and his queen. Swayed by the entrancing tune of the lyre, Hades relented to the bard's plea and let the two lovers depart the chthonic realm of darkness on the express condition that Orpheus would not turn around and look back until he had reached the outside world. Thus, the temerarious youth led the way while the soul of Eurydice followed him in silence. Yet, just as the first, pale glimmer of the surface world filled the cavernous exit from underground, the young man beset by doubts could no longer endure the painful incertitude: he took a furtive back-glance to confirm his companion was close behind. Alas, having so broken the promise he had made to Hades, Orpheus helplessly glimpsed the shade of his wife receding in the darkness to be engulfed forever in the bowels of the earth.

Inconsolable, the orphan of the wind returned to his native forest, but he no longer sang the songs that had once lifted the spirits of all the creatures in the woods, the mountains, and the pastures. Soon afterward, he left the country and set off on journeying beyond the horizons. It was reported that he settled in Egypt for twelve years, during which he studied mysteries with the priesthoods of the strange Egyptian gods.

One day, Orpheus reappeared in the land of his birth. He was now a man whom hardly anyone recognized, and his knowledge and wisdom were without peer. He shunned the raw bacchanalian ways of his youth and founded a mystery cult with a new form of devotion to the two-natured god. This drew the ire of the Thracian women who now plotted his death. One evening, while the mystagogue was reflecting alone by a gurgling rivulet, a group of frenzied Maenads fell upon him, severed his head, ripped his body apart and threw the fleshy pieces in the waters downstream. Orpheus, however, had a great secret. Because he was the only man ever to descend on his own will into the underworld and come out of it unscathed—from the living to the dead, back to the living again—he had thereupon become immune to death. As the river carried away the dismembered body, little by little the flesh was made whole again: bones and sinews, muscles and skin, and every organ reassembled together. Thus was the orphan of the wind transported by the river to the sea, and then farther, by the marine currents and the waves until he was marooned on the shore of Ogygia. There, he was rescued by the nymph Calypso, Mistress of the island. It was Orpheus' fortunes that inspired Homer to write a similar story about his hero Odysseus.

At once, the nymph was smitten with the figure, the cleverness, and the skills of Orpheus, resolving to make him her eternal lover. She knew that his music could command the creatures of the sea, and she would not allow him to touch any instrument out of her presence, forcing the musician to play for her enjoyment only. Calypso thought the beautiful castaway was powerless in getting help out of the island, but a clever orphan of the wind is never without resources. Orpheus crafted a simple pipe out of a reed and with its tune attracted to the beach two porpoises and a turtle. The animals made the stranded bard's escape possible, but in the morrow, Calypso realized the ruse. She flew into a rage, cursing the waters and calling on Poseidon to intervene so that no sea would ever bring back Orpheus to the land of his birth. Hence, the immortal renegade set out on foot, traveling through multitudinous nations and kingdoms, and unsettled parts of the world, never resting too long in one place, preferring the life of the wanderer to that of the sedentary man. Sometimes he followed the nomadic tribes and went as far as he could in the four cardinal directions. He visited unknown people, acquainting himself with their mores and lore, languages and beliefs, and their music and magic. He took back his first profession and everywhere offered his services as an enchanter, a musician, and a storyteller. Everywhere, the people marveled at the enchantments of the magical pipe. And when the orphan of the wind played his music and sang, the butterflies of the fields and the forests, and the bees and the dragonflies would all alight on his clothes, making it seem as if he was wearing a multicolored garment. Whence the legend grew of a piper, a wandering enchanter with a cloak of many colors.

> *Like drops of moonlight in the heart of the night*
> *the Spirit fragments and falls to the earth*
> *but will rise anew with the souls*
> *in the amber glow of dawn.*

The piper sang.

The Legend of the Piper of Hamelin

His fame as a raconteur and an enchanter had spread throughout the empire before he reached the Duchy of Saxony. Having heard he could rid the town of the dreadful rat infestation that plagued them, the people of Hamelin unwisely decided to hire the wizard. The exacting compensation he demanded matched the severity of the affliction. The Piper required that once the job finished, he would leave the place with both the most beautiful maiden and handsome lad known by the townsfolk from amongst themselves. Reluctantly the citizens agreed, and out of his pipe, the Piper played an eerie tune that lured all the rats away from Hamelin thus keeping his end of the bargain. Now, it so happened that the mayor had twins who were the fairest daughter and son in the whole of Saxony, and when the nameless musician vagabond came back to collect his payment, the council reneged on their deal. The watchmen escorted the Piper out of town and threatened him with prison if he ever set foot again in the vicinity. But twelve days thereafter, at midnight, he returned with a terrible vengeance. Strolling down the narrow streets of Hamelin when everyone was asleep, the Piper played a magical composition that no adult could hear. The children, however, bewitched by the music, followed the bard in the darkness. A hundred and twenty boys and girls disappeared into that moonless night, never to be seen again.

* * *

Dear Dominique.

The Piper is invariably a boy. His music is the celebration of unconditional freedom; the phallic pipe symbolizes the untroubled thrust of Eros. The secret of the tune lies in the

409

nature of things unseen, and it would speak volumes to whosoever is not afraid of opening that book. Do you remember the story of the Pied Piper of Hamelin? Seek to unlock its timeless riddles. It harks back to an age when the old pagan lore still played out in the psyche of the common people, and the chants of ancient mystery cults resonated faintly in their memory.

The rats the Piper led away from Hamelin represent that which we fear the most. The children of the story are the souls of humanity; why would they be lured away from the borough and their families? What could be their fate? Why did the townspeople refuse to pay the price there was to pay? Why were the lame, the deaf, and the blind left behind?

Who is the Piper, with his attire of many colors?

Let his melody enchant you and guide you wherever it might lead, without fear or consideration for what you are forsaking.

* * *

The journey was long toward their destination, and to spur the orphans of the wind onward, every evening, when the light of the day mystically fades into the glimmer of the night, the Piper told them a story often interrupted by the strange melodies of his pipe. "Listen," said he, "when the moon is seen closest to the sun, you will hear the tales she tells to entertain the king of the orbs before he retires to sleep. And the stars too gather round to hear their sister as well. "Listen then to the moon, as she tells the story of the wandering bee."

— Having toiled a lifetime for an autocratic queen, a weary bee decided to break away from servility. Surely, she thought, there is more to life than feeding the ruler of the hive. She tried to communicate the notion with a new waggle dance, but all the other bees buzzed her off: "There is no greater virtue," they said, "than hard work and conformity to the purpose of the colony." So, the rebel bee took off on her ultimate journey and none ever heard of her again. "To think outside the swarm is an odd and foolish thing to do," the company of the bees voiced as one. "Only together can we thrive and prosper."

The homeless bee traveled for a long time and far away, seeking to learn hidden things from the flowers, the trees, the blades of grass, the other insects, and even the birds who were chasing her on all occasions. One day at last she alighted exhausted on the heart of a morning-glory, feeling quite alone and wondering if it had been right to leave everything behind. With that consideration in mind, she expired. At the instant, the flower delicately folded her crown over the small, withering body, shielding the bee from the last burning ray of the dying sun.

The stories were the cadence that replaced human time on the march of the orphans of the wind. The youngest in the troop delighted in the legends of brave knights on a quest to free a kingdom from a tormenting troll and of clever twins outsmarting a black-hearted sorceress. Some stories made the older children blush and giggle. The more mature adolescents among them debated with knowing airs the meaning of the fables, arguing they were doors to friendly wonders the elders feared and grossly misunderstood. Had not the Piper explained that the adults always dissimulate or distort that which they do not understand? "The wolf and the fox never deceive their progeny," said he, "yet the parents of the human child do."

Parents however were no longer problematic to the cortege that followed the Piper and had left the borough weeks, perhaps months ago—time was irrelevant now that they lived through the rhythms of sempiternity.

One day, the orphans of the wind asked the Piper where he was taking them. He answered they were journeying to a place of light. And to satisfy their curiosity, he told them the legend of the land of the twelve thousand gleaming arrows.

— In the distant reaches of the past beyond the memories of men, the godlings had their own kingdom in the verdant regions of the far north before they were dispersed throughout the lands and the seas of Earth. One of them was a hero of considerable height and strength, renowned for his supernatural skill with the bow and arrows.

Reg'eikelom—as he was called—had an unquenchable thirst for discovery that set him on a journey to see what lay beyond the mountain range that protected his native soil. His wanderings took him to faraway shores and to a province of bounty on the edge of a great ocean. There, he taught the inhabitants how to perfect the art of archery. So impressed and grateful was their king that he offered his youngest daughter in marriage to Reg'eikelom. It was the coup de foudre for the young man who wedded the ebony-skinned princess at once. With the blessing of the king, the groom resolved to take the newlywed back to the land of his birth. They left the coastal kingdom with a haul of precious gifts and a retinue of servants and warriors. So lengthy was the traveling back home that the couple had a male child in the intervening moons.

The archer's return was greeted with much merriment and wonderment from his people, but the ruling assembly of the godlings had mixed feelings. They were pleased with the adventurer's feats but displeased he had married into a foreign human tribe and weakened the blood of his race. Reg'eikelom, however, remained undaunted. He was determined to carve a kingdom for his heir, who was of royal descent, and give his wife and her son a share into immortality. In the following years, the hero accomplished numerous admirable deeds and prowesses throughout the land, but these new exploits failed to move the rulers or abate their scorn. Then he pleaded mightily and fervently with the gods, but his pleas were met with silence. At long last, he recognized that the only path to have the gods accede to one's heartfelt desire is to beat them at their own game. Thereupon, Reg'eikelom devised a ruse and presented a challenge to the entire pantheon of immortals. He proclaimed that he Reg'eikelom, who had traveled farther than anyone among his kin, who had seen the wonders of the world, could produce a realm more radiant than the divine abode. And the gods whose greatest weakness is always curiosity about their own creatures could not resist the challenge. So it was that, by a pellucid night, in presence of the mighty host of Earth and Sky, Reg'eikelom climbed the highest peak and turned toward the gentle, fertile slopes of the Orient. He aimed at the sky and shot three thousand of his arrows. They grazed three thousand stars and fell, engorged with celestial luminescence. The hero shot another three thousand arrows. They brushed the moon and stole its gleam before hitting the ground. At dawn, another round of arrows was shot. They flew past the rising sun, drawing multi-hued rays of the kingly orb down to the land. Then, Reg'eikelom waited for a light rain and, with a lower aim, sent the last arrows flying through a rainbow, bleeding the arch of its luminous colors. All twelve thousand arrows embedded themselves in the soil, the crags, and the trees, encircling and setting the boundaries of the kingdom Reg'eikelom would present to his son. And the light on the land was such a marvel to behold that the gods assented to all the wishes of the formidable archer.

Nowadays the arrows have ceased to shine. But some globetrotters with dubious claims say they can still be found planted in the very spots where they fell. The truth is that those favored by providence with a keen introvertive, evocative power will chance upon the kingdom of Reg'eikelom. And for them only, the arrows will again display the spectacular light plays that once stupefied the gods themselves.

Withered Fragrance

I sought you in adolescent reveries and awoke bereft.

With the faith of Candide, I endeavored to untangle the knots of romantic love and applied myself to the proper codes of courtship. How frightfully fruitless is the modern man's most feverish and obstinate pursuit. Adrift on the sea of Eros, I drew closer to your shore.

I sought you in religions: such is the fool who prays for answers without knowing what queries hold value.

Through solemn archetypes, I received the first inkling of your presence. Even so, the artifices of the mind still enthralled me more than the silence.

I visited the museums and the haunted alleys of old cities where I imagined glimpsing your spectral train; I only caught a withered fragrance wafting on your path.

I sought you in nature, and I saw my solitude in relief.

I wailed in crushing despair, but no angel or daemon carried me through the ashen vale.

At all times, in all places, I gave you shape and substance; my pain was your strength, the wanderings of my soul were your inroads to my heart. One day at last, in the arabesques of a cigarette's smoky veil, you appeared—what an odd place where to play. Your first offering was as precious as a small daisy plucked by a child and withering quickly. A garden of silence I will tend well, as I grow older and you gain vigor, until the dawn in this very garden when I will give myself to your embrace.

Le Génie Voilé

Life originates and persists in struggle; incidental to that struggle is ephemeral beauty and a fragile harmony that are continuously under attack by entropy and chaos. This natural observation might have brought man to conceive of a superior realm where harmony remains untouched. "What is art, after all," asked Aldous Huxley, "but a protest against the horrible inclemency of life?"[8] I suggest that the artistic endeavor came about not to duplicate or placate nature but as an act of magic, an original attempt to bridge the gap between our incoherent, unpredictable world and a perfect, invisible one. Alas, the bridge is crumbling. Since the ancestors' magical sallies into the arts, Art itself has evolved together with its definition to the extent that it is now thinning out of existence like an infinitely inflating balloon. When nearly everything and anything can be

---

[8] Aldous Huxley, *Antic Hay*, 1923.

considered artistic, where does that leave meaning in the arts? Moreover, while the forgone makers of Art effaced themselves humbly behind the source of their inspiration, a thirst for reward, popularity, and fame spurs many a modern would-be artist; they have joined the crowded mansion of the fraudulent prophets of our time.

The task of defining Art has become an impossible one, but I need not tread those waters at the risk of drowning. The craft that chiefly concerns itself with deliberateness, intellectuality, cleverness, innovation, originality, trendsetting, or provocation can only result in something of and for the mind; though it may occasionally elicit praise and in some contexts respect, it is bereft of numinous passion. To me, short of being intoxicating, art is simply not art.

Aleister Crowley once wrote that "Magick is the Science and Art of causing Change to occur in conformity with Will."[9] The only Art to which I am drawn is magical: it elicits emotions and feelings unparalleled in the natural world and spurs one's will to align itself with a mystical will, casting a spell akin to divine madness. Socrates anticipated that someone overwhelmed by beauty would be drawn to the divine. While prayer and worship may open the gates of heavens, numinous Art is itself a vortex to the realm of the gods, and its masterpieces reveal the hitherto unseen, divine generative desire. "Art does not simply reveal God," declares Hegel, "it is one of the ways in which God reveals, and thus actualizes, himself."[10] I will always remember the day I discovered for the first time Van Gogh's *Café Terrace at Night*. I was inexplicably and completely mesmerized by the painting.

---

[9] Aleister Crowley, *Magick in Theory and Practice*, 1929.
[10] Georg Wilhelm Friedrich Hegel, *Introductory Lectures on Aesthetics*.

I have since found the work to be pregnant with esoteric meaning, but even before that, it had on me an indelible mysterious effect.

Numinous Art possesses its facilitators who have no choice but to become proficient interpreters of the divine mysteries, and the vessels from which the hidden, unpolluted stream of the supersensible breaks onto the sensible plane. For this reason, no amount of skill or training can ever substitute for the inner power that takes hold of the artist engaged in a work of Art. No matter how vulgar, coarse, or reckless their personalities might have been, Mozart, Beethoven, Wagner, Caravaggio, Gauguin gave us masterpieces that relieve the soul from the heaviness of the material world.

Art should pulsate at the core with ethereality and otherworldly energy. Anything that anchors the senses in the world or takes back one's thoughts to reality is at best skillful or aesthetic propaganda. Thus are set apart the artists seized by their genius and those with mere talent or skills: the latter fancy being masters of the landscape whereas the former, knowingly or not, are only the gardeners.

Eros and Psyche

The designs of the uncreated generative Desire are often revealed through an interpretation of allegories in myths and art. The tale of Eros and Psyche was an inspiration in antiquity, during the Renaissance, and until the end of the 19th century. Then, the narrative nearly disappeared from collective consciousness while, coincidentally, the nocuous notion of romantic love took the center stage and the longing for one's *syzygos*, or "Mate of the Soul," misleadingly morphed into the commonplace compulsion to find a "soulmate."

To Eros, the primordial Desire, the graceful youth-god with "glittering golden wings," everything gushing forth from Apeiron owes its existence. In our modern, degenerate perception though, he is the mischievous cherub who adorns Valentine's cards, a mere projection of our misplaced concerns with immature, romantic attachments. Removed from his primal splendor, his fate is more tragic than the fall of the Morning Star.

The modern idea of free will is completely absent from all the ancient epics and romances. In the story of Eros and Psyche, the uncontainable, mutual passion of the young immortal and the maiden-soul is compelled by their intertwined destinies. Under the spell of Fate, the soul wanders the world, facing many trials, yet irresistibly driven to Eros until a providential denouement opens for the eloping couple the gates of Elysium. Throughout the soul's adventures, her guiding beacon is the glimmer of the god within, Eros in Hyle, the uncorrupted Desire signified by the oil lamp Psyche carries along to illuminate the darkened chamber where her betrothed is asleep. The scene is often portrayed in classical paintings and alludes to the human soul guided by divine light, searching the obscured alcoves of the heart. When the god awakens at last in the bridal chamber, the lover and the beloved fall in a coalescent embrace. The marriage of Eros and Psyche bestows immortality upon the soul who has escaped the enclave of the flesh and is free to live forever with her mystical companion.

The Marine Eros[11]

Clasped in the coiled embrace of a serpentine, marine creature, the aerial youth plunges into the waters. Spirit into matter, light into darkness, Desire into chaos, he becomes at once Hylieros to satisfy Providence and answer Necessity. In the fated company of each other, the two beings play and struggle, now emerging from the psychical expanse, now diving back in its depths. At last, a child no longer but in form only, the god rises alone like a young sun out of the silent sea: Eros-Harpocrates, Lord of the two horizons.

Angels

From ages immemorial, when they first appeared in circumstances unknown, angels have fascinated humankind. Their influence can be traced as far back as the Babylonian empire and the Zoroastrian religions. Though they assumed many shapes and donned many disguises, we follow over the millennia the flight of those resilient and commanding beings who mediate between the psyche and the beyond. The scholar mystics determined their place in the hierarchy of the heavens; the master glaziers and illuminators of the middle-ages gave them their luminescence; the Renaissance and baroque artists refined their androgynous allures while strengthening their bearing.

When the powerful messengers reached the peak of their rule, the Abrahamic God grew jealous and fearfully of their equivocal, transcendent beauty, and their unique bond with

---

[11] Inspired by a 2nd century Roman marble statue from the Farnese Collection, displayed in the Naples National Archaeological Museum in Italy.

mankind. So it was that the reformation made them disappear from one third of Christendom. The vanished would eventually return but under strict gender lines with the incoming engineers of morality stripping them of sexual ambiguity: the pre-Raphaelites of the Victorian age feminized the divine ambassadors while the propagandist imagery of the 20th Century militant churches virilized them. And that wasn't the end of their curse. New-Agers drew the celestial beings down to the common place while the digital age vulgarized them, sealing the gates of their kingdom. The classical angels suffused with exquisite grace have been displaced in our imagination by tawdry, fantasy creatures devoid of quintessential presence—a reflection of our increasingly clouded and erring minds. A hideous new breed of supernatural messengers, repulsive to aesthetic sense, brims with artificial light and colors to compensate for its hollowness. But light is not always beautiful, and when it is glaring, the beautiful angels are dying.

An Angel without Wings

Was it Zeus, Aphrodite, or the Rex Mundi who clipped your wings and forced you to abide in the human world? Though your lot may seem unfair, you have inspired through the ages the art of the Renaissance man, the devotions of the ancient pagan aristocracy, the seraphic visions of the mystic, the verses of the poet.

The aethereal grace trapped into this world—for those who behold it—floods the heart and deranges the senses, separating the soul from the shell. The curse on an angel without wings is our blessing as well.

Scapegoat[12]

'tis better to carry the sins of men than to live by the rules of their lords. 'tis better to pick the dry, bitter flowerets of the desert than to feast on the dead foods of mankind. 'tis better to die an unfettered spirit than to linger an entombed soul.

Your cousin Aries was placed first in the stars, you only reaped Jehovah's spite. Yet, an earthy god took you in his embrace, and the pastures of Arcadia are your reward at last, with wine, laughter, and the rondes of the shepherd boys.

Youth with Ram[13]

Who is hiding behind your audacious, knowing smile, young Baptist? Certainly not the crazed prophet of a Judean desert; not even a playful shepherd in Arcadia, but the genius of youth, timeless, free as the wilderness wind, unfettered and flouting, boldly conniving with the ancient god of fertility, the sacred ram who imparts vital strength and euphoria.

The Eighth Work of Mercy[14]

Two angels in embrace dominate the canvas with ravishing twirls. In a coalescing ascent, unconcerned by the earthly plane

---

[12] Inspired by William Holman Hunt's *The Scapegoat*, 1854-56

[13] Inspired by *Saint John the Baptist*, a masterpiece painted by Caravaggio around 1602 for the Mattei family and displayed at the Capitoline Museums in Rome.

[14] Inspired by Caravaggio's masterwork *The Seven Works of Mercy*, completed in 1607 as an altarpiece for the church of Pio Monte della Misericordia in Naples where it has been housed to this day. In 1969, radiographs of the painting were taken that indicate Caravaggio originally planned to include three angels in the upper section. The depiction of Mary and the Infant Jesus came as an afterthought, most likely at the request of the artist's patrons. Caravaggio's intended focus wasn't on the Madona and child, or the acts of mercy per se, but on the angelic powers on high.

below, their glance is for one another only. With a commanding hand, the mightier of the dioscuric beings separates the aethereal from the gross, sealing after their rapture the vortex of the seventh heaven. His soul-companion, lifted out of the vale of tears, abandons himself between the lofty wings like a Renaissance Ganymede hanging on the neck of the august bird.

Caravaggio knew light and beauty are trapped in the irredeemable world. He resolved to set them free, becoming the artisan of an eighth work of mercy.

Zephyr[15]

The wind bloweth where it listeth, and thou hearest the sound thereof, but canst not tell whence it cometh, and whither it goeth: so is every one that is born of the Spirit.

—The Gospel of John

Playfully, gracefully, a youth balances himself above the liquid element. He is Zephyr, softest of the winds, messenger of spring. Unaffected by the raging waters parting the somber forest about him, his nature is to skim freely above fields and ponds, never to be hampered, never to be bound to anything but a Larkspur flower as spirit is bound to soul. And yet, when remorse and melancholy over the loss of his beloved overwhelms him, Zephyr lingers ever so gently by a young king or a shepherd, fanning their summer dreams, carefully shifting the twigs and the season's foliage to let the cooling ray of the moon caress their skin. Then does he pass, taking away their memories with him on his further journey.

---

[15] Inspired by Pierre-Paul Prud'hon's *Jeune Zéphyr se balançant au-dessus de l'eau*, a painting presented in 1814, and by Anne-Louis Girodet de Roussy-Trioson's *Endymion-Effet de lune, ou Le Sommeil d'Endymion*, 1791.

The Idol[16]

Creamy skin, golden curls, and rosy cheeks, erect and naked as a sprout, a boy on the tip of his toes stretches his lithe frame to reach the higher end of a pedestal. With the aplomb of Cupido, he inspects irreverently the object of a fervent commotion. The statuesque deity looks down on him with stony silence while the zealous and frenzied crowd around hears a voice like the thunder:

"What impudent child dares to approach the feet of the mighty?"

Swift and spirited as a summer rain, the genius of youth rejoins with an antiphon:

"Your enthralled devotions and devout conventions, your clamored morals and affected mores are the rubble and rust of the past. The primeval gods were power in themselves; your idols only have power over your minds. The daring of light and Desire will take precedence and wash away all chimeric icons when the sun of Phanes rises in the heart of the young in Spirit."

Enfants au Bain dans les Rochers[17]

When the mist of grief lifts and the tide of isolation recedes, a fellow traveler may appear on the shore of existence where one has thought himself forlorn. Thus, the artist's evocative landscape reveals two lads where the lens of a reprobate photographer had captured a boy alone.

---

[16] Inspired by *The Idol,* "to the Unknown God" (a reference to the Acts of the Apostles 17:22-3), painted by Agnes Clara Tatham.
[17] Inspired by *Enfants au Bain dans les Rochers*, a painting by Georges Maroniez after a photograph by Guglielmo Plüschow.

Who is this kindred youth reclining beyond the rocks of life's rivage? What mysterious embarkation is he anticipating, his sight drawn to the horizon? Step into the painting and you may recognize the stranger. He is the heavenly twin, the shield and the vessel, waiting to take the soul of the heirs across the abyssal sea.

The Great Serpent[18]

In the Good Book, you were at first vilified as a liar, and then the afflicted worshipped you as a healer. You descended from heavens as a wondrous seraph and paced the stary expand. You murmured secrets in the soul's ear, and a prophet in Galilee called you wise. The priests of the ancient Egyptians enacted your ritual slaying, and their magicians cast a spell of trampling your head with the left foot. Yet, their Kings made you the symbol of their sovereignty. Reviled or revered, demonized or deified, you slither everywhere through time and in man's psyche. You raise your head and spew your milky venom. You are the embodiment of life force and death; your power is fertility and destruction. You bite your tail and become a blessing and a curse, the cycles of incarnation, the binding of the soul and her release; the guardian of the "pearl that lies in the sea."

O awesome Serpent, I followed you in your fall. I saw you in a dream, uncoiled and crowned, crawling through the original convulsions and the turbulence, reigning over the

---

[18] Inspired by *Madonna and Child with St. Anne (Dei Palafrenieri) or Madonna and the Serpent*, a masterwork by Caravaggio, painted in 1605–06.

primeval elements. But you consume yourself, and you seal your fate.

O Apophis, Lord of Chaos, foe of he who lords over the two horizons, you sought to crush the Protogenos in his egg, but a holy child instead would crush your head.

The Visitant

So assertive, pervasive, and persuasive is the Abrahamic creed, it gnawed at my heels even as I strived to swim away from the shores of militant Christianity. Unavowed terrors kept me on the long leash of religiosity. Until one day, a visitant dissipated my fears. It happened in the most mundane whereabouts and circumstances, and I did not immediately perceive who he was despite his striking allure. Favored with a caress from the sun's rays, his skin glowed like the sand of the dunes under the morning light, and the effect on the curls of his hair recalled the rippling dance of a field of ripe wheat swayed by the wind. With his earrings and bracelets, he looked as if bedizened for a bygone pagan festival, yet, on a chain around his neck he wore a crucifix, the dying sun-god of the Christians, tortured and nailed to the cross. Then and there, I fathomed in the image of his countenance the very distillate of my own being.

So it was that the preternatural encounter created a bridge I crossed between the dead and the living. Henceforth, an introvertive backward glance would suffice to show me that my visitant always follows in my steps from a short distance. He was with me as I traveled back to the recesses of the ages to meet the abandoned primeval gods of forgotten cults and, even farther, to plunge in the core of our very existence and contemplate the ruling principles of its manifestations. That journey to the innermost was a new baptism, albeit not for a remission of the sins: a clearing of the mind and a purification of the will in preparation for the offering of my soul to her rightful heir.

I know him better by his timeless guise now, the puckish god, fairest among the deities; the veritable god who subdues the hearts of men. His wings and his arrows are the symbols of his sovereignty and power: the wings for he knows no boundary; the bow and the arrows because he is Desire and Life. He is the shine in the rising sun, the benevolent healer and preserver in love with the silence, who responds only to the most ardent of the mystical pleas.

THE VESSEL

The Gate at the End of the Bridge

Long ago, the mighty ruler of a distant land once built a wondrous edifice as a testimony to his lasting grandeur. In centuries past, many a weary traveler must have rested at the foot of the monumental gate and let himself be filled with awe and wonder. The most erudite visitor may have pondered the ancient inscription etched in the stone by the prudent monarch and found in its wisdom reward enough for an arduous journey. The modern tourist attends to his selfies and pays no attention to the carving on the wall. Well advised would he be though to heed the warning of the Mughal:

> *The world is a Bridge, pass over it, but build no houses upon it. He who hopes for a day, may hope for eternity; but the World endures but an hour. Spend it in prayer for the rest is unseen.*

The days of mankind are spent structuring their abode on a fragile arch and striving to consolidate their dwelling as if it could be permanent. We marvel at our achievements and crowd the bridge but are oblivious to the gate of magnificence at its farthest reach.

The Path and the Gate

Dear Dominique.

People habitually show an inclination to follow well-worn pathways that herd them in a common direction like so many ants moving along the scent-marked tracks of one lone scout-ant. They would sooner be funneled and directed than pace and consider the limits of their territory, alone. Thus, we must question the wisdom of seeking the Christian "narrow way that leads to life," which sounds like the half-truth in a leader's expert repertoire of deception. Despite the lofty promises, the institutionalized religions' "narrow way" is circular and never bifurcates to free the soul from the clutches of the cosmic god.

In the most inspired declaration of his rather strange career, Jiddu Krishnamurti famously remarked that "truth is a pathless land." Pathless as it is, the truth has multiple entrances, and man's tragic mistake is to miss the gate for the overabundance of road signs.

Abandon the notion that a coveted paradise is reached at the end of a harrowing and demanding route, with hard work, abnegation, moral fiber, and obedience. The empyreal sovereignty is within; pack nothing but the keys. Almost without exception, the theologies and creeds of the world will tell you what to expect beyond death. At the same time, you will hear that life is what you make of it. But the apotheosis of Desire turns those claims around: life is pre-determined, conditioned, and predictable, but for the liberated soul, the beyond is the realm of unbound aetherealization.

Glimpse of the Aeons

The stifling monism of the Abrahamic religions that have directed the piety of the West in the past 2000 years vastly benefited worldly institutions and powers but offered scarcely little to the human soul in compensation. For the unfettered seeker with the fortitude to chart a forgotten landscape, the metaphysical dualism embraced by free religious thinkers, heretic mystics, and philosopher poets, holds loftier promises.

In the 12th Century, the Cathars found in biblical exegesis the fundamental truth that *all things came into being through God save for the nihil that did not originate in Him.* This gnosis was untenable to the old Roman Catholic Church as it would be to the new religious establishment. It outlined a path for a radical understanding of the universe as the battleground of two everlasting opposed principles above the creator himself.

Gushing out against the conceptual backdrop of nothingness is the primal reason: the idea that must be thought, the image that must be seen, the melody that must be sung, the equation that must be manifested. It is Desire, omnipresent, omniscient yet bound by his own nature. There is no greater god than He, except Necessity; their offspring is Fate.

When Fate is born, she stirs in the bosom of Night, and a brilliant speckle appears. Time begins His course. Concurrently, two roads branch out: one is the route taken by the Protogenos, the other, preferred by Erebos, winds down through entropy. Thus are perpetuated the two principles, irreconcilable and working at cross purposes, the dominant twin forces, dyad of the absolute, clasped in a contest for supremacy without mercy. The clash engenders physicality, then man, forging his destiny torn between Desire and Death.

The gods are many, and I believe in them all, but I only worship and honor a few. For those are the faces and the masks of the unfathomable One, the undivided divine. They come into being through our passion and longing; our worship gives them vigor. They copulate to give us birth again and again thus ensuring their own immortality. Gazing and breathing into the procreant Apeiron, the undivided divine perpetually seeds reality with his projection like Narcissus who, contemplating his exquisite beauty reflected on the surface of the waters, plunges into the depths to be reborn as a delicate perennial.

Trinity

Brethren! We have a message from another world, unknown and remote. It reads: one... two... three...

—Nikola Tesla, Christmas 1900

Dear Dominique.

We do not come from the stars but from the seas. The other world "unknown and remote" from which triadic patterns are surging is not in the luminous firmament, but in the numinous center of our being. While mankind increasingly seeks a meaningful connection with alien life, their sight drawn to the stars, they are dangerously misguided in that endeavor. The prodigious odds that allowed the proper conditions for life to develop on the planet are commensurate to the uncountable sterile worlds that arose in the process. In the cosmos, humans will only find the lowest forms of existence, deceitful entities, and the unsoundable dread of their own estrangement, for none of which they are prepared.

You, my young friend, will receive the veritable good tidings from that strangest world, the empyreal sovereignty, distant and near, familiar and surprising. From the undivided divine proceeds a dyadic seed, and from the twain a third will be born. This is the secret of the Christian trinity:

1. The Father: originator of our being, who seeds the generative Apeiron, whence comes the Mother, the

creation, birther and destroyer, encompassing life and decay.

2. The Son: the individual soul, the outcome and *raison d'être* of biological and meta-biological evolutionary forces.

3. The Holy Spirit: Light and Desire, the angelic power abiding in the center of our being, transmuted by the theurgist of the inner mysteries into the soul's savior-twin, guide and guardian of the heirs, the preserver, the vehicle of our liberation.

Crossroad of the Gods

Two routes we follow in life: one is desire, the other is detachment.

We set off on the first gently with a simple evocative stroke on the introvertive canvas, quickly followed by complex designs and enticing landscapes. Paved with creative intentions, desire is ever beguiling, leading us farther along, making slow, imperceptible turns in the direction of order, structure, and obligations until it develops into acquisitiveness, the insatiable hunger to possess. From there the road goes down, and the monuments we built for our gratification crumble under their own weight, pulled by the gravity of Nihil. Our mind next enters a frantic state, a frenzy to preserve what inevitably escapes us before chaos overtakes those who have grown deaf to the original uncorrupted Desire.

Detachment begins as an ideal, a pure, otherworldly vision of infinity that draws us like a spell toward an "enlightenment" that soon blinds us. Believing spirituality frees the soul, we do not see that the soul must free the Spirit. We seek universal consciousness, yet we do not even understand ourselves. We enthusiastically embrace oneness with "the All" not realizing our supposed liberating ascent is the descent *à rebours* into the amorphous collective mind of our origins. Cosmic oneness is the severing of spirit from soul and her absorption into the very universe she sought to leave behind. Detachment in itself will never take anyone past the cosmic gates unless it is replaced by an uncompromising renouncement of everything material and a passion of the soul for her trans-physical *syzygos*.

At the intersection where the two roads meet, a youthful god, guardian of all the crossroads, is waiting. The wings on his sandals are for detachment, the staff in his hand is for Desire. Seeing from a higher plane, he contemplates the pattern below that no mortal can observe: a lemniscate—two serpents biting each other's tail in an 8-shaped clasp. The two roads combine into one, each beginning where the other ends.

We live our lives in a loop, at times coming to the fulcrum where the two ways cross and still facing the same riddle. Only those who pause and sit by Hermes' side will understand the signification of his finger pointed skyward: finding Desire in detachment and detachment in Desire we reach the end of the two roads to meet the supreme individual, immaculate and immortal.

The Names of the Gods

They were once incanted through awe and ecstasy within the secluded walls of temples, in underground crypts and sacred grottoes, and in the hallowed groves, but the true names of the immortals have been sullied and rendered vulgar. Dragged down from their holy abodes, the residents of the empyreal realms first crossed the lands of dreaming and mythmaking before ending their journey destitute in the most parched cul-de-sac of the mind. Peddled by merchants of religious commodities and preachers of morality, paraded by apostles of lies and the CEOs of corporate mega-churches, the few surviving gods are now shades of their former countenance, ghosts of their lost glories.

My dear Dominique.

The living gods had abandoned us even before they became our dead icons. If perchance one is calling you from the luminous innermost, you must call his name in return. Let the materialist and the faithful revel in psychic and spiritual waste, but you, invoke the true name of your god ceaselessly as I have shown you. Usher your heavenly twin patiently toward your heart until he fills your whole being. Let him become the governing and organizing principle of your life.

Protogenos

We call him Amor, but truly he is Desire, the thrust of life infinite on its course. Before the god of Abraham was, Eros is. His arrows are the nails, his wings are the cross. The tortured, suffering Jesus is the soul crucified to the world; the risen Christ is the sovereign Self. The moralists invented a cosmic ruler for laws, commandments, and precepts enforced by the lawgivers and religious leaders to keep us in chains. But Eros wells up from within and never summons anyone from without. To follow his promptings is not the same as to heed the edicts of the capricious Rex Mundi or his minions; it ought to be a passion for the incorruptible lover of freedom and justice who dwells in the core of our being. Hear his whispers in the depth of a silent heart; turn yourself into a conduit for the transformative numen that will grow into your aethereal, eternal nature and divine individuality. The uncreated generative Desire has been severed from our souls by a jealous god who makes demands and takes more than he gives, but the victorious youth will reclaim that which he owns.

Phanes

Like the thousand suns in the vault of heaven, the dandelions of June put on their fiery crowns to reign. Who dressed them with such flamboyant apparel, adorned them with golden rays? Who lit the fire in their color?

From the lightless abyss comes the torchbearer, offspring of Desire and Fate. His flambeau bursts into the myriad fragments of a kaleidoscopic rush and ignites on the aether the spiral-dance of the galaxies. At last, the august spheres rule the cosmos, and the dragonflies performing their aerial ballet make a great show of prismatic iridescence over a patch of dandelions.

Abraxas

Abraxas is the liminal god of the entirety who, like Dionysos before him, partakes both of the physical and non-physical worlds. His fearsome, triform body situates the heirs of the divine who await their liberation from the cosmos where they must abide just a little longer. The fierce creature's rooster head welcomes the morning sun as a portent of the rising Liberator seeking to fulfill his destiny. The crowing rooster represents the awakened soul. Abraxas holds a disk-shaped shield, a solar symbol representing the protection of a numen or daimonic power within. In his other hand is a whip, the symbol of subjugation under the lawgivers, and the tyranny of the material world. His legs in the shape of two serpents are the duality of discontinuous and continuous eternities, the anchoring of Desire in matter and its release from physicality.

The rest of Abraxas' body, his torso and pelvis encasing the heart and genitals are human-like, delineating the path of the uncreated generative Desire rising against decay. The genital area (male or female) is the crucible of Hylieros who ascends to meet the soul. In the vaulted chamber of the heart, the soul and her savior are joined in a mystical union.

The Desireless of Tartarus

Beyond the depths of the psyche, past the gates of the primeval mind where darkness and chaos still reign, dwells Abaddon the Desireless, denizen of Tartarus. To seek them is to enter a maze one rarely escapes. To woo them is to make a formidable ally who will faithfully help you succeed in your reckless quest while slowly devouring you from the inside. They are anti-Hylieros, the face of calculated, emotionless evil, violence, destruction, viciousness, and hate. They are without desire because their sole function is to be servant of the mind's most tenebrous and twisted impulses, carrier of ire, instrument of revenge, sower of discord, fountain of filth and decay. Summon the creature and they will do your bidding diligently, but the grip of their tentacles will slowly tighten on your mind and rob you of the light. Yet, ignore the Desireless and they will persist in dividing your house.

There cannot be two kings overseeing the kingdom: one must grow, the other weaken. When Hylieros ascends, the pellucid Desire ushers the soul to a numinous sphere. In its center, Abaddon the Desireless forever is confined, infinitely receding and yet, never to perish.

Adonis

Before, the petty, jealous, and sadistic mountain jinni Yahweh appropriated the title "Adonai" in a bid to lord over our sphere, the handsome, ever-young fertility god Adonis was worshiped by the Phoenicians, and in the unspoken mysteries of the Greek women. A myth telling us how a wild boar killed the graceful ephebe becomes an allegory for our time. The boorish one-god has supplanted and murdered the many classical gods of passion and ecstasy. We created a lawgiver to justify the abuses of society; we pray a Heavenly Father to bless our wars and our armies, to grant victory to a politician or a sport team; we have conjured a Rex Mundi who revels in our hysteria and oversees our slow, steady, descent into the crushing gears of a materialistic system.

The Son of Dawn

There was the son of God, and there is a son of dawn.

The former came to do the will of the Father, the latter descends to free us from His tyranny.

One wanted to save mankind from sin, the other takes our pains and suffering.

A child of privilege was born king, the disenfranchised one is sovereign by his own making.

The messiah asked his followers to fall upon their knees, a liberator tells the heirs to rise to their destiny.

The lord was tortured to please a cosmic entity, the rebel wouldn't stand for the demiurge's hypocrisy.

One is honored and revered, the other is despised and slandered. But the first will be last and the last will be first in the true order of the heavens: Son of dawn, heavenly angel, my shield and my vessel.

The Garden of Adonis

There is a garden without gate or fence, not at the end of a narrow, harrowing, or secret path, but on the broad, easy slopes of a wide, verdant valley. There, the primordial gods and the demigods, the godlings and the gentle daemons, the angels and the benevolent nature spirits, the peaceful earthly creatures and the mythical ones mingle in harmony and ecstasy. The human souls, too, are invited and welcomed to this mystical realm, though few are found among its inhabitants.

No road leads to this beguiling place; it is reached when all routes have been abandoned. Sadly, the mortals need a pathway to roam endlessly, an object to pursue. Dreams are considered worthless unless they are "achieved"; aspirations are not enough: we devise goals, targets, timeframes, and deadlines. Then we smugly announce we are going somewhere and making progress when, in truth, we are walking in circles. We understand efficiency and productivity, but our mind is not fruitful.

Forbidden Fruits

There are fruits so sweet, they are forbidden; there are gnosis and wisdom so vast, they are interdicted. The false gods and their servants bar entry to the orchard. They are like the dog who sleeps in the manger: neither does he eat, nor does he let the oxen eat. And whosoever dares to share with our kind what we are not meant to have—whether he be a Titan or the noblest of the angels—is severely punished indeed. Yet, a dissenter brings forth fire and light and makes his abode in the receptive heart. No ruler is potent enough to fetter him or nail him to a cross. He is like a zephyr blowing where he wishes; and who will stop the soul eloping with the wind? Love the torchbearer and you will be transported on his wings, by his promise bound to aethereality.

There are sweet, forbidden fruits you must steal. No authority can decree what is for you to harvest, not even the pretenders who hide in the cosmos. Uncreated Desire is pure knowledge and infinite life in the shapes of a youthful genius, or an angel who flouts and defies. Seek him, and he will set you free from the lies and the rage of those who are unable to taste the sweet and leave the bitter behind.

Solitude

Dear Dominique.

I was at the park in the afternoon. Hummingbirds were fluttering from cherry blossoms to pine trees, and a man was rehearsing a nostalgic melody on his accordion. The sun was out yet tempered by the briskness of a Northwest spring morning. The extraordinary thing about the moment was not the improbable postcard cliché, but the realization there exists sublime states (albeit ones that interject themselves rarely in our ordinary lives) when or where nothing seems more desirable. If a limited set of parameters may elicit such an instant in the physical world, think of what prodigious possibilities can be educed in aethereality. I will tell you what the gods do to occupy eternity: they create myths they can stage endlessly. And they have learned to forget their own stories so that the pleasure they derive from them is always renewed. That is also the power of the child.

I thought of you.

I know what it is to be in a place of deep anguish and to feel fathomlessly alone. I was fortunate to sense in my core a distant, yet persistent resilience seeking to reach my heart and my mind. It is to this inner fortitude superior to hope that you must give your attention. It will grow, taking the form of lofty archetypes to make itself recognizable and desirable, and then developing into the inexpressible.

Individuals who are vulnerable have a consequential advantage over those who feel invincible: from their vulnerability, they have a surer grasp of man's exploitive tendencies and the snares of megalomania. Theirs is the chance to rise above the frailty of human nature and heed their numinous self rather than squander their energies playing the power games without.

Many persist in carrying their pain because it is the best companion they can find: an abusive friend who will not go away, whom they won't let go. They surrender to others the power they have in themselves to heal in order to sustain a search that fills the void of their existence. Meanwhile, those we invest with superior authority and advanced knowledge make a living out of our misery, thus perpetuating our never-ending quest. But remember, the knights died on their quest for the grail because they sought something external to themselves that did not exist. The grail has always been in the temple of our innermost. Seek the answers you already have in you, and the questions will no longer overwhelm your life.

You can never give or receive love. Every fiber of your being is infused by Desire—the self-sufficient determination that prompts all existence—and refined through the inherent love that bonds soul with Spirit. And if the human notions of love are fickle, the ineffable passion breathed by your heavenly twin can never fail you. Be still and thorough; before the rising sun, a morning star must shine.

Quietude

The thrum of a dragonfly's wings and the buzz of the honeybees; the crisp crack of a twig under the foot and the crunch of the snow in the thick stillness of a winter night; the soft hoot of an owl calling from the dark and the mysteriously unsettling cry of the cuckoo in a grove; the song of the summer cricket leading me in a game of patience to uncover its earthy burrow; such are the sounds etched in the silence that dissipate in the brouhaha of our time to linger only like a faint echo of a distant, parallel life.

Man is afraid of quietude because without noise he must own his crushing uncertainties. Accordingly, we invent devices we can carry along or fit on our ears to ensure every second of remaining no-noise is at last blotted away. Even the image is loud nowadays with its digital complexities, minute details in high definition, and aggressive omnipresence in the new media. Yet, silence persists as my hierophant, my preferred companion, and my expertise. I like to write, I speak little; and though I use the words to expound nuances, it is the hush between the lines that ought to be read.

The Ronde of the Unseen

There is a past etched in the collective psyche, built from the reminiscence of each passing soul. What we remember fills the perception of what we are. Memories are the primordial root of emotions, judgment, and desires. As they accumulate, our psychological profile and psychical make-up increase in complexity.

There is a future made of all that is but has yet to enter perception. Our meta-individuality will be distilled from the experiential perception of a past and the educing of a future.

Consciousness is the perception of movement, and movement engenders time. Timelessness may abide outside consciousness but there is no consciousness without a perception of time. Time is not the illusion; the illusion is that we are in time when, in truth, time is in us.

Everything arising from Apeiron, the dormant sea of *protoeidoi*, is in a constant flow. When you reach the dot at the end of this sentence, it will already be in the past. Was the present in the dot? Did you see it, feel it? The present is without substance or reality and has no breadth or depth. It does not exist except as a mildly convenient construct. Everything you have read so far in this book is in the past; all you have yet to read is in the future. Nothing exists in between, not even a period or a comma. The "now" can only be defined by the past and the future, and to focus one's awareness on the "now" is to allow the wings of Desire to be clipped by Chronos. To live in the present is to overlook the harmony of cyclical time. The passing of time works for us more often than it works against us; "to everything

-- a season, and a time to every delight under the heavens," sang the psalmist.

We cannot possibly live in the past, the present, or the future because we are time itself, reborn with each passing instant into something different. We can only meander with the river of the coursing moment[19] and dance the ronde of becoming and being. Understanding this notion (and motion) helps us seek the drifts of existence that are the most favorable. The little swifts in the sky know the atmospheric currents that carry them almost effortlessly over vast distances.

Life will always be full of unforeseeable dangers, obstacles, and setbacks no matter what we do. It helps to know that the soft sand on the beach and the smooth pebbles of the creek were once massive rocks on the run of a river. The water never strives to dislodge or fracture a boulder, instead, it flows incessantly around, washes over unremittingly until the boulder has dwindled to a grain of sand at the bottom of the sea.

Be like the water! Embrace the wind! Let yourself be carried away by the ronde of the unseen and find your rhythm in infinite movement.

What Is the Soul?

Dear Dominique.

In times long foregone, celibate, pious scholars would spend a lifetime of solitude pondering the nature of the soul. They

---

[19] Even taking one day at a time is to project oneself in the future. To be successful, survival, the defining impulse of our species, demands not just an adaptation to what is but the ability to anticipate what is to come.

came out of seclusion only to engage their rivals in metaphysics jousts that could last several days. What do we have now? Self-proclaimed experts of the soul who dispense the clichés and trite sound bites that catch fire among New Age and "conspirituality" gullible believers. Let the masses hear them and their audience buy tickets to their "mega-events." You, my young friend, should know that the most widely espoused and vaguest conceptual propositions are the least likely to be of any value to you. Naturally, for the seekers with an attention span no wider than their smartphone, the pompous would-be professors of mysticality cut an awesome figure. With a serious face or a beatific smile, and much pausing for dramatic effect, the spiritual influencers can utter the broadest vapidities and pass them for epoptic profundities, making a popular talk show host drop her jaw in amazement (yet they lack the panache, the presence, and the learning of their predecessors, the old-school occultists and esoteric writers who died with more questions in their mind than they had answers on their lips). Do not let yourself be enthralled by the posers who speak lightly and insubstantially of soul and spirit, essence and energy, consciousness and awareness, light and love, the All and the Universe, dropping mystical words as if they were magic spells; out of their mouth they are just drivel. Tarot reader, aura healer, astral traveler, lightworker, cult leader, or pastor, none are such eminent authorities on things unseen that they may arrogate a right to be bolstered in that role by a crowd of worshippers at the altar of credulity.

So, what is the soul you may ask? Her mysteries are the riddles of anamnesis. Solve the latter and you will understand the former. The creature with a capacity to form explicit reminiscences and to dream is a sentient being with a soul. How foolish is the man who chases the remembrance of past lives when the threads of his present existence escape him. Wherever your memories go and hide, there is your soul.

The pieces of our soul are remembrances, and the hold of the mind over them is attachment. The hides and stores most memories in a locked basement, rewriting and enriching them before letting out and exposing on the main floor those that are best suited to give us a persona in which we will believe. They are masks behind which our self is concealed from ourselves. Our soul is like a bright iceberg floating in a deep, dark sea: we only see its tip; the rest is submerged.

To untether the soul, the grip of the mind must be broken and the anamnesis let to drift away from its physical restraints. On its own accord, it will moor at the safe harbor of its new, aethereal host. It is in the luminous attic, not in the dark, damp basement, that we'll come to understand ourselves at last, when all the memories of the many worlds are gathered and sealed unto the legitimate heirs of the souls. And hear me now: the foundation of eternity is not fall and redemption, or death and rebirth; it is memory and forgetfulness. Without those two, there would be no conceivable endlessness.

Thoughts & Silence

Dear Dominique.

Without the capacity to think, we could not build a perception of individuality with our memories at its core. Thoughts began their odyssey as our friends and the bedrock of our soul before turning their inherent toxicity on us. Soon, they demanded all our attention and erected a wall around our consciousness to keep us from seeing what lies beyond them.

Beyond ordinary thoughts is the reach of the *noumen*, the thinking through the gods. Early in my life I listened for the rustling of angelic wings. I felt my way in the darkness of the maze until I found the thread that ushered me through the confusion of political and religious ideas, the cultural disagreements, and the social discursions. By age 15, I had already posited rudimentary philosophical tenets and wrestled with the mystical apprehensions that would help shape in later years a metaphysics of the sovereign self and the inner mysteries of the savior-twin. Perhaps your sensibilities too have been sharpened by Hylieros, the glimmer of your true destiny, the bestower of your freedom who will progressively illuminate your path through life. If you have been so inspired as to seek him, you will hear his call as he seeks you. Let your worries and anxiety melt and dissipate in him. Let the embodiment of uncorrupted Desire absorb your concerns and own will until the time your earthly mind fades out completely and your whole being rises over physicality.

Thoughts can refine the mind and grow the soul. Unfortunately, the best sort—philosophical, existential, and introspective—has been mostly eroded out of the modern man's mental landscape. His reason is molded by social media and news outlets, his cogitations herded in the many corrals of mass-thinking. Incertitude, doubts, unanswered questions have grown unbearable to his enfeebled intellect. Only those who traverse the fog will emerge into the light; only those who face the chasm within themselves will receive the transcendent awareness hidden to others. Grown-ups demand fast and simple answers to everything; children are no longer interested in challenging literature and fall under the sway of "influencers" groomed by corporations or of the loudest social media fads and trends. It is common of course for a youth to be tugged in several directions at once and to go with the stronger pull. But under wiser guidance, they would learn to recognize the whispers of a mystical twin within and to rely on such rather than heed the clamors of the material world.

I surmise a 6th century person did not have to contend with the latest pop song playing itself unceasingly on her mind, or with the perpetual worry fed by instant national and international news, or with her electronic devices' constant demand for attention. Our age is the tyranny of noise and chatter, but you can escape it by creating within yourself a refuge of silence. To open your sanctuary and propel your awareness into its center, away from invasive psychic disturbances, you will need a key. That key could be anything you like as long as it triggers a sense of stillness, quietude, and solace, and ideally calls to mind your numinous self. Spend as much time as you can every day with your idea, and you will soon realize there is relatively little that requires serious, constant, or focused thinking. Then you will find yourself paradoxically in two worlds at once. One is the earthly, including your unrestrained thoughts, the other is the aethereal where silence is sovereign and your soul walks with the gods. You will hear the earthly noise but follow the gentle rustling of angel wings. (The angels are conspicuously fond of stillness and silence—their preferred mode of communication—as opposed to their adversaries, the archons who thrive in noise and chaos). Your awareness will no longer be on the physical plane but through it, held in silent awe. There, your only task will be to uphold a state of determined, open expectation. The aethereal world is not like the world of imagination. The latter remains in your mind, but the former exists as a separate reality, an existence of your own that is taking place as an alternative to the mundane and laying the foundations of your eternal dwelling.

Imagine yourself on a cozy winter day at home, watching from the window the rain or the snow fall: you do not count the snowflakes or analyze the chemical composition of the raindrops; you let your thoughts drift away from your mind, fall with the rain, disperse in the puddles, and vanish into the rivulets. To find stillness, use your mind as a window, not looking in it but through it. And to see clearly, you will need to keep the window panes free of spatter.

The expression "to have something on the mind" is quite appropriate because our thoughts are like ware on a table: we can clear the table or put whatever we wish on it. When the solution to pressing problems seems unreachable, it is a salutary habit not to revolve worries before going to sleep. Imagine a drawer and empty your mind in it before retiring to bed at night. Then close the drawer and go to sleep. All your concerns are already affixed in the psyche; you can retrieve them at any time if necessary. And your heavenly twin too has access to the drawer. Trust in his ability to sort out and answer your needs better than you would.

Knowledge of the Gods; wisdom of the Soul

The curse and the blessing on mankind is its capacity for abstract thinking. It is the two-edged sword that can destroy man or make him a god. It is the plight and the promise of Eden, a story of dangerous knowledge and the wisdom it necessitates. What differentiates advanced civilizations from pre-industrial societies is the degree of abstraction in perception. The primitive, like children, do not conceptualize and relate only to what is directly observable. Their gods are humans or animals with superpowers; their art is imitative; their technology levels with a sufficient provision for basic needs; intellectual exploration is irrelevant; expansion is unnecessary. The life of the primitive is in the now, adapted to the rhythms of a nature that cannot be controlled. What is not seen or understood is magical, and magic is the primary means to alter unfavorable conditions. When his environmental conditions become unbearable though, man had an inherent ability to switch strategy and develop notions to supplement mere observations. The primary import of abstract thinking is the capability to anticipate the future. Whereas the past and the present are specific (peremptory), the future is conjectural. Hence, long ago, hunter gatherers discovered they could offset the vicissitudes of the nomadic life by forming sedentary communities based on agriculture. Cultivating and storing grain and fruits in lieu of collecting seeds and berries was the result of forward planning born of the mind's ability to project itself in the future. Abstract thinking was never a product of evolution; it was a gift to enable man to rise to its divine destiny. Homo sapiens was endowed with a godly attribute intended to liberate him from physicality; instead, he turned it into the means of dominion over the

448

physical world, of intemperate increase and acquisitiveness. Our gift turned into our curse, a pandora box that let out materialism, greed, and violence. To be sure, the conceptual faculty allowed for admirable developments in the arts, literature, and philosophy, culminating with the concepts of soul and spirit that are fundamental to our liberation. Yet it is now almost exclusively dedicated to solving the problems we have created for ourselves, and to the survival of our species.

The forbidden fruit of Eden was the power of abstract thought. On the one hand, it gave our first parents the recognition of good and evil and opened the door to becoming gods (Genesis 3:5); on the other hand, it led us on the path of suffering, *working by the sweat of our face* (Genesis 3:19), and imposing our rule over nature (Genesis 1:28). Good and evil, along with love, are the epitomes of abstraction, tenets without substance, as intangible as the mind itself. The primitive does not understand good or evil; he knows only what is taboo and what isn't. Nor does he have any need for love; he knows what creates discord and how to preserve harmony. The primitive relies on the Magna Mater like a child relies on his mother. He lives in the Embrace of Gaia but can never escape her clutch. His sky father and earth mother will not let him evade parental control and rise above them, beyond the boundaries of the cosmos. Life in Eden was the prototype of archaic existence. The god who walked in the garden guaranteed his progeny peace, comfort, and delight for as long as they would not endeavor to be anything more than well-provided-for birds in a gilded cage. There certainly is something to be envied in the condition of the "noble savage": he is unbothered by the strictures and burdens of civilization, with a vastly diminished propensity for neuroses, acquisitiveness, and violence compared to his counterpart in the modern world. I remember hearing the Tahitian man being belittled for his indolence and "loose" morals, when I was in French Polynesia (at the time, remnants of genuine Polynesian culture were still observable). But why would the islanders want to acquire a taste for toil, enterprise, or artificial morality? Before the arrival of "progress" with its mental and physical diseases, its compulsory, tendentious education, societal structures, and moralistic religions, life in the South Pacific was quasi-idyllic: tropical roots and fruits grew abundantly without being cultivated; innumerable fish could be easily caught; the climate did not call for extensive sheltering and clothing; chores were turned into play; energy was saved for dancing, chanting, and copulating.

Man in Eden is free from the vagaries of abstract thinking, but physicality consistently conditions his choices. In any case, the last little pieces of Eden are nearly all gone, and to seek the primeval garden is an impossible walk backward. Outside of Eden, man misused the loftier capacity of his mind to fashion his own prison. Only by combining the wisdom of the soul with a transcendent awareness offered by a personal inner savior can mankind lift itself above and beyond matter.

Dreaming

Dear Dominique.

Millennia of revolving the riddle of his dreaming has not brought homo sapiens closer to an answer. Perhaps it is better thus: should he penetrate the oneiric territory not as a lone, daring visitor but with cohorts of experts in tow, they would bring into it the same devastation the conquistadors brought upon their new world.

The dreaming is a reverse process; it is to the wake what the ebb is to the tide, leaving onto the beach of our consciousness countless debris alongside the occasional gem or a rare treasure. While we are awake, our environment and the images of our lives translate into memories, emotions, feelings, and impressions; when we dream, memories, emotions, feelings, and impressions create a new world of images and project its atmosphere onto the back of the mind.

Dreams are both the playground of Hylieros and the feeding ground of the archons. In that lot, the mind is an old, tenacious chaperon unwilling to let go of her charge. She sits on a side bench watching, unwelcome among the strange and familiar beings, the new or ancient types and patterns, the representations and symbols, the dispersed reminiscences that linger unsupervised in the dreamy hills. Hence, dreams give us that strangest, unsettling impression of being split in two, both actors and observers, puppets and puppeteers, looking at ourselves from the extra-dimensional viewpoint of two opposite perspectives at once. We experience a reluctant involvement as if moved by uncontrollable impulses or governed by an alien will. The "I" still identifies with waking consciousness while a youthful player, unformed and immature, finds his early bearings on an ascent to assume a shape and sovereignty of his own: roaming semi-free in the fluid and transitional sublunar regions between the material and the aethereal, striving to elope with our soul, he experiments with forms and narratives. But Mind's conditioned mechanisms are set as traps to prevent a would-be fugitive from escaping her grasp. Memories cling to the vault of the flesh, and our mystical sibling's efforts to sever the ties create confusion and distress in the landscape, and among the inhabitants and visitors of the dream. With only a handful of hazy memories under his wings, and lacking a complete sense of individuality, his march is haphazard and delirious, while the chaos left behind generates archons like maggots on a carcass.

The dream journey is fraught with terrible dangers because it is not the natural domain of the lower self attached to the physical plane. The fact that dreams are notably fickle and easily altered by environmental factors as well as what we eat, drink, or otherwise ingest shows they are not meant for self-help. Besides, we only remember a smattering of what we actually dream in an entire night. By necessity, the unremembered vast portion of the dreaming ought to have other functions than being interpreted (most often erroneously) by the conscious mind for dubious benefits. The ancients knew that not all dreams were relevant, that they were just as likely to deceive as they were to tell the truth. Wisely, they concerned themselves exclusively with those dreams recognized as being sent by the gods, which were the exception, not the norm. We cannot steal from the Oneiroi, we can only accept the ambivalent gifts and be thankful when one of those relays a message from our numinous self or carries beneficial knowledge. The dreaming is a gauge of life, which explains why so much of it is disturbing. It is wise to be consistently attentive to and learn from the gauge when opportune; it is foolish to temper with it. In the wild, mammals never interfere in their offspring's play, knowing that it is how they will learn to survive; they only ensure the environs are without danger.

Likewise, your only care should be to ensure the playground of the night is safe by tidying your landscape of the day. Would the feeble mind that can hardly govern its own kingdom in the daylight claim dominion over the nocturnal province? Should the mind that cannot even manage affairs in her own house concern herself with a getaway? Let the intermittent dreaming take care of itself and redirect your intentions instead to the constant numinous companion in the core of your being.

The Thorns

I dreamed of a child who could leap, fly, and do all sorts of wonders. Poised on the top of a high wall, he walked the crest merrily, when suddenly, like the tentacular arm of a giant marine creature, a thorny vine thrust out of the desolate field on the left of the rampart to strike and grip the youth's shoulder, paralyzing me—for I was the lad, a stranger to myself.

The thorns penetrated my flesh, and I was brought to a halt, momentarily. But my body would not bleed or feel pain, and with one hand I ripped the herbaceous intruder, throwing it back to the parched ground. Laughing and running, my youthful self, fresh resident of the realm, rushed down to the splendorous land on the right side—a nascent, anarchic world of awesome possibilities—to garner the anamneses and seal them as his own.

Over written stories, an unspoken, eternal myth takes precedence; over the decaying world, bolder realms are rising; over the ashes and blood of the Titans, the Liberator is reborn.

Illumination

In my youth, my mentor showed me an exquisitely decorated page from her private collection of antiquarian books and manuscripts. She pointed to the miniature set as the background for a dropped initial:

On a yellow saffron background, patterns in silver, vermilion, and malachite twirled and effloresced, enfolding two putti in front of an azurite curtain. They sat face to face on a couch rendered in golden leaf, and each one's two feet touched the other's sole to sole. The twins gave unto each other the sign of Harpocrates, putting the tip of the left index finger to their lips. With an open right hand, each presented to the other an amber gemstone. "This," my mentor said, "is the secret of the codex."

She had the most extraordinary personal library I have ever seen; with an extensive array of old books and comparatively few still in print. Once, she remarked in passing that her most invaluable volumes were the "veil-like ones."

> *They may look pretty, be well written, or sound interesting; they may appear unfocused or random; but if one sees only the veil, one doesn't see what the veil could dissimulate. Now, if you see all the threads woven into the fabric, how they are connected, and if you ravel them out one by one, then the veil falls apart and you can see what it was hiding.*

Cupid on Earth

You fell on a deserted sandy beach, little prince of the sky; your fate is that of the Morning Star banished to the desolation of

Earth. You lost your bow and your arrows; Psyche herself is mocking you.

Do you remember being worshiped from the groves of Thespiae to the temples of Rome? Even Apollo must have been envious of your glance "ardent and gentle," your "locks shining with the brightness of youth," and your pair of golden wings to carry you through the pellucid expanses.

There is no room left for you in the inns of the land. However, when you find the "truthful and believing heart," you make your abode within and become at once true lord of the heavens.

The Two Arrows

Listen, youth! Do not let the morals of mortals shackle you: your love is free, and your soul is already bound. On the day of your birth, two bowmen pierced your heart with their arrow. When you remove one, the head of the other will break inside, sealing your fate to the will of the shooter. You may choose between the wound of Eros or that of Artemis, but remember: no worldly vows or oaths, no human promise or blessing can supersede the arrow from the quiver of the archer you are compelled to follow.

Cupid at the Door

Jesus has been knocking on my door all day; incessantly, brashly, desperately, like an obsolete traveling salesman. He wants me to accept him, to adore him, to make him part of my life. He loves me unconditionally, forgives me for everything, and would never abandon me no matter what. With the 21st century militant Christianity, the once Pantocrator and Healer has been reduced to a stalker in need of a hug.

I put foam plugs in my ears and pretend I am not home.

So delightful is the soft knock of timid Cupid on the shutters of my window in the late hours of the night. I must listen attentively not to confuse his motion with the stirring of the mice in the attic. He has nothing to offer; he needs shelter, and maybe a bowl of soup as well. He was a bit cold and hungry out there. He sits by the fire and watches the flames dancing to the tune of their own crackle. He does not say much but, from time to time, gives me a coy, furtive glance. He has not come to teach or give love because true love cannot be given or received: it can only be, and we see it, or we don't. Now and then, we may receive a little help from an arrow out of the young god's quiver.

Tears of Cupid

This secret no one knows: the tears of Cupid are in the rain when the children born of the mud, in the image of their creator, forsake the young god made of aether, in the image of their soul, and follow the primeval usurper.

Yesterday, I walked past a cemetery and heard the song of the robin. I recognized in his melody the call of the winged Eidolon, not for the dead but to the living.

The Kingdom

With a concern to satisfy orthodoxy and none for truth, an anonymous cleric muddled the holy writ with one stroke of ink. Whence there would be two churches: one visible for the senior Apostle, one invisible for the youngest of the Twelve. Is the kingdom "within" or "among us?" The answer would not come until the handle of the jar broke, and the meal emptied on the road. Rightly was it said truth would spring forth from the earth: Lo, "the kingdom is inside of you, and it is manifest."

Seeing through

Dear Dominique.

In the great play of life, no matter how much we believe in our character, at the end it will be shown to have been but a stage act directed by Necessity.

There are those who will tell you to count your blessings; but what blessings does the world that is your prison have to offer? A well-fed bird in a golden cage cannot fly until it escapes. Yet, the lawgivers and leaders expect you to be satisfied with the accommodation they devised for you.

There are those who will tell you to smile and think positively; do you want to resemble them who build a psychic wall to escape their awareness of the inescapable realities of injustice, greed, wanton destruction, deception, and hypocrisy? When your apprehension of suffering is pure, pain passes through your entire being without harming your soul.

There are those who surmise you are free to make your own decisions; the reality is, nothing in space-time has ever had an agency of its own. By some estimates, we may make as many as 35,000 decisions in a single day. Even if this number is disputed and conservatively reduced to a tenth, we still face thousands of choices daily—a notion borne out by diligent self-observation. The bulk of those choices will be made automatically, under the pressure of conditioning factors, and without a full range of pertinent information or the requisite time for thorough examination. Your fate was sealed with the primordial thought that gave you birth. Indubitable freedom can never be found in any form of agency; its essence is in the absence of struggle. Once you surrender to the uncreated, uncorrupted determination at the origin of all things, the struggling ceases and you are liberated.

There are those who insist you think too much; but ills and evils thrive in the steps of those who think too little or reduce everything to moralistic simplifications to avoid being disturbed by uncertainty. In truth, from the place of uncertainty, you will return stronger.

Logic is your first line of defense against misleading eductions from the automatic mind, but oftentimes it won't be enough. You must seek the light of your numinous self to illuminate the recesses and corners of the psyche until there is no darkness left. Over logic and a profound, inner cognizance though, the do-not-think-too-much crowd favors relaxing, reacting, or rationalizing, and they would sooner judge than process. Naturally, the vast, digital ant mill of the Internet has become their universe. They swapped a sound intellect and genuine introvertive intimations for an overconsumption of simplified information. They dispense with complications and relish sound bites, one-liners, screenshots, and memes that intensify the wasteful excitement that already floods their brains. They live vicariously in a virtual sphere tailored to disguise reality and distance soul from Spirit.

There are those who parrot that the cosmos is beautiful and that strife on Earth is only a consequence of our inability to see we are one with all life. Everything is connected, they say, yet the modern world has entirely disconnected them from the realities of the natural world. Their view is restricted by the protective walls of civilization or the bends that suit their beliefs. The fact that everything is connected does not mean all boundaries are illusions and all is one; it does not bespeak universal harmony and undifferentiation. That is a new perspective of the human entity who has come to dominate the world entirely. The 1000 pieces of a large jigsaw puzzle remain clear-cut even though they all connect, and they are not "one" with the big picture they shape. Idyllic, benevolent, and cooperative mother Earth is the fiction of latter-day, naïve idealists just as the noble savage was that of 18th century sentimental primitivism; both were embraced by a privileged class to make them feel better about the vacuousness of their lifestyle. Pre-industrial tribes were mindful of the connection of all things; they also saw strict boundaries that cannot be dissolved. They participated in the violence intrinsic to nature and amplified it with the unique cruelty that typifies the human species. Amidst the chaos and horror all around us, that which is lovely and harmonious is just a fleeting glimmer trapped by the material world. If there is indeed beauty in the midst of existence, it strangely feels like the echo of a distant call and suggests an aethereal plane distinct from physicality. There is much saccharin talking nowadays about living in harmony with nature, but we mistake harmony for balance; they are not the same. Life never strives for harmony; life is the struggle for hegemony that sometimes achieves balance. Man, with its superior intelligence and cognitive capacity, has the upper hand for now. But so did the dinosaurs once; our earthly reign is not eternal.

There are those who will attempt to disorient you with high-sounding, incomprehensible philosophical jargon and endless abstract discourses. They think they can prove the superiority of their point if they can manage to dazzle you with the breadth of their impressive knowledge and discursions. Their aplomb is as high as the unverifiability and unprovability of their convoluted concepts; the only thing they achieve is the self-satisfaction of feeling more enlightened than everybody else. But what is the point of asseverating if the asseverations can be understood by none other than the asseverators? Their conceit and pretense at helping you only masks the vacuousness of the notions they advance. They fancy themselves flying high above the summits of enlightenment but lost are they in the labyrinth of their metaphysical delusions of grandeur.

We all lie. And the more complex the social frame is, the more inevitable the lying gets. To disguise the truth is not always wrong because dissimulation developed as a natural, often necessary social strategy. But, when we continue misleading and falsifying to gain a personal advantage at the expense of others, duplicity turns into a way of life.

There are three distinctive traits of human nature that seem to surface in tandem often. When we encounter any one of those in a person, the other two cannot be very far: idealism, greed, and a propensity to lie, not least to oneself. A society that understood this principle would improve considerably. Malicious deceit mirrors the mechanisms of the archonic powers that hoodwink humankind in order to ensure their own survival. Even worse perhaps are the flaws of denial and self-deception: we can hardly conceive of anyone honest with others who isn't at first honest with himself. Such is the conclusion reached by the novelist and philosopher Fyodor Mikhailovich Dostoyevsky in his novel The Brothers Karamazov:

> *Above all, don't lie to yourself. The man who lies to himself and listens to his own lie comes to a point that he cannot distinguish the truth within him, or around him, and so loses all respect for himself and for others. And having no respect he ceases to love.*

In an age when anyone's life can easily be thrust in the spotlight, we witness on a daily basis the pathological liars whose naturalness at lying becomes an expertise as they increasingly come to believe their own lies (especially about themselves). Deceit is often the first step in seeking to impose a direction, a choice, or a condition on someone else. Significantly, we often try to avoid for ourselves that which we try to compel our fellow beings to accept for the sake of a belief or an ideology. There is also an inherent problem to the so-called Golden Rule: what one may find good, reasonable, or fair is not as a matter of course that which another would perceive to be such. Moral codes inevitably give legitimacy to fanatics who seek to thrust on entire populations their views of what is best for everyone. Indeed, religious extremism is a consequence of the Golden rule carried out to its logical end. Wealthy industrial nations wish to see other countries follow in their political and economic path for their "own good," and are not above forcing the hand of reluctant people. But the original good intentions turn into ill-thought policies and lack of foresight that pave the roads for unforeseen problems and misery. It is common for charitable acts to have disastrous corollaries. Governments and political leaders as a matter of course always "know" what's best for you.

But what is needed most and yet is sorely lacking is radical self-honesty. Once you truly know yourself, understand your motives, realize whence come your decisions, and are aware of your thought process, then only can you avoid being embroiled in well-intended meddling that wreaks havoc. What's more, you will have no need for manufactured moral compasses. Self-knowledge is the true knowledge of good and evil and the maze of deception into which we move has its origin in the great lie of Eden:

> *But of the tree of the knowledge of good and evil, thou shalt not eat of it: for in the day that thou eatest thereof thou shalt surely die.* (Genesis 2:17)

Whether we are sold a pill to cure our ills, an elected official to care for our ills, a system to prevent our ills, or a moral philosophy to make our ills acceptable, we can suspect ulterior motives with roots in the genesis of mankind. Self-knowledge is the antidote to the poisons that trickle into our minds. It reveals who crafted our chains and how to break them. It clears our mind and paves the way for the manifestation of our numinous self as a heavenly twin who gives us freely and unconditionally the means to become the instrument of our own salvation.

I have nothing to teach you; my words are a mirror for you to see who you are. Once you recognize your true nature, your destiny will take care of the rest without me telling you what to do or change. I am a sower; you are the gardener. The first teacher of life is life itself, but the sovereign one rests in the innermost, nested between order and chaos, confined behind the earthly walls of your mind, waiting to be roused. Evoke him in the shapes of an angel; usher him patiently toward the center of your heart to meet your soul; inquire about his name from the silence to call gently with a holy invocation. Keep your awareness effortlessly on these sacred words without analyzing, imagining, or making yourself feel anything. Let the words be feeling in themselves, carry you, and become you. Let the amber light of your heavenly twin outshine your troubles, burn your fears away, and purify the altar of your inner sanctuary. There is no other truth than that found within yourself.

There are those who, for a fee, will tell you how to manage your life; learn from your own life before you learn from the counsel of others. Therapists, spiritual advisers, and self-help books have their time and place. But they should come with a warning label: like natural supplements, they too may trigger unwanted side-effects; and they are certainly not an ultimate panacea for all that ails us. Beware lest you become a serial seeker: they follow so many roads, they end up nowhere; they find meaning only in never finding what they seek. Be a student of yourself. Beware of the purveyors of spirituality who are like the proverbial dog resting in the manger of the oxen; it doesn't eat and does not let the oxen eat either. Stay clear of anyone who claims to be spiritually awakened. And remember, even worse than considering yourself perfectly sane is thinking you can cure the folly of others.

My writings are not mine per se, and essentially, I am a scribe. My function is to document accurately the effluences of a volition beyond my mind, but inevitably the writer betrays his inspiration to some degree. If you discover contradictions in my observations, try to reconcile them. The effort alone will steer you toward that place where contradictions collapse. My speech is not rehearsed or stilted; it is authentic, thus fallible.

William Blake wrote:

> *The man who never alters his opinions is like standing water, and breeds reptiles of the mind.*

And, to quote Theoretical Physicist John Archibald Wheeler:

> *We live on an island surrounded by a sea of ignorance. As our island of knowledge grows, so does the shore of our ignorance.*

What inspirational teacher can claim on his deathbed to exemplify the aims of his own words? How many self-appointed gurus honestly empower their disciples? Where are the spiritual posers who edify their followers instead of satisfying their narcissist streak? What religion gives more to the faithful than it requires of them? Which so-called magi, occultists, or mystics genuinely enlighten the powerless without accepting fees or gratuities or duping the elite for favors and prestige? To let yourself be led by an outer influence is to go on a blind's errand. To carry on with scheduled, structured, contrived spiritual disciplines or exercises is to further immure the Spirit. Concern yourself not with enlightenment or mystical oneness; your sole intent should be for the liberation of your soul, which will be brought about spontaneously when you have no longings left save for your heavenly twin. You only need to concern yourself with the weaving of your own myth to generate an aethereality that will ripple with transcendent awareness throughout your inner life. The way of liberation is uncharted because it is followed for the first time differently by each individual.

Faith is not virtue but foolishness, a dead end, and a trap. You can inspire people to reflect and ponder, but the byways to liberating cognizance can only be walked singly. Khalil Gibran poetically summed up the sentiment of the faithful when he asserted that "faith is an oasis in the heart which will never be reached by the caravan of thinking." Yet, the oasis is oblivious to the grander geological realities and constantly at risk of drying up. The caravan of thinking, however, moves forward steadily in the thick of the sandstorm. I was a man of faith once, but truth is a friend of logic, not of emotions, and even holding a mere opinion is far better than clutching to a solid belief. The strength of your opinions is that you can change them at any time with the accretion of information, experience, and wisdom; you are not bound to them as you are tied to your convictions. Trust the angel of your destiny, and you will have no need for hope or superstitions.

A cornerstone of human nature is that we would sooner buttress our rationales than seek to unearth their roots. When we believe to have freedom of choice and discernment, we are mistaken: our minds are incessantly assailed by manipulative influences superior to the little factual and objective understanding we can salvage. Aggressive, powerful interests from everywhere seek to promote uncertain, short-term advantages at the expense of authentic, long-term benefits. The propaganda of yesterday has been replaced by an overload of information, the purpose of which is to overwhelm our processing ability. And people often confuse an ultra-abundance of claims for a mark of authenticity. In that climate, trite and fresh "alternative truths" abound. But subscribing to them does not necessarily make anyone aware or vigilant; it draws the adherents deeper into someone else's cast of mind, luring them into a jungle of disquietude and anxiety where the "revelations" supposed to disperse the fog of falsehood become the clouds that obscure their thinking. Those who masquerade as the authenticators and sole guardians of truth weave strings of preconceptions, hearsays, and plain guesses into extravagant narratives that distract the listeners' attention away from the real perpetrators of deceit (closer to them than they think). They use reason but no logic, and there is a vast difference between the two. Reason is the skill of a mind that makes room for all prior knowledge and accumulated information. It easily accommodates bias, half-truths, and especially self-deception. Logic is a gift, and a virgin process that starts anew every time it is applied. This is why we acknowledge that truth often comes out of a child's mouth. Children scarcely reason because their knowledge is limited, but they are adept at implacable if imperfect logic. Adults who grow complacent favor reason. The earliest philosophers understood that logic is a means to give back to the mind what belongs to the mind and to the gods what belongs to the gods.

Humankind is sometimes justifiably compared to an ant colony with its denizens unreflectively following the imperatives of their society. But the serial "truth-seekers" and conspiracies aficionados bear comparison to an ant mill that crashes the functioning of the anthill: having severed themselves from the body, they follow one another in circles until exhausted, and they die without having arrived anywhere. This confused lot has embraced so many "truths" that they will often affirm something and its opposite in one breath and with a straight face. So attached are they to absolute truths they would gleefully see innocents suffer if it validated their claims. To be proven wrong would not be a relief for them that no one was harmed but a sore disappointment.

When you are busy chasing secret schemes and cover-ups in a world ripe with duplicity and machinations, you risk missing the greater, unclouded truths available within you. Truth cannot be found like a pearl in an oyster, and you will not get it from those who profess the most loudly and insistently to have it. The most defining and pertinent truths derive from a laborious inner alchemy that engages the numen as much as the mind. Pour yourself in the vessel that your numinous self is, and you will not be found lacking; let it be your shield, and you will be protected throughout your life.

Higher primates have the ability to look persistently for patterns from which they can form assumptions about their environment. This very efficient adaptive strategy has helped propel the human species from mere survival to world domination. Having reached the apex though, adaptation is no longer our concern, but our need to find patterns endures. Thus, we unintentionally reversed the process, starting with our assumptions and subsequently striving to find patterns that would confirm them. This insane, unproductive, and potentially destructive approach will only accelerate our downfall. Proof of my argument can be found in the way information is now increasingly processed and distributed via algorithms that feed you what pleases your mind in lieu of impartiality and objectivity. The social media in particular have become expert at hijacking user engagement based on our propensity for bias.

Historical conspiracies are universally relevant, but conspiracy theories are highly idiosyncratic and without relevance for as long as they remain a psychological mechanism, and they generally do. The easy believers who delve entirely into a soil of speculation are full of anger and apprehensions over what they cannot control. (And no threat is more persistent than a nonexistent one.) Hence, they find comfort in tribe identity, in vituperating, scapegoating, and becoming addicted to the emotionally charged scenarios that compensate for being unable to remake the world as they wish. Those individuals are obsessed with pseudo-revelations about secret worldwide hierarchies of absolute power they are powerless to unseat. Yet, while they blame and castigate remote, caricatural villains, they are oblivious to the closer, direct influences that hijack their thinking: the church leaders they revere; the public figures they legitimize; the social orders and economic systems they support.

In effect, we are all conspirators because it is in human nature often to protect one's perceived interests and further one's aims through deception. Hence, deceit has always been and will always be with mankind. We are all deceived, not least the deceivers themselves who are primarily self-deceived. You must elevate your ability to respond critically and raise a shield of skepticism to protect your psychical and physical wellness. It is better to exhibit rational doubt toward all things than to pit absolute conviction and unconditional disbelief one against the other; there is nothing more crippling than certitude. Next, you must yield the sword of the profound cognizance bestowed by your numinous self. The heavenly twin is the capstone of a pyramidal temple only you can build. From its apex, truth will radiate down onto the square base of materiality. Its four walls are prudence, silence, profundity, and lucidity.

Posturing appraisers and dealers of unquestionable truths short-circuit the easy believer's ability to think logically by exciting his emotions, heightening his suspicions, and feeding him increasingly outlandish myths to make sense of a world he no longer understands. But, unlike the ancient myths, the newest ones are devoid of metaphysical meaning and their concern is strictly material. Instead of giving the assurance that our destiny is in the hands of the gods, they reinforce the frustration of the weakest minds who call the skeptics sheep, not realizing they themselves are part of a herd dominated by its own egregores. Every generation, it seems, needs a freshly baked or reheated batch of lurid, speculative, and spectacular fantasies as a source of cheap thrill to distract them from the ordinary—like a bad odor they cannot stop smelling or a car wreck from which they would not avert their eyes.

Spiritual sleep is a state of confusion, and most individuals are deeply invested in confusion because it fills the void they cannot face. They say they want to see clearly, but they are not honest with themselves. They say they are awakened, but they have swapped their confusion for that of someone else. Keep your sight beyond the horizons of worldly preoccupations, towards unknowing, where your numinous consciousness remains unaffected by the forces exerted on our minds.

The reason ideas are so powerful is that the same idea can both enlighten or delude just as well. From the seeds of beliefs planted in our minds come the choices we erroneously believe to be ours. That is why it is so easy to manipulate small minds, especially when the idea is couched in simplistic or emotional form. The easier and the quicker an idea can penetrate the brain, the more likely it is to grow unprocessed and cause untold damage. The more demanding the idea is, the longer it can be exposed to the rigors of logic before being accepted, discarded, or held in the limbo of skepticism.

There are two types of inquiry: first, queries that bolster findings of our own; second, those that lead to accepting formulaic, regurgitated answers. The work-family-country paradigm is geared toward the latter. Children behave responsibly when they seek the information they do not have from those who (they assume) are knowledgeable, and they respond well if taken seriously, without patronizing. Unfortunately, the grown-up's advice and solutions soon prove rather unsatisfying and unpropitious. Youths grow suspicious of the elucidations arising from the adult milieu; adolescents are inclined to reject them. Having reached their late teen years, our charges and pupils are thrown ill-equipped on a shaky vessel for the arduous journey to discovery of the total self and its place in creation. For most, the odyssey turns into a wreck. Once we are conditioned to customize our asking to a predictable answering, we are deemed a decent citizen, apt to be a conservative or a progressive, to vote, to handle vital decisions. We think we are well informed whereas we have lapsed into mass thinking. Even sub-systems self-styled independent, anti-establishment, fringelike, non-conformist and so forth, conspicuously match the rigid templates of the group to which they belong.

Rarely has any truth been unearthed where the masses rush to listen. At the same time, the idea that the majority is not always right gives credence to lunatics who think they are geniuses because their follies are rejected. The gate out of that impasse is to question scrupulously and perpetually all the assumptions you live by. Doubting everything still prevails as the prerequisite to the questions that elevate our mind, and the answers that liberate our soul. Therefore, your first line of defense is logic, as I have already said. But the surest guide throughout the meanders of life is your numinous self who whispers from the innermost. And the more you heed those whispers, the more you will understand yourself and the world, drawing closer to the truth. Always remember: if you are consumed (or even, merely distracted) by anything but a love for your inner liberator, you cannot transcend the world; you are only burned on the altar of Magna Mater.

Truth is not relative, and yet it can never be apprehended impartially or dispassionately because we do not stand outside of it but move within its embrace. Forever and by necessity, truth must be tailored. To find one's own truth, as the expression goes, is to dance with the gods in whose image truth offers itself to us; it isn't a discovery but a gift.

The Mythmaker

Dear Dominique.

Upon re-reading your latter missive, I decided to offer a few more pointers that I hope will be of some help.

You say you are worried sometimes that you are missing something or need to do something before it's too late. This is a common plight of those who are looking for answers beyond mere physical existence. It's also the spiritual tourist's bane. Even if you were able to absorb and process the utterly astounding variety of religious, spiritual, esoteric, mystical, and occult currents in the world, you would still be left wanting for more. And in spite of the sheer number of claims and promises made by the proponents and leaders of those various movements, none—I repeat, none—has bridged the gap that separates them from the divine (which is not the same as claiming to have been on an astral or psychedelic trip, to have had visions, or to have felt "at one with the universe") for the simple reason that they are still here standing among us, prisoner of the flesh, subject to pain, fear, and death. Therefore, they are still divided, and none can tell the taste of the unmixed divine wine.

It might sound counterintuitive, but the better approach to save you a seat at the banquet of the gods-beings when that day comes isn't "knowing" but "unknowing." Get rid of the metaphysical clutter and leave behind all dogmata, beliefs, and preconceptions so that you may reach a blank state in which you can no longer utter a single word to anyone with regard to the nature of spiritual realities. (A rare thing indeed nowadays, especially on the Internet.) There and then, all that remains are the utmost longings of your soul for numinosity and divine passion. There is nothing else to do, really, because the very minute you long for the numen, the numen is born in you, and the god you seek is seeking you. It is that simple and worth repeating: your longing is all that matters. Now, if you feel your yearnings need focus, there is an easy way about that. Pick something you can easily sustain in the center of your being: a word (a name or an evocative word), a few words (e.g. a short prayer, a verse, an affirmation, an invocation, etc.), an image, or any combination of those (keep it as simple and unencumbered as possible though); even a fond feeling that you can effortlessly bring back will do. Anything uncomplicated will work as long as it triggers only the most uplifting, comforting, and joyful sentiments in you. You decide. And do not let any remnant of false morality or propriety deter you in your choice. The sacred motif you choose will be a gate for the numen, a bridge between your soul and spirit. That is the same rationale behind icons, talismans, mantras, except that your chosen motif is held within. Make it a substitute for unwanted thoughts, undesirable emotions, and mental junk. Keep it as a safe dwelling for your heavenly twin to grow. All the supernatural beings, angels, devils, idols, or objects of reverence in the world are projections of our desires and our fears; no more, no less. No divinity ever was who had not been born from the heart of man. And we create myths to keep alive the gods we want. Therefore, there is no reason why you should not determine where to funnel your desires. In similar fashion, rather than adopting someone else's salvific myth, you owe it to yourself to create your own. Swedenborg, Blake, Blavatsky, Rudolf Steiner, George William Russell, Aleister Crowley, Gurdjieff, Carl Jung (to name only a handful of them), all built a personal myth of salvation, as did the myriad of self-appointed gurus and prophets whose followers think vicariously. And although the many myths we have inherited can be inspiring or useful, none will do more for you than the one you dream up yourself. Make it an unexacting and delightful task. "My yoke is easy, and my burden is light!"

The End of the World

The end is upon us, not sudden, apocalyptic, or cataclysmic, but slow, debilitating, and merciless. We mocked a would-be prophet and his followers when, on the day he had appointed, his promised Messiah did not return, and nobody was taken up to Heaven. Still, the distraught, old fool found reconciliation in extremis, claiming everything he predicted had indeed happened, but on a spiritual, not an earthly plane. We laughed, not realizing the irony was on us:

Nothing new, nothing original, nothing different is coming up to surprise us. The past has been copyrighted, trademarked, franchised, and the present is a copycat. The 60s were the last fertile decade as evidenced by its wealth of innovations in culture, the arts, social experiments, spirituality, and exponential technological advances. All that plateaued in the 70s, and the 80s signaled mankind had begun its steady descent from the peak of creativeness down to a dearth of ingenuity and originality concomitantly with the rise of the new Internet culture. By the start of the new millennium, progress was mostly defined by unhinged, consumer-driven commercialization and high-tech improvements on what had been previously invented. Vulgarity, the commonplace, the asinine, and the ugly are filling the vacuum left by our extinguished brilliance. The collapse of ideas into a vapid, amorphous muddle of culture in the joint custody of the state and the corporations alarmingly accelerated the engrossment of individuality into matter. The sublime archetypes have been drained to the last; the future belongs to cyber-fantasies that will relieve our minds of anguish while tethering our souls without redemption. In that bland climate, it isn't surprising to find indications human intelligence had already passed its climax and may be regressing. As noted by researchers, IQ scores worldwide have been declining since the 70s. The New-Age gurus continue to speak of a transformation and expansion of human consciousness, but that proposition does not hold water in view of the world recent political developments, the increasing horror of localized conflicts and terrorism, the random violence, the unabated rush to armament that reaches even into Western households, and an all-around hateful atmosphere that knows no age, race, or borders. Despite the spiritual tourist's weird obsession about "oneness" with the All or the universe, the only places where we become one with anything is in the digital sphere, or in front of an electronic screen. In that artificial space, a melding of minds is speedily dragging mankind on the dangerous path of transhumanism.

Air is toxic, Water is poisoned, Earth is polluted, and devastating fires rage. The elements are out of balance and the sickness is beyond healing. The rich and the powerful retreat behind their walls and fences like the wealthy of ancient city-states trying to avoid the plague. They parceled the land in myriad little oases, nonetheless their fortune is as shifty as the desert sand, as tenuous as a mirage. We persist in working to "build" our future, but apocalyptic visions and dystopian scenarios have replaced futuristic utopias in our collective consciousness.

We can wait for the rapture, suffer, and die with hope as our sad companion. We can wait for a Mahdi and follow the lunacy to our demise. We can wait for the visionaries of transhumanism to fulfill their promises and lull us to acquiescence with the sound of their electronic melodies. I have learned from the beliefs gone by. As Ganymede and Psyche once did, I seek the redeeming wings to transport me, not to a mythological heaven or an artificial paradise, but to the impossible depths and heights where the gods abide.

Non est mortale quod opto.

Apotheosis of a Soul

When the sky melts into the sea at the darkest hour, and the lights come dancing on the varnish of the night, it is as if one could behold the scintillas of life, liberated at last from their earthly dungeon, journeying in procession to their abode of shine. At the sight of the joyous cortege, an enthralled soul is moved by a rhapsodic illumination; she strips off her garment of skin, slips through the nocturnal veil, and joins in angelic henosis her lucent companion.

Part Five

Without the higher and finer sentiments man does not live;
he merely exists.

—Manly P. Hall,
What the Ancient Wisdom Expects of Its Disciples

I am an Image in the heart.
When an image enters your heart and establishes itself
You flee in vain: the Image will remain with you —
unless it is a vain fancy without substance,
sinking and vanishing like a false dawn.
But I am like the true dawn, I am the Light of your Lord …

—Rumi,
The Masnavi

VEILED ILLUMINATIONS

A Passerby's Mystical Contemplations

There are many ways to learn. One may read books, pose questions, reflect, experiment, or heed teachers. We can even dream answers or consult oracles, perhaps. Yet another method of gathering knowledge is to listen to conversations: the calls and songs of the warbles, the murmurs of the brook to the pebbles, the whispers of the wind to the foliage. Less fruitful but more frequent of course, are the discussions held by acquaintances and strangers.

The following are colloquies between spirit and soul. Because those two are no ordinary interlocutors, the language you will hear is unusual as well. The verses of the fool invite you to follow the two conversationalists into their extraordinary plane of perception where each line is a small tear on the backdrop of the physical world. To peek through these slits is to gaze into the aethereality obfuscated by the mundane that plays in our reality.

YOUTHFUL & MYSTICAL APPREHENSIONS

À la Belle Étoile

On the byways to Caraman I met a lad
His mood was too somber, and he would not speak much
We slumbered *à la belle étoile* by the campfire
I could sense in his sorrow a wishful desire
To free the captive bird from a family clutch
And I offered him my verses to make him glad.

The Chestnut

Long ago I saw you reigning over your kind
In the majesty of a moist, mysterious wood
Lit by the ocher of your leaves, without a sound
Once more I met you forlorn in the school playground
Watching my first, uncertain steps out of childhood
Sharing the nostalgia concealed under your skin.

The Teacher

Your name is forgotten; your legacy is shame
Your sole skill was to torment and humiliate
You were embittered, and your heart was sorely blind
You scorned the weak, but the sickness was your own mind
Was there in your pupil a sin to castigate?
What did not kill my soul set my spirit aflame!

The Swifts

From a classroom window, in the first hour of school
A boy watched the swifts free of curricular angst
Tracing invisible arabesques with their tail.
He longed to join them, to play and defy the gale
But he would sit, bear the teacher's jabs, and be mocked
Envying the bird who could eschew any rule.

Childhood Dusk

The hour daylight resists the assault of the night
Charmed by chants of the waves to the Protogenos
Drunk with the scent of the pine trees, sea, sand, and salt
I heard his call from the depth; reason came to halt
My soul drowned into the soothing spell of Eros
At last with her Master, eager to reunite.

The Source

Ambling on a dust path to a small church afar
I heard at a trail's bend a dribbling melody
Wafting on the summer heat, calling from the shade
"Come; draw near my cooling water," the fountain bade
I the boy surrendered to the spell willingly
Like Abramelin's angel bound by the grimoire.

Van Gogh's Shadow

When I was a young student, I stumbled upon
Van Gogh's mystic vision of a café at night
Of Chartres blue, lambent halos, and yellow glow
And my soul was beguiled by the furtive shadow
Evanescing through a portal of orange light
To evade the mundane before the break of dawn.

Manhood

I began to cringe at the wetness of the rain
The drench of the storm I would no longer enjoy
And the quixotic youth I was became adult
Leaving behind the byways I sought as a boy
In the vain pursuits of manhood I would exult
I traded the lure of errant life for a chain.

The Kid

Once I found a kid hiding behind a boulder
I'd heard the stray whimper and thought to carry him
But he was too quick to evade my grasp and flee
He didn't need rescue: a little beast must run free
Yet the waif returned to the clearing on a whim
Leaping, hoping, nudging my back and my shoulder.

The Young Poet

His head tilted down with dark hair brushing the page,
Spellbound by the genius within who guides his hand
The pupil writes; his thoughts spill down to the paper
Dictated by muses from a loftier sphere
Words aethereal like a mandala of sand
Dedicated to graceful gods who never age.

Ode to the Moon

I .

The Representative

The things I promised you, I will promise again
No lie is too bold to keep you numb and content
I assure you, I can really change your lot
Trust me with your vote and rush to cast your ballot
Remembering is futile; live in the present!
With hope aplenty, of thinking you may abstain.

The Town Crier

Perched on the upmost branch of a bare tree, a crow
Laments from his lofty seat the sins of our kind
Punctuating absurd scenes down below with caws
And still we scurry, oblivious to our flaws
Making a great display of our ludicrous mind
Forever pursuing a receding rainbow.

The Impudent Seagull

Aloft on the finial where it alighted
It relishes having no manner or master
And shits on the unfurled standard without a care.
Wretched is the earthbound, I am lord of the air
Reckons the cheeky seagull with scornful laughter
Eying a garbage pile nearby it had sighted.

Back Alleys

I relish walking in the back alleys of town
That harbor a spirit free from strict compliance,
Where stale memories rise and linger in the air
And the inscrutable, blind windows seem to stare
When rats and strays learn the ropes of self-reliance
And the street noise comes to abdicate and wind down.

The Prayer Rug

Bastet knows the hour: a she-cat keeps out of sight
'til the humans leave the place vacant and silent
To present on the kitchen mat her offering
The humble rug is now a station for praying
The queen gives up her favored toy for a portent
And calls on with a wail the goddess in the night.

There Was a Hill

There was a hill on the outskirts, not far in sight
Where the road seemingly ended, and the sun rose
No redeemer on its slope died in agony
'twas a vision and a promise of harmony
A hallowed high ground, a sacred place of repose
Where my secret desires like the swifts would take flight.

Lure of the Window

A window may trigger for me strange ingressions
Lit by the moon, the sun, or veiled by a shadow
The vexing impression resists my inquiry
Beguiling my wistful soul with a mystery
Open or shuttered, conjuring a subtle flow
Of introvertive, evocative expressions.

The Windowsill

Who has leaned contemplative on the windowsill?
The thinker, the lovelorn, the weary and forlorn
Gazing absently, transfixed in their paradigm.
I have sat on the narrow edge many a time
Begging the moon at night for a prick of her horn
To make me her slave and free me from Gaia's will.

Angst

I have felt our forebears' primeval, piercing fear
And the terror of an alien existence
We do not understand nature's hostility
We traded our deep instinct for servility
Behind walls we no longer look in the distance
To rent the veil of things as they falsely appear.

The Portent on Valentine's Day

A rebel balloon escapes from Valentine's Day
And ascends swiftly buoyed by a biting gale
A crimson portent in the February gray
Staging pirouettes in an aerial ballet
To please the master of the hearts and to regale
The winged Eros who spirits the lover away.

The Parting of the Dream

Your sweet farewell aroused my wistful emotions
For in the parting of the dream was much sorrow
You gave me a kiss; your trust was unshakable
Our vows of reunion are now unbreakable
You softly asked for a letter in the morrow
May these versed lines convey my tender devotions.

LES VRAIS MYSTÈRES DES TAROTS

At the height of his power and glory, the great architect of the universe gathered round his retinue for a wondrous celebration.

To entertain his guests, the sovereign asked his jester to compose a series of verses that would unmask with verve the mighty archetypes who had come to the fête under the guise of Lords and Ladies in the royal entourage.

These are the words spoken by the feisty Fool at the court of the supreme, cosmic ruler.

Le Bateleur I

You are called Magician, master of the unseen
But the Fool sees through the illusions of your game
In truth, you were always a deceiver at heart—
A mountebank, a performer; *c'est dans les cartes!*
You delude and cheat the gullible without shame
Concealing your dupery behind a smokescreen.

La Papesse II

I am Joan, custodian of the Church of John
Hailed by the beloved at the gnostic altar
I vowed to conceal his mysteries with my veil
I am drunk with the thick honeyed milk of the Grail
I am the anointed soul who will not falter,
A Priestess in the cult of the arriving dawn.

L'Impératrice III

I am the Empress, the fertility of Earth
I am the bounties and cruelties of matter
In the folds of my mantle play the timid fawns
On the watery glaze of my tears glide the swans
I am the passions of the Nymph and the Satyr
The mother of the soul, the cycles of rebirth.

Le Pape V

What god made you Vicar in the Church of Peter?
You relish the power and the pomposity
You hold many a key but let no one enter
Your reach is mighty, but empty is your center
The mark of the papacy is atrocity
From a throne in the Holy See reigns a cheater.

L'Amoureux VI

Twin torches illumine the temple of "I AM"
One is Ecstasy, and the other is Desire
The sempiternal flames of the divinity
With the burning of love bear no affinity
And if at your altar one of them lights a fire
Seek not the false god of Abraham, but the lamb.

Le Chariot VII

The soul is a chariot pulled by two horses
One represents Movement, the other stands for Rest
But who is the charioteer holding their reins?
Sprung from the innermost, Eros removes all chains
He is the mystical Desire behind our quest
To understand whereto our memory courses.

La Justice VIII

I am the law of requital and rectitude
'tis my sword that severs the spirit from the soul
But heed *le Fol* and you will not be torn apart
The scales of justice will discern the truthful heart
Behold, the divided god-seed will be made whole
To free the elect from his earthly servitude.

L'Ermite VIIII

I am the withdrawn heretic and the doubter
He who solemnly wowed to seek until he finds
Holding high the lamp of gnosis to light my way
I look at the phenomenal world with dismay
In my refuge there is no need for walls or blinds
I have abjured man's ways and *folie de grandeur*.

La Roue de Fortune X

I am Necessity, the ronde of destiny
And the cosmic origin of fluctuation
My rim is a circumference that is nowhere
And my hub is the center that is everywhere
Your fortune in life revolves without cessation
In the work of the Fates there is no clemency.

La Force XI

Blessed is the soul who has tamed the roaring lion—
The force of creation turned into her servant,
Lending her the secret of immortality
But none will break the chains of physicality
Who has not acquired the gnosis of the serpent
Woe to the soul who is vanquished by the lion.

Le Pendu XII

If you contemplate my fate, do not pithy me
You see my scourge, but do you realize your plight?
Hanging upside-down I have a new perception
I am no longer sharing in your deception
Can't you feel the noose on your own neck holding tight,
Dragging you through the delusion that you are free?

XIII

I follow in your steps from beginning to end
I nourish the life that thrives on putrefaction
The thief and the jailer must surrender to me
Of the sufferer I heed and answer the plea
I am both a promise and its satisfaction
Why would you shun me who am your most loyal friend?

Tempérance XIIII

I am thymos in the breath and blood of mankind
Your angel and the archons alike I nourish
The vessels in my hand are the heart and the mind
In each cup the poison or the salve is refined
Drink of the one: the cosmic rulers will flourish
Apply the other: the angel you will unbind.

Le Diable XV

My fathers are many, my mother is the Earth
I am the two-horned in *Tempérance's* shadow
Reviled by the engineers of morality
Keeper of the byways of sexuality
From my vessels the libations to the gods flow,
The day my followers are led to a new birth.

La Maison Dieu XVI

I am *Maison-Dieu*, temple of Hylieros.
The house divided against itself will not stand
And ought to fall amidst the storm's roar and thunder
Inevitably, Mind will be rent asunder
Our bedrock of beliefs needs crumble into sand
And man must pass through the narrows of Erebos.

L'Étoile XVII

Our birthplace is not on high, we sprang from the sea
The stars of heaven are the markers of our fate
Like the pots fired in the oven of the potter
We are only vessels made of clay and water
And all human lives on Earth stream from the same gate
Following Ananke's immutable decree.

La Lune XVIII

I gather the glimmers rising from the meadow—
The anamneses drawn to the mystical light
That I will wheel into the sun at early bright
I am the Moon, sovereign over the crystal Night,
Heralding the Beloved as is my birthright,
Caressing the Lover with the beams of my glow.

Le Soleil XVIIII

In the innermost sanctuary of the heart
The soul is drawn to her sibling the savior-twin
'tis the ever-blooming garden behind a wall
Where the shimmering rays of the rising sun fall
And when the exiles from Eden embrace therein
Never again the two lovers will stand apart.

Le Jugement XX

Between Death and Life, from many a universe
The individualities rise from the clay
And awake from the transitory, earthly dream.
One will waft on a lucent, aethereal stream
The other will be tossed in the wind like the hay
Thus memories ascend, or in matter disperse.

Le Monde XXI

Earth, fire, water, and air swathe and cradle the soul
Yet the elements also fashion her prison
'til the shattering of bones on the earthly plane.
Will the soul evanesce through the cosmic membrane?
Behold, the heir of the memories is risen!
Destiny's last chapter is about to unroll.

The Emperor was stunned and displeased by the words he heard. It dawned on him he had turned into an unwilling participant in his own game now out of control. Having listened to the wisdom he would not heed, his thoughts were agitated, and he feared the truth he had not sought. Yet, overwhelming curiosity compelled him to contain his anger and inquire defiantly:

"Do you imagine the cleverness of the fox can outmatch the might of the wolf? Tell us then, what are the true faces of your sovereign and his slave?"

L'Empereur IV

Your throne is the cosmos symbolized by the square
You rule supremely over the plane of matter
And proclaim your reign to be the terms of the All
But you are the blind god; your true name is Samael
The leader of the archons I will not flatter
The wise initiate you can no longer ensnare.

Le Fol

I was born with the moon and will rise with the dawn
I stand both in the beginning and at the end
I am the prudent elder and a daring youth
I gather the memories and distill the truth
I reveal my holy name to the soul my friend
I am the daimon to whom my chosen is drawn.

GNOSTIC RHAPSODY

The Two Principles

We were the battleground even before our birth
Of two principles vying for domination
Reality is a theater for their play
One commands the pull of entropy and decay
The other is the thrust of manifestation
Their tug of war begot the cosmos and the earth.

The Game of Life

Alpha is Desire, the descent into the dark
Omega is Passion, the rising of the Son
'tis the sequence of life in Heaven and on Earth
Eros-Dionysos, the dance of endless birth
In matter they play; on the track of time they run
And then, on their Elysian journey they embark.

Dioscuric Angels

They did not fall proudly from the heavens on high
They do not plan their escape by reaching the sky
In the labyrinth their mortal parents remain
But the Sons of Zeus are destined to flee and reign
Without wings of feathers and wax they learned to fly
Icarus died; they will live when the sun draws nigh.

The Arrow of Light

If a sharp, swift glint, in daylight or in the night
Suddenly passes, like gold through a dreamy mind
Know that an arrow of Desire will pierce your heart
No longer would Eros and Soul be kept apart
His enchanted darts are the bolts that seal and bind
Psyche to her Lover in abiding delight.

The Gnostic Altar

On an alabaster altar the soul lies bare
Overshadowed by the holy Spirit-essence
She beholds the sanctuary of the angels
And in the nave and sacred edifice's aisles
Through the apse and chapels spreads out the warm
fragrance
Of a reassuring incense wafting on the air.

The Impious Sprite

I dreamed of a lithe sprite keen on laughter and dares
Who defied and mocked the regnant power and might
While bathing naked in their temple's baptismal font
I dreamed of the archons enraged by the scamp's taunt
The sprite is real; his nemeses he will smite
To unburden my soul of her tormenting cares.

The Passion of Marguerite M.

Marguerite Magdalene was thirty-three years old
And five was the number of fellows she had loved
Her passion for the sixth would be the most steadfast
Though but twelve seasons their mystical bond would last
The secret of the mother and her beloved
In her lifetime would outshine gems, silver, and gold.

Spirit and Soul

Spirit is silent like the breath, untamed like youth,
Passionate and willful, yet shapeless like water
Through the gentle devotion of Psyche—the soul—
Spirit grows, takes flight, and brightens his aureole
Soon as an angel, he rises over matter
Now a lover, he guides the soul to her own truth.

Silence

He is a youth with a fingertip to his lip
His wide eyes are carved to see beyond mortal sight
The locks of his hair are a veil for his secret:
A gnosis greater than any book can transmit,
The wisdom the hierophants searched in the light
Silence: the charming god I revere and worship.

The Two Lights

Merciless light that scorched Daedalus' hopes and dreams
Maddening light that robs the prophets of their sight
Dazzling light that keeps Sophia concealed and veiled.
Lambent light that welcomes the elect who prevailed
Light stolen by the day but reclaimed by the night
For an archangel's aureole and the moonbeams

Free Will

Free will is a masked pretender, a charlatan
O the fools who believe they are born free to choose
To shape their world, their life, and their reality
The True Will abides beyond our capacity
To do right or wrong, or to pay our god his dues
Of our fortunes the stars are the sole artisan.

The Key

In the beginning, her parents fashioned a key
Yet the soul frets and searches for meaning in vain
Seeking prophets and looking for a messiah
The key is no longer with Dyēus or Gaia
But buried in the body of sorrows and pain
It is the winged eidolon, the twin of Psyche.

The Children of Hamelin

Waddling ahead, the piper pipes his merry tune
Endearing the children of the bourg who follow
The heedless and fickle grown-ups have lost their chance
And the child alone will learn the mystical dance
Who of the winding byways becomes a fellow
Willed by the pipe to share in the piper's fortune.

The Flight (a dream)

I fly over wilderness and stunning landscapes
With my fingers the waters of a lake I graze
Then I reach the heart of a venerable wood
Where among sentinel trees He spends His childhood
Always followed by the guardian's watchful gaze.
I will bid my time and return when He escapes.

The Window of the Entirety

Life is a view afforded to a god-being
Gazing at many vistas in infinity
There is no paradise or divine election
There is no Gehenna or blessed resurrection
Through intermittent and ceaseless eternity
He stands at the window from which we are seeing.

The Eagle and the Rooster

Lo, the Rex Mundi's days are coming to an end
Woe to the bird of the clouds who reigns from the sky
With an all-seeing eye and the threat of his claw
Behold, a child rises to elide Yahweh's law
And the bird of dawn is His relentless ally
To the spur of the rooster the eagle will bend.

The Owl

With magnetic, dark eyes ensconced in a white heart
She who dwells in the night, companion of Wisdom
Entices the soul to journey through ills and pain
Looking upon life with neither joy nor disdain
Knowing the god of silence will give her freedom
When, by the claws of Death, the corpse is ripped apart.

The Optimists

By his god the very first optimist was cursed
But we followed with each passing generation
Trusting the false promises of revolutions
Placing too much faith in worldly institutions
Our fate will be captured by a mere quotation:
"We were expecting everything except the worst."

The Call

Shatter the regnant carnival mirrors of life
And see with your inner eye the pellucid truth
The nameless god you are seeking is calling you
On the wall of your heart he has written the clue
To unlock the secret of harmony and youth
In a place of repose, far beyond worldly strife.

The Design

Life is a blessing wearing an ugly disguise
What creator sent us here to suffer our plight?
Did we have any choice but to accept our lot?
There is nothing to learn and nothing to be taught
We come from the light and will return to the light
Necessity demands our fall before we rise.

The Heretic's Book

Penetrate my hidden corridors if you dare
Listen to the whispers and consider this claim
'tis better to face doubt than pray for salvation
Or fear a demiurge's threats of damnation
Take one bold step and jump through your dogmatic frame
Free yourself from the twin bonds of hope and despair.

The Color of Incertitude

Robe your soul in the color of incertitude
Like the angelic ephebe who incurred God's wrath
And sat with the goats on the left side of the Son
Blue pigments the ether before the rising Sun
'tis the shade of the night upon the Lovers' path,
The dye of the water wherein life is renewed.

Anagoge

I am the soul, born of forlornness and wisdom
Rise anew winged eidolon with this child your twin
Come eternal Self in an aethereal shape
That from the dark reach of Hades I may escape
And, with Ganymede, an immortal's share may win
In solar triumph over the earthly kingdom.

Destiny

Through the fabric of time and many lives entwined
Runs a thin, golden thread spun and cut by the fates
In such a way destiny is set to unfold
Child of Night, read the portents hidden in the world
Ananke drew your path to the Elysian gates
Even through the walls raised by the god of the blind.

Sophia

Counselor, protector, provider and reprieve
Most precious gift sought with mystical intent
In the midst of Eden by the serpent unveiled
Loftier than the gnosis of those who prevailed
Never-ending Wisdom thrice called in a lament
Sophia: Holy Mother of motherless Eve.

The Vow

When the Lord of the horizons erodes the night
When the morning star surrenders to her master
And when a rose takes on the color of amber
The seal on a holy vow will be their anchor
From the Beloved's cup Soul will drink hereafter
For his Lover, Spirit will yield the sword and fight.

Parting Words

I have cast a fire upon the world, and I watch over it until it blazes.

—The Gospel of Thomas, Logion 10

Dear Dominique.

Everything I was bound to disclose, I have now told you: what was passed on to me and what I stumbled upon; what can be transmitted and what must remain a secret between those of the same amber blood—the companionage to which you now belong.

I have opened a door; I have lifted a curtain; I have crossed a bridge. I have given you a sign and a token. Now we stand on the threshold of the 6th arcanum; it behooves you to increase, and me to become less.

I have made my offering; you will have to make your own as we all have. I do not claim to have all the answers, but I gave you the keys to the treasury and, at the very least, I showed you how to ask yourself the right questions. This is my legacy to you, and my task is complete. Nothing else is forthcoming but that which you will infer or discover on your own. Manly P. Hall, whom I will quote, had much wisdom to offer with regard to our responsibility:

> *If a man should ask me who I am, I shall answer that I am a voice crying in the wilderness. If he should ask who sent me, I shall answer that my soul sent me. If he should ask by what authority I teach men, I shall answer that I am my own authority. If he should ask what message I bring, I shall answer that I bring no message, but only interpret according to my light that*

message which is eternally here. And if he should ask, 'What reward have we if we follow you?' I shall answer that the accomplishment of labor is the reward of labor.

Now, remember this: the moment you are led to believe you must evangelize the world, or that you are invested with a spiritual mission to change it, is the moment you veered off transcendent awareness and fell prey to the world. Your preeminent concern should be with your numinous self until he becomes in a profound intimacy the ruling and saving principle of your life. They only can seal a vow that you will live eternally among the god-beings as a god-being. He is the *devenir dans l'être*, and there is no power on earth or in heaven greater than that which is already in you.

I was hoping to see you in person before you embark on the rest of your journey; but I recognize your mind is steady and clear, and you must follow the thread Clotho has spun for you. May this resolve steer you again one day, if only so briefly, to sit by my side as you once did; only this time I will be the one listening attentively, and the insights you share I will collect to illumine the night before me.

My shield; my vessel.

Printed in Great Britain
by Amazon

29721631R00292